POLITICAL POWER

AND THE PRESS

POLITICAL
POWER
AND THE
PRESS

WILLIAM J. SMALL

W · W · Norton & Company · Inc ·
New York

COPYRIGHT © 1972 BY W. W. NORTON & COMPANY, INC.

First Edition

Library of Congress Cataloging in Publication Data

Small, William J
    Political power and the press.

    1. Government and the press—United States.
2. Press and politics. I. Title.
PN4738.S6   323.44′5   72–3102
ISBN 0–393–05339–3

PRINTED IN THE UNITED STATES OF AMERICA

1 2 3 4 5 6 7 8 9 0

For Tami and Willa,
who bring their father
more joy and pleasure
than one man deserves.

CONTENTS

PREFACE

I am always impressed by the courage of people in journalism.

They are a diverse lot but if there is a single characteristic they share it is a tenacious determination to stand tough against any encroachments on a free press. They may disagree with each other—even about the other fellow's practices—but they are as one in asserting the absolute necessity of a free press in a free society.

Each generation has its free press battles. Sometimes they come not generations apart but at intervals of a year, months, or even weeks. Often there is limited or almost no public support for the position of the press, particularly when emotions run high, tension becomes endemic, and the public gets nervous. When the nation runs a fever, free press is more difficult to retain but more vital to uphold.

It would be easy to buckle under pressure or succumb to the seduction of powerful forces which would manipulate or suppress the news. There is rarely an accounting later of the stories we never saw, the facts we never knew about, or the items that were slightly modified. A culpable press could permit that to happen, at least in the short run, safe in the silence that attends the word not spoken. But the American press is rarely culpable no matter how much security silence offers. One is reminded of the cartoon Ed Murrow used to have on his wall. It showed two people on a deserted island and the woman says to the man, *"I'd* know, that's who'd know." Reputable news people take the same view when there is a temptation to tamper with the news.

While I am in awe of the courage of journalists, I am not without concern over the shortcomings of the news communicators and should explain that though this volume deals with many of those shortcomings, it is not meant to be a balanced measuring of government on the one hand and the press on the other. There is a history, longer than the history of the Republic, of government meddling with the news. This book means to examine that meddling.

There is need for a word of apology to my friends in government. Some very good men run the nation's affairs. Many easily fit the usual cliché descriptions of hard-working, dedicated, patriotic, sacrificing, etc. I'm glad they are there. I think they are good. I am proud that many are my friends. But I don't trust any one of them for one minute when it comes to news.

Men in government, for good reasons as well as suspicious ones, are compelled to minimize or suppress information, to try to mold it by the amount they release and the timing of that release. Men in the press, by practice and tradition, want to publish all they can learn as quickly as they can. The two groups must differ in this key element to their relationship and as a result are compelled to become adversaries. But I apologize to my friends in government for this book won't make them look good. I await their books to tell me all that's wrong with the press.

I also apologize to two other groups for the convenience of shorthand expressions. First, I refer to the press as a generic entity including broadcasting. Many of my fellows in broadcasting bristle at the word "press" because of its print connotation. They have tried for years to get press conferences called "news conferences" and to have press secretaries called "news secretaries." They are probably right, but this book is my capitulation to custom. I surrender to those who call us all members of the press.

The other group I probably have offended for reasons of convenience and shorthand embraces half our world and most of my personal household. I refer to females. In this volume there is a tendency to refer to *men* in government or the *men* of the press. It means, of course, men and women both. I recognize that and I am sympathetic but beg to be excused on the grounds of sloth—

I am too lazy to write *men and women* of government or *men and women* in the press or the typical American *man and woman*. I risk the wrath of the ladies but again succumb to custom.

The men (and women) who made America in the first place, made sure that we were to have a free press. They knew that the country was easier to run without a nagging from the sidelines, that premature or excessive reporting did injury to efficiency. In some primitive societies, they say the greatest curse is the past. In America, we are blessed by the past. It gave us the tradition of a strong press standing up to government.

There is a danger, in reviewing the record of the last two hundred and fifty years, a danger in concluding that it was always thus and a free press threatened always survives. It is true that the greatest excesses of government, during the Alien and Sedition Acts of the John Adams era or the newspaper burnings of Lincoln's time or the Espionage Act under Wilson, failed to eliminate a free press. It is true that the tradition of the American press has survived the witch hunts and the extremes of patriotic fervor, attacks from people in high places and temptations from within in times of high tension. The danger in assuming that it has always been such and always will be is that the test of the theory might be terminal. As Hitler showed us, a press suppressed does not make a recovery. As Lenin indicated, a press controlled does not revert to a critic's role. As history reminds us, free speech surrendered is rarely recovered.

My own views on the heart of American free speech, the First Amendment, tend to be close to the absolute views expressed by the late Justice Hugo Black. I can recognize the moments when compromise of the First Amendment obviously serves a greater social goal but I am not willing to surrender to that recognition. With rare exception, every time a journalist concedes greater social goals and adjusts his reporting accordingly, he shortchanges the people he is truly responsible to, the public, and has not really served any greater good. Government *ought* to be difficult for the governors. The scales *ought* to be weighted against the people's servants and for the people. It *should* be made harder for the cop to convict the culprit in a democratic state where men and ideas are considered innocent until proven guilty.

The job of the newsman is not to make government easier but

at times to make it more difficult. He must begin with the premise that the more the people know, the wiser they will be. He must end with the conclusion that the role of the press is not to be popular with either the politician or the public but rather to be honest with both.

I happen to think that the current press is holding to the premise and sticking with the conclusion better than the press has in the full history of this nation. If they are willing to spend the time and the effort, Americans today can learn more about what's going on than could any other people in history. The press presents more material and, despite constant criticism, presents this more fairly than it ever has in the past. America is flooded with the word and it is only through the word that Americans can seek the truth that shall keep them free.

In preparing a book such as this, one is indebted to many of his colleagues and ends up, as I do now, with the cliché of being grateful to "too many to mention by name." I should like to offer particular thanks to Sylvia Westerman, Elizabeth Midgley, Richard S. Salant, and Max Frankel for their comments on various portions of this volume. I am once again indebted to Mrs. Marjorie Geddes for her tolerance and good counsel in the preparation of the manuscript.

One is compelled to thank his wife for her understanding during the long hours a writer is married to his manuscript. My wife Gish, to be candid, hated every moment spent at a typewriter rather than at more pleasant, more familial pursuits. She thought the idea of doing another book a bad idea, a view that I hope will change after she reads this volume. On the other hand, the love and perceptions of nearly twenty-five years of marriage prevailed and another fool was suffered gladly. I am grateful to her for that and for those years together. She is a remarkable person and I am a lucky man.

William J. Small
Washington, D.C.

POLITICAL POWER

AND THE PRESS

I

POLLUTING THE
INFORMATION STREAM
The Politician and the Press

To the politician, the press is irresistible.

It is his mirror in the morning. It is his glimpse at himself. It is a judgment of his actions, his image. It is the link to his constituency, a line to his public, the avenue to the electorate. The only thing that spoils this link, this line, this avenue is that the politician cannot travel it freely—the press is not in his hands, but in those of the journalist.

News reporting is too important to be left to news reporters alone, so politicians try to help. The press is too important to be the private domain of men who are by profession skeptical and, by temperament, cynical of politicians. The press is too important as a means, the most important means, of moving political information to the public. And so the press is irresistible, so much so that the politician cannot keep his hands off.

Even in their darkest moments, politicians were never in favor of a press that is actually censored, controlled, or captive to government. They may have wanted to mold it a bit but they all be-

lieved in a free press. After all, the very first of all amendments
to the Constitution established a free press.

It is accepted doctrine that editors and publishers and broadcast
executives speak in defense of the First Amendment whenever it
seems threatened. There are those in journalism who find such
defenders of the faith tiresome and sneer that instead of professing
the rights of a free press, the defenders would do better to simply
engage in tough reporting. They sometimes hint that the loudest
defenders of the First Amendment run the worst newsrooms.

The criticism is unfair, no matter what the quality of the newsroom in question, for the need to meet each challenge to press
freedom is a very real one. Some of the worst excesses of government, during the Civil War and World War I, were tolerated because of a complacent press, because of an editor whose ox was
not being gored. The press must itself protect its right of free
speech for no one else has the means to do so except the very ones
in government who would compromise the press.

It is tempting to portray politicians as venal men in their attitudes towards the press. As the documentation in this volume
shows, no era in American history has been without its attempts to
manipulate the news. The accumulated evidence is especially sobering since one can only catalogue failure. When politicians succeed in perverting the press, in suppressing news or changing it,
that success generally goes unrecorded. The politician has gotten
the coverage he desired and the press is not about to confess its
failure to challenge that. The nation will never know how many
times the press has been gulled or intimidated or has simply played
willing accomplice.

The freedom of the word—freedom to speak it or print it or
broadcast it but most especially, freedom for others to hear it—is
crucial to any democratic state. It is, as Mr. Walter Lippmann
once observed, not so much a privilege as an organic necessity in
a great society. Each time a branch of the press fails to publish
the word, to hear the word and pass it on, then society is deprived
of one essential to its very being.

Politicians profess to want the public informed, for they all believe in a free press. While it is frequent that they dabble in form-
ing the information, it is rare that they tinker with the flow of
information for personal gain or to cover up unethical or criminal

acts. History has seen some of that but usually political news management comes from purer motives. Public men, without exception, feel that the public is best served when it learns about actions and decisions at the right moment. The press wants to put it out now, the politician wants to hold it for the right moment, premature exposure being damaging. Public men, without exception, also feel that it isn't always in the public interest for the populace to know everything about decisions or actions and so they would leave some matters to remain hidden. The press would hide nothing short of the most intimate matters of national survival.

The politician can be persuasive in arguing the need to delay the word or to protect the public from some of the facts. Newsmen are sometimes persuaded and become willing accessories. Whenever they do, they violate the trust that the Founding Fathers placed in the press. The First Amendment is a protection for the public, not the press alone. It is implicit that while Congress is forbidden from abridging free speech or preventing the public from the redress of grievances from the government, the press is similarly proscribed from doing injury to free speech or the public right to know when government has aggrieved it.

The persuasiveness of the politician comes from his relationship to news media. The curse in the geography of journalism is the newsman's proximity to the public man. Cronyism, flattery, sharing of confidences all work in favor of the politician. Only the tradition of independence and of skepticism by news people works against him.

Often, from his position on the inside, the politician is convinced that he knows best. He is not out to fool the public but really to protect it. He feels that his knowledge of the public's business is such that he can be sure when premature publication or publication at all is more damaging than helpful. He can be terribly righteous, wrapped in the flag. Marcel Proust once warned us to "love those who seek the truth; beware of those who find it."

Truth, of course, is not the substance of news reporting. The general public finds this difficult to believe because they so want to have the truth in each day's newspapers, on every newscast on radio and television. So does the press but it can't be done. Events reveal themselves spasmodically. Despite the best efforts to provide continuity by reflecting reporting, news interpretation, and backgrounding events, the fact remains that on no single day is all revealed.

As Walter Lippmann put it, "The theory of a free press is that the truth will emerge from free reporting and free discussion, not that it will be presented perfectly in any one account." What is truth anyway? Is it the same to all men and at all times? The failure of the press is reflected in the failure of the historian. He deals in yesterdays as the press deals with today but the historian is often revised by later historians or the revelations of later fact. Even if there were one truth to be had, the public is cheated if it fails to have opinions at variance with that one truth. No one said it more eloquently and more properly than did John Stuart Mill in 1859:

> If all mankind minus one were of one opinion, and only one person were of the contrary opinion, mankind would be no more justified in silencing that one person, than he, if he had the power, would be justified in silencing mankind. Were an opinion a personal possession of no value except to the owner; if to be obstructed in the enjoyment of it were simply a private injury, it would make some difference whether the injury was inflicted only on a few persons or on many. But the peculiar evil of silencing the expression of an opinion is, that it is robbing the human race; posterity as well as the existing generation; those who dissent from the opinion, still more than those who hold it. If the opinion is right, they are deprived of the opportunity of exchanging error for truth: if wrong, they lose, what is almost as great a benefit, the clearer perception and livelier impression of truth, produced by its collision with error.

Politicians will not have this. The more thoughtful understand it but they are imbued with the righteousness of their cause and disturbed by the troublesome nature of other opinions being reported. The reporting of other opinions is an affliction imposed by the press for which true believers have a low tolerance.

All of this, the public man notes, is fine in theory but less attractive when one sees the daily distortions inflicted on its public by a free press. He knows the real story and the press only approximates it and often falsifies it.

Why this failure to report "known" truth? First, the newsman usually has access to many sources, some of them hostile to the politician. They contribute to his reporting. Even friendly sources or those in the employ of the political leader don't always have the facts as their leader would want them. Further, the reporter must measure his material with critical eye and with the background of other known fact. The result is not the same as material viewed with the eye of the converted.

There are special problems in the press. One is time. It reports now rather than later so it must report from an incomplete dossier. In addition, there is the pressure of competition which further inhibits delay in searching for additional fact. There are technical impositions on print and broadcast news which also serve to foil the objectives of the public man, the main one being the great need in news to condense and simplify.

It is also possible that a politician, despite the advantage of his position on the inside, might sometimes be wrong. It is rare that a public man sees this possibility for after all he has access to material and is witness to events that no journalist or historian can match. Still he might be wrong. Lyndon Johnson recognized this when he wrote his postpresidential memoirs and called them *The Vantage Point,* explaining in his opening words "I have not written these chapters to say 'This is how it was,' but to say 'This is how I saw it from my vantage point.' "

The press functions as a device to report on the view from that vantage point but also to question whether a president might be wrong. It also functions to report opposing points of view even when the president is right. The press is to provide the common man with the views of different vantage points, right and wrong, true and false.

It is little wonder that the press and the politician throughout our history have had a love-hate relationship. There is permanent tension; what both call an adversary relationship. Where that does not exist, where they are happy with each other, either the press or the politician is not doing its job.

The adversary relationship is sometimes misunderstood. Some newsmen think it compels them to become prosecuting attorneys. To assume guilt by profession in viewing politicians is unfair to them and improper for the journalist. The public is cheated as much by this as it is when the politician in power is always assumed to be right.

On the other hand, politicians, on their side of the relationship, must recognize that they, too, are not to be prosecuting attorneys. Most politicians find the press as venal as some reporters find the politicians. They cannot excuse error lightly, they cannot suffer the press gladly. They are tempted to take strong action, convinced that there is a press conspiracy against them. The society remains great to the extent that they fail. As Albert Camus wrote, "A free press can of course be good or bad, but most certainly without freedom it will never be anything but bad."

In the summer of 1971 the *Wall Street Journal* solemnly noted, "The press of America is under governmental attack as never before." The instances it cited are explored in detail in this volume. The unprecedented move by the Nixon administration to impose prior restraint on the publication of a series of articles in the *New York Times* was a key battle in 1971. The *Times* revealed a secret study ordered by a previous defense secretary to determine the pattern of decision making in our Vietnam involvement, a study popularly known as the Pentagon Papers.

Another important event in 1971 was a congressional move to subpoena unused film, the outtakes, of a CBS News documentary, "The Selling of the Pentagon," and the subsequent debate over whether Congress should cite CBS and its president, Dr. Frank Stanton, for contempt because he refused to submit to the subpoena. The broadcast press has never fully staked out its position under the First Amendment and the collision with the Congress was a milestone in the continuing fight for broadcast freedoms.

The year also saw a climax over moves by government to use subpoenas with increasing frequency in demand of news material not published. The subpoena controversy was also essential to the struggle of the press to steer clear of government interference. This, and the many other devices of government to deal with the press, will be examined in the course of this volume.

Confrontations between the governors and the press increased greatly in the late 1960s and early 70s. It was a period in which the public questioned many of the institutions of American society, the government, the church, the schools, and the press. In a time when the nation was bogged down in an Asian war, there was bitterness and divisiveness and established institutions seemed incapable of restoring unity and good will. The questioning of the press by a frustrated public was spotted by some politicians, notably Vice-President Spiro Agnew, and political capital was sought in strong, frontal attacks on the credibility of the news media. The press stood up against the Agnew attacks and parallel ones from others in the Nixon administration. There was a rare display of newspaper support for television, considerable editorial defense of the competitors in the electronic media.

Despite the tough and courageous words of the defenders of the faith, there was apprehension that the many and varied attacks on the press—from the executive branch, from subpoena-wielding law enforcement agencies, from congressional committees —might compel an unseemly caution, a crippling self-censorship. The popular judicial phrase was "a chilling effect." In an American Civil Liberties Union report on the press in September, 1971, Fred Powledge wrote,

In the final analysis, the magnitude of the chill is difficult, even impossible, to measure accurately. It is possible only to say it is there and to point it out when it is obvious; when a newspaper or television station do not cover a story that ordinarily would have been covered; or to wonder if a story that *has* been covered has been "toned down" somewhere along the line, and if so, whether the result is a story that is closer to the truth or more distant from it.

It is not so easy to measure other chills: A wire service reporter who thinks one of his editors is a conduit to the F.B.I. says he warns his black military sources not to tell him anything they wouldn't tell the police. A television producer says he has a colleague who decided not to invite a rejection, and so he didn't suggest a project that might be termed "too controversial." A black newswoman for a radio station says she wants to do a story explaining what people in the ghetto are really thinking, but she knows that "the management wouldn't sit still for that."

A newspaperman might want to do a story on marijuana use among his town's youth; he knows that in order to do a proper job of research he must interview young marijuana users. But there is a chance (and, if the government prosecutors are successful in the Caldwell case, a likelihood) that he will be subpoenaed to testify in secret to a grand jury. Does the reporter decide not to do the story?

The decision *not to do the story* appears to be multiplying, all over the nation, and before long there will just not be very much interpretation of complex events and social movements. What will be left will be the relatively safe "hard" news of speeches and statements, and that can be easily manipulated.

It is in these ways that the First Amendment is being lost, a little each day.

Just as one will never know the success a politician has in perverting coverage of a story, so it is with self-censorship. Largely unknown are the successes of a chill on free reporting. The reader or the television viewer will never know what he has missed if it is not reported in the first place.

After the House of Representatives voted not to cite CBS for contempt because of the documentary, "The Selling of the Pentagon," the *Boston Globe* noted in an editorial: "We are glad, for the people's sake, that CBS has won its latest battle, however temporarily. But what will really count is whether CBS will be emboldened to give the public more such documentary films as 'The Selling of the Pentagon.' "

The stake that every man has in a sturdy and flourishing press is enormous. Considering the tools that men of power have to weaken and wither the press, it is a tribute to journalists that they have survived the intrusions of politicians and governments so well for so long. When Senator Sam Ervin of North Carolina, chairman of the Senate Subcommittee on Constitutional Rights, opened a series of hearings on government and the press in late 1971, he said, "Our Founding Fathers were wise enough to know that there is no way to give freedom of speech and press to the wise and deny it to fools and knaves. Certainly, they did not intend for the government to decide who were the wise and who were the fools and who were the knaves."

The stake is enormous. Fred W. Friendly, the great television documentarian of the Murrow years at CBS, used to say, "What you don't know can kill you." Those familiar with Friendly's fondness for the dramatic might tend to dismiss that. When the Pentagon Papers emerged with fresh evidence that much of what the public didn't know about decision making in Vietnam led to deeper and more costly involvement, continued and increasing casualties, there was fresh evidence that what one doesn't know *can* kill. In this case, literally.

If the press is chained to reporting one day at a time, it will certainly lead to abuses but if the consumer of newspapers and broadcasts understands the nature of the product, the abuses are tolerable. Again, Senator Ervin:

> Our historic commitment to freedom of the press means that we must tolerate absurd, misleading, and vindictive reports which sometimes appear in newspapers and magazines and on radio and television. It means that thoughts and ideas which we hate and despise will appear in print and be broadcast across the land. James Madison recognized that "Some degree of abuse is inseparable from the proper use of every thing; and in no instance is this more true than in that of the press." Most Americans have come to understand that the irritating excesses of the press are a small price to pay for a press independent of government control.
>
> They realize that only an independent press can vigorously and effectively contribute to that wide-ranging and critical discussion of public affairs which is a prerequisite to a democratic society.
>
> This view of the role of a free press in a free society necessarily means that there will be tension and sometimes hostility between the press and government. Indeed, it is the conflict between the press and government which attests to the vitality of the First Amendment.
>
> This conflict exists today. It is manifested in a number of relationships between government and the press.

The tension between press and government, the adversary relationship, is fundamental to any honest measuring of public decision making by the journalist. Government, like any of us, cannot be counted on to announce errors that it has made. Government won't expose thievery or fraud or ineptitude. The rogue is always the first to protest his innocence. When conducting the people's business it is easy to rationalize the errors of the bureaucracy, easy to cover them up with the excuse that it serves no useful purpose to undermine public confidence. Only the press and political opposition see useful purpose in exposing government's imperfection. If the unpleasant aspects of government go unreported, the public is not simply uninformed, it is misinformed.

During the congressional debate on "The Selling of the Pentagon," a Republican congressman from Ohio, Clarence Brown, told his colleagues that it didn't matter that many were displeased with the reports on television newscasts and documentaries. "The plain fact," he said, "is that the First Amendment is not limited to the truth. That amendment guarantees the right to print and speak— but the right of expression thus assured may be the truth to one and lies to another. It is up to the individual citizen to make the discrimination of which is which. Rather, the First Amendment merely guarantees that someone dissatisfied with the version of the truth he is hearing may select another version of the truth as he sees it from other outlets among the various media or even tell his own version of the truth."

While others may agree with the congressman's insistence that the truth of one and the lie of the other be revealed, that sunlight— as Justice Brandeis noted—is the most powerful of disinfectants, it is in the nature of governments to operate in the shadows, to provide only revealed truths, to resent the probings of the press. It is not a new phenomenon. The framers of the Constitution met in secret in 1787. Even the U.S. Senate, in its beginning years, sat in secrecy, holding its debates behind closed doors.

It is little wonder that politicians ever since have yearned for as much privacy as conditions would permit. The result can be devastating. Secret government takes damaging steps to "protect" the public. Only free and public discussion can be the disinfectant. Again Louis Brandeis: "Men feared witches and burned women. It is the function of speech to free men from the bondage of irrational fears." It was a thought echoed by the *London Observer* in 1968 when it said, "You begin by suppressing witchcraft. You end by suppressing Galileo."

Inspiration for the earliest advocates of a free press in America came from two London newspapermen, Thomas Gordon and John

Trenchard who, early in the eighteenth century, wrote under the pen name of "Cato." They had tremendous impact on their own countrymen and those in the colonies who would some day start a new nation. Their writings, *Cato's Letters,* were published in four volumes and enjoyed tremendous popularity on both sides of the Atlantic. "Cato" also became a popular pseudonym for defenders of liberty in America for the next one hundred years.

Cato wrote that "only the wicked governors of men dread what is said of them" and "whoever would overthrow the liberty of a nation must begin by subduing freedom of speech; a thing terrible to public Tyrants." In colonial America, many editors, including Benjamin Franklin, quoted Cato (Franklin himself using the pen name "Silence Dogood" at the time). Said Cato, as quoted in Franklin's *New England Courant,* "Without freedom of thought, there can be no such thing as wisdom; and no such thing as public property, without freedom of speech: Which is the right of every man, as far as by it he does not hurt and control the right of another; and this is the only check which it ought to suffer, the only bounds which it ought to know."

The newspapers of the eighteenth century were very little like those of today. They scorned objectivity and were highly partisan, highly opinionated. Facts were not permitted to interfere with a point to be made, an enemy to be castigated, a favorite cause to be pushed. The very first newspaper in North America, Benjamin Harris's *Publick Occurrences, Both Forreign and Domestick,* outraged the government so by two of its items that it was suppressed and all copies destroyed. It expired after a single issue.

James Franklin, Ben's older brother, angered those in authority in Boston when in the *New England Courant* he attacked the experimental use of inoculations to combat smallpox, an editorial position that infuriated Cotton Mather and ended a year later with James Franklin's jailing for contempt of government. He also angered the government itself by criticizing its campaign against piracy. Ultimately he was forbidden to publish anything again and seventeen-year-old Benjamin came from the back shop to take charge of the paper.

Ben Franklin was far wiser, considerably more subtle, and managed to keep out of the path of the authorities. He moved on to publish the *Pennsylvania Gazette* and while engaging some in criticism, remained careful not to anger authorities enough to put him out of business. He did notice, at the time, "If all printers were determined not to print anything until they were sure it would offend nobody, there would be very little printed."

Few printers were as cautious as Franklin and, increasingly, journals of political comment appeared. They were highly opinionated and as little concerned with factual reporting as was Benjamin Harris when he invented wild stories about Indians torturing captives or immorality in the royal family of France. Such publications were irksome to the rulers of the colonies but they became very popular with the public.

Protecting the right of such publication was, early patriots felt, vital. In 1776, largely thanks to the ideas of George Mason, the Virginia Declaration of Rights was adopted in Williamsburg by the House of Burgesses. Jefferson drew upon them when he wrote the Declaration of Independence. Strangely enough, such a delineation of individual rights was omitted when the Constitution was adopted. A number of early leaders said it was not necessary to spell it out because it was inherent in the rights of men.

There was a popular movement, however, to introduce a Bill of Rights as the first amendments to the Constitution. Pennsylvania had done so in its state constitution of 1776. John Adams had led the fight to include it in the Massachusetts Constitution—"The liberty of the press is essential to the security of freedom in a state; it ought not, therefore, to be restricted in this commonwealth."

Goaded by Jefferson, who was abroad at the time, and Washington, who made it one of the very few specific recommendations in his inaugural address, James Madison led the fight for a Bill of Rights. In one of his speeches to that effect, he asserted, "The freedom of the press and rights of conscience (are) choicest privileges of the people." Fisher Ames of Massachusetts and Roger Sherman of Connecticut led the opposition, calling it unnecessary and unwise, such rights in English common law being considered inborn and inalienable.

Madison found enough support in the Congress and even more in the general public. At first, he wanted to incorporate the Bill of Rights in the actual text by changes, omissions, and additions but this was abandoned in favor of a collection of amendments at the end of the Constitution. On June 8, 1789 Madison introduced a series of constitutional amendments of which the House of Representatives accepted seventeen, the Senate fifteen. Out of conference came twelve which were submitted to the states. Eleven states had to approve. In a matter of weeks ten states ratified and on December 15, 1791 Virginia approved, bringing in the first ten amendments as a Bill of Rights. The two amendments dropped would have fixed the size of the House of Representatives and would forbid congressmen from raising their own salaries.

The first of the ten was, of course, the brief fifty-four word protection of free belief, free speech, and free press: "Congress shall make no law respecting an establishment of religion, or prohibiting the free exercise thereof; or abridging the freedom of speech, or of the press; or the right of people peaceably to assemble, and to petition the government for a redress of grievances."

While the prohibition on abridging free speech is, on its face, absolute, the courts have sometimes construed it otherwise and have, in effect, changed it to mean Congress may make "some laws" abridging freedom of speech as Justice William O. Douglas has observed. There were numerous convictions involving antiwar publications and speeches during World War I (under the Espionage Act) and these were sustained by the Supreme Court. In the 1920s, the Court upheld convictions dealing with advocating the overthrow of the government by force and communist leaders were convicted of a conspiracy to do just that. The courts, it has been noted, sometimes follow the ballot box. They often follow the temper of the times.

The exceptions Douglas cites are all the products of national stress, of national fear, concern, hysteria. Woodrow Wilson would tell us, "The wisest thing to do with a fool is to encourage him to hire a hall and discourse to his fellow citizens. Nothing chills nonsense like exposure to the air." But under Wilson, the Espionage Acts flourished in legally sanctioned, and Supreme Court upheld, defiance of the First Amendment.

Permitting fools to hire a hall may not be the inevitable cure for nonsense but forbidding them the opportunity of a hall is an inevitable detriment to intellectual growth. Ideas need to be tested by other ideas, even foolish ones. Communication in a democracy must carry concepts of all kinds, opinions, beliefs, sentiments,

impressions, conceits that are popularly accepted and those that
are not. There must be enough room for robust debate.

The worst excesses of the press are not enough to diminish the
breathing space needed for a variety of ideas. At the end of the
nineteenth century yellow journalism emerged and the newspaper
war between Pulitzer's *World* and Hearst's *Journal* illustrated how
two giants in competition for circulation could whip up a hysterical public. While it is argued that they were not alone responsible
for America's entry into the Spanish-American War, they certainly were major contributors to war fever in 1898. Pulitzer even
claimed that his newspaper's evidence was responsible for the rise
in "war spirit" and, similarly, after Congress voted for war in
Cuba, Hearst told his staff it was "our war." A *Journal* headline
read "How Do You Like the *Journal's* War?"

Other New York newspapers were appalled. The *Evening Post*
editor wrote "A yellow journal is probably the nearest approach
to hell existing in any Christian state" and Adolph Ochs of the
New York Times called for a law to prohibit "freak journalism."
The worst of yellow journalism was enough to recall the French
poet Baudelaire's earlier admonition, "I am unable to understand
how a man of honor could take a newspaper in his hands without
a shudder of disgust." The abuses cannot always be forgiven,
but in a democratic state they must always be tolerated.

It is difficult for some to reconcile the worst of yellow journalism
with any national purpose, yet the press, even when dead wrong,
is an important goad to a democratic state. Leaders feel compelled to set the record straight and that alone is a significant
contribution to public understanding. John F. Kennedy once noted
that while a totalitarian state has many advantages in being able
to move in secret, "there is a terrific disadvantage in not having
the abrasive quality of the press applied to you daily."

As president, Kennedy found plenty to dislike in the press coverage he received (he was known to talk back to a television set
when the news disturbed him), but he said, "Even though we
never like it, and even though we wish they didn't write it, and
even though we disapprove, there isn't any doubt that we could
not do the job at all in a free society without a very, very active
press."

In a not-so-free society, the very, very active press is the first thing to be eliminated. Totalitarians hold the press in disdain.

In the 1860s, when Otto von Bismarck became Germany's "Iron Chancellor," he quickly took after the press. Even mild criticism resulted in the jailing of editors and German newspapers would have "sitting" editors to serve out Bismarckian sentences while the real editors remained under disguised titles. In 1890, it was estimated that he had inflicted more than one hundred years of jail terms on editors. In one year alone, 1878, Bismarck suppressed 127 periodicals. Those he did not suppress, he kept in check with threats or bribes. With the aid of an immense fund for such expenditure, he bribed both domestic and foreign journalists to carry out his propaganda and to engage in unprincipled attacks on his enemies. The Iron Chancellor had little respect for the client press he had created. He called it a "reptile press" and said its editors were "press cattle." As he summed it up, "Decent people do not write for me."

The lessons of Otto von Bismarck were not lost on Adolph Hitler some forty years later. He used the same techniques, development of a kept press, suppression of all criticism, and the use of bribes and honors to influence journalists, domestic and foreign. For the development of the Nazi press, he had Max Amann. For the use of domestic and foreign press to conduct propaganda, he had the evil genius of Joseph Paul Goebbels.

Amann, who was Hitler's old sergeant in World War I, headed the publishing house *Eher Verlag,* which started with a small, four-page anti-Semitic weekly, the *Voelkischer Beobachter.* It became the Nazi party organ. Amann, when Hitler took power, was given the authority to open or close or expropriate for the party all other German publications. By 1936, he had seen to it that the Nazi daily press grew to over one hundred newspapers with a total circulation of more than four million. By the forties, *Voelkischer Beobachter* alone had a daily circulation of a million copies. Amann wiped out the leftist and much of the moderate press, expropriated the property of all Jewish publishers, and merged or took over hundreds of Catholic newspapers under the wing of *Eher Verlag,* the publishing empire.

As for Goebbels, he became minister of propaganda and under

the infamous Editor's Law of 1933, compelled all journalists to register with the state, all editors to accept appointment as officials of the state, and all publishers to follow Nazi discipline or face closing down. Of course all persons engaged in communications had to be German Aryans.

Foreign correspondents inside Germany were expelled if too critical, were given every courtesy including bribes if favorably disposed towards the Nazis. In time some left Germany, some became little more than publicists for the Nazis, and all suffered from the self-censorship that comes with a Goebbels nearby, ready to reward or punish.

Goebbels did not limit himself to foreign reporters in Germany. His influence reached reporters in other countries. Using an immense slush fund, he subsidized foreign journalists, especially in France. In 1936, according to Édouard Daladier, as many as four-fifths of French journalists were taking money from the Nazis. When the Nazis entered France, the combination of kept newspapermen and the stupid excesses of France's own military censorship, resulted in few Frenchmen being aware of the extent of the Nazi threat. As the government prepared to flee Paris, newspapers there were able to report that the public was still "completely ignorant of the fact that the German advance has suddenly assumed such gigantic proportions."

For Goebbels, the use of journalism was part of the weaponry of his government. Years later, when supporters of the Kennedy administration wondered why the press should react so strongly because the assistant secretary of defense talked of news as one of the weapons in government's arsenal, they needed only to have noted that virtually the same words were spoken by Goebbels when he said, "News policy is a weapon of war. Its purpose is to wage war and not to give out information."

In time, Goebbels' master, Adolph Hitler, observed that "the organization of our press has truly been a success. We've eliminated that conception of political freedom which holds that everybody has the right to say whatever comes into his head."

In like vein, Benito Mussolini eliminated one-third of Italy's newspapers and compelled all remaining newsmen to join the Fascist Party. He was to proclaim, "I consider Fascist journalism as my orchestra."

So it always is in totalitarian states. By their very nature they cannot permit a critical press and will not permit a free press. V. I. Lenin, in 1920, asked

> Why should freedom of speech and freedom of press be allowed? Why should a government which is doing what it believes to be right allow itself to be criticized? It would not allow opposition by lethal weapons. Ideas are much more fatal things than guns. Why should any man be allowed to buy a printing press and disseminate pernicious opinions calculated to embarrass the government?

In the Soviet Union no man is so allowed. The press is part of the government's apparatus. It publishes only approved matter.

When the hated head of the secret police, L. P. Beria, was executed, there was no announcement in the Soviet press. Readers learned about it by reading between the lines of a society announcement. The list of Soviet leaders attending the opening of an opera failed to include the name of L. P. Beria. That was the first hint that he was out of power. He was already dead.

When ex-Premier Nikita Khrushchev died, it was forty-eight hours after the rest of the world knew it that *Pravda* was permitted to mention the passing of a leader who had fallen from grace. The obituary was exactly fifty-seven words long.

Pravda (Russian for "truth") is the world's biggest daily newspaper with a circulation of 9.3 million copies. *Izvestia* is second in Russia with a seven million circulation. Both are read carefully by Soviet citizens and foreign diplomats for clues as to what is happening inside Russia but one needs to know how to read the newspapers in Moscow. Front page stories often are simply long, dreary official directives on factory production or farm techniques. On the other hand, *Pravda* publishes a daily nine hundred word article on the left column of the front page which deals with a current problem in party doctrine. The column was conceived by Lenin himself years earlier. Here one finds the most overt word of changes in foreign or domestic policy, and so the "lead" editorial is read with avid interest.

Pravda, which sells for three kopeks—a touch more than three cents in U.S. money—is generally six pages long. Page 1 deals with serious articles or proclamations on domestic and international subjects. Page 2 covers internal party affairs such as new appointments and letters to the editor which themselves are read for a grasp of what the editor, and thus the government, approves. Page 3 is devoted to science, literature, and the arts. Page 4 generally deals with reports on Communist parties in other countries. Page 5 carries reports from *Pravda's* forty-two foreign news bureaus including those in New York and Washington. *Pravda* not only uses *Tass,* the Soviet press service, but also has access to the AP and UPI. The last page of the paper deals with sports and leisure activities.

Throughout the paper are those verbatim accounts of official documents and statements. As official party organ, its editors explain, *Pravda* is obliged to print major documents in their entirety even though readers find it a bore. It may be dull, but it is required.

Readers of the Russian press are a special breed, watching to see which leaders and which policies are mentioned with increasing prominence and which are mentioned not at all. Douglass Cater has noted, "In this reversed image form of journalism, the intelligent Soviet citizen must learn as much from what is not in his newspaper as from what is there." He observed that there are "occasions when an entire issue is quickly sold out because of an apparently inconsequential story tucked away in the paper. . . . Its meaning is lost on the foreigner, but the Soviet reader evidently perceived deeper implications."

Khrushchev, when still in power and anticipating more than fifty-seven words of obituary, proclaimed: "The press is our chief ideological weapon. It is called upon to rout the enemies of the working class, the enemies of the toilers. Just as an army cannot fight without weapons, so the Party cannot successfully carry on its ideological work without such a sharp and militant weapon as the press." In the words of Cater, "Curiously, the press, in quite different ways, is indispensable to government in both Washington and Moscow."

Current history is dotted with regimes that would like to emulate the Soviet example or, failing that, try to inhibit the press where it cannot be fully controlled. General Ayub Khan permitted only closely supervised newspapers in Pakistan and would jail editors and take away their printing plants if they offended him.

When he was overthrown in 1969, his successor General Yahya Khan restored some freedoms to the press but within a month clamped down a censorship tighter than before. On Formosa, Chiang Kai-shek employs a policy of tight control and self-censorship which, if violated, leads to jailing of editors. South Vietnam's Nguyen Van Thieu took office in 1965 and immediately closed down thirty-six daily newspapers. In Peru, the new regime in 1970 decreed fines and jail terms for any newspapermen deemed to have insulted the government. Prison terms for journalists were reported from Brazil, Cuba, Haiti, and many other Latin countries.

Considering the propensity of governments to seize control of the press and to suppress even modest opposition, it is all the more remarkable that the free press tradition should survive in western democracies and be admired by those, particularly in Latin America but elsewhere as well, who see the values of unrestrained publication. The American tradition has been a beacon to others though there is a continual battle to keep the U.S. press free and flourishing. It remains the strongest and freest press on earth.

The beginning of the American press tradition precedes the beginning of the nation. We must go back to 1734 and the arrest of John Peter Zenger.

Zenger is the name that comes most quickly to tongue as American editors speak on freedom of the press; it is now a cliché for editorial courage. The case of John Peter Zenger is worth examination for it is important, cliché or not, and tells much about the American attitude toward the press even in the pre-Revolutionary colonies.

He was an editor in name only; he was really a printer. His *New York Weekly Journal* was a newspaper in name only; it was really a propaganda organ to oppose a noxious governor. While Zenger had the courage to go to jail, the heroes of his story include an elderly lawyer named Andrew Hamilton and the true editor of his paper, James Alexander.

John Peter Zenger came to New York City in 1710 as a thirteen-year-old boy and served an eight-year apprenticeship to printer William Bradford. In time, he moved to Maryland and became a public printer on his own but returned to New York after the death of his first wife. Zenger remarried and in 1725 rejoined Bradford in a very brief partnership which produced a single book. He then struck out on his own as Bradford's rival.

William Bradford was the official printer of New York and served the needs of the governor, printed the accepted newspaper, the *Gazette,* and handled all printing contracts for the government. In an earlier day Bradford had himself fought a battle for press freedom. He was a public printer in Philadelphia until he was brought to court for some indiscreet speculation about the honesty of the Quaker authorities. He argued his own case and fought for the right to challenge obviously biased jurors and to shift the burden of proof to his accusers. Bradford's eloquence, though unsupported by English common law of the day, prevailed. There was a hung jury and he was freed. His career in Philadelphia was over, however, and he moved to New York where his actions were more discreet, his official support more firm, and his business more prosperous.

When John Zenger struck off on his own, there was room for a second-class printing shop catering to New Yorkers with reason to avoid the official printer. For a number of years Zenger published critical pamphlets, open letters of complaint, and religious tracts. His authors were those who Bradford could not or would not print for fear of official censure.

In 1732 a new governor arrived in New York—Brigadier General William Cosby, colonel of the Royal Irish, equerry to the Queen, and now governor of New York and the Jerseys. He was a haughty, petty tyrant with a taste for intrigue, a passion for connivance, an appetite for power, and a penchant for worldly goods that could only be summed up as insatiable greed. Cosby surrounded himself with sycophants and quickly made enemies of some members of the established class including Lewis Morris, chief justice of the supreme court. Morris, a commanding figure in the politics of both New York and New Jersey, irritated Governor Cosby with a ruling on the question of monies due Cosby. The governor, to avoid a jury, had named the supreme court a court of equity and Justice Morris, in open defiance, had declared this unlawful. In an intemperate and insulting letter, the governor demanded the text of Morris's judgement. It was supplied but was also published (by Zenger) in a further gesture of defiance by the chief justice.

William Cosby was furious. He said the king's authority was trampled on, and vowed to replace Morris as chief justice. He knew that Morris's chief rival was Stephen DeLancey, New York's leading merchant prince who had battled Morris on the floor of the Assembly in an angry controversy over trade with the Indians. The governor named DeLancey's young son James as the new chief justice of the supreme court.

Lewis Morris swore he would have revenge and became leader of the anti-Cosby Popular Party. His colleague there was James Alexander, the true editor of Zenger's *New York Weekly Journal*. Alexander created that newspaper on November 5, 1733 to report the results of the previous week's assemblyman election in West-chester. Lewis Morris had run against Governor Cosby's candidate, William Forster. The sheriff tried to fix the election by disfranchis-ing all Quakers, supporters of Morris, because they were forbidden by their religion to take an oath. Custom permitted them to vote but Cosby's sheriff would not. Unfortunately for him, Morris had enough votes anyway. The *Weekly Journal* then appeared with Alexander's biting story of the Westchester election victory.

Every Monday beginning November 5, Governor Cosby could expect attacks on his administration. He was called a "Nero," ac-cused of voting as a member of the council which violated the rules of his governorship, of adjourning the assembly in his own name instead of the king's, of being "governor turned rogue." The articles were signed anonymously by Thomas Standby, Philo-Patrie and, of course, by Cato. The true authors were, primarily, James Alexander and Lewis Morris.

The governor bitterly wrote the Board of Trade in London that Alexander was "the head of a scheme to give all imaginable un-easiness to the government by infusing into, and making the worst impression on, the minds of the people. A press supported by him and his party began to swarm with the most virulent libels." Of Lewis Morris, the governor wrote, "His open and implacable malice against me has appeared weekly in Zenger's *Journal*."

The attacks in the *Journal* continued. Cosby was accused of suppressing trial by jury, of undermining "fundamental laws." His high sheriff was ridiculed as a monkey who "fancied himself a general." Another Cosby associate was called a "large spaniel" whose mouth was "full of fulsome panegericks."

The governor could take it no more and early in 1734 sought to have a grand jury move against the "seditious libels" of Zenger's publication. Two grand juries refused to bring an indictment and finally the governor had his own Council issue a warrant for seditious libel. The sheriff took John Peter Zenger into custody on November 17, 1734. He was to be held there, incommunicado, for ten months before his case came to trial. Throughout that period he remained silent about the men who really wrote and edited the *Journal,* an enormous contribution to the tradition that sources of information be kept sacrosanct.

His wife bravely took over publication and Anna Catherine Zenger not only kept it going—it missed only one issue during his imprisonment—but knowing how eager the authorities were to find the real editor, how gladly they would trade a printer for that man, she protected James Alexander's identity even as her husband did. The one issue that failed of publication was on the week of Zenger's arrest and a first person editorial the following week explained the lapse, the arrest, and concluded "I doubt not you will think me sufficiently excused for not sending my last week's *Journal* and hope for the future, by the liberty of speaking to my servants thro' the hole of the door of the prison, to entertain you with my weekly *Journal* as formerly."

On August 4, 1735 John Peter Zenger came to trial before young Justice DeLancey and an associate judge. His defense was said to have been planned by James Alexander (Some say that Benjamin Franklin made contributions) and was conducted by one of the most distinguished lawyers in the colonies, the elderly Andrew Hamilton, almost eighty years old.

Charging seditious libel was an old device of unhappy officials. English custom, they felt, prohibited printers from publishing anything that offended the king or his representative. Truth was no defense for "the greater the truth, the greater the libel." Since the king's rule was absolute, any criticism of it was illegitimate and thus criminal. If true, it was all the more criminal for it could cause disturbance in the populace, a breach of the public peace. Truth was no defense in libel matters.

A jury was quickly chosen. Attorney General Richard Bradley read the formal charges. Zenger pleaded innocent. Then the white-haired lawyer from Philadelphia dramatically rose and appeared to give away his case. Andrew Hamilton announced that he confessed for his client that he had published the newspapers named in the charges. Bradley quickly rose and said, "If Your Honors please" the case is over, the jury can bring in a verdict of guilty.

"Not so, neither, Mr. Attorney," said Defense Counsel Hamilton, "There are two sides to that bargain. I hope it is not our bare printing or publishing a paper that will make it a libel. You will have something more to do before you make my client a libeler. For the words themselves must be libelous—that is false, malicious, and seditious—or else we are not guilty."

Justice DeLancey admonished the defense: "You cannot be admitted, Mr. Hamilton, to give truth of a libel in evidence. The court is of the opinion you ought not to be permitted to prove the facts in the papers." Hamilton said that would make it a Star Chamber case. The flustered justice asked Hamilton to mind his manners—"You are not permitted to argue against this court."

Lawyer Hamilton bowed to the chief justice courteously, saying "I thank you," and then turned his back to both judges to address the jury. "Then it is to you, gentlemen, that we must now appeal for witnesses to the truth of the facts we have offered." DeLancey interrupted—juries had no right under law to decide anything other than what Hamilton already admitted, that Zenger had published the papers. Judges, not juries, decide whether such papers are libelous. Hamilton simply said juries may indeed do so and continued to argue before the jury.

He began by noting that the suppressing of evidence by the state was itself the strongest of evidence, "and I hope it will have that weight with you." He lectured them on jury prerogatives, saying it was their right to rule on the truth of the alleged libels, to respond to "men who injure and oppress the people under their administration, provoke them to cry out and complain, and then make that very complaint the foundation for new oppressions and prosecutions."

Justice DeLancey kept objecting but the wily old lawyer ignored him. He continued his appeal to the jury directly: "Old and weak as I am, I should think it my duty, if required, to go to the utmost part of the land where my service could be of any use in assisting to quench the flame of prosecution upon information, set on foot by the government to deprive a people of the right of remonstrating and complaining too of the arbitrary attempts of men in power."

The record shows that he rested his case with this plea for a free press:

> The question before the Court and you, Gentlemen of the Jury, is not of small nor private concern, it is not the cause of a poor printer, nor of New York alone, which you are now trying: No! It may in its consequence affect every Freeman that lives under a British Government on the Main of America. It is the best cause. It is the cause of Liberty; and I make no doubt but your upright conduct this day will not only entitle you to the love and esteem of your fellow-citizens; but every man who prefers freedom to a life of slavery will bless and honor you, as men who have baffled the attempt of tyranny; and by an impartial and uncorrupt verdict, have laid a noble foundation for securing to ourselves, our posterity and our neighbors, that, to which nature and the laws of our country have given us a right —the Liberty—both of exposing and opposing arbitrary power (in these parts of the world, at least) by speaking and writing truth.

Justice DeLancey tried to force a directed verdict but did not succeed. After short deliberation, the jury returned with a verdict. Foreman Thomas Hunt shouted defiantly, "Not guilty!" and cheers rolled across the courtroom, the crowd ignoring angry Justice DeLancey's attempt to rebuke it.

The verdict was an extremely popular one. A dinner was given in honor of Andrew Hamilton and the city council voted him the freedom of the city of New York and gave him a gold box to contain the document. The proceedings of the trial were published and shared the popularity of Cato's *Letters*. It was even published in England with an editorial footnote that the American trial "having made a great noise in the world, is here inserted: though the doctrines advanced by Mr. Hamilton in his speeches are not allowed in the courts here to be law." The Zenger case established rights of juries which would not become valid in England until 1792.

Zenger was a landmark in the history of a free press. In that tiny courtroom in New York's city hall, a major blow was struck against the doctrine that public officials are immune from criticism. It was the foundation for setting truth as a defense in libel. It was the precedent for editors in the next two hundred years to fight for the right of publication. Gouverneur Morris, one of two grandsons of Lewis Morris to sign the Declaration of Independence, traced the beginning of American liberty to the trial of Zenger rather than the Stamp Act, for it established the inborn right of free thought and speech. In his words, "The trial of Zenger in 1735 was the morning star of that liberty which subsequently revolutionized America."

There are those who say the Zenger verdict broke the will of Governor Cosby. Rebuked by a jury of men who were typical of his constituency, he gave up his battle against Zenger, Alexander, and Morris and on March 10, 1736 died in office. The following year Zenger was named public printer in New York and one year after that, thanks to the political power of Lewis Morris, public printer in New Jersey as well. He died in 1746. Elderly lawyer Hamilton returned to Philadelphia and made one final contribution to the men of the new world. He designed the new state house which was used as the meeting hall for the Revolution forty years later and became known as Independence Hall. Hamilton died on August 4, 1741 exactly six years to the day after the trial of Zenger.

The popularity of the Zenger decision and the widespread discussion of the case were woven into the fabric of a free press in America. And so it was when the Constitution, conceived in secret deliberation, made no provision to guarantee freedom of speech except for congressmen, popular demand hurried approval of a Bill of Rights. The press, the people felt, needed protective shelter from the government.

The history of the official and the journalist in this country is not a record unblemished since Zenger. As we shall document in this volume, excesses against newspapers occur increasingly in time of national strain, including time of war, when newspapers have been stopped of publication, of mail privileges, of distribution, and, even on occasion, put out of business, the editor jailed or expelled from the community.

The companion to such direct action against the press is an intimidation that chills free speech. That, too, has been felt in the years since Zenger. During the early 1950s, in the prime of Joseph McCarthy, America faltered and so did its free press as fear and hysteria gripped much of the nation. The late Arthur Hays Sulzberger spoke out at the time saying, "Freedom cannot be trifled with." For his fellow publishers in the age of McCarthyism he noted, "There has been dropped upon utterance and thought a smoke screen of intimidation that dims essential thought and essential talk and begets a fog through which we wander uncertainly. Nor is it the superzealots who bother me so much in all this—it is the lack of plain, old-fashioned guts on the part of those who capitulate to them."

The third partner in government's advantage over the press is the right to protect state secrets. While direct action against the press is rare and intimidation not always successful, the habit of hiding the actions of government from the public is general and persistent. It is done in the name of efficient operation of the people's business. But the power to operate in a closed room is the power to cover up error or worse. Knaves blink in the sunlight, they smile in the shadows. Good men don't fear the light of publicity, but they find it counterproductive and they go to the shadows where corruption is the resident temptation.

The right to have secrets is extended down through all levels of government and lesser men are even more likely to abuse the privilege. Sometimes it reaches absurd levels. Gaylord Shaw of the Associated Press tells of an experience with Pentagon classification:

> We submitted fifteen written questions to the Pentagon. They answered numbers one, two, six, ten and thirteen and totally ignored the others. When we inquired as to the reason for the absence of answers to two-thirds of our questions, we were told the material we requested was classified. One of those classified answers was the date of the founding of Fort Benning, Ga.
>
> So we placed a call to the public information office at Ft.

Benning. The officer who answered the phone gave us the date immediately. The following exchange then ensued:

OFFICER: "Why didn't you just ask the Pentagon and save the price of a long distance call?"

REPORTER: "I did ask the Pentagon. They wouldn't tell me."

OFFICER: "You're kidding! Why?"

REPORTER: "They said the information was classified."

There was a moment's pause and then, obviously nervous, the officer pleaded: "Well, for God's sake, don't tell them you got it from me!"

Current America is full of amusing anecdotes about foolish exercise of the right to mark something "secret" but that power can be a damaging one. As the late Justice Hugo Black said in his final opinion, appropriately one dealing with the free press, "The word 'security' is a broad, vague generality whose contours should not be invoked to abrogate the fundamental law embodied in the First Amendment. The guarding of military and diplomatic secrets at the expense of informed representative government provides no real security for our Republic."

The government's powers to punish the press, to intimidate or inhibit the press, and to keep its secrets from the press are the powers to hide from the people, the masters to whom government is ultimately responsible. As noted earlier, when one examines the documentation regarding intrusions into a free press, one would do well to think of the record as necessarily incomplete. It is a record of failures, of the attempts to intimidate or manipulate the press which failed because they became known. What we must lack of necessity is the record of times when politicians succeeded in getting a story killed or changed or distorted just enough to take the edge off. We know the father of failures in media manipulation, we are ignorant of the orphans because their parentage has successfully been kept secret. How many times have politicians succeeded? We rarely know. We can only know when they fail or are challenged.

Still there is value in examining just that—the attempts that we know of, the failures, or, at least, the publicized successes. This we now do. We take as our first subject of examination, the actions of presidents. Much of what public officials do or would do has been done or attempted by the most powerful of all men, the American president. His relations with news media tell us much about both institutions, the presidency and the press.

II

HOW FAR WILL THE PRESIDENT GO?

To an aide, John F. Kennedy once said of the press, "Always remember that their interests and ours ultimately conflict."

Presidents don't like the press.

Almost every president professes to be a defender of press freedoms, particularly in the early days of his presidency. Inevitably, he pledges an "open" administration. Almost every president comes to develop a strong distaste for the press and an urge to malign, manipulate, and manage the press very soon after his early days.

Perhaps the only exception to this rule of presidents and the press was William Henry Harrison. He died one month after his inaugural.

Presidents of longer tenure have been quick to anger over press excesses. George Washington wanted a State Department clerk fired because he edited an anti-Washington newspaper. Teddy Roosevelt brought libel suits against newspapers both during and after his presidency. Jefferson once suggested that a few good prosecutions would help restore the integrity of the press.

Presidents hate news leaks. Teddy Roosevelt and Herbert Hoover used the Secret Service to find the source of unwanted news reports. The Kennedy, Johnson, and Nixon administrations used the FBI similarly.

Presidents love to and sometimes lust to have power over the press. Andrew Jackson placed fifty-seven reporters and editors on his payroll. Woodrow Wilson once considered a federal news service to make sure the public got the "real facts." Harry Truman suggested that in an emergency he had the right to seize the nation's newspapers. John F. Kennedy was the master of "news management," Lyndon B. Johnson the overseer of "credibility gap," and Richard Nixon the patron of Spiro Agnew.

No president has been able to ignore the press. It is like walking past a full-length mirror several times a day. One can't resist looking into it and seeing what it has to reflect.

Modern day presidents do more than look into the matter of what the press reports. From George Washington, who "managed" the publication of his final address in a hand-picked newspaper, on to Franklin Roosevelt, who used radio to circumvent a hostile press, presidents have dabbled in media manipulation. In the television era, beginning after World War II and flourishing in the presidencies of Kennedy, Johnson, and Nixon, presidents did not have to dabble; they had tremendous room to maneuver. Ironically, they have had mixed success.

Consider the press coverage of the modern presidency. A large group of newspaper, magazine, and broadcast reporters are "permanently" assigned to the White House and travel wherever the President goes. Television alone has two correspondents per network assigned to the White House. Still photographers and television camermen by the dozen supplement the reporters. On presidential trips, the press plane carries dozens of "regulars" or up to hundreds of reporters depending on the nature and scope of the presidential travel.

Newsmen are at the president's side as long as he permits it; for twenty-four hours if he wants it or if a crisis demands it. Television time is his at his mere request. As ex-presidential Press Secretary George Reedy once put it, "There is no other human being on the face of the globe who has any comparable facilities for projecting every thought, every nuance, that is in his mind."

Bill Moyers, one of Reedy's successors in serving Lyndon Johnson, said, "Modern Presidents have realized that they can never effectively govern unless they learn to reach the people through the mass media, and the wise ones have discovered how to go through or over the press to the people."

While the opportunities for presidential power to "go through or over the press" have increased in the electronic age and the sophistication of a president's "media advisors" has grown with the development of that art, modern presidents don't do better than their predecessors did. They don't do as well as the first presidents did in eras when there were "kept" newspapers, some for you and some against you. Richard Nixon, in the third year of his presidency, was given to complain "It is probably true that I have less, as somebody has said, supporters in the press than any president. I understand that and I do not complain about it."

Of course, the Nixon administration—as has its predecessors—has complained mightily and frequently, if not directly the president then pointedly the vice-president, Cabinet members, national party officials, and supporters in the Congress. The president, they would say of their man in office, just doesn't get a fair shake from the press.

Nixon's press secretary, Ron Ziegler, is fond of referring to the "adversary" relationship between press and president. He is right. They are not allies and when there is a healthy press, politicians will fail to make them members of "the team." Frustrated presidents sometimes turn to patriotism as an appeal for support. Yet, from this nation's earliest days the role of an independent "censor" of government, as Jefferson put it, was the most vital role of the press. The newsman was not meant to be "on the team," he was meant to view that team from the sidelines.

The result of press "censoring" of government can be frustrating and usually is galling to presidents. Their image makers search for that magic way to make it come out "right" in the press. Complete success, however, is self-defeating. When the press succumbs to presidential seduction, its constituency develops its own skepticism and the press is not believed. Only in totalitarian states is the press unabashedly friendly to a nation's leaders and there the press is never believed.

They will never be compatible, American presidents and the press. That is something that citizens should be grateful for.

This is not a new development. It has been so from the start.

Thomas Jefferson knew the bite of a newspaper. He knew that in public life, no matter how much "purity of conduct," a president could be attacked in the public prints. He wrote Dr. James Currie that it is "an evil for which there is no remedy, our liberty depends on freedom of the press, and that cannot be limited without being lost."

Jefferson knew the temptation of politicians (There are rights "which governments have . . . always been fond to invade"), but he felt, to his final years, that government should be kept out of the press. As he wrote Lafayette in 1823, "The only security of all is a free press. The force of public opinion cannot be resisted, when permitted freely to be expressed. The agitation it produces must be submitted to. It is necessary, to keep the waters pure."

Jefferson is worth reviewing. He is responsible, as much as any man, for the First Amendment.

An early and strong advocate of a bill of rights, Jefferson kept petitioning Madison and others to include it in the Constitution. He said the people are entitled to such a defense "against every government on earth" and added that a bill of rights is what "no just government should refuse." From Europe, he wrote Madison and Washington again and again, often giving a series of "short answers" to objections raised against a bill of rights. He was very disturbed at the omission of such guarantees in the original Constitution.

In one letter to Madison, Jefferson's defense of a Declaration of Rights warned that government might not like it. In words that are especially pertinent today, he addressed himself to office holders frustrated by what they consider the excesses of the press and the intrusions of press opinion into the operation of government. Wrote Jefferson, "The inconveniences of the Declaration are that it may cramp government in its useful exertions. But the evil of this is short-lived, trivial and reparable. The inconveniences of the want of a Declaration are permanent, afflicting and irreparable." At no time did Jefferson, who wrote as bitterly as anyone about press excesses be they short-lived, trivial, or reparable, suggest that freedom of the press be unlimited. He always insisted on "the liability of the printers for false facts printed," but those facts must be printed first and publishers suffer the consequences later.

Precedent for opposing prior restraint on publication was found in Blackstone's commentaries. That such precedent is still not fully accepted is found in actions of the U.S. Government in current times. Blackstone wrote: "The liberty of the press is indeed essential to the nature of a free state; but this consists in laying no previous restraints upon publications, and not in freedom from censure for criminal matter when published."

Twenty years later, in 1789, Jefferson wrote similarly in a "Proposed Charter for France" suggesting "printers shall be liable to legal prosecution for printing and publishing false facts, injurious to the party prosecuting, but they shall be under no other restraint." Blackstone had written, "Every freeman has an undoubted right to lay what sentiments he pleases before the public; to forbid this, is to destroy the freedom of the press: but if he publishes what is improper, mischievous, or illegal, he must take the consequence."

In time, and largely because of Jefferson's insistence, the Bill of Rights was added to the Constitution as the first ten amendments, the first embracing free speech and free press. "I am persuaded," said Jefferson, "that the good sense of the people will always be found to be the best army. They may be led astray for a moment, but will soon correct themselves."

It is remarkable how Jefferson anticipated the many arguments relating to the press and dealt with them in the earliest days of the nation. Years later Woodrow Wilson would note how much better it is to have free speech, free press, and let off steam rather than have it build up. Similarly, Jefferson told Thaddeus Kosciusko of "the newspapers, which serve as chimneys to carry off noxious vapors and smoke."

He considered his relations with the press a "great experiment" conducted while "the artillery of the press has been levelled against us, charged with whatsoever its licentiousness could devise or dare." He said such abuses of press freedom were to be regretted but public duties were more urgently pressing on a president's time, any punishment must be left to public indignation. In 1804, in a letter to Judge Tyler, he wrote of the great experiment and noted that if man is to be governed by reason and truth, all avenues to truth must remain open. The most effectual is freedom of the press—"It is therefore the first shut up by those who fear the investigation of their actions."

The most extravagant statement Jefferson ever made about the press, one quoted frequently by newspaper editors in their Freedom of Information declarations, dealt with public opinion as the basis of government "and were it left to me to decide whether we should have a government without newspapers, or newspapers without a government, I should not hesitate a moment to prefer the latter." Lyndon Johnson once quipped that Jefferson said that before he became president! In retrospect, Jefferson would have enjoyed that observation.

Yes, it is true that Jefferson said that while in Europe and it was nine years before he became even vice-president. It is also true that Jefferson's interests in newspaper freedom were less for their publishers than their readers for he had added, after saying newspapers without government are preferable to the reverse, "I should mean that every man should receive these papers, and be capable of reading them."

In his mind, the important thing was moving information to the electorate. This not only made man better equipped to choose and understand his leaders, it made the leaders more responsible to the public. "As men become better informed," wrote Jefferson, "their rulers must respect them the more."

Though the beginning years of the nation were witness to some of the most glowing rhetoric in support of a philosophical basis to press freedom, it was an era of newspapers unlike any we know. There was far less news than opinion and papers were usually vitriolic in tone, irresponsible in substance. Further, it was an era of kept newspapers and Jefferson himself had a hand in backing one such paper before and another after his election.

Jefferson's greatest rival in the Federalist camp was Alexander Hamilton who had backed James Fenno's *Gazette of the United States* into a position of power, the voice of the Federalists during George Washington's Presidency. Jefferson sought to counteract the *Gazette* by inviting anti-Federalist editors to set up shop in the capital.

Failing to get Benjamin Franklin Bache, who later became a key figure in the Alien and Sedition Act controversy, Jefferson found an equally talented, equally outspoken editor in Philip Freneau. He wooed him but was turned down. Then Jefferson offered a subsidy: "The clerkship for foreign languages in my office is vacant; the salary, indeed, is very low, being two hundred and fifty dollars a year; but it also gives so little to do as not to interfere with any other office one may choose."

Freneau consented, came to New York, and founded *The National Gazette* which quickly became the young nation's leading anti-Federalist voice and, in the course of it, a vicious critic of President Washington. For two years, Fenno and Freneau competed. Freneau's superior ability was a constant irritant to Hamilton and the Federalists. It also exasperated George Washington who called the attacks an him "outrages of common decency."

In May 1793 Washington could take it no more and confronted Jefferson with the excesses of Freneau who, the president said, had attacked every single act of government. He asked Jefferson to withdraw Freneau's appointment as clerk. Jefferson declined and at the time noted privately, "I will not do it. His paper has saved our constitution which was galloping fast into monarchy."

It should be noted that while Jefferson's editor was drawing a government salary and had access to official documents, Hamilton's man was not wanting for support. Fenno was made printer for the Senate and also did printing for the Treasury Department. His paper was used increasingly for Hamilton's counterattacks on Jefferson.

Washington was running out of patience. One account tells of the day that the president "was much inflamed, got into one of those passions when he cannot command himself." Washington defied anyone to prove that he had ever acted with other than the purest motives. He said he'd rather be in his grave than in his present situation, would rather be on his farm than be emperor of the world.

Finally, Washington appealed to both Jefferson and Hamilton to stop the press war for the sake of the government. Hamilton promised cooperation but noted that Jefferson had started the *National Gazette* for political purposes, namely attacks on Hamilton.

Jefferson pleaded innocence in a four-thousand word letter (which may have been truly protesting too much), in which he recognized the dissension but pleaded that no one was more distressed than he. Hamilton had attacked him in the *Gazette of the United States* under the pen name "an American" and had made a number of false charges, notably that Jefferson had written from Europe in opposition to the Constitution and that he advocated nonpayment of the public debt.

As to Hamilton's main charge that he was the patron of Freneau, Jefferson admitted encouraging the beginning of the newspaper but denied influencing the editor. At the same time, Freneau went before the mayor of Philadelphia and signed an affidavit that Jefferson had neither directed, controlled, nor tried to influence him, nor had Jefferson written a line for the *National Gazette.*

In his long letter to Washington, Jefferson waxed eloquent as to the role of the press. "No government ought to be without censors and where the press is free, no one ever will. If virtuous, it need not fear the fair operation of attack and defense. Nature has given to man no other means of sifting out the truth either in religion, law, or politics. I think it is honorable for the government neither to know, nor notice, its sycophants or censors, as it would be undignified and criminal to pamper the former and persecute the latter."

While this was a fine defense of press freedom and strong reason not to fire Freneau from his clerkship, it was also part of one of the cloudier declarations by Thomas Jefferson. He wrote that he never, directly or indirectly, had any influence in Freneau's newspaper. He also insisted, "I never did by myself or any other, directly or indirectly, write, dictate or procure any one sentence or sentiment to be inserted *in his, or any other gazette,* to which my name was not or that of my office." Unfortunately, Jefferson's role as patron was too well known for that to be fully believed. Years later, Freneau would charge Jefferson with not only writing much of his publication but with being author of some of the worst articles. He produced a marked file of paper as proof.

When Jefferson resigned as secretary of state in 1793, Freneau faded from the picture. The *Gazette* was suspended from publication during the yellow fever epidemic that year and never regained its former stature.

During the Adams administration, there were many papers friendly to the president and John Adams wrote for a number of them under the pseudonym "Novanglus." He actually made plans to publish a government newspaper but never succeeded. In his outline of what such a paper would be, Adams talked of restraint from publishing libel and a ban on all paragraphs "offensive" to individuals, public bodies, and other nations. He added an exception; it need not forbid advertisements.

Jefferson, on succeeding Adams, did come close to establishing a government newspaper. He prevailed on a young Philadelphia editor, Samuel Harrison Smith, to move the *National Intelligencer* to Washington, now the national capital. It became the voice of the Jefferson administration and was kept on through the two terms of James Madison, though Madison did not share Jefferson's great interest in it or the press generally.

Just as Jefferson had introduced competition to the Federalist paper, Hamilton introduced strong counterpoint to the *National Intelligencer* (which had now added "and *Washington Advertiser*" to its masthead). Hamilton's new vehicle was the *New York Post,* which has passed through many different lifetimes to become the longest-lived daily in the United States though philosophically far from the paper that was started in November of 1801. Hamilton remained aloof from the *Post* publicly but privately wrote for it, as he had for the *Gazette of the United States* in earlier years.

The *Post,* by the way, started a sad chain of circumstances which led to the end of Hamilton. Its editor, William Coleman, wrote an article accusing Jefferson of paying a Richmond editor, James Callender, to slander John Adams. Callender had called Adams a hoary-headed incendiary. In the habit of that day, other newspapers picked up Coleman's story including the *Wasp,* edited by Harry Croswell in Hudson, New York. The government took action against the *Wasp* and, under New York law, Croswell was indicted and found guilty of libelling the president.

He appealed his conviction to the state supreme court and his lawyer was none other than Alexander Hamilton. Hamilton, in the spirit of an earlier advocate named Hamilton who had defended John Peter Zenger, gave a stirring defense. He talked of "the right to publish with impunity truth, with good motives, for justifiable ends, though reflecting on government, magistracy, or individuals."

The judges were evenly divided so the appeal was lost but the defense was so impressive that the New York Assembly passed legislation to provide that juries judge the law as well as the facts, that truth be admitted as evidence in libel cases. These issues were the same as those Andrew Hamilton had argued for Zenger. They were now passed into law.

There was a sad finish to the story. While in Albany to argue the case, Alexander Hamilton visited a tavern and during a discussion had some unkind words for Aaron Burr, Jefferson's vice-president. They were old enemies, Hamilton and Burr. The differences went back many years, Burr having defeated Hamilton's father-in-law in a U.S. Senate race in 1791. Hamilton called Burr "dangerous" and said he might offer "a still more despicable opinion" later.

Reporters were in the tavern with Hamilton since he was the center of the case then before the state supreme court. His remarks were picked up in an Albany newspaper and read by Burr. At the time, Burr had wanted to run for governor of New York but Hamilton had rallied opposition to that. Now the insult. Burr challenged Hamilton to a duel and they met at ten paces at Weehawken. Hamilton was killed.

The press grew in power over those early years and many political leaders recognized it. By the time Andrew Jackson was elected, the influence of the press was quite marked. Jackson subscribed to twenty newspapers. Further, to make sure of friendship among newspapers, he put fifty-seven journalists on the government payroll. One historian wrote that Jackson "ruled the country by means of the newspaper press."

"Old Hickory" was often criticized for loading his administration with newspapermen and would reply, "It is the object of all who really take an interest in the honor and welfare of our country to elevate the character of the press and make it a vehicle of truth and useful knowledge. What scheme can be more subversive of this object than one which virtually withdraws from the service of the press those who aspire to some higher character in life than that of mere agents for the advancement and distinction of others?"

One newspaper editor warned, "Invade the freedom of the Press and freedom of Election, by showering patronage too much on Editors of newspapers and on Members of Congress, and the rights of the people themselves are exposed to imminent danger." Jackson replied that he would not discriminate against his friends simply because they are just that, his friends. As so many presidents after him, he asked to be judged by the results not the fears and forebodings, "before he condemns the Tree, he ought to wait and see its fruit."

Its fruit was a powerful "Kitchen Cabinet" of five men, three of them journalists. The most powerful were Francis P. Blair and Amos Kendall. The latter, a Kentucky editor before joining the government payroll, was described by one congressman as the president's "thinking machine, writing machine, aye, and his lying machine." As for Blair, it became a cliché for Jackson to say, "Take it to Blair."

Blair, a tall, very thin Marylander was editor of the *Washington Globe* which joined the *United States Telegraph* as the kept papers of the Jackson administration. Subsidized by official advertising and government printing contracts, the *Globe* was quickly spotted as the voice of Andrew Jackson. It was read abroad as well as at home for official views. The Russian foreign minister once complained to the American ambassador there about a matter in the paper and asked that President Jackson see that it be corrected in the *Globe*.

Blair also had a knack for news management beyond the confines of his own, obviously pro-Jackson publication. He would plant pro-Jackson articles and editorials in other newspapers and then reprint them as signs of public support for the president.

The idea of an official administration paper finally died out in the administration of James Buchanan. Others would hire newspapermen and newspapers would, some of them, continue to have a strong political bent but the era of the kept newspaper as such died by the beginning of the Civil War.

Abraham Lincoln, in keeping with that earlier tradition was once a partner in a Springfield, Illinois, German language newspaper which was pledged never to offend his political beliefs. As the silent partner and financial supporter of the *Illinois State Anzeiger,* Lincoln signed a contract with publisher Theodore Canisium stating that if the paper should "in political sentiment" depart from the Republican platforms and if it should ever print "anything opposed to, or designed to injure the Republican Party, said Lincoln may, at his option, at once take possession of said press, types, &c. and deal with them as his own."

The *Anzieger* never departed and served the Republicans well. After his election as president, Lincoln withdrew and Canisius became full owner. Shortly after that, the paper was discontinued as President Lincoln had another reward for his friend, appointment as U.S. consul on Samoa.

Lincoln had no reservations about the role of the press in supporting a president and had no reluctance to make demands to fit. The most powerful paper outside of New York was the *Chicago Tribune,* which had supported Lincoln from the start. When its publisher, Joseph Medill, and other Chicagoans came to Lincoln in August of 1864 to protest an increase in the draft, Lincoln turned to him and said, "Medill, you are acting like a coward. You and your *Tribune* have had more influence than any paper in the Northeast in making this war. You can influence great masses and yet you cry to be spared at a moment when your cause is suffering. Go home and send us some men." As Medill wrote later, "We did."

One wonders what would happen today if a president spoke so bluntly to a publisher, if a politician made so large a demand on a newspaper.

From the very start, the newspapers of America have been hard on the leaders of the land. While there were kept newspapers and pledged newspapermen, there were just as many in opposition. Their style was virulent and presidents—as John Kennedy said many years later—were reading more and enjoying it less.

George Washington said he couldn't understand the torrent of abuse from "factious" newspapers because he was doing his duty. He added, in remarks to Gouverneur Morris, "I have nothing to fear from invective." He suffered in silence as newspapers of that day called him despotic, treacherous, an imitation of the English Georges, a frail mortal, one who put on royal airs, and a man of "spurious fame." Privately, Washington complained of the "willful, artful and malignant misrepresentations," but publicly said nothing.

It especially hurt when Tom Paine, the pamphleteer who aroused the country for revolution, turned on Washington and blamed him for the hard times that had befallen Paine. He accused his former friend of falsehood, ingratitude, and pusillanimity, and called Washington a hypocrite, an imposter, and one who has abandoned good principles. Washington made no response to these published slanders.

In the end, Washington said he stopped reading newspapers and the few he looked at were really for the advertisements "as being the only truths we can rely on in a newspaper." After his retirement, he wrote Rev. William Gordon, "I suffered every attack that was made upon my Executive conduct . . . to pass unnoticed while I remained in public office; well knowing that if the general tenor of it would not stand the test of investigation, a Newspaper vindication would be of little avail."

It was said that Washington felt the sting of newspapers so strongly ("We have some infamous papers calculated for disturbing if not absolutely intended to disturb, the peace of the community."), that he considered not running for a second term.

Jefferson, who late in his presidency wrote Baron Alexander Von Humboldt that, "When a man assumes a public trust he should consider himself as public property," similarly said presidents should not respond to the press. He frequently sprinkled his correspondence with reference to a desire to keep out of print. "My greatest wish is to go on in a strict but silent performance of my duty, to avoid attracting notice, and to keep my name out of the newspapers."

He wrote that to answer the "calumnies of the newspapers" would take more than all his time and that of twenty assistants and "while I should be answering one, twenty new ones would be invented." It was Jefferson who wrote John Norvell (in a letter that he insisted not get into the press) that newspapers could be divided into four chapters—truths, probabilities, possibilities, and lies—the first chaper being very short and the second not much longer. Such papers, Jefferson feared, would have few subscribers—"Defamation is becoming a necessary of life; insomuch, that a dish of tea in the morning or evening cannot be digested without this stimulant. Even those who do not believe these abominations, still read them with complaisance (and) betray a secret pleasure in the possibility that some may believe them, tho they do not themselves."

Despite his championship of a free press, he wrote Monroe that "my scepticism as to everything I see in a newspaper makes me indifferent whether I ever see one." He wrote of "A truth now and then projecting into the ocean of newspaper lies."

Many years later, another president said much the same. Woodrow Wilson wrote Mary Hulbert, "Do not believe anything you read in the newspapers. If you read the papers I see, they are utterly untrustworthy. . . . Their lying is shameless and colossal!"

Few presidents felt the sting of a partisan press more than Lincoln. He was called a "half-witted usurper" and a "slang-whanging stump speaker." He was accused of needless slaughter of men in search of victory ("the head ghoul in Washington"), of granting pardons to win votes, of drunkenness, and of treason. Lincoln rarely showed anger at the venemous attacks. He did once, however. A New York report accused Lincoln of insisting that he be paid in gold while Jefferson Davis was taking his pay in Confederate money and Lincoln's soldiers in depreciated dollars. Lincoln reacted angrily and said, "If the scoundrel who wrote that don't boil hereafter, it will be because the devil hasn't got iron enough to make gridirons."

Wilson is often quoted for his famous phrase "open covenants . . . openly arrived at" but he hardly meant press coverage. He was speaking of the processes of diplomatic negotiation, not reporting of that diplomacy. The latter would horrify him. Indeed, in 1913, he shouted at a reporter, "Damn it, man, can't you take me as you find me?" and then quickly calmed down with, "Pardon me for blowing up. These stories about Cabinet appointments are all false, and to keep on questioning me about it is to doubt my veracity."

From the limited viewpoint of the presidential office, his veracity *is* always being doubted and the press *is* frequently publishing the lies that Washington, Jefferson, Lincoln, Wilson and so many others complained about. "Limited" is the presidential view, for just as the press has access to only part of the facts, so does a president. Only so much about any event reaches a president's desk and that is filtered through many hands. These internal "censors" are inclined to be sycophants, for few men on his staff are willing to tell a president he is wrong.

Even when a president has a clear idea of a set of events, he does not know the difficulties that the reporter encounters in gathering them. Politicians usually suspect that the reporter's bosses, his editors and publishers, are molding a reporter's impressions. Franklin Delano Roosevelt was continually attacking publishers, calling them the *real* threat to press freedom. "I have little fear," he wrote, "that freedom of the press will be abridged from external assault in this country. The danger is from internal corruption."

Harry Truman felt much the same and told an interviewer in 1951, "I think a publisher, or any newspaperman, who doesn't have a sense of responsibility and prints a lot of lies and goes around slandering without any basis in fact—I think that sort of fellow actually can be called a traitor."

While some publishers, increasingly fewer by Truman's time, might have engaged in personal journalism, most of what presidents consider "lies" and "slander" is simply all a reporter can get at the time. Politicians want to control not only the content of what is made public but also its timing. Reporters are continually struggling to make public more than politicians want sooner than they'd like. As Kennedy said, the interests of the one and the concerns of the other are ultimately going to collide.

It is thus that an adversary relationship is inevitable between a searching press and a government in power. Each is suspicious of the other. Each sees the weaknesses of the other. The press suspects government of wanting to lie and to cover up while government suspects the press of wanting to expose, embarrass, and entrap it.

Since the pull-and-tug in America is not simply press and politicians in office but also the competition between politicians, those in and those out of office, there is reason for the "Ins" to hold another view of the press. It works the same in its treatment of the "Outs." It is a censor for all, a check on the established order and on those who challenge it. For all its frailties, the press is the only such check. Its information is often incomplete, sometimes inaccurate, and almost always sporadic, coming in fits and starts, but in the long run it is the primary source for politicians to know of each other and for the public to know of politics. It can be supplemented but it can never be replaced.

The president who smarts under the reporting of the moment can take solace in knowing that his political opponents will suffer from the same examination. A president can also be sure—if he is sophisticated enough—that any distortion is likely to be more a failure of his administration's handling of the information than of any press determination to distort or lie. The best pattern,

George Washington noted in his time, is "plain dealing." When he asked that citizens be well-informed, Washington said, *"Concealment* is a species of mis-information; and mis-information and false alarms found the ground work of opposition." Franklin Roosevelt rejected any suggestion that he place restraints on the press at a time when his advisors warned that the press might hurry the nation into World War II. Roosevelt said no "sensible" man or woman believes that the press should be curtailed or threatened; "The influence of the printed word will always depend on its veracity; and the nation can safely rely on the wise discrimination of a reading public which, with the increase in general education, is able to sort out truth from fiction. Representative democracy will never tolerate the suppression of true news at the behest of the government." Jefferson had said it much earlier of the people, "They may be led astray for a moment, but they will soon correct themselves."

That doesn't mean that presidents don't feel the press callous towards the heavy responsibility they bear. As Lincoln noted to Thurlow Weed in 1861, "Do you gentlemen who control so largely public opinion, do you ever think how you might lighten the burdens of men in power—those poor unfortunates weighed down by care, anxieties, and responsibilities?"

The press rarely did lighten the load. Presidents, on the other hand, frequently engaged in their own lightening of the load, their own molding of public opinion. "News Management" as a phrase entered the scene during the Kennedy administration but as a practice began with the very first president.

George Washington even managed to have his Farewell Address published in a hand-picked newspaper and exclusively at that. He sent for David Claypoole, a partner in the *Pennsylvania Packet and Daily Advertiser,* which was the nation's first morning daily, and asked him to publish the address, even setting the date of publication (the following Monday). Tobias Lear, his secretary, would deliver the copy on Friday.

In the first draft of his Farewell, Washington snapped at his critics in the press whose publications "have teemed with all the Invective that disappointment, ignorance of the facts, and malicious falsehood could invent to misrepresent my politics and affections; to wound my reputation and feeling; and to weaken, if not entirely destroy the confidence you have been pleased to repose in me."

Alexander Hamilton had given him advice in the publication, Washington asking him which editor would be best to go to and did he think the length of the Farewell was too much for newspaper publication. After Washington sent the draft to Hamilton for comment, he decided to drop the references to the press.

News management, as we have noted, was also practiced by Jefferson. Prior to his presidency, he wrote a Richmond editor in response to a story that Jefferson's name be considered for the next presidential election. The story disturbed Jefferson, who authored a correction and told the editor, a close friend, "You will oblige me by inserting in your paper some such contribution as below in a form not importing to come directly from myself." It was done just that way.

Jefferson, while in office, was accused of an improper expense account during his stay in France. That story appeared in the *Baltimore Federal Republican* and the president wrote a reply, demanding that the editors publish it. They did. He warned that the printers, having committed libel, should consider this publication only small retribution and he emphasized that he would pay no further attention to this "palpable misinformation" about his French expenditures. The printers were not contrite and printed a second story which accused Jefferson of receiving double payments. Jefferson was not loyal to his pledge to pay it no further attention. He wrote, and they published, a second and even longer defense.

Presidential anger often involved leaks of information that he either does not want published, does not want published in that form, or does not want published at that time. Even Washington, in the dark days of 1777, complained of the leaks and expressed the wish "that our printers were more discreet." His successor, John Adams, was angry—as was Washington—when newspapers printed the story that Adams would ask Washington to come out of retirement to strengthen the army during the war scare of 1798. The story happened to be true but Washington read it in print before Adams talked to him. He was considerably irked by the indelicacy. He told Adams so.

Jefferson, in his later years, complained bitterly when some of his letters somehow ended up in print. He wrote John Adams that it ought to be made a crime. One senses the fury of his reaction to such leaks when he writes, "Although I know it is too late for me to buckle on the armour of youth, yet my indignation would not permit me passively to receive the kick of an ass."

A news leak that shocked Abraham Lincoln was the publication, before he ever delivered it to Congress, of a portion of his first State of the Union address. It appeared in the *New York Herald* in an article written by Chevalier Henry Wikoff, a reporter who had befriended Mrs. Lincoln. The suspicion was that the first lady had leaked the speech to Wikoff. When a congressional committee investigated, a White House gardener took the blame, offering a far-fetched story of having seen the speech on a library table as he arranged flowers, memorized sections, and passed them on to Wikoff. Lincoln paid a surprise visit to the committee to declare under oath that his wife was innocent. Wikoff was jailed and later returned to his newspaper but not to report at the White House.

Herbert Hoover, as so many presidents, hated stories about his personal life and, when they began to leak out of the White House, took strong measures to stop them. The offending stories included Hoover's dog biting a Marine guard, the president's auto travelling too fast, and a report that some of the White House curtains had patches on them. Hoover assigned the Secret Service to find the source of the leaks and placed a ban on all White House news other than official and approved announcements. The Secret Service failed, the restraint on news failed.

Teddy Roosevelt, on taking office, called in the chiefs of the three press associations. The new president had barely returned from McKinley's funeral. He told them that he would be accessible and would trust the reporters who possessed his confidence but if the confidence were violated, the president would punish the guilty by withholding news from them. The bureau chiefs argued against the policy but Roosevelt simply said, "Now we understand each other." Roosevelt twice tried to impose the ban, once on a reporter who irritated him with a story about Roosevelt children teasing Thanksgiving turkeys on the White House grounds and the other against a London correspondent who misused a letter of introduction. The president found that he could ban them from the White House but he couldn't keep them from the news.

Ridicule was the tool that Roosevelt used more frequently. He had an "Ananias Club" for reporters he considered liars and who would be felled as was Ananias when Peter rebuked him. Roosevelt was sole founder of the club and its full committee on membership. The Ananias Club grew over the years and while largely a joke in the early days, tested the tempers of news people after a while. Membership was usually the final, public rebuke. The president also made a habit of calling a reporter's editor and complaining about stories and even suggesting the reporter be replaced.

Franklin Roosevelt carried on the spirit of Ananias when he would tell reporters—Robert Post of the *New York Times* was one—to stand in the corner and put on a dunce cap. F.D.R. took it a step beyond the caustic and gave chills when he rebuked another reporter, John O'Donnell of the *New York News* during World War II. Someone had brought the president a souvenir of the battle in Europe and suddenly FDR awarded it—a German Iron Cross—to the offending reporter.

Post's offense was simply to ask the president if he were thinking of a third term. O'Donnell's offense was a story dealing with lend-lease which Roosevelt found damaging to Anglo-American relations.

Another to feel the heat of FDR's anger was a former friend and biographer Ernest K. Lindley, who irritated the president early in 1940 when he wrote a column for the *Washington Post.* It said Roosevelt had told a southern congressman that he did not expect to seek a third term. Roosevelt called a news conference, said not a word of Lindley's was true. He went on to attack all columnists; some are wrong twenty percent of the time and others are wrong eighty percent of the time.

Presidential anger is fury matched only by a woman scorned. When *Time* magazine did a story about the retirement of President Auirre Cordo of Chile, who the magazine said was spending more and more time with the wine he cultivates, Roosevelt called it a "disgusting lie" and a "contribution to Nazi propaganda." Roosevelt insisted on direct quotation as he announced that the U.S. government had been forced to apologize to the Chilean government. Publisher Henry Luce said the president's attack was unwarranted by the facts and unwise as an attack on the free press.

Reporters do not enjoy the personal attention attendant to a presidential blast. It is a strong man who is not somewhat shaken. Reporters do not relish presidential ridicule. They get no satisfaction from presidential lectures. On the other hand, there is little evidence that presidents get better treatment after they badger or belittle reporters. Generally they simply increase antagonism from the offending reporter and his sympathetic colleagues. Presidents can't really win in such confrontations. As Oscar Wilde noted long ago, "In America, the President reigns for four years, but Journalism will be reporting again tomorrow."

Many presidents reserve their strongest censure for the personal matters. Even here the president cannot win. Woodrow Wilson with fire in his eyes, bitterly dressed down reporters for speculating about his oldest daughter's romances. "I do not see why I should permit representatives of papers who treat the ladies of my household this way to have personal interviews with me. They are entitled to all the news there is, and so far as even the ladies are concerned they are welcome to all that is true, but beyond that there is something that I cannot and will not endure."

Finishing his lecture, Wilson admonished the reporters to "put yourself in my place and give me the best cooperation in this that you can, and then we can dismiss a painful subject and go to our afternoon's business." Professor Wilson's stern admonition worked —for a few weeks.

Perhaps Harry Truman had a better idea. He recognized that he couldn't do much about news reports dealing with his family while still president but "I'm saving up four or five good, hard punches on the nose, and when I'm out of this job, I'm going to run around and deliver them personally."

Whether the excesses of the press deal with personal lives or public policies, presidents don't go around punching reporters or columnists in the nose. They rarely even resort to calling them "sons of bitches" though—as Truman's term testifies—that has been done.

Jefferson once suggested strong action against the worst of the press, which he said had reached a "degree of prostitution" in its licentiousness and its lying. He wrote Thomas McKean, "I have long thought that a few prosecutions of the most prominent offenders would have a wholesome effect in restoring the integrity of the presses. Not a general prosecution, for that would look like persecution, but a selected one."

Andrew Jackson had another way to get at the wayward press. Jackson's editor-advisor Kendall, now appointed postmaster general, suggested that one way to inhibit the troublesome antislavery publications of the day was to seize them in the mails. Jackson ordered him to do so until the Congress could pass legislation to deal with it, to take down the names of all subscribers, and then expose them "thro publik journals as subscribers to this wicked plan of exciting the negroes to insurrection and to massacre." Those patronizing such "incendiary" works, wrote Jackson to Kendall, should be exposed so that they either stop or get out of the country.

In 1835, in his seventh annual message to the Congress, he called for legislation to prohibit any circulation in the South of "publications intended to instigate the slaves to insurrection." Such a measure was introduced, one that gave the postmaster the right to burn such material if not withdrawn from the mails. It was too much for Congress, however, and was defeated 25 to 19.

Editors were momentarily protected from postal seizure but the abolitionist writers found there were other perils. In Alton, Illinois a resolution was passed demanding an end to the publication of Elijah P. Lovejoy. Mobs had destroyed his presses. The date was November 3, 1837 and Lovejoy addressed a hostile public meeting, "If the civil authorities refuse to protect me, I must look to God; and if I die, I have determined to make my grave in Alton. I have sworn eternal opposition to slavery and by the blessings of God I will never turn back. With God I cheerfully rest my cause. I can die at my post but I cannot desert it."

Four days later, he did indeed die at his post. A mob attacked the warehouse where his new press was stored. Lovejoy, trying to protect his property, was killed.

Lovejoy's death was only a hint of things to come. The slavery issue did not abate and finally led to the Civil War which saw editors jailed, presses destroyed, postal powers used, censorship, expulsion of reporters, and more.

III

IT'S TOUGHER IN TIME OF WAR

Censorship of news dispatches began April, 1861 in Washington with the government assuming control of all telegraph wires. The responsibility floated back and forth from the Treasury Department to the War Department to State and back to War. Washington correspondents complained mightily. The censors, they said, were stupid and ignorant and eager to spend all their time in saloons.

The complaints led to a congressional investigation to see if the censorship had not gone beyond the "laudable objective" of withholding information from the enemy and had gone on to "restrain wholesome political criticism and discussion." Washington correspondents testified and complained about the restrictions of General McClellan. In March of 1862, the Judiciary Committee filed a formal report and said, "Dispatches, almost numberless, of a political, personal, and general character, have been suppressed by the censor." It said, "The telegraph has become a most important auxiliary to the press of the country, and should be left as free from government interference as may be consistent . . . in a time of war."

At about that same time, however, Secretary of War Stanton

ordered a reporter arrested as a spy and the capital was distracted from the censorship matter. The man in question was Dr. Malcolm Ives of the *New York Herald* who, according to Stanton, came without invitation to a conference Stanton was holding for some members of Congress. Ives, additionally suspicious because his brother had quit the U.S. military service to join the Confederate Army, was there "for the purpose of spying and obtaining war news and intelligence in regard to Cabinet consultations, telegraphs, etc. for publication, which he knew was not authorized to be published."

Dr. Ives, assigned by the *Herald* to set up a Washington news bureau, when told to leave, had said that the full power of his newspaper would be turned against the Lincoln administration if he failed to get his story. He was arrested and jailed at Fort McHenry. Stanton kept him there until the following June, never filing a charge against him. The *Herald,* in a display of newspaper cowardice, did nothing to defend Ives and simply dropped him from the staff. As for Stanton, he loudly announced that others would be treated similarly if they committed similar breaches of conduct.

Edwin M. Stanton, Lincoln's secretary of war, was gloomy, ill-mannered, vituperative, intolerant, harsh, and hated by almost all subordinates. Lincoln also found him hard to take but admired him as a man who got things done ("Folks come up here and tell me that there are a great many men in the country who have all Stanton's excellent qualities without his defects. All I have to say is, I haven't met 'em! I don't know 'em! I wish I did!"). It was Stanton who demanded the rigid censorship and the press despised him. Lincoln often had to intervene on their behalf but in the end he supported his secretary.

The generals had their complaints. Lee and the Confederate generals read northern newspapers regularly and gathered much information on the movements of the Army of the Potomac. It was said that a *Philadelphia Inquirer* story tipped Lee off as to McClellan's moves, permitting him to pull troops out of Richmond and use them to counter McClellan. Ulysses S. Grant protested strongly to Stanton that the *New York Times* in November, 1864 had published a story giving the exact strength of Sherman's army as well as his campaign plans. The *Indianapolis Daily Journal* re-

ported the exact maneuvers of Sherman's forces as they marched
through Georgia. The worst transgression was a *New York Tribune*
story which suggested to Confederate General Hardee that Sherman was moving to meet his supply ships at Morehead City and
resulted, Sherman was convinced, in a heavy loss of men in the
Carolina campaign.

Sherman's feelings about news gatherers were expressed on
December 26, 1864 when he issued a special field order on occupying Savannah: "Not more than two newspapers will be published in Savannah; their editors and proprietors will be held to
the strictest accountability, and will be punished severely, in person and property, for any libelous publication, mischievous matter,
premature news, exaggerated statements, or any comments whatsoever upon the acts of the constituted authorities."

Under these conditions, why bother publishing at all?

General A. E. Burnside, whose whiskers from ear to ear ended
up as part of our language, went Sherman one better—he once
ordered a newspaperman shot. It was during the Wilderness campaign and only intercession by Grant saved the reporter. William
Swinton was the man and he gained access to Grant's headquarters
at Spotsylvania by passing himself off as a "literary gentleman,"
writing a history of the war. When Grant read a full account of
his own orders to one of his officers in a Richmond paper he began to suspect Swinton. A few nights later, Swinton was found
eavesdropping on a staff meeting. After that, Swinton was picked
up by Burnside at Cold Harbor and was arrested. The general
issued orders to have him shot that afternoon. Grant heard about
it, countermanded the order, and expelled Swinton from the front.

Grant himself grew increasingly harsh with reporters. In 1863,
Thomas Knox of the *New York Herald* committed a technical offense and Grant had him court-martialed and sentenced to banish-
ment from the military department under the general's command.
A committee of correspondents pleaded on his behalf and Lincoln
reversed the sentence permitting Knox to remain if he did not anger Grant again.

At one point, General Henry W. Halleck expelled all correspondents from the Union forces in the East. The *New York Times*
said it was because they had exposed the "military blunders, im-
becilities, peccadillos, corruption, drunkenness, and knavery" and

had failed occasionally "to puff every functionary as much as he thinks he deserves." The Halleck order didn't hold long.

General Sherman won honors as the roughest of all on reporters. He never missed a chance to chew out correspondents, to attack newspapers, to blame news leaks for his troubles. When a *Herald* reporter filed a story in violation of censorship, Sherman had him arrested as a spy and only Lincoln's intervention kept still another general from ordering execution of a reporter.

The views of Sherman probably reflect the military's historic view of the press from Valley Forge to Vietnam. One correspondent pleaded with Sherman, who seemed to throw reporters out of his lines almost as fast as he found them, that he should not be expelled because he was only seeking the truth. The angry Sherman said, "We don't want the truth told about things here—that's what we *don't* want." When he learned that an explosion had resulted in the death of three news reporters, Sherman said "Good! Now we shall have news of hell before breakfast."

Lincoln sometimes intervened but not always. A *London Times* reporter, William Howard Russell, wrote a lurid account of Union Army panic at the battle of Manassas and Lincoln's aides insisted that he be deported. Lincoln agreed.

Rough as were Lincoln's generals and secretary of war, there was no passion quite like that of the mobs, many of them Union soldiers, who attacked newspaper offices across the North. The army, with a discipline something less than perfect, turned the other way as soldiers destroyed presses and threatened editors.

In June, 1861 soldiers completely wrecked the Booneville, Missouri, *Observer*. The following year in Kansas, Union soldiers ran wild in a campaign against dissenting editors. About forty men from Fort Riley went to the *Kansas Frontier* office in Junction City and gave George Dummer, the editor, twenty-four hours to get out of town before taking axes to all his furniture. Dummer complained to the Fort commander who mustered his entire command on the parade ground to find the guilty men but failed. The soldiers returned to town that night, filled Dummer's bedroom with bullets (he wasn't there but another man was wounded by a stray bullet), and destroyed his press.

The *Rockport Democrat* in Indiana was invaded early in 1863 by soldiers who destroyed the type cases and smashed the furniture. The Keokuk, Iowa, *Daily Constitution* got the same treatment at about the same time from seventy-five soldiers from a nearby army hospital. In March of that year, a troop train *en route* to St. Louis stopped in Richmond, Indiana, where they wrecked the plant of the *Jeffersonian*. The train went on to Indianapolis where the soldiers read about their Richmond actions in the *Sentinal* and marched on *that* newspaper. Only a heavy guard around the office saved it.

Similar treatment was given the Fairfield, Iowa, *Constitution and Union,* the Sunbury, Pennsylvania, *Democrat,* the Youngstown, Ohio, *Mahoning Sentinel,* the *Dayton Empire,* the *Gallatin County Democrat* in Illinois, and others.

These actions were illegal, of course. Much more damaging because they had official if not constitutional sanction, were the actions of the federal government. It practiced suspending newspapers from publication and arresting their editors.

In the summer of '61 three Baltimore papers, the *Republican,* the *South* and the *Daily Exchange* were barred from the mails. The editors of the last two, Thomas W. Hall and Frank Kay Howard (who had written in the *Exchange,* "We can afford to despise Mr. Lincoln's warnings and menaces.") were arrested as "a military precautionary measure." The *Exchange* responded the next day, September 14, with a blistering attack on the government and a pledge to continue supporting the South. The publisher, W. W. Glenn, was arrested and joined his editor behind bars in Fort McHenry.

In Missouri, Major General John C. Fremont had little patience with newspapers. He suppressed two newspapers in 1861 for reporting false statements regarding military maneuvers and barred five New York papers and the Louisville *Courier* as being "disloyal." When the St. Louis *News* criticized Fremont's military strategy, he had the editor arrested, all copies of the offending issue seized and destroyed.

One of the most publicized incidents took place before dawn on June 3, 1863 when General Burnside's troops marched into the offices of the *Chicago Times,* stopped the presses, and took possession of the premises. The editor, Wilbur Fiske Storey, had been warned the day before, in a telegram from Burnside, that he was stopping publication of the paper based on General Order No. 84

accusing the *Times* of "repeated expression of disloyal and incendiary sentiments."

Storey appealed to Judge Thomas Drummon of the U.S. circuit court. The judge directed that troops not carry out Burnside's order until application for a permanent injunction be heard in open court. Burnside responded with an order to his troops repeating that the *Times* was to be suppressed. The judge, in court the next morning, said he wanted to give every aid and assistance to his government "but I have always wished to treat the government as a government of law and a government of the Constitution, and not a government of mere physical force. I personally have contended and always shall contend, for the right of free discussion, and the right of commenting, under law and the Constitution, upon the acts of the officers of the government."

Meanwhile, at the state capitol in Springfield, resolutions were passed condemning Burnside's order as "despotic" and "destructive of good government, and subversive of constitutional and natural rights." Prominent Republicans, including Senator Lyman Trumbull, a confidant of Lincoln, telegraphed the president, asking that he revoke Burnside's order. He did, embarrassed by the suppression of the paper. Even Stanton was displeased with Burnside and said he must be personally consulted on all questions relating to newspapers.

Editor Storey was not impressed. He regretted Lincoln's intervention, feeling that the matter should have gone to the courts where he felt sure he would be vindicated.

In New York, the most famous press incident during the war involved the suppression of two papers—the *World* and the *Journal of Commerce* for publishing a fraudulent story. The author was Joseph Howard who, on May 18, 1864, engaged in a bizarre plot to make money in gold speculation.

Howard concocted a story in which Lincoln allegedly declared May 26 as a day of fasting, humiliation, and prayer for the nation. The spurious proclamation also called for another four hundred thousand men to be drafted. It had the flavor of virtually admitting the war was lost. Once published, Howard knew, gold prices would shoot up as a hedge against collapse of the Union.

He and an accomplice, Francis Mallison, prepared the story just as the Associated Press might and had it delivered to the New

York newspapers just before they closed the presses for the morning's printing. It appeared to be a formal document from the White House transmitted by the Associated Press and delivered by messenger in the usual manner. The New York *World* and the *Journal of Commerce* both carried it.

Lincoln had his own opinion of gold speculation. At an earlier moment, he said of "those fellows in Wall Street who are gambling in gold at such a time as this" that "For my part, I wish every one of them had his *devilish* head shot off." On the morning of the eighteenth, there was feverish activity in the New York Stock Exchange and the price of gold shot up.

Stanton immediately issued a statement calling the "proclamation" false and suprious, an absolute forgery. The statement said that Lincoln had signed orders directing Major General John A. Dix to stop publication of the *World* and the *Journal of Commerce* for "wickedly and traitorously" publishing the false story, to seize their offices, and to arrest the editors. The papers were not permitted to print for two days.

Meanwhile, General Dix's men found Joseph Howard and jailed him at Fort Lafayette. The general wired Stanton that Howard had confessed all. Stanton replied that President Lincoln, upon hearing that, was ordering the editors free to publish again. Lincoln, said Stanton, felt that the editors could not hide behind a plea of ignorance or good intent but that he was not disposed to impose "vindictive punishment."

They did publish again, the *World's* editor, Manton Marble, writing a signed editorial naming Lincoln the tyrant and despot who had destroyed freedom of the press.

The would-be gold speculator, Joseph Howard, remained in a cell in Fort Lafayette until August of that year. Howard was once secretary to the Reverend Henry Ward Beecher who interceded on his behalf. Lincoln told Stanton that he wished to oblige Beecher if Stanton approved. Stanton agreed and Lincoln issued the order: "Let Howard, imprisoned in regard to the bogus proclamation, be dismissed."

The Civil War was witness to some of the greatest excesses against the press in American history, greater in number and manner than even the worst excesses under the Alien and Sedition Acts which at least cast a legal patina over such actions. At the end of the eighteenth century, the country was still small enough for government actions against newspapers to be passed on by word of mouth. By the Civil War, that was no longer possible and news exchanges had not grown to the point of giving the incidents widespread currency. Only a few, the closing of the *Chicago Times* and the actions against the two newspapers in the Howard case, received wide publicity. It is significant that in those cases the papers were closed down for only a day or two.

Periods of war and national hysteria lend themselves to political moves against the press. Unfortunately, a troubled electorate at such times is willing to look the other way when this happens.

In 1848 when John Nugent of the New York *Herald* broke the story of the terms of the Mexican Peace Treaty (Some say Secretary of State James Buchanan leaked it), President Polk was furious, called in several senators to discuss it, and told them the treaty was in jeopardy as a result of premature publication.

The senators called Nugent to a closed hearing of the Senate Investigating Committee and quizzed him for five hours, then had him held in custody at the home of the Senate's sergeant-at-arms. Nugent was held for four weeks before being released. His boss, James Gordon Bennett, headed for Washington to seek release of the reporter but on learning that the Senate planned to apprehend him, turned around and returned, announcing he would fight his battle from the *Herald's* New York offices. The Senate, ultimately, quietly released Nugent.

During the Philippine Insurrection of 1899–1902, advisors to President McKinley were angry at the treatment they received from *The Nation,* the New York *Evening Post,* the *Boston Herald,* and the Springfield, Massachusetts, *Republican.* The president's cabinet spent one very long meeting in serious discussion of whether or not to prosecute the publications for treason.

Less than twenty years later the nation was at war and hysteria in the populace was such that press freedoms and other freedoms were once again endangered. Despite some depressingly oppressive legislation, the actions against the press in World War I were far less extreme than those of the Civil War. Woodrow Wilson, while shrinking from the White House press corps, stood firm in defense of press freedoms.

One week after America entered the war, he created a Committee on Public Information headed by George Creel, former editor of the *Rocky Mountain News* in Denver. From the first, Creel looked upon his task as winning the "fight for the minds of men," but he felt that voluntary actions were better than any formal censorship and told Wilson the need was for "expression not repression." Within two months, various legislation would be passed and censorship would be created but Creel's deft treatment of the generally cooperative press was such that few complained during his tenure in office. The villains, as time went on, were the attorney general and the postmaster general.

Creel tried to stick to voluntary censorship at home, issuing guidelines that dealt with troop movements and ship sailings. At the war front, Frederick Palmer was appointed by General Pershing to oversee censorship. The former New York *Herald* correspondent was disliked by reporters for censoring too much while distrusted by the military for censoring too little. Major Palmer lasted less than a year.

Something like sixty war correspondents were at the front. Five of them, including Heywood Broun of the New York *Tribune,* lost accreditation for offending the censors.

Just weeks after he appointed Creel, Wilson had written a prominent journalist to assure him that he had no great enthusiasm for censorship. "I can imagine no greater disservice to the country than to establish a system of censorship that would deny to the people of a free republic like our own their indisputable right to criticize their own public officials."

At the same time, the administration put forth the Espionage Act which became law on June 15, 1917. This law, which the government was to quote in its case against the *New York Times* over half a century later in the Pentagon Papers controversy, provided for penalties up to ten thousand dollars and long jail terms for interfering with the draft or encouraging disloyalty or exposing secrets to foreign powers.

This was followed by the Trading with the Enemy Act of October 6 and the Sedition Act of May 16, 1918. The three formed a direct threat to the press and came close to nullifying the First Amendment. Despite this, in unanimous decision the Supreme Court upheld the Espionage Act where there was "a clear

and present danger." Wilson wrote that he approved of the legislation but "I shall not expect or permit any part of this law to apply
to me or any of my official acts, or in any way to be used as a
shield against criticism."

The Trading with the Enemy Act formalized censorship and
made it punishable to convey any false report or statement that
interferes with U.S. military success or encourages disloyalty or
mutiny or obstructs enlistments or the draft. Wilson offered his
views to senators considering the legislation. He urged "a mild
form of censorship . . . more than a moral obligation upon any
newspapers that might tend to print news by which the enemy
might profit."

The Sedition Act went beyond the Espionage Act and listed
nine additional offenses including the use of disloyal or profane
language about the United States, its constitution, its flag, and the
uniform of its army or navy. The fine, as with the others: up to
ten thousand dollars and/or up to twenty years imprisonment.

While the president wanted a mild form of censorship, his Post
Office, under powers given it by the Espionage Act, barred over
seventy-five publications from the mail, most of them socialist in
philosophy or German-American. The foreign press had to provide
a proper translation in English to be filed with the postmaster at
the point of entry. If offending foreign-language or political newspapers and magazines agreed to drop all discussion of the war,
they could resume Post Office privileges.

The Espionage Act reflected an orgy of hate across the country.
There was unofficial spy hunting by ordinary citizens, state laws
passed to forbid the teaching of the German language, others to
ban the playing of German music, etc. Under the provisions of the
Espionage and Sedition Acts, over fifteen hundred persons were
arrested for disloyalty including Eugene V. Debs, the Socialist
candidate for president on four occasions, who was jailed for
threatening that Socialists would not support the war. He was
not released until 1921.

Another prominent Socialist, Victor L. Berger, was convicted
of sedition. He was the first Socialist elected to the Congress and
in 1918 was re-elected, then expelled by the House. Berger's Milwaukee *Leader* was among the publications banned by the Post
Office. The president wrote the postmaster general about the case

and said he did not find the evidence against Berger's newspaper very convincing. Said Wilson, "There is a wide margin of judgment here and I think that doubt ought always to be resolved in favor of the utmost freedom of speech."

The president defended Postmaster General Albert S. Burleson when a Hearst executive, Grenville S. MacFarland, said he thought Burleson was going too far. Wilson said Burleson was being "misinterpreted" and was really anxious to see freedom of criticism exercised to the limit.

On the other hand, the Post Office chief tested Wilson's limits in the case of Max Eastman's radical magazine, the *Masses,* which was banned because of four antiwar cartoons. Wilson called the editors "well-intentioned" and suggested that it was well to let them "blow off steam." The postmaster general agreed, as long as they did not violate the Espionage Act, but informed the president that the law will be followed to the letter and if not enforced, the postmaster general's resignation would be on the president's desk.

Wilson, on December 4, 1917, expressed his tolerance for free speech even during crisis and his firm belief that criticism is better exposed to the air than bottled up. "I hear the criticism and clamour of the noisily thoughtless and troublesome. I also see men here and there fling themselves in impotent disloyalty against the calm, indomitable power of the nation. . . . They do not touch the heart of anything. They may safely be left to strut their uneasy hour and be forgotten."

The Sedition Act was repealed in 1921 but the basic Espionage Act still applies.

Wilson, despite his wartime intercession on behalf of some newspapers and his proclamations in favor of open criticism, was still irked by the coverage of his day. When he declared Memorial Day as a day of prayer, he was furious to see distortions of his remarks in the Hearst press published over his signature. He condemned it as "something very like forgery" and asked the attorney general to report back on what legal process could "bring this habitual offender to terms."

Theodore Roosevelt, writing in the Kansas City *Star,* defended the Hearst papers and expressed displeasure with the treatment of the press by the Wilson administration. He said it was anxious to punish newspapers which told about the failure to conduct the war efficiently. The ever-present Postmaster General Burleson issued a statement saying that he had received more complaints about Roosevelt's letters violating the Espionage Act than he had about the Hearst newspapers.

Burleson was not about to cite a former president for such violations, of course, but it would have been interesting irony to have Roosevelt in court on such charges since he was personally involved in taking newspapers to court, suing for libel.

The incident happened in the last years of Teddy Roosevelt's presidency but it began before he even took office. There had been years of debate over whether a canal should go through Panama or Nicaragua. A French engineer named Philippe Bunau-Varilla, who had gone to Panama at the age of twenty-six when the deLesseps Company tried to build a canal, became the leading Panama advocate and—along with a New York attorney and manipulator named William Nelson Cromwell—succeeded in getting a Panama Canal built.

Theodore Roosevelt entered office and declared himself in favor of the Nicaraguan route. The New Panama Canal Company was willing to sell its holdings for forty million dollars but the Congress seemed to be inclined to agree with Roosevelt and go to Nicaragua. Bunau-Varilla engaged in a massive lobbying effort to get the Panama route approved and urged the Congress to look into the question of volcano eruptions in Nicaragua.

By a stroke of luck, Mount Pelee in the Caribbean erupted and destroyed St. Pierre and a week later Mt. Monatombo in Nicaragua blew, though with much less damage. Bunau-Varilla found a Nicaraguan postage stamp showing a volcano behind a wharf scene. He bought ninety of the stamps and placed each in the center of a pro-Panama propaganda piece which was sent to each member of the U.S. Senate. Panama won 42 to 34. Bunau-Varilla repeated his stamp act for members of the House where there were only eight dissenting votes. Roosevelt signed the bill on June 28, 1902.

It was necessary now for Colombia to agree since Panama belonged to it. Within a year the New York *World* published a strangely prophetic article, believed to have been planted by William Cromwell, predicting a Panamanian secession from Colombia if agreement were not reached. The revolt was planned in Bunau-

Varilla's hotel room. It began at 5 P.M. on November 3, 1903 and within an hour the Colombians were out, the Panamanians in. American diplomats walked in the victory parade. Within days, the United States recognized the *de facto* government. Two weeks later, the canal treaty with Panama was signed with the Panamanian signatory being its new ambassador to Washington— Philippe Bunau-Varilla.

The Louisville *Courier-Journal,* an advocate of the Nicaraguan route, had been charging corruption in the forty million dollar payment—"twenty are for thieves in France and twenty for the grey wolves of the American Senate." It lectured Roosevelt on the "Forty Thieves of the Forty Millions" and dismissed Bunau-Varilla as "Vanilla Bean."

The real attack on the Panama arrangement came in January of 1904, however, when the New York *World* published the first of many articles, this one headlined "Panama Revolution a Stock Gamblers' Plan to Make Millions". The report charged that a Paris and New York syndicate with Bunau-Varilla as its "clever agent" engineered the revolution. The article flatly contradicted President Roosevelt's special message denying any U.S. involvement, directly or indirectly. Bunau-Varilla threatened to sue.

The *World* ran similar stories in the months that followed, pretty much ignored publicly by Roosevelt, but in late 1908 the Indianapolis *News* ran an editorial based on the *World's* exposé. The October 9th editorial was entitled "The Panama Scandal" and credited "an able and observant newspaper in the East" as its source. This was followed by other editorials and cartoons.

On November 29, a Richmond, Indiana, author, William Dudly Foulke, wrote President Roosevelt, noting that the *News* had written a series of accusations against Roosevelt, before and after the recent political campaign. What were the facts? Teddy Roosevelt replied against the "abominable falsehood . . . a slander, not against the American government, but against the French government" and accused newspapers like the *News* of practicing "every form of mendacity known to man from the suppression of the truth and the suggestion of the false to the lie direct."

The exchange of letters was published. The *New York World* then called Roosevelt a liar who never addressed himself to the question of who got the forty million dollars but simply engaged in "a string of abusive and defamatory epithets."

Roosevelt began talking about libel suits. He wrote Henry L. Stimson, then U.S. district attorney for Southern New York, "I do not know anything about the law of criminal libel, but I would dearly like to invoke it against Pulitzer of the *World*." He also asked for action against the Indianapolis *News*.

A grand jury was impaneled in Washington early in 1909 and machinery was set up to obtain an indictment against the Indianapolis editors while a similar grand jury began hearing testimony in New York against the *World*. The Washington grand jury returned seven counts against the *News* people and warrants went out for the arrest of the editor and publisher. They went before U.S. District Judge Albert B. Anderson, who heard the government contend that the men must be tried in Washington, D.C. since copies of the *News* could be found there and thus the crime was committed there. Judge Anderson said a newspaper has a duty to publish the news and, editorially, to draw inferences from that news. As for moving the defendants to Washington, he said the government has no right to "drag citizens from distant states to the capital of the nation, there to be tried" and said, "If the history of liberty means anything—if constitutional guarantees are worth anything—this proceeding must fail." He dismissed the charges.

In New York, the *World* case came before Federal Judge Charles M. Hough on January 25, 1910 on the technical charge that twenty-nine copies of the offending *World* had been circulated at West Point, in the New York federal building, and other areas under federal control. Judge Hough, as Judge Anderson before him, found this argument strained and "a novelty." He quashed the indictment. It went to the Supreme Court which, on January 3, 1911 ruled that Hough had been correct, that federal enclaves in the states are not treated as separate from the state unless expressly provided to the contrary. Some weeks later, the attorney general ordered all actions still pending in Washington dismissed.

Joseph Pulitzer, who had remained offshore on his yacht during part of the controversy to avoid being taken into custody, had won a victory. A president of the United States had tried to use the court to punish two newspapers that nettled him and he had failed. As the *World* said editorially in its evaluation of their individual roles, "Mr. Roosevelt is an episode. The *World* is an institution." Or as Wilde had suggested, journalism governs forever.

Roosevelt had somewhat better luck in 1912 during his Bull Moose campaign for the presidency. A Michigan Republican weekly, the *Iron Ore,* had written, "Roosevelt lies and curses in a most disgusting way; he gets drunk, too, and that not infrequently, and all his intimates know about it." Roosevelt sued on both civil and criminal libel counts and asked ten thousand dollars in damages. When the paper admitted it could not substantiate its charges and offered to print a correction and apologize, Roosevelt asked the court to instruct the jury to bring a verdict for only nominal damages. It did—six cents and court costs.

Roosevelt is credited with being the first president to institute modern press relations in the White House and while he was the innovator of many customs that remain today, the White House press evolved over several presidencies to its present state. Grover Cleveland, for example, experimented with the advance distribution but-hold-for-release speech at the suggestion of George F. Parker, an editor who served as a prime speech writer for the president. Parker suggested they be distributed seven days in advance. Cleveland agreed to five while expressing serious reservations, telling his advisor, "You will find yourself betrayed by someone and I will be speaking an address which has been published somewhere."

William McKinley knew all White House reporters by name and let them work in an outer reception room of the mansion. McKinley's closest aide was thirty-three-year-old George B. Cortelyou. It was he who handled press releases for the president, a new information practice instituted by McKinley. The president also introduced regular briefing sessions for reporters, most of them conducted by Cortelyou.

It is indicative of McKinley's faith in his man that he turned to him with the most difficult assignment of all. When the president was shot in Buffalo, Cortelyou bent over his fatally wounded chief and the president raised a hand to the aide's shoulder to whisper, "My wife. Be careful, Cortelyou, how you tell her. Oh, be careful."

In an efficient manner which was to be remembered when James Hagerty played a similar role after President Eisenhower's heart attack, Cortelyou conducted the immediate business of state. He telephoned Washington to suggest that Vice-President Roosevelt and the Cabinet come to Buffalo. He notified relatives and personal friends. He issued releases on the President's condition. It was said, as it was said of Hagerty later, that he was virtually an acting president.

When McKinley died, George Cortelyou served as a one-man transition committee, familiarizing Roosevelt with the job. The new president was grateful. He appointed Cortelyou to his Cabinet as the nation's first secretary of commerce and labor. Roosevelt's choice for press secretary was William Loeb, Junior, who had been with him when he was governor of New York.

Theodore Roosevelt loved publicity. He knew what it was, how to create it, how to manage it. The press releases were timed for maximum effect, all checked by the president and some even authored by him. Roosevelt would brag that he "discovered Monday," that traditional slim day for news, and T.R. would often hold up releases for Sunday night, knowing how much better play they would get in the news-hungry Monday editions.

He is credited with introducing the modern news conference, a give and take question and answer session which he usually worked into a late afternoon hour, sometimes while he was being shaved. He did not hold these regularly but when he did, he spoke to reporters briskly, bluntly, colorfully—there was no stuffiness to the relationship.

Roosevelt could, as was noted earlier, be very rough on reporters. He often issued strong denials. One story tells of a publisher who told Roosevelt that he believed the president really told a French newspaperman certain things which Roosevelt denied. Said the president, "Of course I said them, but I said them as Theodore Roosevelt and not as president of the United States!"

Roosevelt also is said to have been the inventor of the "trial balloon," sending an idea aloft and then deciding whether the reception of it warranted approval or whether he had to disown his own idea. He played favorites with reporters and to the chosen few were leaked new presidential policies or proposals. When they appeared in print, TR would embrace them if they met with acceptance or drop them if they were criticized, his name never linked to the losers.

He invited newspapermen to White House dinners and on one such occasion when he heard a reporter criticize his railroad policies, he sent the reporter abroad to study European railroads and report back to him. He gave newsmen a permanent press room in the West wing of the White House after seeing them standing in the rain to interview official visitors as they left. He then encouraged presidential visitors to stop by the press room.

He looked after the reporters on the road. Once at a banquet of the Illinois Bar Association, he discovered that the correspondents were dining in a small room below the banquet hall. He announced that they were members of his party and, if they were eating below, so would he. The flustered Bar Association people quickly set up a table for the press, apologized to both them and their patron, the president. The White House regulars, in T.R.'s affectionate description, were "my newspaper cabinet."

William Howard Taft, on the other hand, disliked the press with few exceptions (namely Gus J. Karger who wrote in Washington for the Cincinnati *Times-Star,* a paper owned by Taft's brother) and was even heard to grumble, "Must I see those men again? Didn't I see them just the other day?"

Woodrow Wilson was different. He looked forward to meeting with the press and became the first president to schedule news conferences regularly and in advance, two a week. His Princeton background was part of it; he saw the sessions as opportunities to give scholarly opinions, a sort of academic seminar. He was stunned to find that the two hundred correspondents in attendance were not the same as his students, that his painstaking preparation for these lectures was wasted.

He soon regarded any questions that bordered on criticism as a slur on his honesty. If there were follow-up questions, he would snap "How many forms are you going to ask the same question in?" His air was condescending, his manner uncomfortable, his style abrupt.

He introduced an innovation—the off-the-record remark—and would often preface a statement with "this is not to be printed but is just to guide you." To his credit, he did not pick the subject matter as Roosevelt had but let reporters ask whatever they liked.

When the Germans sank the Lusitania in 1915, he discontinued news conferences to protect national security. His press secretary, Joe Tumulty, then became the conduit to the press. Years later Wilson would complain that while some reporters were able, "the interest of the majority was in the personal and trivial rather than in principles and policies."

During his first year as president, Wilson considered starting a federal news service. He wrote Harvard's President Charles W. Eliot that it was needed to get the "real facts" to the people. "The real trouble is that the newspapers get the real facts but do not find them to their taste and do not use them as given them, and in some of the newspaper offices news is deliberately invented."

He said he wondered how the public ever got the right impression regarding public affairs.

Warren Harding, a genial Ohio publisher, became president in 1921, restored regular news conferences, played hearts (nickel a point) at the National Press Club, played golf with reporters, and had them over to the White House socially. Warned to be careful of the press, he said, "That's nonsense. I'm a newspaperman myself and I know all about reporters."

All was well for all of nine months. Then the president appeared at the National Press Club and committed a *faux pas* by saying that the upcoming Four-Power Treaty on Naval Arms Limitation did not contain a pledge to protect Japan. A furious Secretary of State Charles Evans Hughes said the president was wrong and submitted his resignation. Poor Harding begged Hughes to remain, soothed things with the Japanese, and told reporters angrily that "all questions must now be presented in writing. None will be replied to until the department affected has been consulted. If no reply is made, there must be no reference to the fact that the question had been asked."

End of friendly relations with the newspaperman-president.

It was his term that created "White House spokesman" as the device for not quoting a president directly. His closing days were bitter ones. The Teapot Dome scandal in which Albert B. Fall, the secretary of the interior, took hundreds of thousands of dollars to permit others to exploit rich oil reserves held by the U.S. Navy, was uncovered by the *Denver Post* and others. Harding spent his final months incensed at press treatment, second-guessing reporters and editors. His press secretary, George Christian, grew similarly hostile and bluntly told reporters that he expected favorable publicity for Harding or none at all.

Calvin Coolidge belied his reputation as "Silent Cal" in that he talked a great deal with reporters; he just didn't say much. Coolidge did restore regular news conferences and set an admirable record of such—five hundred and twenty in six years, almost twice a week on the average. He was honest but parsimonious in what he would say. Questions were submitted in advance and chosen at the president's discretion. When a dozen reporters submitted the same question—would he run for reelection in 1928?—Coolidge thumbed through them slowly until he found a different question. He answered it and ended the conference.

It is ironic that Coolidge, of all people, was condemned for news manipulation by the Institute for Public Affairs. Meeting in Charlottesville, Virginia the group accused the uncommunicative president of using the press for "propaganda purposes."

Herbert Clark Hoover arrived at the White House basking in a "good press" as the great engineer responsible for the European relief program in World War I. He started out with twenty-three news conferences in his first year and ended with half that number in his last. Questions were submitted in advance. Once the president startled reporters by wondering why so few questions were submitted. Fifty to sixty were turned in each time. It turned out that Hoover's aides were pulling out those which might provoke or embarrass their chief.

Relations degenerated in the usual pattern and got much worse when the president bogged down in the economic crisis. He suggested that reporters should exercise self-censorship in writing about the depression. He even went the next step and suggested that such stories be submitted to the White House for clearance before publication. He called it a crisis second only to war. In 1931, Hoover tried to get reporters to stop "waylaying" visitors attending an economic crisis conference at the White House, promising he would give them more information the next day if they would bear with him. Reporters, represented by Richard V. Oulahan of the *New York Times,* told the president that it was improper to expect reporters to do anything other than try to get as complete a story as possible and as soon as they could.

What a contrast was Hoover's successor. Franklin Delano Roosevelt came into the White House as cousin Theodore had years earlier, a breath of fresh air for reporters. His very first news conference of nearly one thousand in his long tenure was a masterpiece of winning over reporters with candor and confidence.

Roosevelt greeted the hundreds of reporters with, "I am told that what I am about to do will become impossible, but I am going to try it. We are not going to have any more written questions."

He proceeded to answer quickly, fully, and informally. He was thoroughly at ease with every question offered, demonstrating a grasp of events and the background of current problems. The new president was gay and confident. He obviously was enjoying every moment of it. When that first news conference ended, for the first time in presidential history the reporters spontaneousy broke into applause.

One old hand in the press corps called it "the most amazing performance the White House has ever seen."

The president truly liked reporters. He knew most of them by their first names. He followed and took an interest in their personal problems. Special favorites would be invited to the White House swimming pool to play water polo with him. Many were invited to receptions, picnics, and Sunday afternoon teas at the White House. He invented the "lid," a device to allow reporters to go home nights or weekends knowing "a lid was on," that there would be no news at the White House for the period of their absence and that they would get calls at home if an emergency changed the situation.

Roosevelt understood the adversary relationship but he also knew that he could get his story across through his handling of correspondents, through the use of radio, through movie newsreels. He would tear the hide off publishers and newspaper owners, some of whom he called "boobs," most of whom he knew to be Republicans, and many of whom he knew loathed him. He called it "the Tory press" and felt it 85 percent against him. When a Gallup poll in 1938 showed that over 35 percent of the nation's press supported the New Deal, FDR didn't believe the figure accurate. He also distrusted a later Gallup poll that showed 82 percent of the public felt the administration was getting fair treatment in the news columns (72 percent of Democrats, 90 percent of Republicans believed this according to Gallup).

Of course, radio had arrived and FDR was superb on the airways. He developed the so-called fireside chat, talking confidentially to millions in their homes. It was the most direct form of presidential communication ever to the public. It also, of course, circumvented the newspapers and went right to the electorate.

Roosevelt, in the memory of Americans of that period, made dozens and some thought hundreds of radio fireside chats but in fact he made very few. Their impact was so great that listeners looked back and remembered many more than actually existed.

Though he gave three such chats between March and July of his first year, he gave only one other that year, two the next year, and only one-a-year during the rest of his first term. He was heard when radio picked up ceremonial affairs or his speeches at political gatherings, but he was fairly infrequent in his use of the fireside chat. It was a special technique, saved for special occasions. Arthur Krock said, "Mr. Roosevelt is the best showman the White House has lodged since modern science made possible such an effective dual performance."

FDR's White House instituted four classes of information for reporters: off-the-record (not for publication), occasional special items for direct quotation, background information, and the indirect quotation—information which could be attributed to him but not using exact quotes. This last, of course, protected a president from his own sloppy use of the language. Roosevelt didn't need that protection but Eisenhower, who lapsed into sloppy syntax at times, was later to permit actual quotes at all news conferences.

White House newsmen on the whole were very fond of FDR but relations grew strained after the first two years of "honeymoon." As for the president, he fashioned himself an expert on how stories should be played and sometimes referred to reporters as "the Class." For example, he would say, "If I were writing the story, I would put it this way: that by no stretch of the imagination has the president or the secretary of state ever been the least bit concerned . . ." etc. He would drop in phrases like "and then, if I were going to write one more paragraph, I would put it this way . . ." He often would say that he expected a question to be asked, would then ask himself the expected question, and answer it.

Raymond Clapper called it the "White House School of Journalism" but he did so cynically—"Never in my twenty years here have newspaper reporters received as much advice as to how to do their work, and as much warning against light-fingered handling of important news situations, as in this Administration." Clapper noted that Roosevelt was quick with ridicule, dismissing newspaper speculation as "a sewing circle story" or a "Monday morning story."

Many respected Roosevelt's newspaper savvy. Raymond P. Brandt of the St. Louis *Post-Dispatch* wrote that the president had "the news sense of a managing editor" and Heywood Broun wrote "Franklin Delano Roosevelt is the best newspaperman who has ever been president of the United States."

Roosevelt also knew how to compose just the kind of language to please the press. Saluting freedom of press in America, he wrote, "I am glad too that our Government never has seen fit to subsidize a newspaper or a news service and I dare make the prediction that it never will." He said the free press is "freer than it ever has been in our history."

The president, however, never departed from his public attacks on the villains in journalism, the bosses. He once held a news conference before the annual conventions of the American Association of Schools and Departments of Journalism and the American Association of Teachers of Journalism and told them, "Lack of confidence in the press today is not because of the editorials but because of the colored news stories and the failure on the part of some papers to print the news. Very often, as you know, they will kill a story if it is contrary to the policy of the owner of the paper. It is not the man at the desk in most cases. It is not the reporter. It goes back to the owner of the paper."

Roosevelt blamed the owners for some of the "perfect fool questions" reporters ask at news conferences. He said he could always tell when their editors put them up to it.

In 1938, the president engaged in a bit of journalistic practice as an author. He contracted with United Features Syndicate to do a series of thirty articles on his own story of the New Deal. *Liberty Magazine* published three similar articles by him at the same time.

It was the first time that a president had ever written for paid publication while still in office and it was strongly criticized. Walter Lippmann wrote, "No sophistry can disguise the fact that state papers and presidential opinions have been sold commercially for private profit."

With the coming of World War II, Roosevelt's relationships with the press became more difficult. He sometimes would "disappear" with no press knowledge of his whereabouts until he returned to the office. His handling of the news media led Raymond Clapper to complain that he was carrying "the whole technique of a controlled press far beyond anything we have experienced in this country." Arthur Krock said the administration used "more ruthlessness, intelligence and subtlety in trying to suppress unfavorable comment than any I know."

The best example of Roosevelt's manipulation of the press was also, in effect, the last. He had for years managed to hide his physical infirmities—reporters never reported and photographers never filmed the president on crutches. At the end, his physical condition was rapidly degenerating but the public was largely unaware of this as he ran for a fourth term. His physician issued reassurances that he was well. A few months after the election, on April 12, 1945, he was dead.

Harry S. Truman's first news conference was just five days later and a record number of three hundred and forty-eight reporters were in attendance. Truman saw no reason that news conferences must run long and often held some as short as ten or twelve minutes. His very first lasted only twenty minutes.

The number of reporters had grown too large for the oval office so Truman moved his conferences next door to the White House, to the Indian Treaty Room on the fourth floor of what was then the Old State Department Building and is now the Executive Office Building. It gave reporters a chance to sit and take notes while not standing up with a question.

In ninety-three months in office, Truman met the press three hundred and twenty-four times. Though he held news conferences frequently, he did not maintain a regular pattern, simply called them when he felt they were justified.

He introduced one minor innovation, reporters had to identify themselves before each question, and one major first step—television film. Truman permitted the networks to shoot about fifty feet of silent film before questioning began. Television correspondents would narrate the substance of the news conference over the silent footage.

Harry Truman had a feisty press personality. His well-known temper was pretty much under control, but it could break loose at times. He knew that Roosevelt at the end had avoided calling on hostile reporters but Truman took questions from anyone and gave back as much as he took. He once snapped at a lady correspondent that she should read the law in question. She said she had. He snapped, "No, you haven't."

He was unpredictable and his propensity for snapping back answers in staccato fashion (some reporters said he spoke too quickly to permit accurate notes) occasionally ended up foot-in-mouth. Secretary of State Dean Acheson said he used to keep a sort of first-aid kit, "a boxful of clarifications" handy to patch up after every Truman news conference.

His quickness of reply sometimes caused him to accept the questioner's choice of phrase. In 1948, when a reporter asked him, "Do you think the Capitol Hill spy scare is a red herring to divert public attention from inflation?," Truman said he did. He, of course, then became the author of "red herring" which did not endear him to the Congress. Acheson was later to note, "We learned from all mistakes but one—the fast answer in that nightmare of presidents, the press conference."

Truman had his habits and newsmen had to accommodate to them, including his daily regime of wakening at 6 A.M. and going for his famous, after-breakfast walks. Newsmen had to trail along. Merriman Smith of United Press complained that the dawn coverage had ruined his life, "By ten-thirty in the morning, I was ready for lunch."

The president also had a sly sense of humor. On a fishing vacation near Tiptonville, Tennessee he once invited reporters out to his lodge for a visit. After a half-hour, and in a mellow mood, Truman suggested they hold a news conference. A big issue of the moment was whether the United States would share its knowledge of the atomic bomb and Truman was asked about it. "We're going to keep it," he said. Press Secretary Charlie Ross, caught off guard, quickly interrupted—"Mr. President, are you on or off the record?" Truman said, "Charlie, I'm on the record."

Newsmen raced for the door. The nearest telegraph office was thirty miles away. Truman grinning, shouted after them, "Wait a minute. I invited you for a social visit and now you're running out on me."

Relationships were not always that gay. Smarting over press criticism of his handling of the war in Korea, Truman denied false cease-fire stories and gave reporters a dressing down, taking the AP to task for a misleading item which he felt came out of the intense competition for news. He said times were too dangerous for that.

On another occasion late in his second term, he wrote a columnist, "You newspapermen have a complex that anyone who tells you of any of your many shortcomings is either anxious to be a dictator or else he is an ignoramus. But you should take into consideration that we are no longer in the Gay Nineties of Ben Harrison, William McKinley, or Teddy the Rough Rider. . . . If Russia would be a good neighbor and use her military expenditures for her own economic development, I would not have to scold the publishers for giving away our military secrets. Wish you'd do a little soul searching and see if at *great* intervals the President may be right. The country is yours as well as mine."

Truman's most controversial exchange with the press came in early 1952 at his three hundredth conference. The federal government had taken over the steel industry days earlier and at his April 17th news conference he was asked, "If it is proper under your inherent powers to seize the steel mills, can you tell us whether, in your opinion, it is proper to seize the newspapers and radio stations?" Truman snapped back that under similar circumstances, the president has to do what is best for the country and "that is your answer."

It was an unusually large audience for a news conference. The American Society of Newspaper Editors was in town for a convention and many editors were among the five hundred and twenty press people at the news conference. They were very upset. One editor said, "If the President can do that, we're pretty close to dictatorship."

One week later, the American Newspaper Publishers Association met in New York and condemned the president, pledging to resist "and defeat" any attempted seizure of newspapers and radio "by any president." There were nearly five hundred publishers present and only four voted against the resolution.

Editorials blasted away at Truman and asked if this was "Goodbye to the Constitution?." The Knight papers called Truman "testy, opinionated and often reckless." The White House declined to clarify the president's remarks. One week later, he held another news conference and called any suggestion that he would seize the press "hooey." He slowly, and carefully, read from notes that such a thought never occurred to him.

Truman marked the end of many things. The atomic era was underway but its implications just beginning. The age of jet travel would change presidential patterns but Truman could still take a train. Most of all, television was just beginning and though Truman's inaugural was televised, the real impact of the medium on the White House came in the years that followed, the years of Eisenhower, Kennedy, Johnson, and Nixon.

IV

AND IF THE PRESIDENT HAS THE USE OF TELEVISION AS WELL?

Truly modern and sophisticated techniques to persuade the press, to manipulate the media, entered the scene with nonmodern, unsophisticated Dwight David Eisenhower. Television was just beginning to take hold and Ike was a TV natural. He was also blessed with Jim Hagerty, an adept press counselor who understood the media, even the new one of television, and gave all political press secretaries everywhere a lesson in how to use them.

Thanks in part to the press, Ike was one of the most popular heroes ever to enter the White House, yet there was a strong suspicion among the press that the new president didn't much care for reporters. It was said that he exhibited a great deal of antagonism towards newsmen during his years in the military and even some testiness during the campaign.

At his first news conference, Eisenhower handled that question by saying of reporters that "through the war years and ever since, I have found nothing but desire to dig at the truth so far as I was concerned, and be openhanded and forthright about it. That kind of relationship I hope we can continue."

His questioner persisted—"Did you feel that reporters had been fair to you, too, in their questions?" The famous Eisenhower grin flashed and he said, "Well, when you come down to it, I don't see that a reporter could do much to a president, do you?" There was laughter. It was predicted that a long, friendly relationship was in store; the Truman era of presidential pique was over.

Before the year was out, however, the president ran into trouble with the press. He had set up a strict "no leak" news policy for his staff, but the attorney general, Herbert Brownell, invited five correspondents to his home with just such a leak in mind. Saying he would like to be good to them because they had been good to him, Brownell told them of the most important Eisenhower appointment of them all, Earl Warren to head the Supreme Court.

When the president confirmed the story at a September 20 news conference by announcing "something that is certainly by no means news any more," reporters demanded to know if the administration's policy was to leak important news to friendly newspapers. Ike replied that subordinates might leak material but he wanted to be fair with the press. He also suggested that if reporters had complaints they should see Press Secretary James Hagerty.

They did. An angry horde of them confronted Hagerty demanding to know if he, Hagerty, or the president, knew that Brownell planned to leak the story. Hagerty, equally angry now, snapped back, "It is none of your business, but the answer is no." The "none of your business" kept tempers hot for some days. A New York *Daily News* writer, John O'Donnell, suggested trouble in the "education of Dwight D. Eisenhower in the sweet uses of publicity."

Eisenhower had one thing working for him, however. He had Hagerty. Despite the brouhaha with Brownell, Hagerty was good. He became history's most influential and concurrently most effective presidential press secretary.

James Hagerty was New York Governor Tom Dewey's press secretary through nine years and both of Dewey's unsuccessful tries for the presidency. The son of the prominent *New York Times* political reporter James A. Hagerty, Jim had spent eight years himself as a *Times* reporter before joining Dewey on "temporary" duty in 1943. Hagerty was tough-talking, chain-smoking, hard-drinking and the very model of a newspaperman at first blush but, as one observer put it, "his instincts toward news manipulation and techniques of mass psychology were as smooth as any Madison Avenue executive."

Hagerty cultivated the press corps as no one had ever before or since. He was available to them round the clock. Unlike many in his position, he was perfectly capable of giving authoritative answers on almost anything the administration was involved in. He looked after their comfort on the road. He personally advanced presidential overseas trips to be sure the needs of the press were met. One story tells of a reporter getting drunk on one trip and Hagerty writing his story for him.

Hagerty was also the master of manufactured news. He would route every government report that might have the slightest public interest, from cost-of-living figures to the vaguest plans for departmental conferences, through the White House and stamp them with the president's imprimatur. No matter where the president was or what he was or, significantly, was not doing, Hagerty made it appear that churning activity was the continuing characteristic of Mr. Eisenhower. Some called it woodworking from Hagerty's laughing admission, "Boy, I sure had to dig into the woodwork for that one."

The press secretary also was the master of minutiae. He could present a stream of little known, or little cared for, facts about almost anything. In 1959, Hagerty briefed four hundred journalists and among other things revealed that (a) Ike was sleeping in a four-poster bed and (b) he had slept in one before. This led Art Buchwald to do a famous column which included this dialogue: "Q: Did the President speak to anyone before retiring? A: He spoke to the Secretary of State. A: What did he say to the Secretary of State? A: He said, 'Good night, Foster.' Q: And what did the Secretary say to the President? A: He said, 'Good night, Mr. President.' "

Reporters howled. Hagerty screamed and barred Buchwald from all future press briefings. He vowed to "get even" with Buchwald's paper and called the offending column "unadulterated rot."

Hagerty may have had trouble seeing the humor of a Buchwald but he had no trouble spotting ways to use an Eisenhower most effectively. One was to place the president's news conferences on radio as a first step and then on television.

The risks were obvious. It meant direct quotation. In fact, it meant more; the president would be heard saying the words himself. A slip of the tongue could do great damage. It was as Acheson had noted, "the nightmare of Presidents, the press conference." On the other hand, it offered the opportunity to get the president's views to the public, directly, without the filter of the press, and with terrific impact.

On December 16, 1954 Ike held a news conference and had what he called a "Christmas present" for reporters and the public. Reporters could quote him directly. The public could hear a tape recording of the news conference. All networks carried it on radio and two used it on television over films of previous news conferences.

The second step was taken on January 19, 1955 and television was allowed to film an entire news conference. Hagerty set the ground rules, namely that the White House reserved the right to edit the film. Was this a form of censorship? Not at all, claimed Hagerty, "We want the White House to remain in control of the spoken word of the president." But Hagerty never used his prerogative of editing film. That first news conference, as all those filmed afterwards, appeared untouched by Hagerty hands on networks the same night. In a way it was silly to reserve the right to edit. To do so would touch off a flood of stories giving far more prominence to any mistake the president made.

The press secretary told reporters, "This is being done so that all media of information can cover presidential news conferences, and so the people of our country can not only read reports of the conferences but can hear and see the discussions the president has with you gentlemen." The era of presidents and television was underway. Hagerty, by the way, on leaving the White House became head of news and later a corporate vice-president of the American Broadcasting Company.

The press secretary is best remembered not for innovations but for his skill in a crisis. Nine months after filmed news conferences began, Hagerty received his greatest challenge as press secretary when the president suffered a heart attack. It happened on September 24, 1955 in Denver where the Eisenhowers were visiting Mrs. Eisenhower's family. Hagerty was in Washington at the time and immediately flew to Colorado. Ike, told Hagerty was coming, said simply "Good, tell Jim to take over."

Jim did. He told doctors that he wanted two medical bulletins a day as long as the president's life was in danger and "I will ask you to explain what they mean in English so I can make them understandable to the news media." Dr. Paul Dudley White, perhaps the nation's leading heart specialist, was called to the hospital. Hagerty ordered twenty copies of White's immense volume on heart diseases. He marked up six hundred pages that applied to Eisenhower and had the books placed in the hospital press room. He held five news briefings a day, seven days a week for three weeks.

While Hagerty had generally been reluctant to discuss personal matters involving the president in the past, he decided that the more information reporters received, the better it would be. He deluged newsmen with details from whether Ike's toast was white or whole wheat to the exact number of hours the president spent in the oxygen tent. He even gave reports of Ike's bowel movements to startled reporters. It was all right, Dr. White told a news conference, "The country is so bowel-minded anyway."

Hagerty's purpose was simple. He wanted to paint a portrait of a president moving toward recovery. He succeeded.

As noted, Hagerty labelled the reports that he was really acting as president as "a lot of bunk." But it was no bunk that Hagerty felt there must be a show of presidential strength, especially with an election just one year away on the political horizon and other nations watching closely on the diplomatic front.

Five days after the attack, Hagerty announced that the president would perform his first official act since he was struck down. He initialed two lists of routine State Department appointments. The next day Hagerty announced further progress—the president had signed his full name. Each day, Hagerty would make similar announcements.

When doctors permitted it, official visitors came—the first being Vice-President Nixon on October 8, then the Secretary of State John Foster Dulles, and in time all members of the Cabinet. Each visitor after seeing Ike would be taken before the press corps by

Hagerty to discuss their private conversations with the president. Much of it was carefully orchestrated by Hagerty in his best "woodwork" manner. The attorney general would come out and tell of Ike's approval of a major court reform program. Skeptics found it hard to believe that the two discussed it at the president's bedside, but the press picked up the story. The image was of an Eisenhower taking hold, running the country even from a hospital bed.

The president returned to Washington finally and Hagerty could relax, having completed a masterful job. From the first days at Fitzsimmons Hospital, the public received Hagerty's picture of a stricken president running things and now back, recovered, and ready for the 1956 elections.

Unfortunately, two months before the 1956 Republican National Convention, Eisenhower was struck again, this time with an attack of ileitis. He had to undergo surgery and again, Hagerty swung into action—fourteen news briefings in two days before the operation. This time, however, it was different. Hagerty decided that the candor which marked the heart attack would not be useful now. He decided to minimize the seriousness of the attack lest questions be raised about the recurring health problems of a man seeking reelection.

So Jim Hagerty compared the president's condition with a man who had suffered a bad cold. It was hardly an accurate description of an inflamation of the lower small intestine, which is fatal if not relieved. Secretary of State Dulles referred to Ike's "indisposition." And this time Hagerty declined to make the doctors available.

Oh, there was the usual Hagerty attention to small details. The president's menu at mealtimes, the number of state documents he had signed, etc., but little on the medical aspects. The press secretary explained, "A President's heart attack is the property of the people. But we did not consider the ileitis something that endangered the president's life."

Marquis Childs observed, "It seemed that the patient had hardly come out from under the anesthetic when he was reported by Hagerty as conferring with Dulles and members of the White House staff."

The press grumbled. It was a cover-up of a serious matter but it worked. About seven weeks after the attack, Hagerty put the finishing touch to the affair as Ike called a morning news conference, the first since the president was taken to Walter Reed Hospital on June 9. The president was thinner, looked weaker, and spoke a bit more slowly than usual but he was well-prepared and did a masterful job. He took more than three dozen questions and handled them. *Life* magazine said, in "perhaps the frankest, most searching interview since Wilson inaugurated regular conferences in 1913."

Hagerty had done his job well. Eisenhower was renominated by acclamation and, of course, won re-election in November.

All told Eisenhower held only one hundred and ninety or so news conferences in eight years, but that one on August 1, 1956 was the crowning achievement of White House handling of the press. James Hagerty, who always said his job was to make his boss look good, had done it so well that another four years were in store for a man who suffered two terribly serious blows to his health in just one year.

Eisenhower's presidency marked the beginning of the era of television at the White House. Hagerty showed superbly how media could be manipulated. It was in the subsequent presidencies of Kennedy, Johnson, and Nixon that television grew as the major stage for presidents, that media manipulation reached even more sophisticated heights.

John F. Kennedy was a marked contrast to Ike. He knew reporters and liked them where Ike was suspicious and never fully trusted them. And Kennedy first saw the full potential of television where Ike had used it sparingly.

In Florida after his election but before his inaugural, Kennedy took Pierre Salinger's suggestion that they consider live television at news conferences and asked for reaction. Foreign policy aides including McGeorge Bundy and Dean Rusk thought it too hazardous. Kennedy, confident of his ability to handle give-and-take, was not concerned about that. He worried about other things. Would there be too much exposure for the new President? Would the networks carry them if there was no special news break? Would newspapers react adversely to the obvious competitive advantage television was getting? On the other hand, newspapers were expected to oppose most of the new president's program, Kennedy noted, and with television, "we should be able to go around the newspapers if that becomes necessary."

Salinger was asked to check out the networks. He found them eager to carry the news conferences. He got a different reaction from the White House regulars, many of the newspaper reporters in Palm Beach raising "a storm of protest." It ended up in a shouting match with the last shout coming from Salinger: the decision was final, take it or leave it. When he called Kennedy to report on the reaction, the president was laughing. "Don't tell me. I already know. I could hear it clear across town."

When the presidential party got to Washington, Salinger was invited to lunch with a group of veteran correspondents at the Sheraton Park Hotel. He described the meeting as having "all the cordiality of a drumhead court-martial." He was turning the press conference into a side show. It would cease to be newsworthy. Reporters would now become a propaganda tool for the president.

Salinger persisted, and on January 25, 1961, just five days after his inaugural, Kennedy walked across the stage of the New State Department Building auditorium, faced four hundred and eighteen reporters, and held the first news conference ever on live television.

As a rule, Presidents prefer to call a news conference when they have "news to make." Somehow presidents never feel that taking questions alone is sufficient. Kennedy expressed that concern when he asked if the networks would carry them if there were no major news break. He wanted his first news conference to open with such a story.

The news break for that first televised news conference was to be that the Soviets were releasing two American pilots who had come down over Russia. Unfortunately, on the night before, David Wise of the New York *Herald Tribune* called Salinger and said he had the story of two pilots being released from Lubiyanka Prison. Salinger told him the story was correct but premature publication would blow the whole deal sky high since the Soviets insisted on simultaneous announcement of the release. Wise was asked to hold up the story. He agreed to call his New York editors. The *Herald Tribune* decided to hold and Salinger later saluted them for their willingness to act in the national interest. It also permitted Kennedy to open his very first news conference with a blockbuster of a story and the Soviets, strangely, chose that the simultaneous an-

nouncement be made at 6 P.M. Washington time just as the news
conference began. It was well past midnight in Moscow.

Kennedy was pleased with the first televised news conference.
"I thought that went very well," he told Salinger on the drive back
to the White House. He asked for an audience rating (sixty million watched). Since a local station in Washington reran a tape of
each news conference at night, the president had the opportunity
to view his work and did so whenever he could, commenting on
his style, on the lighting, the camera angles.

He was a master of the electronic medium and knew it. He also
knew what it permitted him to do to offset newspaper reaction.
Said Kennedy one evening in the White House, "We couldn't survive without TV."

Salinger felt the wire services, AP and UPI, were the single
most important client he had since they serviced all newspapers
and broadcasters but he considered the networks "the second most
powerful faction in the establishment." He started adding a network reporter to the small presidential pools and dealt privately
with the three network bureau chiefs to arrange presidential appearances on television.

The combination of wire services and networks, he noted, permitted the president to communicate with "unbelievable speed to
the nation and the world." In ten minutes, a presidential announcement of importance could be on the airwaves and on the
teletype machines. This was especially important to have during
the Cuban crisis, as Salinger himself has recalled:

> There were desperate moments during the Cuban missile
> crisis when communications between JFK and Khrushchev were
> running hours behind because of the total inadequacy of
> diplomatic channels. We decided to release JFK's statements
> directly to the networks and wire services, knowing that
> Moscow was monitoring our radio frequencies and news wires
> and would have the word hours faster. Khrushchev did the same
> with Radio Moscow and Tass, and the speed-up in communica-
> tions may very well have been a factor in preventing escala-
> tion of the crisis. This necessity for instantaneous communica-
> tion was the reason for prompt agreement, after the Cuban

crisis, on installation of the hot line (teletype system) between Washington and Moscow.

Cuba, of course, both during the abortive Bay of Pigs adventure and the later missile crisis, gave the Kennedy presidency its most dramatic moments. The first was his greatest embarrassment and the other his most satisfying accomplishment. The role of the press in both confrontations involving Cuba is important.

The *Nation* on November 19, 1960 published an editorial, "Are We Training Cuban Guerrillas?" It told of a U.S. financed, "Guatemala-type" invasion, with forces being trained in Guatemala to invade Cuba. In January, the *New York Times* reported such training but said authorities explained that it was to meet any assault from Cuba, not to go into Cuba.

In April, Gilbert Harrison of the *New Republic* sent presidential aide Arthur Schlesinger, Jr. the galley proofs on an article "Our Men in Miami," which Schlesinger called "a careful, accurate, and devastating account of CIA activities among the (Cuban) refugees." Schlesinger took the article to Kennedy who expressed the hope that it could be stopped. Harrison agreed, Schlesinger wrote, in "a patriotic act which left me oddly uncomfortable."

Meanwhile Tad Szulc, the able Latin American correspondent for the *Times* was developing the same story in Florida, a story of recruiting men to engage in an "imminent" invasion of Cuba. Turner Catledge, the managing editor, called James Reston to ask advice. Reston cautioned him against pinpointing the time of the landing. Szulc recalled that the editors dropped mention of the CIA involvement as well. At the *Times,* editors Ted Bernstein and Lew Jordan protested. Never before had the front-page play in the *Times* been changed for policy reasons. They appealed to the publisher, Orvil Dryfoos. He said national security and the safety of the men going ashore were involved.

Ironically, there was a "shirttail" to the Szulc story which said some of the things that were dropped. A separate item was printed just below the end of the Szulc report telling of a CBS News report of plans for the invasion of Cuba in their final stages, ships and planes from Florida preparing for the assault.

Kennedy was reported to be furious at stories about the upcoming invasion. At one point he told Salinger, "I can't believe what I'm reading! Castro doesn't need agents over here. All he has to do is read our papers. It's all laid out for him."

The April 17, 1961 invasion was a complete failure and an extreme embarrassment for Kennedy. Officials, once the landings started, told reporters in Miami that five thousand men were involved. They hoped to encourage the Cuban people to rise up and support a large invasion force, but when the landing of a thousand (not five thousand) men ran into trouble, the same officials tried to minimize the defeat and said there was no invasion, that two hundred to four hundred men had landed simply to deliver supplies to anti-Castro guerrillas already in Cuba. James Reston wrote in the *Times*, "Both times the press was debased for the Government's purpose. Both times the Castro government and its Soviet advisers knew from their own agents in the anti-Castro refugee camps and from their own observation on the beaches that these pronouncements were false and silly. And both times the American people were the only ones to be fooled."

Newspapers attacked the White House for hiding the facts. Ambassador Adlai Stevenson, himself ignorant of the invasion plans, had gone before the United Nations to deny U.S. participation in the Bay of Pigs.

The president was criticized for his refusal to speak on the Cuban question at his first news conference afterwards ("I do not think that any useful national purpose would be served by my going further into the Cuban question this morning"). Bitterly he told Salinger, "What could I have said that would have helped the situation at all? That we took the beating of our lives? That the CIA and the Pentagon are stupid? What purpose do they think it would serve to put that on the record? We're going to straighten all this out, and soon. The publishers have to understand that we're never more than a miscalculation away from war and there are things we are doing that we just can't talk about."

On April 20, the president had an opportunity to straighten out the press when he appeared before the meeting of the American Association of Newspaper Editors. He spoke on Cuba but made no reference to press aspects of the Bay of Pigs other than to say "There are, from this, sobering lessons for us all to learn."

A week later, however, he spoke at a New York dinner of the

American Newspaper Publishers Association and this time the president did go to the press issue. "Every newspaper now asks itself with respect to every story, 'Is it news?' All I suggest is that you add the question, 'Is it in the interest of national security?' "

In a harsh indictment of the press, he said: "This nation's foes have openly boasted of acquiring through our newspapers information they would otherwise hire agents to acquire through theft, bribery, or espionage; details of this nation's covert preparations to counter the enemy's covert operations have been available to every newspaper reader, friend and foe alike; the size, the strength, the location, and the nature of our forces and weapons, and our plans and strategy for their use, have all been pinpointed in the press and other news media to a degree sufficient to satisfy any foreign power; and, in at least one case, the publication of details concerning a secret mechanism whereby satellites were followed required its alteration at the expense of considerable time and money."

He asked the publishers to recognize their own responsibility, to reexamine standards to see "our country's peril." Even the First Amendment, he asserted, "must yield to the public's need for national security." He then offered to cooperate in something he called "the voluntary assumption of specific new steps or machinery" to do this.

The audience took that to be a call for some form of self-censorship. The St. Louis *Post-Dispatch* warned that this could "make the press an official arm of the government somewhat as it is an official arm in totalitarian countries." The Indianapolis *Star* said Kennedy was trying to intimidate the press. The Los Angeles *Times* said it was a Kennedy "smarting with chagrin" who angrily sought to make a scapegoat of the press. Noting that the press had accepted the administration denials prior to the invasion, the *Times* said instead of a president chiding the press, "it should have been twitted for having its leg pulled."

A group of editors and publishers arranged to meet with the president to see what he had in mind. They met for over an hour, the president saying he didn't want to restrict the publishing of news but stressing the critical period of history of the moment. Kennedy's staff had listed a series of allegedly harmful disclosures that had appeared in print.

The president asked the editors if they did not agree that it was a period of extreme peril to the nation. He was surprised to get the blunt answer: "No." They said they saw no need for censorship short of a declared national emergency. Kennedy said he had no intention of making such a declaration. The meeting ended with the puzzled committee agreeing to think about it, unclear as to what Kennedy had in mind and convinced that the president himself had only a vague notion of what he wanted.

Clifton Daniel, the managing editor of the New York *Times,* revealed details of the *Times'* involvement in the Bay of Pigs when he spoke in June, 1966 to the World Press Institute meeting in St. Paul. Daniel says that Kennedy turned to Turner Catledge at the White House meeting and, in an aside, said, "If you had printed more about the operation you would have saved us from a colossal mistake." A year later, the president told the *Times* publisher Orvil Dryfoos much the same: "I wish you had run everything on Cuba."

Daniel himself agreed. In his St. Paul speech, he said, "My own view is that the Bay of Pigs operation might well have been cancelled and the country would have been saved enormous embarrassment if the *New York Times* and other newspapers had been more diligent in the performance of their duty." He reported however that James Reston did *not* agree: "If I had to do it over, I would do exactly what we did at the time. It is ridiculous to think that publishing the fact that the invasion was imminent would have avoided the disaster. I am quite sure the operation would have gone forward. The thing had been cranked up too far. The CIA would have had to disarm the anti-Castro forces physically. Jack Kennedy was in no mood to do anything like that."

But five years earlier, on the day after the editors met Kennedy to discuss the lessons of press coverage of the Bay of Pigs, Reston had written in a different vein. "The trouble with the press during the Cuban crisis," he said then, "was not that it said too much but that it said too little. It knew what was going on ahead of the landing."

A year after Daniel's detailed account of the *Times* and the Cuban crisis, Senator Robert F. Kennedy spoke before ASNE and said, "Clearly, publication of U.S. battle plans in time of war would irresponsibly imperil success and endanger lives. On the other hand, President Kennedy once said that wider press discussion of plans to invade Cuba—known to many reporters and patriotically withheld—might have avoided the Bay of Pigs. . . . In looking back over crises from Berlin and the Bay of Pigs to the Gulf of Tonkin, or even over the past fifteen years, I can think of few examples where disclosure of large policy considerations damaged the country, and many instances where public discussion and debate led to more thoughtful and informed decisions."

President Kennedy faced an even more serious crisis on Cuba when, late in 1962, it was discovered that the Soviets were placing missiles on the island. There, too, the press was involved but this time the president took direct and personal action to preclude what he considered premature disclosure.

The election campaign in the fall of 1962 was full of charges that the Soviets were moving missiles with atomic capability into sites on the island of Cuba. The president's chief national security advisor, McGeorge Bundy publicly denied this just one week before it became public, stating, "I know there is no present evidence and I think there is no present likelihood that the Cubans and the Cuban government and the Soviet government would in combination attempt to install a major offensive capability." At the time he said it, the White House was already examining aerial photos of the installations under construction. John F. Kennedy was to return from a campaign appearance in Chicago, allegedly to nurse a bad cold as the last weekend of Cuba crisis planning began. On Monday he went on television and told the American people about it.

Earlier, however, James Reston had talked to Bundy about the matter and it was clear from Reston's questioning that he knew what was up. Bundy told Kennedy and the president telephoned Reston. He told him of his plans to go on television Monday night and said publication in advance would result in a Khrushchev ultimatum before the president could personally report to the people. Reston said he understood and would recommend that the *Times* hold up publication but he also recommended that Kennedy talk to the publisher. He did. Dryfoos then put the issue up to Reston and his staff. The story was withheld. At the time of the publisher's death, the president wrote Mrs. Dryfoos that "this decision of his made far more effective our later actions and thereby contributed greatly to our national safety."

Some say that the Bay of Pigs marked the end of Kennedy's very brief honeymoon with the press. Others say it lasted longer. In either case, his administration gave rise to the phrase "news management" and both Cuban affairs were very much a part of that.

It is odd that Jack Kennedy should be tagged with "news management." He was well liked by most of the press, counted reporters and columnists among his closest friends, mingled with news people socially and professionally, and is said to have considered buying a newspaper after he ended his presidency. He had even briefly worked as a newspaperman and when he became a member of the National Press Club during his presidency, the bulletin board calmly noted that "John F. Kennedy, a former newspaperman now in politics, was approved for membership." The president held frequent background sessions with reporters, had exclusive chats with certain favorites or particularly influential newsmen, had publishers and editors to lunch at the White House, and did much to endear the working press to his presidency.

Yet this was the administration of "news management."

It was James Reston, testifying before a congressional committee who created the term. He said he wasn't worried about suppressing the news as much as managing the news.

Reston's colleague Arthur Krock wrote a famous article in *Fortune* magazine in March of 1963 entitled "Mr. Kennedy's Management of the News." In it, Krock says that based on his fifty years of Washington news coverage, he found the administration guilty of a news management policy "enforced more cynically and boldly than by any previous Administration in a period when the United States was not in a war." He defined news management as suppression, concealment, distortion, false weighting of facts, threats, shutting off sources, and even the "off-the-record" device which operates "without the imprint of authority and responsibility, and is open to repudiation by its very source if repudiation becomes expedient." He said, "This is a public relations project and the president is its most brilliant operator."

The president, asked about managed news, professed no knowledge. The press secretary, Pierre Salinger, said that he, too, was ignorant in the matter—"I don't know what managed news is. Nobody ever defined this to me."

The press didn't need a definition. *Newsweek* polled forty-three top Washington correspondents. All but three found the administration guilty of news management. While the same number said it believed the Eisenhower administration also guilty, the vast majority felt Kennedy worked harder at it. The correspondents were equally split as to which president was the more successful.

What was the bill of indictment?

1. Every aspect of the Bay of Pigs preparation was hidden. The official investigation of it was never made public. Portions of a congressional investigation later were leaked by the administration to make it look better.

2. A State Department briefing just before the Bay of Pigs misled a large group of editors and publishers, some of whom later called it a "mockery."

3. The Defense Department gave out false information during the invasion to mislead the enemy. It, of course, misled the American public.

4. In the search for news leaks at the Pentagon, lie detector tests were considered and, in the words of one newspaper, there was the "humiliating public picture of top presidential appointees being asked to swear to their innocence."

5. Questions were planted at news conferences.

6. The FBI was used to wake up reporters in the middle of the night to determine sources for stories during the 1962 steel-price crisis.

7. Reporters were heavily criticized, sometimes by the president and sometimes by his staff. Fletcher Knebel wrote an article for *Look* about halfway through the Kennedy years and could already list the following: "Jumped on by Jack"—reporters from the Washington *Evening Star,* the *New York Herald Tribune, U.S. News and World Report,* Hearst Headline Service, *Newsweek* and *Time;* "Bawled Out by Bobby"—reporters from *Newsweek,* the *Herald Tribune* and two syndicated columnists; "Probed by the F.B.I."—reporters from the Washington *Evening Star,* the *Wall Street Journal,* the Wilmington, Delaware, *Journal,* the Associated Press, and *Newsweek;* "Sat On by Salinger"—reporters from the

Herald Tribune, the Gannett Newspapers, the North American Newspaper Alliance, United Press International, the *Detroit News,* and the *London Times.*

One reason for the growing number of those "Jumped On by Jack" or "Sat On by Salinger" (and the list above is far from complete) was that Kennedy read so much—"every damn thing written" complained one reporter. At the same time, it was said "his skin is as thin as cigarette paper."

Once, irritated by the *New York Herald Tribune's* extensive coverage of the Billy Sol Estes scandal while that newspaper was ignoring a stockpiling scandal that traced back to the Eisenhower years, Kennedy announced that he was cancelling the White House subscriptions to the paper, all twenty-two of them. The cancellations brought the wrath of editors down on Kennedy's head and political opponents chided him for the move. Richard Nixon, even years later, would boast that he never cancelled a newspaper subscription.

The move was a mistake. Kennedy missed many of the *Trib's* writers. Mrs. Kennedy wanted the fashion columns smuggled into the White House. While publicly standing by the cancellations, the White House began reading the paper again. One White House aide told this author that a staff messenger went to the railroad station each morning and brought copies back to the mansion. One could read the *Trib* in your office, he said, as long as you kept it covered on your desk. In time Kennedy relented and public word went out that the paper was back on the White House reading list.

Kennedy's troubleshooter in all of this was portly Pierre Emil George Salinger, who smoked ten cigars a day, played poker with the boys, and was known for the quick quip (example: "I am not a textual deviate"). "Plucky Pierre" courted reporters even more than his boss and was candid as much as could be without compromising administration ends. He even admitted an occasional mistake. Once he banned three antiadministration newspapers from a background briefing and then denied there had ever been a briefing. Said a contrite Salinger later, "It was stupid."

Salinger, by the way, once prematurely passed on an unconfirmed report that the Dominican dictator Rafael Trujillo had been assassinated. Kennedy was furious as the hours passed without confirmation. At one point, the president told his press secretary, "We now have later intelligence that Trujillo may not be dead." Said Salinger, "Mr. President, if he's not, I am."

After the Cuban missile crisis, Pierre Salinger insisted, "We did not lie to the American people." He said the only legitimate place where news could be managed was at the editorial desk. He suggested a study was needed to see if news was being managed in the public interest. At about the same time, Kennedy with a nice, light touch of self-ridicule, spoke to the Gridiron Club dinner and began "Fellow managing editors . . ."

Theodore Sorenson, Kennedy's confidant in the White House and later his biographer, defended the president against the news management charge, saying Kennedy never withheld privileges from unfriendly papers, never tried to intimidate reporters, never deliberately falsified facts to cover up errors. Sorenson said while the administration would occasionally arrange for planted questions, the president "preferred" that interviews not be staged in advance.

He did, Sorenson admits, after a crisis like steel or Cuba request that all reporters' inquiries come through the White House but that did not work. He did let the press corps know, through phone calls and notes, of stories he especially liked and those he disliked. He did ask staff to do the same.

Sorenson also tells of Kennedy noting newspaper criticism of news management and saying, "Does anyone think we'd get 'belted' every day if we could control it ourselves?" Did he feel that the issue of news management had bite? No. Kennedy said privately "We aren't losing any votes on that one."

When assassination snuffed out his presidency after only a thousand days, Kennedy left two disparate images in regard to his press relations—that of news management on the one hand and of the pioneer in a truly open news conference on the other. He held fewer, on the average, than even Eisenhower but television made them vivid and won him tremendous public support. It was his most dramatic innovation and was done over the protest of many publishers (he reassured them sarcastically that he wanted America to "observe the incisive, the intelligent, and the courteous qualities displayed by your Washington correspondents").

There are those who considered the televised news conferences the great legacy of the Kennedy years, the measure of the man, his policies, and his thinking. The brilliant appearances on television presented Kennedy's successor with a problem that haunted him all through his presidency. Lyndon Baines Johnson was not young, handsome, witty, and a television natural. He had every confidence that he could handle the job of the presidency; he was far less confident of his role before the cameras.

He inherited Pierre Salinger as his first press secretary (Salinger departed with very little notice in 1964 to run for the U.S. Senate in California but overestimated his popularity in his home state and was defeated by movie actor George Murphy that November) and the question of news conferences came up early. Johnson held his first on December 7, 1963 but it was very sudden, very impromptu. Salinger ended a press briefing by inviting the White House regulars into the president's office for a cup of coffee. They suddenly discovered a news conference was under way.

Johnson was simply putting off his first appearance before the cameras. The press play after the coffee-'n-conference was very good and he braced himself for one before the cameras. One thing was sure—he would minimize comparison between him and his telegenic predecessor. He never held a conference in the familiar auditorium at State where Kennedy had all of his, opting instead for the International Conference Room in another part of the building. Ultimately most news conferences would move to the East Room of the White House (where Richard Nixon would hold his), the front porch or airplane hanger of the Johnson ranch in Texas, and even, outside on the south lawn of the executive mansion. At the last, on a pleasant summer day, Johnson invited wives and children of correspondents to come and "see how Daddy works."

This president was concerned about his appearance on television, he was also close to paranoid about mistreatment at the hands of the press. In the Senate, especially in his years as Majority Leader, he could orchestrate press coverage with comparative ease since he rarely sought personal publicity. In the White House he was, as Kennedy once described it, right in the center of the bull's-eye. Further, he suspected that much of the press, particularly the Eastern press which he distrusted most of all, was always aiming at that bull's-eye.

Part of it was his Southern, nonurban, non-Eastern, background. He told one distinguished columnist: "I don't know whether we are far enough away from Appomattox that a Southern President can really unite the people of this country, particularly against this big, Eastern, intellectual press. They're trying to cut me up."

He called the press "the least-guided, least-inhibited segment of U.S. Society." He complained that "they warp everything I do, they lie about me and about what I do, they don't know the meaning of truth. They are liars and cheats." On the other hand, in the spirit of the love-hate relationship of so many chief executives toward the press, he could when the news was favorable say things like "I trust the press. I trust you just as much as I trust my wife."

If Kennedy wooed the press fervently, Johnson did it passionately. He constantly had reporters, publishers, broadcasters, bureau chiefs in to lunch or for sherry in the living quarters. He briefed reporters alone or in groups. He even invited some media executives to swim in the White House pool (until reports came out that the men, unprepared and without bathing suits, engaged in naked dips). He almost always had reporters at formal White House dinners, as guests not working press, and danced indefatigably with their wives. Christmas might mean a gift of bookends with the presidential seal or deer sausage from Texas.

It didn't work. Embarrassing stories seeped out. Washington reporters, always heavy on gossip, seemed eager to pass on an inside story that would show the warts and all. The president would get testy. He once snapped at a reporter for a "chicken-shit" question (involving the White House payroll) and told some magazine reporters, "Someone ought to do an article on you and your damn profession, your First Amendment."

After just one month in office, he summoned the administration's chief press officers to the White House and gave them a tongue lashing. The White House had made the front page only once that week, no thanks to them. It was the annual lighting of the national Christmas tree. That was to change, there had better be more. "You are working for me now," he reminded them and he was going to Texas for the holidays and he wanted them to give Salinger as many stories as possible, all to be released at the Texas White House. He said he had been checking the budget and almost a billion dollars was being spent on people like them and they had better start earning it.

Unfortunately no matter how much money or how many men the government had to help, on television the president was on his own. This president wanted to do television well and wanted to do it often. He did it often. He used television for not only news conferences and speeches but for bill signings and settling railroad strikes and even for declaring war on the Ku Klux Klan. In time, he wanted it always available, nearby and quickly, so the networks, at great expense, installed a television studio in the East Wing, in what had been a small movie theatre placed there by FDR.

Requesting time of the networks was easy. The three television networks have a permanent "pool" committee to handle presidential appearances and other pooled coverage, each Washington bureau chief rotating in the three-month chairmanship. A president could request time and, though not required by law, the networks never failed to provide it.

Lyndon Johnson had a fetish about not "asking" for time. His press aides simply would tell the bureau chief-chairman that the president was making an important appearance and it was "available" for live television. George Reedy, LBJ's second press secretary (he had four in all), has observed that no medium used to communicate with the public could possibly turn down such a presidential suggestion and he could not conceive of such an appearance not having journalistic significance. "If the President uses the time for an unworthy purpose, that in itself becomes a newsworthy event. It is not up to the television networks on such occasions to decide whether the President is appearing for substantial or trivial reasons. As long as the networks do not waive their right to comment on the appearance after it is made or to present adversary material, they should merely acquiesce to the request. Of course it is conceivable that such requests could get out of hand, in which case the whole subject would have to be reexamined."

Philip Geyelin, in his book *Lyndon B. Johnson and the World,* wrote: "He and his closest advisors made no bones about their concept of how a President's thinking ought to be conveyed to the public—by Presidential appearance on television, without comment or interpretation or analysis." That might have been considered desirable, and LBJ often hated the postpresidential analysis, but he never even remotely suggested the networks stop the practice. That was left to Spiro Agnew in the Nixon Administration.

Johnson, particularly in 1965, made numerous television appearances and his critics felt he abused the privilege but the presidential appearances were always somewhat, and usually very, newsworthy. It is assumed that though a president is "always political," his television appearances as president should be nonpartisan. Johnson's one departure from this came in December 12, 1967 when the White House told the television pool that Johnson's appearance before the AFL-CIO in Bal Harbour, Florida, that night would be "major." All networks carried the speech which turned out to be a highly partisan attack on congressional Republicans. The networks were embarrassed and angry, one executive saying, "We were led down the path." The Republicans were even angrier, they asked for and received television time to reply to the president.

Despite Johnson's aversion to placing himself in a setting which invited comparison with Kennedy, he did pick up one of JFK's most effective television experiments—the three-network "Conversation With the President." On December 17, 1962 Kennedy appeared on all networks for one hour, interviewed by Bill Lawrence of ABC, George Herman of CBS, Sander Vanocur of NBC, the White House correspondents. They taped about seventy-five minutes of material the day before and a three-network committee edited it down to one hour. The producer for the pool was Fred Friendly of CBS.

Kennedy had received tremendous praise for his performance. It revealed a different side of the man than did news conferences or any form of "hard news" interview. A second such "conversation" was in the exploratory stage when Kennedy was killed.

On March 15, 1964 Lyndon Johnson appeared in "A Conversation With the President" on all three television networks. The reporters this time were Lawrence of ABC, Eric Sevareid of CBS, and David Brinkley of NBC. Friendly was again the producer and dramatically opened the broadcast with a tight shot of the metal plaque on the back of LBJ's leather chair: "The President,

November 22, 1963"—a graphic reminder of the transition from JFK to LBJ. The broadcast, very well received, dealt with his first hundred days in office and, in the words of Salinger later, "did a great deal to underline the fact that he had the reins of government firmly in hand."

While the audience was less than that attracted to the first "conversation," an audience of thirty-eight million versus forty-eight million for Kennedy, it was very large indeed and the networks were as pleased as the White House. The exclusive interview by television reporters of these "conversations" was a significant boost to network prestige and marked deference to the importance of television.

It would be over three and a half years, however, before the president did another and this one ended up in bitterness. The network-White House agreement, from the first Kennedy "conversation," was that the networks would have a free hand in editing the material down to an hour but that the White House could make suggestions if the president made an error affecting national security. In the "conversation" of December 19, 1967 the White House went far beyond that in its suggestions for editing.

The reporters this time were the then White House network correspondents, Frank Reynolds of ABC, Dan Rather of CBS, and Ray Scherer of NBC. The producer was Robert Asman of NBC and the tri-network editing committee was in New York to cut the tape back to an hour. The taping was done on Monday morning, the day before the broadcast. After ten minutes was taped, the "conversation" stopped so that the president, his advisors, and network people could watch a playback to "see how it looked." The taping then resumed, almost a full hour of it. They decided to take a break and the president disappeared for about fifteen minutes to do business in another room. He returned and another twelve minutes was taped, which brought the broadcast to a natural ending with a "Thank you, Mr. President." Presidential aide Marvin Watson entered the room a moment later, however, and said the president would be available for some more taping on the farm problem. This was done but produced nothing that would end up in the final broadcast. Johnson left again and returned again, suggesting he tape a tribute to the late Australian prime minister Harold Holt. This was also taped but not used since

Johnson was flying off to Australia the next day and the tribute seemed dated.

The editing committee in New York had about eighty-five minutes of material to cut back to less than an hour for three-network use. There were other editing committees, however, at the White House, at the State Department, and finally aboard Air Force One as the president flew across the Pacific on Tuesday.

Bill Monroe, the NBC bureau chief and chairman of the Washington pool, started getting phone calls. William Bundy's office at State told the White House press office that there were five deletions needed on security grounds, each a sentence or two dealing with Vietnam. This was passed on to the editing committee. Since national security was a proper ground for White House involvement in editing, the committee agreed to make the deletions.

Bundy also passed on the suggestion that one section of the material on Vietnam was redundant and they could cut it out if they liked. The networks chose to keep it. The White House suggested that the rest of the Vietnam material be kept intact because it contained a careful and deliberate balance. Some of this was cut.

Later Monday night other suggestions were phoned in. It was recommended that two questions relating to the meeting with Kosygin at Glassboro and the Mid-East be cut because they were "stale" and contained nothing new. The White House was straying far from limiting itself to matters that jeopardized national security. The proposed cuts were denied. It was suggested that a section on taxes be dropped because the sound was bad. The networks replied that on their tape the sound was fine.

Another call, this from the aide to the press secretary suggesting a factual error in the president's description of the vote to make McNamara head of the World Bank. The material involved had already been deleted in the New York editing. Still another call with two more editing suggestions. Monroe argued that these fell far short of the agreement dealing with national security and didn't even pass them on to New York.

On Tuesday, the day of broadcast, calls from Air Force One through Bromley Smith of the National Security Council staff at the White House. This time a request that two items earlier deleted be restored. One dealt with conditions for a Middle East peace and it was said that deleting it gave a misleading impression on an important foreign policy matter. This was restored by the editors. The other suggestion was denied.

The networks rankled at the torrent of editing suggestions. CBS added a brief on-air announcement to its presentation: "Portions of Mr. Johnson's remarks were edited at the request of the White House on the grounds of policy and national security." The other networks made no such announcement, explaining later that they felt the essential journalistic integrity of the broadcast had not been compromised.

It rankled network newsmen to have such a heavy hand laid upon their work. The thought of Johnson and his aides flying across the Pacific on Air Force One, with a videotape machine aboard and transcripts in hand, convinced at least one network news chief that all future "conversation" broadcasts would be done to time, never again edited. That point was moot. Richard Nixon, who may have had different reasons to avoid network editing, insisted that his "conversations" not only be to time but that they be "live" which, of course, means no editing by anybody.

Johnson, as had Eisenhower and Kennedy before him, recognized that television and the other tools for capturing center stage could be used to blanket the opposition if one knew what was coming. There is a much-cited example of a presidential blizzard of activity designed to obfuscate something else in the news. In March of 1967, Senator Robert F. Kennedy was about to deliver an attack on the administration's Vietnam policy which the White House was determined to snow under with headlines of its own.

On that single day, Lyndon Johnson (1) called an impromptu news conference, (2) revealed that Soviet Premier Kosygin had just written and had agreed to negotiate antiballistic missile limitations, (3) rushed to Howard University to give a civil rights speech (which, incidentally, was one of the finest of his presidency), and (4) ended the day speaking about the state of American education in an appearance at the U.S. Office of Education. At the same time, three steps were taken to defang the Kennedy speech in whatever press play was left for it: (a) Senator Henry Jackson produced a long letter from Lyndon defending his Vietnam policies, (b) Secretary of State Rusk called Kennedy's proposals old stuff and (c) in Saigon, General Westmoreland took issue with New York's junior Senator.

Kennedy wasn't fully snowed under but for twenty-four hours his much-heralded speech was buffeted about in the mighty winds of a White House publicity storm, fully unleashed. The tactic didn't work, however. In the days that followed the transparent maneuvers of the White House were exposed in a series of press commentaries. George Reedy once suggested that if a president didn't make news, that was news of itself. Now a president made too much news and that too was news. Johnson was similarly rebuked by pundits for his hurried Honolulu war councils a year earlier to take headlines away from Senate Foreign Relations Committee hearings on Vietnam.

Johnson also suffered when engaged in a bit of news management in the timing of an appearance during the Six-Day War later that year. U.N. Ambassador Arthur Goldberg, on the afternoon of June 6, called to tell the president that an agreement on a Middle East cease-fire resolution seemed assured. Johnson decided to issue a brief statement after the former Security Council vote and the networks were alerted to get the small TV studio in the East Wing ready.

The president arrived at 7:45 P.M. and noticed that the networks were carrying the United Nations proceedings and that Soviet delegate Nikolai Fedorenko was speaking. "I want to follow him," said the president. He was insistent that the networks not switch to him earlier, giving the appearance of interrupting the Russian. After some minutes, however, the president grew impatient—he was not a man for standing around, waiting—and demanded that the networks tape his remarks but hold them for broadcast until Fedorenko finished.

The networks, after some debate with the press aide to the president, agreed but Fedorenko suddenly finished and Johnson decided to start immediately. He rushed to the podium and began. Unfortunately the networks were now in station-break time and the president was "upcut." He returned from the studio only to hear his wife complain that she was watching TV and only heard four sentences. The full statement was six. It was carried later that evening during network special coverage.

Lyndon Johnson's attempts to manipulate coverage strained his relations with the press. "News management" was the phrase for the Kennedy years; in Johnson's time it was "credibility gap"—the

White House was not to be believed. Press resentment poured forth.

Newsmen resented his funneling all important announcements through his office. One weekend at his Johnson City ranch on the Pedernales River there were forty-two news releases from the White House press office, quickly dubbed the "Pedernales Press Service."

Newsmen resented the twists and turns of administration statements reflecting, obviously, the whims of the president. They resented the critical calls, sometimes from the president but usually from his aides. On one occasion network bureau chiefs received a call from a press aide, Bob Fleming, calling attention to a UPI report of a communist mortar attack in Vietnam which killed twenty-seven women and children. Fleming said, "Everybody is doing so much reporting about other kinds of killing" and neglecting the brutality of the enemy. The bureau chiefs were convinced that the call was prompted by the president.

Newsmen resented publicity barrages to distract the public eye from administration problems. Saul Pett of the AP called it "the Lyndon Johnson school of window dressing."

Newsmen resented the president's passion for secrecy. It was a common joke that the best way to kill a presidential appointment in advance was to leak it to the press because LBJ would never make an appointment first mentioned in print.

Newsmen resented the president's insistence that things be announced only when he wanted them announced. He told an impromptu news conference one day that he had not begun to consider a replacement for Arthur Goldberg on the Supreme Court. The very next day it was announced that Abe Fortas would succeed Goldberg.

Bill Moyers, LBJ's third press secretary, explained much of this to the press as the president wanting to keep his options open—"the president doesn't believe that speculation about his intentions is accurate or justified because he himself often does not know until the very last minute what he is going to do. It is *very* important for a president to maintain, up until the moment of decision, his options, and for someone to speculate days or weeks in advance that he's going to do thus and thus is to deny to the president the latitude he needs."

Reporters admired Moyers but did not readily accept his defense. If an appointment or policy is right, discussing it in print or on television before it is announced makes it no less right. Press speculation doesn't really commit a president. Further, presidents use the press as a trial balloon. All modern presidents had, including Lyndon Johnson who was known to have personally leaked a National Security Council memo dealing with nuclear weapons when he thought it would serve his purpose.

And so "credibility gap" became the damaging byword of the Johnson years. Republicans loved it. Editorials seized it. Articles were written analyzing it. Historians frowned upon it (Henry Steele Commager said, "The habits of deception carry the danger of self-deception; you can begin to believe your own propaganda"). Lyndon Johnson hated it.

One high official in his administration bitterly complained to the AP that the White House had "never lied to the press" but that the president had a right to protect his options, his secrecy, his decision making. "The American people," he said, "have a right to know but they also have a right to have dangerous problems handled properly by responsible officers and not by the press. Nobody elected them."

The usual, final resort of the wounded politician: nobody elected the press.

The LBJ credibility gap was especially wide in 1965 during the revolt in the Dominican Republic. It was news manipulation at its most extreme as the White House tried to manipulate news reporting of U.S. involvement in the uprising by followers of Juan Bosch on April 23, 1965.

The administration was fearful of a take-over from the left though they insisted, in the early days, that it was not Communist coups that worried them, it was protecting U.S. citizens on the island. A right-wing military junta opposing the rebels was invited by the United States to ask for U.S. troops to protect those U.S. citizens. They did. On April 28, President Johnson went on television to announce that he had ordered four hundred Marines to "give protection to hundreds of Americans who are still in the Dominican Republic and escort them safely back to this country." Top officials, on a background basis, again denied reports that it was to offset a Communist take-over.

In time, twenty-four thousand American soldiers were on the island. The administration still insisted their role was to protect Americans. The president himself spent hours convincing individual newsmen of the danger to our citizens there. At one point he said, "Some fifteen hundred innocent people were murdered and shot, and their heads cut off." He also told of phoning the American ambassador who "was talking to us from under a desk while bullets were going through his windows, and he had a thousand American men, women, and children assembled in the hotel who were pleading with their president for help to preserve their lives."

No one was beheaded. Only a few Americans, and they the soldiers, were shot by the revolutionary force. Ambassador W. Tapley Bennett, Jr., didn't remember being under the desk as he talked and there were no bullets coming through his window. As Hugh Sidey of *Life* magazine described the president's use of "excruciating detail" in telling his story—"The more he talked, however, the more the story ceased to resemble the facts."

At one point, Ambassador Bennett called in newsmen to report on "rebel atrocities" which included heads cut off and carried on spikes through the streets, against-the-wall executions, and machine-gunning of the innocent. All of these stories were untrue, including Bennett's account of how one of the military junta's leaders, Colonel Juan Calderon, was murdered. Reporters found Calderon that very day, alive and well, and ready to take questions.

The administration now switched course and decided to raise the Communist issue. They started feeding stories, in direct contradiction to earlier stories, that the real danger in the Dominican Republic was of another Castro coming into power. The State Department issued a list of "known Communists" involved, carefully seeing that the list was printed on white paper with no identification indicating an official source. The list included the names of children, of the same person spelled different ways, and of dead Dominicans. One reporter said it looked like a ward heeler's vote registration list in Chicago.

In Santo Domingo, Ambassador Bennett also released such a list. Reporters there noted that some on the list were out of the country, others were actually in jail throughout the period, and some were obvious non-Communists including one supreme court justice.

Much of the fakery attendant to the Dominican fiasco was made public by Senator J. William Fulbright in a major Senate speech. It was before Fulbright's committee, in executive session one year after the affair, that Undersecretary of State Thomas Mann complained about "slanted reporting" of the U.S. intervention. Mann's testimony was never made public but the Los Angeles *Times* obtained a transcript and published the story.

Mann confirmed that the junta had secret support from the United States and had been invited to request U.S. troops to protect Americans, something the administration denied at the time it happened. Nevertheless, Mann was bothered by press coverage and said he used the word "slanted" advisedly, that a small group of reporters "emotionally committed to Bosch" went looking for facts to support their own preconceptions. He said the U.S. image was soiled in Latin eyes by "assertions and insinuations that United States government officials were lying about what the facts were."

Ambassador Mann said he was shocked. So were reporters at the suggestion that the insinuations and the lying were on their part.

At the end of Johnson's term of office, the journalism society *Sigma Delta Chi* in its 1968 Freedom of Information report was to say, "The Credibility Gap, which has reached awesome proportions under the Johnson Administration, continued to be a grave handicap. Secrecy, lies, half-truths, deception—this was the daily fare." It quoted one White House correspondent as saying the president considers himself not only commander-in-chief but also editor-in-chief.

The report concluded, "President Johnson is leaving office with perhaps the worst record for credibility of any President in our history."

Into that office came a man who believed the press's credibility to be as bad as any in history. Richard M. Nixon had had his problems with the press for many years and was convinced that it was hostile to him and his party. After his election defeat in 1960, he told a *Chicago Tribune* reporter, "Republicans will get better treatment in the press only if and when more reporters, like their publishers, take a more favorable or at least a more tolerant view of Republican policies and principles and not before."

He felt that his troubles with the press dated back to his role in the congressional investigations of Alger Hiss, the former State Department official who was convicted of perjury after the investigation. Nixon was to write, "One of the personal aftermaths of the Hiss case was that for the next twelve years of my public service in Washington, I was to be subjected to an utterly unprincipled and vicious smear campaign. Bigamy, forgery, drunkenness, insanity, thievery, anti-Semitism, perjury, the whole gamut of misconduct in public office, ranging from unethical to downright criminal activities—all these were among the charges that were hurled against me, some publicly and others through whispering campaigns which were even more difficult to counteract."

The press, he was convinced, was party to an anti-Nixon movement and his pent-up fury at a prejudiced press bubbled forth on November 7, 1962 in the famous "You won't have Nixon to kick around any more" news conference. It happened the morning after he was defeated in a race for governor of California, the hoped-for first step back after losing to Kennedy in 1960.

Reporters gathered in a hotel ballroom waiting for Nixon's concession remarks. A car was waiting at the rear exit of the hotel for the defeated candidate. Nixon advisors decided that his press spokesman, Herb Klein, would give the concession messages while a very tired Nixon could leave the hotel. As Nixon watched television, he saw Klein enter the roomful of tired, surly reporters who shouted "Where's Nixon?" and implied the candidate was afraid to face them. Impulsively, Nixon stormed out of the room and headed for the press room. He interrupted Klein and snapped at the reporters, "Good morning, gentlemen. Now that Mr. Klein has made his statement, and now that all members of the press are so delighted that I have lost, I'd like to make a statement of my own."

In a rambling monologue he went on for seventeen minutes, sometimes straying to national issues or to the race just finished, always returning to the press. He had never cancelled a subscription, "unlike some people." He wanted to read criticism. He never complained to an editor or a publisher.

But he noted that the press was quick to pick up his flubs (he had made a campaign speech about running for governor of the United States!) and not those of his opponent. "I think it's time that our great newspapers have at least the same objectivity, the same fullness of coverage, that television has. And I can only say thank God for television and radio for keeping the newspapers a little more honest."

Finally, he came to the end: "As I leave you I want you to know—just think how much you're going to be missing. You won't have Nixon to kick around any more, because, ladies and gentlemen, this is my last press conference."

On the way out, according to *Time* magazine, he turned to Herb Klein and said, "I know you don't agree. I gave it to them right in the behind. It had to be said, goddamnit. It had to be said."

It was the general consensus in the press that Nixon had marched off the national stage forever. They were, of course, wrong. It was the general consensus that this would guarantee a bad press into the hereafter. That, too, was wrong. In the 1968 campaign, though it was not generally known, the Democrats made an extensive search for film of the "last" news conference but after finding a copy and viewing it, decided not to use it against him. Looked at six years later, it only developed sympathy for Nixon.

If he needed evidence that he had not committed political suicide, Richard Nixon had it just five days after his California defeat. ABC broadcast a documentary, narrated by Howard K. Smith, unprophetically titled "The Political Obituary of Richard M. Nixon". Among those interviewed on the broadcast—Alger Hiss. ABC was flooded with complaints, eighty thousand letters and telegrams as well as thousands of phone calls (Nixon issued a statement—"What does an attack by one convicted perjurer mean when weighed on the scales against the thousands of wires and letters from patriotic Americans?"). There was evidence enough that a strong body of Americans did not consider him "dead."

An interesting sidelight to the broadcast was the attempt by sponsors to boycott ABC. James Hagerty, fortunately for that network, was now its vice-president in charge of news and stood tough against the pressures. The man who had played such an important role during Nixon's White House years said, in defense of the broadcast, "If we are weakened, you are weakened, for if through fear or intimidation, we fail to provide all the news—favorable or unfavorable—then you, the citizens of the nation, cannot be properly informed."

California and the "last" news conference, Nixon felt, were good in the long run. In 1967, he told the *National Review,* "It was a bad night. The press sniping, all through the campaign, had been fierce. So I blew up. I regretted it later, but I'll say this: It cleared the air. I get along with the reporters, and they seem to get along all right with me." He told a reporter, "After '62, the press could have said, 'Let's give it to the S.O.B.' but they didn't do it."

In a *Saturday Evening Post* interview with Jules Witcover in February of 1967, Nixon—not yet a candidate—said, "California served a purpose. The press had a guilt complex about their inaccuracy. Since then, they've been generally accurate, and far more respectful. The press are good guys, but they haven't basically changed. They're oriented against my views."

Nixon took office in January of 1969 and, on the whole, found a friendly press. That changed in the months that followed and by November of that year, his vice-president was to unleash the most bitter, perhaps the strongest attacks on the news media ever made by such a high public official. At the end of eleven months, *Editorial Research Reports* was to say, "The Nixon Administration and the press are beginning to live together in almost mutual hostility."

It wasn't that Nixon ignored the press and its needs. While there was none of the camaraderie of Kennedy or flattery of Johnson, no invitations to state dinners or lunches in the White House, Nixon did offer reporters improved working quarters, wiping out the presidential swimming pool to build a rather lush, two deck press room with cubicles for reporters and a wide open area for briefings. There was none of Lyndon Johnson's hurried travel (once reporters left a White House correspondents dinner to fly to Texas, the press plane filled with still tuxedoed newsmen). There was careful observance of news lids, advance warning of news conferences and, when travelling, rooms in some of the very best hotels in this country and overseas.

Mary McGrory noted cynically "While it is not necessary to give reporters news, it is smart to make them comfortable." *Editorial Research Reports* quoted her and observed, "As a Yale football coach once remarked about the alumni, keep them sullen but not mutinous."

Nixon, unlike Johnson who watched television constantly with three sets in his office to switch quickly from network to network, viewed television rarely except for sporting events (and would sometimes telephone the winning coach after a big game). Unlike Kennedy, he was not a voracious newspaper reader. The president, however, had a means to keep track of both broadcasters and newspapers.

Under the direction of Patrick Buchanan, a young, ex-editorial writer for the St. Louis *Globe-Democrat* who caught Nixon's eye some years earlier, *The President's Daily Briefing Book* was "published" six days a week in the White House. It consisted of a four to ten thousand word critique of what television, newspapers, and magazines were saying about the Nixon administration and the problems which confront it.

Buchanan himself wrote "the news top," a five-hundred word summary of the latest news which was the last thing entered in the *Briefing Book* one hour before it reached the president's desk at 8 A.M. The rest of the book, which was stamped "For the Eyes of the President Only" and limited in circulation to some fifty copies for top White House staffers, contained summaries of what the media has to say. The Buchanan staff monitored all networks, the wire services, fifty newspapers, and thirty-five magazines. With the help of video-tape machines in the Executive Office Building, every network newscast or news documentary was recorded for review by the staff. Television was also measured as to what was covered, "how it's played," and how the administration came off.

Few copies were ever viewed by outsiders, giving rise to the speculation that the analysis "for the president's eyes" had a politically conservative, biased viewpoint. This author saw one edition which was largely objective though it referred to NBC's David Brinkley as reporting "in his usual snide fashion" and in a report on Eric Sevareid, said he was "on our side for a change." The flavor of it was "us" versus "them."

In March of 1970, a Columbus, Ohio, *Dispatch* story told of a White House survey rating the three networks as to favorable, unfavorable, and "fair" stories. The breakdown, as the *Dispatch* reported it, showed ABC—favorable, 29 percent, unfavorable 29

percent, and fair 41 percent; CBS—favorable 24 percent, unfavorable 25 percent, and fair 51 percent; NBC—favorable 15 per-
cent, unfavorable 44 percent, and fair 40 percent. The survey said
NBC was guilty of periodically "crusading and generating news"
unfavorable to the administration.

The president's view of news coverage, in the internal *Briefing
Book* or in White House evaluations, seemed always colored by
the idea of "favorable" or "unfavorable." As with so many of his
predecessors, he obviously wanted newsmen on the team and measured them accordingly. In time, he was to turn the wrath of the
administration on those who didn't measure up—primarily the
networks and the liberal press.

Nixon watchers began to spot a trend in certain asides about
the press which they felt illustrated the president's pique or anger
or distrust. He told Helen Thomas of UPI about her colleagues,
"The tendency is to report the exciting things. You don't win a
Pulitzer Prize writing about peace."

He told reporters in the East Room, "We can all, of course,
here in a press conference—we can debate as to whether or not
my view of it is right or the rest. I hope for the good of the country
mine is, and if it is right, what you say now doesn't make any
difference." Here the president had summed up his feeling that
hard questions from reporters meant a "debate" and suggested
that their interpretations meant little, that the nation depended
on the rightness of his decisions.

He told nine women reporters that he was correcting a CBS
report for accuracy—"I don't care whether anybody at CBS,
NBC, or ABC says 'Nixon is wrong on ABM! That is fine. But if
they say Nixon expressed doubts about ABM to a group of people
when no meeting ever took place, that has to be corrected. That
is what I mean. You can't allow a little lie." He hastily said it was
"unfair" to call the CBS report a lie because the reporter "just
probably had the wrong information." The reporter, Daniel Schorr,
got his information from a man who was present at the meeting, a
Nixon appointee.

He told Howard K. Smith, in an exclusive interview on ABC
on March 22, 1971, that the press had distorted coverage of the
Laos invasion, concentrating on four South Vietnamese battalions
that were in trouble while not showing eighteen others that were

not. "That is not because it has been deliberate," said the president, "It is because those make news."

He then showed his reliance on the *Briefing Book* for views of press coverage. "I just saw a summary of two weeks' coverage by the television networks and by the newspapers, and I do not claim that this was deliberate or distorted or anything. Let's understand that. I am not here to bait the press and you are not here to bait me. We are just trying to get the facts. But for two weeks, and there were some notable exceptions we don't need to go into—for two weeks the overwhelming majority of the nation's press and television after Cambodia carried three things: One, the Chinese might intervene; second, American casualties would soar, the war would be expanded and; third, there was a danger that the American withdrawal would therefore be jeopardized. None of these things happened. . . . Now what does this prove? It doesn't prove that the press was trying to deliberately make America look bad. That wasn't the point. But, naturally, they were seeing it from one vantage point. I had to see it from another."

A disinterested examination of the press coverage in Cambodia would result in a different analysis than that of the president's advisors. The question of Chinese intervention was very low on the list of implications that the press drew from the Cambodian intervention.

In that same interview, by the way, President Nixon told Smith that he had less support in the press than any other president. When pressed to compare with Truman and Johnson, he showed his concern with style and his insistence that he never complained about poor treatment.

"Yes, as a matter of fact," the president said, "I think President Johnson did get a bad rap from the press and for the wrong reasons. His style, for example. Now, when you take a man on because of his accent and because he happens to be from Texas or something like that, that is the wrong reason. If you take a man on on his policy, that is something else again.

"Understand, I am not complaining about my treatment from the press. I think it is a philosophical difference. I have many friends in the press, personal friends, as you are quite aware.

"I have never taken on a member of the press individually. I have never called a publisher since I have been president. I have never called an editor to complain about anything. I have never called a television station to complain about anything, and I never shall, as long as I have the opportunity to talk to the American people on a program like this directly. Then if I fail to communicate, it is my fault.

Robert U. Brown, writing in *Editor and Publisher* in the June 5, 1971 issue, observed that the president had been "patronizing" in his news conferences. Brown made references to "our listening audience" and "as I've often pointed out to the press corps" as if reporters should know better; it was "like a school teacher lecturing children for asking impertinent questions." Mr. Nixon said he was not going to use press conferences to comment on political matters. Asked Brown, "Why blame reporters for having political questions in their minds? Isn't that what they are supposed to have?"

Earlier in the year, Mr. Nixon spoke at a White House Correspondents Association dinner and there used a different tone. He invited reporters to ask tough questions—"I guess Winston Churchill put it best when he said, several years ago, that he had always found he benefited from criticism, and he never found that he did not have enough of it. I am in somewhat of that position. . . . Don't give me a friendly question. Only a hard, tough question gets the kind of an answer—you may not like it—but it is the one that tests the man. And that is the responsibility of members of the press to test the man, whoever he is. . . . I can only say I benefit from it. I benefit from your probing, from your criticism, and, if I succeed, and that means if the country succeeds in these great goals, then it will be due . . . in great part to the fact that the members of the press examined searchingly everything I suggested, every recommendation that I made, and made it necessary for me to come up to the mark and do just a little bit better than I would have done if somebody there hadn't been pressing."

He concluded, "So thanks for giving me that heat. And remember, I like the kitchen. Keep it up." The reference was to Truman's famous "If you can't take the heat, get out of the kitchen."

No member of his audience could argue with those sentiments. Many, however, wondered if the glowing rhetoric meant anything in an administration that engaged in greater frontal assaults on the press than any other in the twentieth century.

The chosen instrument was the vice-president. The chosen moment to kick off the campaign was 7:00 P.M. EST, November 13, 1969.

Vice-president Spiro Agnew, still bitter about the press treatment of the 1968 campaign which he felt was meant to make him look like a clown, rose before a Republican meeting in Des Moines and launched a thirty-minute attack on the networks followed, seven days later, with an attack on the *New York Times,* the *Washington Post,* and *Newsweek.* In time, many others would be added to the list.

The president had addressed the nation about Vietnam on November 3. This was followed with the usual analysis by network commentators. The White House staff was convinced that they had unfairly chopped up the president; "There was fairly widespread dismay and unhappiness around here." Pat Buchanan supplied much of the raw material for a counterattack, some say he wrote the speech though he accepts credit only for "some thoughts and ideas." Agnew was assigned to make the speech.

According to the *National Journal,* H. R. Haldeman, the president's closest assistant, coordinated the decision-making group that worked on the rebuttal. The president knew about it but made no contribution other than to permit the counterattack. James Keogh's White House speech-writing team participated along with Buchanan. The final draft was first checked by Agnew's speech writer, Cynthia Rosenthal, and then polished by the vice-president himself, who is said to have toughened several sections.

An appropriate forum was needed. A Midwest Republican Conference was starting in Des Moines and two days before the speech, the vice-president's office called the chairman of the conference, McDill Boyd—a Republican National Committeeman from Kansas—and suggested that Agnew speak on Thursday night, November 13. "I said 'great'," Boyd later explained, "and we set about fitting him in."

On the morning of the thirteenth, network bureau chiefs were sent copies of the speech, alerted by phone that it was coming and it was important. The calls came from Agnew's press secretary, Herb Thompson. Hurriedly the texts were passed on to New York and one by one, the networks decided to preempt the 7 P.M. feeds of network news to carry the vice-president live. An audience of four hundred loyal and enthusiastic Republicans interrupted him with applause seventeen times as he tore into the nation's television networks.

Agnew said the network commentators "and self-appointed analysts" came on the air having "inherited" the president's huge audience and expressed their hostility to what he had to say. He accused them of being prepared to attack, lying in wait for the president. One twice contradicted the president on his exchange of letters with Ho Chi Minh. Marvin Kalb of CBS, noting Mr. Nixon's claim that the letter was intransigent, said it contained "some of the softest, most accommodating language" yet. Agnew said another challenged the president's ability as a politician. Bill Lawrence of ABC said that the president was obviously appealing to the silent majority but "there was nothing new in it politically."

Agnew said another asserted that Nixon was "following the Pentagon line." Bill Downs of ABC suggested that Defense Secretary Melvin Laird comes out pretty well among those "shaping the president's thoughts."

Agnew accused correspondents of sarcasm and a tone of sharp disapproval. He was particularly bitter at ABC for interviewing Averell Harriman whom Agnew compared with Coleridge's Ancient Mariner. He said Harriman was under "compulsion to justify his failures" as Johnson's chief negotiator with the Vietnamese in Paris. It is interesting that ABC, which thought it a coup to get Harriman, assigned Diplomatic Correspondent John Scali to do the interview. In 1971, Scali went to work in the White House as an advisor on relations with the press in matters of foreign policy.

Agnew said the people had a right to digest the president's thoughts before the "prejudices of hostile critics" descended on them. He said Churchill didn't have "a gaggle of commentators" raising doubts about his actions, a contention that would surprise Churchillian students, and that Kennedy rallied the nation in the Cuban Missile Crisis without a round table of critics chewing over his words.

Agnew charged that a "small group of men" determine all network news and decide what forty to fifty million Americans learn of the day's events. He charged that they elevated Stokely Carmichael, the black militant, and American Nazi George Lincoln Rockwell "from obscurity to national prominence." He spoke of a raised eyebrow, an inflection of voice, and a caustic remark raising doubts in the minds of millions about the veracity of public officials or the wisdom of public policy.

Agnew said Americans know little about these few men who run TV news, men who work in the geographic confines of New York and Washington, yet they have "a concentration of power over American public opinion unknown in history." Agnew insisted that he was not asking for censorship but accused the men of "this fraternity" who "do *not* represent the views of America" of engaging in a form of censorship themselves.

Agnew decried the fact that "bad news drives out good news. The irrational is more controversial than the rational. Concurrence can no longer compete with dissent. One minute of Eldridge Cleaver is worth ten minutes of Roy Wilkins. . . . Normality has become the nemesis of the evening news."

"How many marches and demonstrations," he asked, "would we have if the marchers did not know that the ever-faithful TV cameras would be there to record their antics for the next news show?"

He closed by saying, "We would never trust such power over public opinion in the hands of an elected government—it is time we questioned it in the hands of a small and unelected élite. The great networks have dominated America's airwaves for decades; the people are entitled to a full accounting of their stewardship."

Applause. End of speech.

And beginning of a raging controversy between the Nixon administration and the news media.

It should be noted that, in a controversy sparked by the networks' use of analysis after major addresses, when Agnew finished there was no analysis on two networks and CBS simply read statements issued by network executives. The statements, however, were strong. Dr. Frank Stanton, president of CBS, called it an "unprecedented attempt by the vice-president of the United States to intimidate a news medium which depends for its existence upon government licenses." Julian Goodman, president of NBC called it "an appeal to prejudice" and added of Agnew: "Evidently, he would prefer a different kind of television reporting—one that would be subservient to whatever political group was in authority at the time." Leonard Goldenson, the ABC president, said his network would continue to rely on the American people—"In the final analysis it is always the public who decides on the reliability of any individual or organization."

Network people, however, were privately appalled at the support for Agnew's contentions and the outpouring of public sentiment. CBS quickly reported 16,000 calls to its stations in seven cities, 9,000 of them pro-Agnew. NBC reported a similar outpouring and ABC reported over 6,000 calls and almost two-thirds of them in favor of Agnew. Before it was over, between them the three networks counted 150,000 phone calls, letters, and telegrams and the tally was two to one in Agnew's favor. Agnew's own office received almost 74,000 letters, less than 3,800 of them unfavorable.

In the mail to the networks: about 2,500 pieces of "hate mail," one-fourth of it accused the networks of Communist affiliation or sympathy and large numbers were anti-Semitic, anti-Negro, or a combination of all of them. About 15 percent included threats ranging from reporting networks to the FCC to bombing the networks.

ABC later conducted a poll which indicated that 51 percent of the 559 adults polled agreed with Agnew about bias in network news. On the other hand, 60 percent felt the networks had not been unfair to the administration and should not ease up; another 67 percent wanted network commentators to continue analysis and comment immediately after a presidential speech.

Variety chided the networks for turning themselves over to the vice-president "for a severe rap at themselves." After Agnew ended, said *Variety's* Les Brown, "The networks' own horror show has left them shaking with fear."

Newsweek published a signed piece by its managing editor Lester Bernstein who said Agnew's "tactic is calculated to sow caution and second thoughts among men who keep a nervous eye on those broadcasting licenses even as they invoke the First Amendment. NBC and CBS have shown courage in meeting the issue publicly, but in small ways the tactic is already working."

Sigma Delta Chi, the journalism society, was in convention in San Diego, California, and passed a resolution just two days after

Agnew's speech calling it a threat to a free press. The resolution rejected moves "by the vice-president or others to control or impede the flow of legitimate comment and analysis of the news."

Agnew was not without supporters. Senator Hugh Scott, the Republican leader in the Senate, said, "I think the vice-president made a very good statement." He referred to television as "that crazy red-eyed monster" and said, "The pious denials of the three networks ring a little false to me. . . . I think the networks need a thorough goosing." Barry Goldwater said he believed that Agnew did not go far enough and the networks had better "start policing themselves."

Dean Burch, chairman of the FCC, said "The vice-president as a citizen, as a public office holder, has every right to let his views be known on how the networks handle anything. . . . Physician, heal thyself." On the other hand, when a lady in Houston wrote the FCC to complain about the networks in light of Agnew's charges, Burch signed the unanimous reply from the commission that it is not the role of the FCC to investigate whether news analysis is biased or true—"No government agency can authenticate the news, or should try to do so. Such an attempt would cast the chill of omnipresent government censorship over the newsmen's independence in news judgement." The FCC sees that different sides of public arguments are aired but can not be "the arbiter of the 'truth' of a news event."

A few days after Agnew's Des Moines speech, CBS' White House Correspondent Dan Rather revealed that members of the president's staff had been calling television stations to check on editorial comment following presidential addresses. The White House said this was a matter of routine—"There is no government plan to intimidate TV news whatsoever." But critics wondered, in the wake of Agnew.

Rather also uncovered the fact that the wife of a member of the Subversive Activities Control Board was calling Miami television stations asking about their coverage plans for pro-Nixon rallies in that city. Her husband said he made similar calls to Washington, D.C. stations—as an individual not as a member of the board. Did it relate to the Agnew matter?

An FCC staff member, Leonard Weinless, called a Phoenix, Arizona, station and asked for the tape of an interview with Eric

Sevareid on the Agnew question. He said he did it on his own, for his own information.

The FCC Chairman, Dean Burch, called the networks for transcripts of those post-Nixon comments by correspondents. Was this meant to intimidate? Nonsense, said Burch, just a quick way to get transcripts and it was "a bunch of hooey" if broadcasters read anything ominous into that.

The *Washington Post* commented on all this editorially and suggested that maybe the broadcasters were a little foolish in their reaction. "After all, what could the chairman of the FCC possibly do to them, except maybe take away their broadcast licenses?"

Herb Klein, the president's director of communication, appeared on "Face the Nation" and said, "If you look at the problems you have today and you fail to continue to examine them, you do invite the government to come in. I would not like to see that happen."

Then, on November 20, 1969, in Montgomery, Alabama, Spiro Agnew let the other shoe drop. He gave a speech before the Montgomery Chamber of Commerce and noted that he had been severely criticized for his remarks of one week earlier. He said, "I am opposed to censorship of television or the press in any form" including censorship "by a little fraternity having similar social and political views."

He then went on to attack the *Washington Post* and the *New York Times,* the former for its ownership of radio and television stations in Washington as well as *Newsweek* magazine, the *Times* for its failure to carry the story of three hundred Congressmen and fifty-nine Senators signing a letter to support the Nixon Vietnam policy. He said, "The day when the network commentators and even gentlemen of the *New York Times* enjoyed a form of diplomatic immunity from comment and criticism of what they said—that day is over."

As for intimidation, Agnew had his own view of that. At a cocktail party before the speech, speaking under a big banner reading Welcome Spiro T. (Tell It Like It Is) Agnew", he said, "If this country is going to remain great, it is important that people in high positions not be intimidated by the news media."

The two targets of the new blast replied. Both said Agnew was wrong. The *Times* said the story in question was carried, though not in the early edition that Washingtonians receive, and the general topic was treated prominently several times. The *Post* said its newspaper, magazine, and broadcast properties do not "grind out the same editorial line" and cited examples of vigorous competition between them, of editorial disagreement. As for monopoly, it pointed out that Washington is one of the few and one of the most competitive cities in news, one of only three with three newspapers under separate ownership, and was a city with seven television and thirty-five radio stations.

A few days later, one of the major figures in broadcasting struck back strongly at the Vice President. CBS President Frank Stanton came before the International Radio and Television Society answering the issues Agnew raised, one by one. Example: the analysis after Nixon's address was hardly "instant" since informed speculation had gone on for weeks, copies of his text were available two hours in advance, and so "if a professional reporter could not arrive at some meaningful observations under those circumstances, we would question his competence." Example: rather than the monopoly of a small fraternity, 65 percent of news on the air was locally produced rather than by networks.

Stanton said, "Everyone has free access to what we do, and everyone sees us do it. We are not unaccountable. We are not clandestine. We have no end product that is not seen and judged by everyone. But such open criticism is a far cry from sharp reminders from high official quarters that we are licensed or that if we don't examine ourselves, we in common with other media 'invite' the government to move in."

Why did Agnew do it? Why did he carry out his assignment with such obvious relish? Reporters who followed Agnew, a proud man, discovered a great deal of rancor towards press coverage in the 1968 campaign. He was furious about newspaper attention to verbal gaffes. They seemed to seize on it when he referred to "Polacks" or when he kidded a friendly reporter of Japanese descent as the "Fat Jap." He once jeered that *Time* and *Newsweek* belonged "at the bottom of birdcages."

"If anyone is intimidated," he told one reporter, "it should be me. I don't have the resources the networks have."

The White House insisted all along that Agnew acted on his own. One spokesman claimed that the Des Moines speech was not sent to the White House before it was released—a contention difficult to accept. It is not likely that Agnew's office, early that morning, would distribute the speech to all the networks, the wire services, and major newspapers and not send one across the road to the White House.

President Nixon was asked about Agnew at a December 9 news conference:

Q. Mr. President, Vice President Agnew in recent weeks has made two speeches in which he has criticized the news media— broadcasting in particular.

A. Yes, I know.

Q. What, if anything, in those speeches is there with which you disagree?

A. Before this audience? The vice-president does not clear his speeches with me, just as I did not clear my speeches with President Eisenhower. However, I believe that the vice-president rendered a public service in talking in a very dignified and courageous way about a problem that many Americans are concerned about, and that is the coverage by news media—and particularly television news media—of public figures.

Now let me be quite precise. He did not advocate censorship. On the contrary, he advocated that there should be free expression. He did not oppose bias. On the contrary, he recognized— as I do—that there should be opinion.

Let me say on that score that I don't want a bunch of intellectual eunuchs either writing the news or talking about the news. I like excitement in the news, whether it's on television or whether it's in the columns.

He did say, and perhaps this point should be well taken, that television stations might well follow the practice of newspapers of separating news from opinion. When opinion is expressed, label it so, but don't mix the opinion in with the reporting of the news.

It seems to me these were useful suggestions. Perhaps the networks disagreed with the criticisms, but I would suggest that they should be just as dignified and just as reasonable in answering the criticisms as he was in making them.

In that same news conference, Nixon indicated that he was not opposed to network analysis after his appearances and that he did not consider the media unfair:

> Q. How fair do you think the news media has been in reporting on you, and on Vice-President Agnew, and on your administration in general?
>
> A. Generally, I think the news media's been fair. I have no complaints about the—certainly the extent of the coverage that I have received. And I also will have no complaints just so long as the news media allows—as it does tonight—an opportunity for me to be heard directly by the people, and then the television commentators to follow me. I'll take my chances.

Despite the president's disclaimer and official White House statements stressing that Agnew speaks on his own, few believed that. Friendly columnists as well as critics were sure that Agnew was unleashed by the president. Crosby S. Noyes, in the *Washington Star,* wrote "there is no question that he speaks with the full backing and assent of the White House." Columnist Richard Wilson, who had particularly good lines to White House thinking, wrote: "This has been a bold and calculated move which can only be seen in its true perspective as a part of President Nixon's attempt to hold public opinion to his measured course of liquidating the Vietnam war at his own pace and then proceeding with broad governmental domestic reforms and his own re-election in 1972. The move is bold and calculated beyond anything previously dared by a president."

Confirmation came from Clark Mollenhoff, a veteran news reporter who was then on the White House staff. Mollenhoff said, "The speech was developed in the White House" and it "represented White House concern" about "getting through to the public." Others recalled a late 1968 background session with Herb Klein, then handling press in the campaign, when he confided that the vice-presidential candidate was assigned "the hard line" and would "do a lot of attacking."

Three years later, in the debate over whether Nixon would retain Agnew as his '72 running mate, columnist William F. Buckley discussed the "heterodox" attacks of the vice-president. Buckley, very close philosophically, professionally, and socially to the White House wrote: "Spiro Agnew spoke sentiments which cannot reasonably be suspected as being his own exclusively. That is to say, it is unrealistic to suppose that he spoke thoughts which lay athwart presidential conclusions. A president needs to choose his rhetoric rather more carefully than other people. The role of the vice-president, on certain occasions, is to give robust expression to a president's point of view."

Efforts were made to see if Agnew really meant it all. Officers of the Radio Television News Directors Association met privately with the vice-president in late December. They met for seventy-five minutes. The news directors, representing local stations primarily, complained of increasing pressures on them as a result of Agnew's speech and the vice-president launched into a long monologue repeating his Des Moines' charges. Agnew then cited abuses during the '68 campaign, the editing of film to make him look like a fool. That, he said, is exactly how history would have portrayed him if they had lost the election. Winning, he went on, gave him the opportunity to put the record straight.

Earlier, Herb Klein, who was present, had indicated that the vice-president might be encouraged to issue a statement that the administration was not trying to stifle controversy on television. At the meeting's end, this was suggested. Agnew said he would do it only after the networks indicated a positive response to his criticisms. The frustrated news directors left.

Three months later, the vice-president was invited to an off-the-record session of the Radio Television News Analysts Association in New York. Again he chided the media for their coverage of the '68 campaign—"No one paid any attention to the ideas I was trying to talk about. They kept reporting little slips of the tongue." Was his antipress campaign political? "I knew this was something the American people would be concerned about, and after all, gentlemen, I am a political animal."

Agnew had suggested to the RTNDA officers that an example of a positive response to his criticism would be to put Secretary Laird on as well as Harriman. He now asked the analysts— "Where was (Secretary of State) Bill Rogers?" One network reporter told him that the White House told the networks on the afternoon of the president's November 3rd. speech that neither

Laird nor Rogers was available to appear on their post-Nixon broadcasts.

At one point the vice-president made reference to Walter Cronkite's "well known patriotism." Cronkite responded that neither he nor anyone else in the room believed that news can be reported on the basis of patriotism. Applause followed.

The meeting ended with the newsmen as puzzled as their RTNDA brothers, calling it an "unbelievable" performance. At the same time, they were convinced that Agnew left more convinced than ever that they were an inbred group of Eastern liberals.

Agnew did find one supporter in the media. Howard K. Smith of ABC News told *TV Guide* in February of 1970 that "I agree with some of what Mr. Agnew said. In fact, I said some of it before he did." While expressing reservations on Mr. Agnew's "tone of intimidation" and "a sense that we do things deliberately. I don't think we do them deliberately."

"Many of my colleagues have the depth of a saucer," said Smith. "They cling to the tag 'liberal' that grew popular in the time of Franklin Roosevelt, even though they've forgotten its content. . . . Quite literally, what Mr. Agnew suggests is all right. . . . The networks have ignored this situation, despite years of protest, because they have power. And you know what Lord Acton says about power. It subtly corrupts."

Many of Mr. Smith's colleagues were displeased. One veteran ABC correspondent recalled Smith's role as moderator when Alger Hiss appeared in the 1962 "Political Obituary of Richard Nixon." The correspondent said he didn't relish criticism from someone "who would use a convicted perjurer as a character witness."

A different view from Smith's was voiced by James Reston of the *New York Times* on the day after Agnew's second speech— "Watchful commentators from the beginning of the Republic have tended to be critical of the party in power, and the greater the power in the presidency, particularly the power to make war, the greater the skepticism and the harder the criticism. How odd of a Republican vice-president to miss that point. It has of course often been abused, but it is at the very heart of the First Amendment. Mr. Agnew is right that we tend to play up the unusual and the contentious, which, incidentally, is why he is being played up now."

On June 30, 1970, the annual FCC report on complaints received showed that Agnew had fattened its mail bag as well. In fiscal 1969 it received just over 2,300 complaints about news coverage. In fiscal 1970, after Agnew, it received 5,139 complaints of news distortion or suppressed news.

As for Agnew, Republican fund raisers had no complaint. He was the most sought after speaker in America, short of the president, for political banquets. The faithful loved to hear him give the news media hell.

His rhetoric did not cool. In February, he told an Atlanta audience that this was his answer to the "liberal news media's" request that he lower his voice—a tough speech citing the "need for a strong voice to penetrate the cacophony of seditious drivel emanating from the best-publicized clowns of our society and from their fans in the fourth estate."

In March, he told a $100 a plate fund-raising dinner in the Virgin Islands that "Pulitzer Prizes are not won by exposing the evils of communism as readily as discrediting American elected officials. Tons and tons of innuendo designed to smear officials are printed every day."

In May, he told a Texas Republican fund-raiser in Houston that the First Amendment "happens to be *my* amendment too. It guarantees *my* free speech as much as it does their freedom of the press." In that speech he criticized the *Washington Post,* the *New York Times,* Anthony Lewis, Tom Wicker, James Reston, the *New Republic, I. F. Stone's Bi-Weekly,* the *Atlanta Constitution,* the *Arkansas Gazette, Life* magazine, Hugh Sidey, Carl Rowan, the *New York Post,* Pete Hamill, Harriet Van Horne—all for their "wild, hot rhetoric" and "irresponsibility and thoughtlessness." Quite a quiver of arrows for one speech.

In Birmingham, during the political campaign that fall, he ripped into the "supersensitive, self-annointed, supercilious electronic barons of opinion." He promised "to keep on denouncing and discouraging the indulgence of social anarchy and economic crisis that flourished during the permissive sixties."

That same October on the campaign trail, Richard Nixon—in a little publicized remark at a rally at the Teterboro Airport in

New Jersey—joined Agnew's attack on television's coverage of protesters:

"I turn now to a problem that concerns many Americans. We see here a number of television cameras. We appreciate their covering this rally. On the television tonight I will predict that what you are likely to see is not this great crowd. You are likely to see a few demonstrators here, or in Vermont where there were a few hundred, and thousands who did not demonstrate. I do not say that critically of television because, you see, that small minority with their obscene language, throwing their rocks, engaging in violence, they come across the television and many, I think, it seems to me, without justification, have gotten the impression that that small minority is the majority of Americans."

When the 1970 campaign ended, there were those who thought Agnew would let up in his attacks. They were wrong. He was scheduled on November 20 to speak to the AP managing editors convention in Honolulu and offered words of praise for the press and seemed to be in a conciliatory mood:

"I have not the least doubt that the United States has the most self-demanding, least self-satisfied, most ingenious, least inhibited, best-informed, least-controlled, most-professional, least-subjective, most-competitive, least-party-line, fairest, and finest journalistic complex in the entire world.

"I have found newscasters and reporters, in large majority, as fair and as objective as they are emotionally and psychologically able to be, and I have found the great preponderance of them very conscientious in their calling.

"I have found most news accounts of my deeds and words adequate and factual; indeed, time and again I have found surprisingly complementary coverage of my viewpoints by journalists who I happen to know do not suffer from ardor for Agnew."

These comments made the newswires and were carried back to Washington. Ron Ziegler, Nixon's press secretary, called the author of this volume, bureau chief of CBS, and suggested that I read the speech. I did and found that Agnew also said, "To the extent that censorship in any form exists in America, it rests solely with the media people, whether broadcast or print. . . . I strongly believe you need to take a good, hard, dispassionate look from time to time at how your great power is being exercised." He

asked newsmen to stop being so hypersensitive. He asked for more
balanced treatment of controversy and again asked that factual
news be segregated from opinion.

After reading the speech, this bureau chief wrote Ziegler—
"Dear Ron: Per your suggestion. I received a copy of Vice-President Agnew's Honolulu speech thanks to Vic Gold. I have read
it. You must be kidding."

An interesting footnote to this appeared in Allen Drury's
"Courage and Hesitation" when he quotes an Agnew aide as saying of the Honolulu speech, "He had about a page and a half in
which he specifically named people like the *New York Times, Newsweek, Time, Look,* and *Life,* NBC, ABC, and CBS as those he
meant when he talked about the Eastern press establishment. This
caused great excitement in the White House staff. They were
horrified that he would name these people.

"His point of view was that he wanted to say specifically whom
he was criticizing, and not make it just the press in general. However, there was great upset about this in the staff, and they took it
to Nixon. He overruled Agnew and asked him to take it out of the
speech, which he did."

The vice-president professed disappointment in media reaction
to his attacks. He told one reporter, "It would have been a useful
dialogue if they had accepted the criticism constructively instead
of going off on this implied-threat-of-censorship tack, which is
basically defensive and shows their inability to cope with criticism
on its merits."

Political observers wondered at the boldness of the administration in taking on the press. They offered several explanations. One,
public dissatisfaction with the unending flow of bad news had developed public antagonism to the news media. Agnew was telling
them that if the newsmen didn't report this distressing news, it
would go away. Secondly, the attacks would increase support from
the faithful. Republican conservatives, long paranoid about the
press, welcomed Agnew's taking them on and exposing them.
Third, the Agnew strictures would get the GOP a better press in
1972. The media would be more careful about its criticism, more
reluctant to criticize, and above all else, their audience will be less
likely to accept media opinions and reports uncritically.

Agnew was not the only critic used by the administration to rebut the press, he was simply the most effective. He once was asked at an off the record meeting of reporters, why he didn't leave such attacks to others, and replied, "I am the vice-president and you have to cover me."

Among others attacking the media, the second most outspoken administration figure was Robert Dole, the Kansas senator and Republican national chairman. Agnew once kidded him at a Gridiron dinner with, "Who do you think you are? Me?" Many in the audience of newsmen felt that Dole thought just that.

Network correspondents and newspapermen who offend Dole's idea of proper coverage could expect a quick attack, usually in a formal statement from Republican headquarters and sometimes in the *Congressional Record* as well. In public remarks, Mr. Dole tried to outdo Mr. Agnew. He referred to the "doom merchants" of the mass media and charged that the president could not get his message "through a political barrier of negativism and defeatism" and "the news media have proven that they won't do it for us and the best product in the world can't sell itself sight unseen."

After Agnew's initial attacks on the press, Dole likened them to speeches by Adlai Stevenson against a one-party press, "Neither suggested federal intervention, censorship or intimidation of any kind." At the very least, the comparison was enough to make Stevensonian Democrats shudder.

In Denver, Dole once charged that "all you have to do to get on network television is to criticize President Nixon." In the same appearance, he suggested that "Walter Cronkite can't even pronounce Republican."

In mid-1971, Chairman Dole found speaking room on two sides of the Pentagon Papers controversy. He said the *New York Times* disclosures prove that two Democratic presidents and "numerous of their cohorts in the White House" conspired to get us into a large war in Asia. Having made his points against the Democrats, Dole then turned on the newspaper for "irresponsible journalism." Said Dole, "No longer can heads of state be sure that their private talks, so essential in intercourse between nations, will remain private. They are at the mercy of every disgruntled person with access to files, they are at the mercy, literally, of common thieves and men who violate their trust, and they are at the mercy of sensation-seeking newspapers that, for whatever reason—commercial or political—disregard the interests of the American people in the interests of something they call "the right to know."

In one of Pat Buchanan's *Briefing Books* for the president, according to syndicated columnist Jack Anderson, there is this reference: "Media criticism by VP Agnew and Dole is being well covered with Veep apparently causing CBS to at least temporarily hold its fire."

In the long history of unhappiness with the press, no administration ever attacked the media as boldly as that of Richard Nixon. *Time* magazine called it the politics of polarization. Its full effect is yet to be measured.

While this lengthy discourse on American presidents and how they dealt with the press reveals a multitude of methods and a plethora of presidential pressures on the press, it by no means exhausts the ways in which politicians try to manage the news. Political pressure and persuasion, manipulation and intimidation come in many forms. We examine them in the next chapter, a look at how the politician does it to the press.

V

FOR POLITICIANS

How to Do It

For any politician who wants to deal with the press effectively, there are lessons to be learned from examination of George Washington and Thomas Jefferson and Grover Cleveland and the two Roosevelts and Eisenhower, Kennedy, Johnson and Nixon, and others. They gave us the techniques of managing the news. Some techniques are simple, some sophisticated.

In the beginning, there is the news release. The official statement, the news release, may be an announcement of action, an explanation of policy, or a rebuttal to someone else's position. It is, in the skeptical eyes of the reporter, a "handout." For the politician, it is a device which gives its author the beginning advantage. Even the most skeptical reporter must begin with the news release. There is no guarantee that he will not seek other views, but when he does, the base of his exercise still is that news release.

The news briefing is similar. The politician or his spokesman fills in reporters on an issue, or at least one view of it. There is a risk that the questioning may stray from the politician's desired direction, that cross-examination may do injury to his objective, but most of the time reporters simply want to dig deeper into that man's thinking. They may later seek counterpoint, but once again this politician has the advantage of having the reporter's ear first. Good reporters will seek other views but the burden of such a search is now their's while the attention to the original was the result of a useful political technique, the news briefing.

Since timing can be important, politicians have developed impressive tools including that favorite artifice, the news embargo. When obliging reporters agree to the politician's "hold-for-release" they follow a custom of many years, one rationalized by the explanation that the embargo permits time to study and digest the contents of a release. Actually it is the politician's method of controlling the timing of the news, either to get it out at the right moment to counteract an opponent or an event or else to get it fuller exposure by catering to Sunday editions or news-hungry Monday newspapers. The modern twist to release time now holds that if it is for a morning newspaper, the actual time for release is the previous evening to accommodate the major television news broadcasts. If it is for afternoon newspapers, it is released in time for morning radio broadcasts.

Obfuscation is another political technique. When used from positions of power, as in a presidential press office, it can snow a reporter under with more than he wants to know about an event. It can give the appearance of extreme presidential activity by unleashing a flood of different announcements. The latter technique, brought to a high polish for Ike by Hagerty, has been used by every president since Eisenhower.

The skilled image makers from Hagerty through Salinger, Reedy, Moyers, George Christian, Ziegler, and Klein have shown how to use the powers of the presidency in trying to overpower the press. Their techniques have become quite slick and are improved all the time, embracing the latest in technology to help "sell" their man. Students of Hagerty, Salinger, *et al* quickly pick up the techniques to sell their own bosses in the Congress, the Statehouse, and City Hall.

But Kennedy was branded with "news management," Johnson with the "credibility gap," and Nixon with "Agnewism." Where did they go wrong?

Fortunately, the techniques of media manipulation only offer, they do not guarantee, success. Some of the best-laid plans of press secretaries float out untouched by reporters or, worse yet, stray off their planned course and result in the "wrong" kind of publicity. There are other forces bearing on the press.

Reporters, particularly in Washington, are sometimes victims of journalistic trends, of news fads. The image makers occasionally create these, more often try to piggyback on them, and sometimes are thoroughly frustrated with fads in news. What causes one political figure to be covered extensively by newsmen and another to be ignored? Senator Eugene McCarthy used to say that reporters are like blackbirds on a telephone line—they sit together in a row and suddenly when one flies off, the others all follow. Then one returns to the telephone line and they all come back, sitting in a row.

News fads may propel individual personalities into the spotlight. They also deal with ideas, innovation, and change. In this, there is the importance of the radical press, of left and right, the small-circulation newsletters and magazines. They hear their own drums to march by and are less likely to succumb to the current news fad than their brothers of large circulation. Thus it is that sometimes the first stirring of new ideas is found off the main thrust of the truly mass media. In time these innovations infiltrate the mass media, find a place on the telephone line.

The genesis of news fad is the preoccupation of journalists with what other journalists are saying, a form of intellectual masturbation. Each says a variant of what he wants to emulate in another's reporting. Often the other returns to the theme having read his imitator.

Those who would manipulate the press use their techniques to start fads or to ride along with them. One advantage they have, if they represent men in positions of power, is the reliance of the press on the official source. This is understandable. If it is foreign policy, reporters want the views of the president, his secretary of state, or a congressional chairman. One doesn't seek the views of a barber, a grocer, a proctologist. Unfortunately, the views of the established order are not always enough.

In a critique of the American press, Tom Wicker of the *New York Times* told a Columbia University audience that the press suffers from its orientation toward establishmentarianism. Said Wicker, "If I had been in Mr. Agnew's place and been trying to make an intelligent, useful criticism of the American press, I think I would have said that its biggest weakness is its reliance on and its acceptance of official sources—indeed, its "objectivity" in presenting the news. That is, that the fundamental reliance of the American news media in my experience has been, with rare and honorable exceptions, on the statement by the official source, be it government or business or academic or whatever. And much of what we mean by objectivity in American journalism concerns whether due credit is given to the official statement, the official explanation, the background explanation from the official source."

Allowing for the honorable exception, allowing for the hard-digging reporter who seeks to expand his understanding of an issue, the advantage still remains with the official source. He is the beginning. He starts the chain with his statement or explanation or news release. On many occasions, it is more than an advantage, it is everything—it monopolizes news attention. Even when the reporter, the honorable exception, refuses to accept gospel, the burden of counterpoint to official sources becomes his; he must disprove the political contention.

The official source is one of a small breed, a member of either the establishment-in-power or the establishment-in-temporary-exile, the political ins and outs, the official source major and the official source minor. Occasionally an outsider will crack the walls of these two groups. Ralph Nader did it with his attack on unsafe automobiles. An outsider with no special credentials, he managed to become the guiding force in new safety standards. He also became, as a result of the publicity, a "quasi-official" person and thus a fully "official source." Reporters could now seek Nader's views as well as others in the establishment, current or potential. He became an establishment himself.

The problem for the reporter is finding such sources outside existing establishments to see if either the official source or his political critic are to be trusted. While it is true that there is no error so monstrous that it fails to find defenders among the ablest men, it is equally true that there is no error so cleverly concealed that it hasn't a critic.

The other thing about official sources, about men in high places, is that they are overwhelmingly attractive to news people. Journalists are drawn to the merchants of power; they are fascinated by men holding important office. Lord Acton, in his letter to Bishop Mandell Creighton in 1887, warned that "power tends to corrupt and absolute power corrupts absolutely." Being close to power can corrupt as well. There is danger in the geography of journalism. There is danger when correspondents find the powerful seeking their friendship and asking their views.

Walter Lippmann warned, "Cronyism is the curse of journalism." There is subtle pressure when the source says, *"You* are a responsible reporter so I can tell *you."* There is social pressure when the source caters to the reporter, flattering him with attention at lunches and dinners. There is the enormous pressure on a reporter who fears to offend his source and thus lose the contact.

Arthur Krock, on his retirement in 1967, warned about getting too close to presidents—"The objectivity of news reporting in the capital depends upon the conscience of the king and the susceptibility of the press corps." Lippmann noted that "the powerful are perhaps the chief source of the news but they are also the dispensers of many kinds of favor, privilege, honor and self-esteem. . . . The temptations are many; some are simple, some are refined, and often they are yielded to without the consciousness of yielding. Only a constant awareness of them offers protection." He warned against "social climbing on the pyramids of power."

In Washington particularly, but in other political centers as well, certain reporters appear to have a direct line to the man in power. They are read carefully by other politicians and by other reporters to see what whims move the mighty on that day. Sometimes these writers accurately reflect the views of their political friend and sometimes they don't. It was Charles Bartlett among others who seemed to reflect John F. Kennedy, Max Freedman and William S. White who were close to Lyndon Johnson. It was said that White occasionally felt compelled to write with diminished vigor since many considered his views as emanating from the Oval Office of the president, his friend of almost forty years.

Favoritism can sometimes backfire on the politician. It is one thing for other journalists to accept philosophical views passed on to a favorite columnist but when real news appears, politicians are quickly damned by those not favored. George Reedy used to recall the old political rule that "every time a man does a favor, he makes nineteen enemies and one ingrate."

Politicians will risk that however. There are always favorites in the press, there is always the social courting of newsmen. More than one Washington bureau chief has urged his reporters to be neither in nor out, far enough from sources to retain objectivity but close enough to be effective. Distance is an excellent prophylactic for reporters dealing with politicians. Familiarity breeds contempt and inhibited reporting.

Intimacy, however, is only one way to fall prey to a publicity-seeking politician. Professional greed is another. If he knows how, the politician can use newsmen by offering stories too delicious to reject, too outrageous to ignore, and too difficult to question if the reporter is to remain his customarily objective self.

The master of this technique was a U.S. senator who dominated the front pages in the early 1950s. The master was Joseph R. McCarthy.

Several things were right for Joe McCarthy. The timing was right—it was the beginning of the Cold War period and there was much concern and almost paranoia about the "Communist menace." His position was right—he was the U.S. senator from Wisconsin and thus a highly placed, official source. And his technique was right—he knew how to play for headlines and how to bury criticism.

He was eager to provide news; he would "create" stories instantly and even nonstories about great exposes yet to come—a sort of journalistic version of "coming attractions." He was, in the words of his biographer Richard Rovere, "the most gifted demagogue ever bred on these shores. No bolder seditionist ever moved among us—not any politician with a surer, swifter access to the dark places of the American mind."

From the start, Joe McCarthy sought out the press. He told reporters, "Don't hesitate to call me, night or day." Just days after he first arrived in Washington in 1947, he spoke to the question of President Truman's trouble with coal miners and suggested that the president draft John L. Lewis and every one of his four hundred thousand members who refused to work. Once in the armed services, if they still refused to mine coal, they could be court-martialed. Military journals protested loudly—"The idea that the Army should be turned into a vast prison camp is ridiculous" but even the *New York Times* ran the story. Junior Senator McCarthy was most pleased. He was the new boy on the block and he was already stealing headlines from his Senate colleagues. He was to discover, near the end of this first term, that wild statements could propel him into greater publicity, would make him the best-known man in the Congress.

It started in Wheeling, West Virginia, on February 9, 1950. McCarthy was scheduled there to make the first of several week-end speeches. Weeks earlier, he had lunched with friends in Washington and told them how he desperately needed an issue on which to base his 1952 re-election campaign. His companions suggested several ideas which McCarthy rejected as things "no one gets excited about." Then Father Edmund Walsh, dean of the Foreign Service School at Georgetown, asked, "How about Communism as an issue?" McCarthy liked it instantly, stating flatly "The government is full of Communists, the thing to do is hammer at them."

In Wheeling, he did just that. Speaking to the Ohio County Women's Republican Club, he said, "I have here in my hand a list of two hundred and five (State Department employees) that were known to the secretary of state as being members of the Communist Party and who nevertheless are still working and shaping the policy of the State Department." That certainly shocked and titillated the Republican ladies of Wheeling. It was also reported briefly in the local papers, the *Chicago Tribune* and the AP. A few days later, it would reach the *New York Times*.

While immediate press attention to the Wheeling speech was slight (it was to snowball in the days that followed), the State Department didn't miss it. The department wired him at once for the names of the accused and promised a prompt investigation. McCarthy was traveling westward to give more speeches and the telegram caught up with him in Denver. Perhaps he panicked for the moment, possibly fearing legal action if he revealed names, and so he told Denver reporters he was misquoted—that he meant two hundred and five "bad security risks," he hadn't said Communists.

In Salt Lake City, before a public audience again, he came out with a new number and a new version of what he said in Wheeling: "Last night I discussed the Communists in the State Department. I stated I had the names of fifty-seven card-carrying members of the Communist Party." It was believed that McCarthy got the number fifty-seven from a 1948 State Department report to the House Appropriations Committee which said of one hundred and eight employees whose files the committee studied, fifty-one were no longer in the department. Of course, fifty-one from one hundred and eight led to the number fifty-seven.

Reporters in Salt Lake City asked to see the fifty-seven names. McCarthy said he would show the list only to Secretary of State Dean Acheson. A radio interviewer asked, "You mean to say there's fifty-seven Communists in our State Department that direct or control our State Department policy or help direct it?" McCarthy's reply, "I don't want to indicate there are only fifty-seven—I say I have the names of fifty-seven."

The State Department issued a strong statement denying McCarthy's charge. It said it knew of no Communists in the department and if it found any, it would fire them. McCarthy then dispatched a telegram to President Truman saying while the records were not available to him, he knew "absolutely" of approximately three hundred "certified to the secretary for discharge because of Communism. He actually only discharged about eighty."

The story was no longer back page. Newspapers all over the country were carrying the charges of Communists at State. McCarthy's numbers wobbled all over the place—two hundred and five in Wheeling, fifty-seven in Salt Lake, ten when he testified before a special Senate committee openly, one hundred sixteen to the same group in executive session, two hundred twenty in the telegram to Truman, one when he limited it—"I'll stand or fall"—on the case of Owen Lattimore, and eighty-one when he spoke for six strange hours on the Senate floor.

That Senate session was late in the day on February 20, 1950 as his colleagues tried to get clarification of McCarthy's charges. He rambled on for hours, dipping into the bulging brief case that was his source for instant accusations, and started to read eighty-one case studies without identification other than a number on each dossier (which turned out to be from those files supplied the House Appropriations Committee by the State Department). The files spilled across two Senate desks and made no sense except that McCarthy kept weaving an air of mystery around the virtually incoherent contents as he read on and on. Majority Leader Scott Lucas interrupted sixty-one times to try to get McCarthy to stick to one set of figures only to be dismissed by McCarthy—"Let's stop this silly numbers game."

Senator Brien McMahon was called in from a dinner (he appeared dressed in white tie) to buttress Lucas and made thirty-four attempts to test McCarthy but got nowhere. When Herbert Lehman of New York tried, McCarthy dismissed him with "If it is not clear to the senator now, I shall never be able to make it clear to him." Lucas tried again and McCarthy snapped, "I must say, if the senator is going to make a farce of this, I will not yield to him. I shall not answer any more silly questions of the senator. This is too important, too serious a matter for that." Lucas gave up and on his motion, the Senate adjourned at midnight. His fellow senators, as the press, could not pin McCarthy down.

When the special Senate committee headed by Maryland's Millard Tydings investigated his charges and concluded that they were "a fraud and a hoax," McCarthy accused the committee of being "soft on Communism." He later took part in a campaign against the chairman, subsidized by right wing organizations, and flowing with false charges, a campaign which defeated Tydings when he ran for re-election.

In time, Joe McCarthy would make one sensational charge after another: McCarthy calls Dean Acheson the "Red Dean of Fashion." McCarthy accuses George Marshall of treason. McCarthy demands lie detector tests for army officers. McCarthy demands that an armored train force its way through the Berlin blockade. McCarthy leads the fight to deny Anna Rosenberg confirmation as assistant secretary of defense. McCarthy calls Charles Bohlen, nominee as ambassador to Russia, a "security risk—and that's putting it mildly."

As Elmer Davis described the technique: "He has a remarkable gift for turning up with stories that would be important if true and a still more remarkable agility in evasive action; as fast as one of his phonies is exposed he hits the front page with another which won't be exposed till tomorrow; and how many people read the second-day story? The newspapers could not have ignored his early attacks on the State Department and the violent Senate debate they provoked; the Senators could not have ignored them either. It does seem that now that it has been amply demonstrated that nothing McCarthy says can be accepted as true without corroboration the newspapers might be more careful in the way they deal with his 'exposures.' One or two newspapers have worked out methods for handling the news about him that might keep the reader from being misled; but this practice has not spread widely, for it conflicts with the doctrine of the American news industry that if a senator says it, it is news, whether there is any truth in it or not."

Reporters covering the Senate knew how quickly McCarthy would produce a story. He was aware of deadlines, conscious of wire service needs for an "overnighter," confident that he could create stories that no newsman could turn down.

He once ran into two newspapermen in a Senate Office Building hallway and asked them if they were looking for a story. They asked if he had one. "Mmmm, now let's see," said McCarthy and after a while he said, "I'll give you something. You can say that I'm going to subpoena Harry Truman, that's what I'm going to do." They said he certainly couldn't be serious. McCarthy reached into his pocket, where he kept blank subpoenas, and started to fill one out right there naming the former president.

It was hard for newsmen to resist. Of course, Truman never testified but the story got to the front pages.

McCarthy knew how to smokescreen stories unfavorable to him. When a Senate subcommittee was asked to study him on Senator William Benton's resolution to expel McCarthy, the Wisconsin senator accused the subcommittee of "stealing the taxpayers' money" to investigate him. He called for an investigation of Benton by that very committee.

Walter Lippmann wrote, "McCarthy's charges of treason, espionage, corruption, perversion are news which cannot be suppressed or ignored. They come from a United States Senator. . . . When he makes such attacks against the State Department and the Defense Department, it is news which has to be published." Richard Rovere added, "It was also, of course, news that a United States Senator was lying and defrauding the people and their government. But—in large part because McCarthy was a true innovator, because he lied with an unprecedented boldness, because he invented new kinds of lies—even those newspapers that were willing to expose him found that they lacked the technical resources."

Was he ever caught in a flat-out lie? In April, 1950 he read from a supposed letter by Owen Lattimore and invited fellow senators to come to his desk and see for themselves. When Senator Lehman, to McCarthy's surprise, walked over to do so, the Wisconsin senator refused to show it to him and brushed him aside. There was reason—McCarthy wasn't quoting from the letter, he was inventing a text of his own.

On another occasion, McCarthy told of conversations with the late Secretary of Defense James Forrestal. Forrestal, from the grave, could hardly deny the claim that he shared McCarthy's views but nothing in Forrestal's diary ever mentions a meeting with the senator.

On television, in 1952, Joe McCarthy held up a "document" quoting his foe from Connecticut, Senator Benton. It later appeared that the quote did not exist; McCarthy had made it up. The network ran a correction.

The problem in correcting the record, of course, was that it never really caught up with the McCarthy charges. As Elmer Davis noted, "McCarthy gets his effects on the front page . . . and if yesterday's front page story blows up today, there is always today's front page story to bury the refutation."

As Richard Nixon described the problem in a different context —when he felt himself the victim of a smear, not from McCarthy but from the left—"A charge is usually put on the front page; the defense is buried among the deodorant ads."

McCarthy was irresistible to the press. Warren Duffee of the United Press blamed competition in the press for the McCarthy buildup:

There is no question that the press in America, the daily press, had a great part in building up in Senator McCarthy the power he eventually held. I don't deny for one moment that some of his remarks were carried in depth and detail beyond what I and many others, at the time, thought justified. The competition between newspapers and the wire services forced them into building him up. The big papers in large cities were even competing against each other for the headlines. If one of them had a pretty explosive story out of McCarthy, even though some reporters doubted that he had facts to back his statements up (sometimes

he did; sometimes he didn't), the competitive newsstand situation forced the others to carry the story, too. Competition feeds
on itself. This is something newspapers ought to be examining.
I'm willing to take my share of blame for adding to the snow-
balling buildup of Joe McCarthy which, in retrospect, I think
he didn't deserve. But once we were swept into it, it's more like
a whirlpool going 'round and 'round getting bigger and bigger.
Joe was smart enough to make the most of it.

Joe would make the most of it. He would call a morning news
conference and might have nothing to offer—so he would simply
announce that another news conference was to be held, later that
day or the next morning, to unveil new revelations. The announcement of "coming attractions" would give McCarthy time to dig up
something new for the press. It gave the afternoon newspapers
headlines that teased the public; McCarthy about to expose new
charges against the State Department or the army.

He would call high government officials, with reporters listening in on the telephone's extension, and discuss confidential information. The officials would never know how the press learned
it. He would show a reporter classified documents and say, "I'm
going to declassify it right now" and still another story would be
born.

The *New York Times* did a study of its own coverage and confessed, "It is difficult, if not impossible, to ignore charges by
Senator McCarthy just because they are usually proved false. The
remedy lies with the reader." The *Times* concluded that it had performed a disservice but an unavoidable one because of the nature
of day-to-day reporting.

President Eisenhower hated McCarthy but never took him on
publicly except by indirection. When he urged newspaper publishers to place less emphasis on the things that divide the American
people, Walter Lippmann wrote that McCarthy provides "news
which cannot be suppressed or ignored" and that the balance can
be provided only "by news about the truth or falsity of those
charges." He then suggested "General Eisenhower himself has a
heavy responsibility for the things he complains about."

In time some and, finally, many elements of the press began
responding to McCarthy. Cartoonist Herblock coined "McCarthy-

ism," showing the word crudely lettered on a barrel of mud. The word would enter the lexicon of that day and then formally in the dictionary itself, along with gerrymander, quisling, Judas, lynch, and other opprobrious words emanating from dark figures in history.

The brothers Joseph and Stewart Alsop wrote at the end of 1953, "McCarthy is the only major politician in the country who can be labeled 'liar' without fear of libel." A poll of reporters ranked McCarthy ninety-sixth in a Senate with ninety-six members, three out of four newsmen calling him the "worst" senator of all.

McCarthy, with the strength of a powerful, national figure, hit back at press critics. His favorite attack was to call a newspaper "closer to the [Communist] *Daily Worker* than any other newspaper in the country." Among his targets were the *Milwaukee Journal,* the Madison, Wisconsin, *Capital Times,* the *Washington Post,* the *New York Post,* the *St. Louis Post-Dispatch,* the *Portland Oregonian,* and the *Christian Science Monitor.*

When the *New York Post* ran an award-winning series on McCarthy entitled "Smear, Inc.," he accused the editor, James Wechsler, of being a Communist. The accusation, as so many of McCarthy's, was made safely from the Senate floor where congressional immunity protected him from libel.

Once John Steele of the United Press found McCarthy chewing him out for noting that McCarthy always promised to but never did repeat his charges without benefit of congressional immunity. McCarthy called that "the Communist line." He told Steele, "You want me to repeat what I said without congressional immunity so they can sue me. That's the Communist technique, to bring suits of libel." Seeing how angry he had made Steele, McCarthy apologized saying he was sure it wasn't "willful" on the reporter's part. Later McCarthy would quote with approval a charge that there were four hundred Communists in press and radio.

McCarthy could seek reprisals against those in journalism who displeased him. After a *Time* cover story in October, 1951, angered him, he wrote Henry Luce that he was preparing material on *Time* to send to all its advertisers.

When he did battle with Drew Pearson, he gave a Senate speech urging that Pearson's radio listeners boycott Pearson's sponsor,

Adam Hats—"It should be remembered that anyone who buys an Adam hat, is unknowingly and innocently contributing at least something to the cause of international Communism by keeping Communist spokesmen on the air." McCarthy left the Senate that night wearing an Adam hat that Pearson had once given him. Pearson ultimately sued McCarthy for libel but Adam Hats dropped Pearson's radio show. McCarthy also sent his speech and two other Senate speeches attacking Pearson to newspapers publishing Pearson's column.

Pearson found himself one of those attacked by McCarthyite publications including *Counterattack, The Newsletter of Facts on Communism*. Published by the American Business Consultants in New York, *Counterattack* went after all enemies of McCarthy in the mass media and also published *Red Channels,* which listed people "linked" to Communist causes, people in the theatre, movies, radio, and television.

The *Red Channels* lists had a profound effect on the networks, the movie studios, and elsewhere in a growing atmosphere of fear and hysteria, a period which soon was labeled "the McCarthy era." *Red Channels* led to widespread blacklisting as it was distributed up and down Madison Avenue—to advertising agencies, sponsors, and network executives.

As for broadcast news people, *Red Channels* mentioned ten, only a few of them well-known. William L. Shirer was convinced that he was dropped as a result of *Red Channels* and blamed network executives for caving in under pressure and resorting to blacklisting. Howard K. Smith, then of CBS, was also listed in *Red Channels* but said it had little effect. Alexander Kendrick similarly said he was not hurt by the listing (though he called himself "one of the fortunate few") and credited Ed Murrow with resisting any pressure, Murrow having told Kendrick "If you're in trouble, we're all in trouble."

The listings and the *Counterattack* campaigns did have their effect even if, in terms of newsmen, they bagged very few victims. Edward P. Morgan said, "The lists, as well as the whole climate of the past few years, put into the minds of even the best men something which was not there before—a care about the words they used, an instinct to cover themselves on controversial issues."

It was a broadcaster who finally struck the most publicized blow against Joe McCarthy. Edward R. Murrow, on March 9, 1954, presented a half-hour documentary on how McCarthy worked. The "See It Now" broadcast on CBS ended with Murrow saying, "We proclaim ourselves, as indeed we are, the defenders of freedom—what's left of it—but we cannot defend freedom by deserting it at home. The actions of the junior senator from Wisconsin have caused alarm and dismay amongst our allies abroad and given considerable comfort to our enemies. And whose fault is that? Not really his; he didn't create this situation of fear, he merely exploited it and rather successfully. Cassius was right. 'The fault, dear Brutus, is not in our stars but in ourselves.' "

Phone calls, letters, and telegrams—seventy-five thousand in all—flooded CBS, ten to one in favor of Murrow. McCarthy demanded and got the chance to rebut Murrow on CBS, calling the broadcaster "the leader and the cleverest of the jackal pack which is always found at the throat of anyone who dares to expose individual Communists and traitors." He, too, had a large audience. A private survey showed that one-third of the viewers believed McCarthy had proven Murrow was pro-Communist.

Editorial comment split unevenly on the Murrow-McCarthy exchange, most newspapers praising the broadcaster while the Hearst papers and pro-McCarthy columnists attacked him. At the Gridiron dinner in Washington, President Eisenhower threw his arm around Murrow, grinned, and said, "Let me see if there are any marks where the knife went in."

Murrow, the nation's most important television journalist, did great damage to McCarthy. He gave dissent from the senator, where others had only limited success, sudden respectability. Within a matter of weeks, television would cover the army-McCarthy hearings and would expose McCarthy's methods to even greater public scrutiny.

Before the year was out, a special subcommittee of the Senate issued a forty thousand word report on McCarthy and recommended that his colleagues reprimand him. Despite popular acceptance of the idea that he was censured, actually the subcommittee recommended something that in Senate protocol was less than that, that he be "condemned." The full Senate agreed in a sixty-seven to twenty-two vote. McCarthy's comment: "I wouldn't exactly call it a vote of confidence but I don't feel I've been lynched."

A few years later, McCarthy died and a service was held in the Senate Chamber. Congressional courtesy being what it is, the service was marked with charity on the part of the men who had voted to condemn him and the speeches were in the spirit of forgiving. None mentioned the havoc he had wrought. There was one exception; oddly enough it came from the long-time chaplain of the Senate. Reverend Frederick Brown Harris said, "Now that his lips are silent in these days of destiny, when the precious things we hold nearest our hearts are beset by subtle dangers such as have never before been faced, may the ancient admonition of God's holy word be heard and heeded with a new alertness by those who guard the nation's ramparts: 'If the watchmen upon the walls see the enemy advancing and give not the warning, then the blood of the people shall be required of the watchmen's hands.' "

Joe McCarthy had strutted across the stage for less than four years, from early 1950 when he first waved his "list" before the ladies of Wheeling to late 1954 when his colleagues condemned him. In that short period of time, he used the press with success unmatched in American history. Lucky as he might have been in seizing the right issue at the right moment and capitalizing on the nervous state of America, he also demonstrated consummate skill in the techniques available to a political figure. He knew the pressures, the competition and the deadlines of journalism. He knew the power of the official source and the attraction of the outrageous charge. He knew how to bend or stretch the truth or even how to desert it completely for effect. As his power grew, he knew how to play on the fears of those around him. As the atmophere of McCarthyism gripped the country, he knew how to switch from cajoling the press to intimidating it.

The press came closer to being intimidated in those four years than it had under the duress of presidential disfavor, congressional browbeating, repressive laws, and bullying courts and prosecutors in all the years of the nation. Courage was in short supply, restraint was commonplace—there was "a care about the words they used, an instinct to cover themselves on controversial issues." Among the exceptions was Elmer Davis, the tough Hoosier broadcaster who gave his colleagues advice on dealing with McCarthy and others like him, advice that is simple but valid to this day:

"The first and great commandment is," he said, "don't let them scare you."

The bottom line on a Joe McCarthy is the sobering conclusion that it can happen here. A clever demagogue can whip up national hysteria and the press can succumb to his technique.

McCarthy's legacy included some lasting side effects. One was instituted by Harry Truman who, by the way, was one of Mc-Carthy's favorite targets—McCarthy denouncing Truman in early 1951 as that "s.o.b. who decided to remove [General] MacArthur when drunk."

Harry Truman refused to sign the oppressive Internal Security Act of 1950, saying in his veto message, "We need not fear the expression of ideas—we do need to fear their suppression. . . . Let us not, in cowering and foolish fear, throw away the ideals which are the fundamental basis of our free society." But a year later, on September 24, 1951 the president issued Executive Order 10290 as a result of the national hysteria, an order permitting all government agencies to classify and withhold all matter relating to national security; it also would empower all agency heads to pass on classifying authority to their subordinates.

Truman denied that he was keeping legitimate news from the press but the press disagreed. Alexander F. Jones, president of the American Society of Newspaper Editors said, "Any time you give a government department head authority to classify as top secret on a security basis, you are placing a potent weapon in his hands. The result, invariably, is further suppression of the news." The *New York Herald Tribune* asked "Security or Censorship?" Professional journalism groups protested.

The day after Truman issued the order, the Office of Price Stabilization issued a staff memo which would have kept all embarrassing information classified. Truman heard about it and two hours later personally ordered it rescinded, fearing that it would be considered the natural outgrowth of his executive order.

Forty-four Republican senators signed a manifesto damning the order and pledging to fight any moves to "conceal facts from the American people." Among the signers was a man who, like all other presidents after Truman, would use variations of the executive order—Richard Nixon, then senator from California.

President Eisenhower, on November 5, 1953 replaced the Truman order with his own, Executive Order 10501, designed to restore "a proper balance" between public information and state secrets. It took classification privileges away from twenty-eight federal agencies and limited them in seventeen others. Only fifteen agencies continued to have full classification authority.

The legal authority for such an executive order was the so-called housekeeping statute, passed during George Washington's administration to permit government departments to keep and safeguard official records. Said Attorney General Herbert Brownell, "For over one hundred and fifty years . . . presidents have established by precedent that they and members of their cabinets, and other heads of executive departments, have an undoubted privilege and discretion to keep confidential, in the public interest, papers and information which require secrecy."

Eisenhower extended this to "executive privilege" in 1954 to keep administration officials from having to face congressional cross-examination. McCarthy was still an element, a goading force. This withholding of administration people was first used in the army-McCarthy hearings when the secretary of the army refused to permit a general to testify.

While such moves might protect a president's people from Joe McCarthy, they also permitted an administration to keep Presidential Advisor Sherman Adams from congressional interrogation when his name was raised in connection with gifts from Bernard Goldfine; it kept the air force from having to submit to a 1958 check of its missile program by the General Accounting Office, and was used during the debate over the controversial Dixon-Yates contract.

President Kennedy replaced Ike's Executive Order 10501 with his own Order 10964 on September 20, 1961—an order designed to downgrade or declassify material. Some of it occurred automatically after a three-year period, other after twelve years, but some would remain classified indefinitely. It sounded good but Kennedy made as much use of executive privilege as anybody. He invoked it during the so-called muzzling-of-the-military hearings to prevent military and State Department censors from testifying on deletions made in speeches of high military officers. He wrote Defense Secretary Robert McNamara in February of 1962 that he should protect his people from congressional inquiry—"I do not intend to permit subordinate officials of our career services to bear the brunt of congressional inquiry into policies which are the responsibilities of their superiors." Kennedy also used "executive privilege" to prevent any testimony before the Senate Foreign Relations Committee by Walt W. Rostow.

Richard Nixon's administration similarly used executive orders, notably in the case of Henry Kissinger. In addition to people, they kept Senate committees from examining Pentagon material including the Pentagon Papers. In the Justice Department move against the *New York Times* in the publication of the Pentagon Papers, it was Executive Order 10501 as promulgated and amended by Eisenhower and Kennedy that was the starting point in the government's case.

Since executive orders cut off the Congress as well as reporters, the press is twice damaged since as much news about a presidential administration leaks out of the Congress as from the White House itself. Senate chairmen complained about the penalty of such presidential power during all the years since Truman first issued his executive order. The executive branch, they protested, was preventing the legislative from gathering the information it needed.

Political leaders, in their collection of measures to manage the news, rarely fall back on something so formal and so forbidding as an executive order. It is usually more effective and far more adroit to use methods less open to public exposure and congressional protest. One such means is counterpoint to cronyism with the reporter; it is the complaint to the reporter's boss.

John F. Kennedy was partial to the idea of "bitching to the boss" despite the protests of his aides that he didn't do that. Sorenson wrote, "Contrary to reports, there were no threats to secure an offending reporter's dismissal or deny him access to the White House."

Kennedy expressed tremendous displeasure over *New York Times* reporting from Vietnam, primarily that of David Halberstam (though the president's wrath could hardly match that of President Diem's sister-in-law, Madame Nhu, who said, "Halberstam should be barbecued, and I would be glad to supply the fluid and the match."). According to the *Newsweek's* White House man, Charles Roberts, Kennedy phoned the publisher of the *Times* and asked that Halberstam be given a change of assignment. On one occasion, the *Times* publisher was with the president in the White House and was told—he thought as a joke—"Why don't you get Halberstam out of Vietnam?" Telling it to his own people at dinner later, the publisher was startled to find they took it seriously.

Kennedy may have run a secret check on the offending Halberstam. One presidential aide, talking to reporters at a bar in Hyannisport, Massachusetts, boasted of a CIA report on the reporter which allegedly showed Halberstam never went out into battle areas. His profession had no doubts about Halberstam's reporting; he won the Pulitzer Prize for his Vietnam coverage.

When *Fortune* magazine did an article about Kennedy's Bay of Pigs crisis, the president was most disturbed and told a news conference that the *TIME* version of that article was "the most inaccurate of all the articles that have appeared on Cuba." He called Henry Luce personally to complain and then dispatched General Maxwell Taylor to New York to see Luce and point out the alleged misstatements. The writer of the article was Charles J. V. Murphy and when Kennedy learned that Murphy was a colonel in the air force reserve at the Pentagon, the president personally ordered him transferred, "preferably out in the desert."

Kennedy, by the way, once had aides prepare an analysis of *TIME*'s treatment of his first year in office as compared with Eisenhower's. He then sent it to old friend Henry Luce. The study claimed Eisenhower was treated with sympathy while Kennedy encountered ridicule in the magazine; Eisenhower's year "was dealt with in only glowing terms and heroic prose—but the Kennedy Administration, in contrast, was nary given a chance and criticism was never spared."

There is no record of Luce's reaction to the analysis provided by the president

Presidents realize that some of what they are "reading more and enjoying less" as Kennedy once put it, is a result of members of their staff telling more than they should or telling it prematurely. Like any other bureaucracy, the executive branch is too large to keep tight rein on what everyone is saying. They try, however.

At various times, the Lyndon Johnson White House tried to find the source of news leaks by initiating a series of checks. The

Secret Service would canvass the staff after an unwanted story broke to see who had seen the reporter involved. At one point, government chauffeurs were to report on all places visited outside the White House including, of course, lunch with reporters. The information went to Marvin Watson who was in charge of spotting staff members making suspicious contacts with the press.

In late 1955, Watson installed a system of telephone checks, the switchboard operators to record every outside call to a member of the staff. Reporters quickly realized this when operators began to ask their names. They simply invented fictitious names. Henry Wadsworth Longfellow was calling most frequently while Hollywood movie stars and international playboys were among other persistent callers. That check was dropped in January of 1966, Press Secretary Bill Moyers lamely explaining that it wasn't meant to be a check on reporters calling in but was simply a study to achieve operating economy and eliminate unneeded telephones.

A typical Johnson administration exercise in searching for news leaks came after Robert Pierpoint of CBS reported an insider's evaluation of the president's reaction to two 1966 primary elections, Oregon and Florida. The report obviously displeased the President. Press Secretary Moyers called Pierpoint in. When the CBS man would not reveal his source, he was warned that the president might call him in with the same question. Pierpoint told Moyers that he could not reveal it to the president either. Moyers said he knew that and had already told Mr. Johnson so. Pierpoint was never called in by the president but others were questioned by the press office to see if they had talked to him and Secret Service guards were asked if they had witnessed staff talking to the reporter.

A *Washington Evening Star* reporter, Roberta Hornig, broke a story in early 1970 about a private letter from Interior Secretary Walter Hickel to President Nixon expressing differences over the administration's attitude toward the nation's youth. The *Star* quoted one Interior staff member as saying an extensive "head hunt" was underway to discover how Miss Hornig got the letter. She, herself, was called in by a press aide and found herself being quizzed as to the source.

One much-publicized search for sources which outraged the journalistic community in April, 1962 was the use of the FBI to check on published stories dealing with the rise in steel prices. Edmund F. Martin, president of Bethlehem Steel, was quoted as telling a stockholder's meeting in Wilmington, Delaware, that this was no time to raise the price of steel. When Bethlehem became the first to join U.S. Steel in increasing the price, Martin issued a statement saying he was quoted incorrectly. The attorney general, President Kennedy's brother Robert, ordered the Antitrust Division of Justice to see if there had been a conspiracy in violation of the antitrust laws.

Lee Linder of the AP in Philadelphia, who reported the original story, was awakened at 3 A.M. by an FBI phone call. He thought it a joke. The agents said they were coming right over and thirty minutes later were at his home, asking him to go over his story with them. He said he stood by his story. James L. Parks, Jr. of the Wilmington, Delaware, *Evening Journal,* who also covered the stockholders meeting, found the FBI waiting at his office when he arrived at 6:30 A.M. A *Wall Street Journal* man was also called in the middle of the night.

The *New York Times* said the matter smacked of a "personal vendetta" by the brothers Kennedy against the steel executives and the *New York Post* complained of a "police operation" better directed at catching spies than in the "invasion of (reporters') privacy." The *Richmond Times-Dispatch* called it an "indefensible abuse of personal power by a hired public servant." Republicans decried the "Gestapo tactics" and "press suppression."

At his next news conference, the president was asked about it:

Q: Mr. President, Chairman Miller and other Republican leaders have focused a good deal of criticism on the nocturnal activities of the FBI. Could you shed any light on that, sir?

THE PRESIDENT: No, they were attempting to—reporters have called up a good many people in the middle of the night themselves—(laughter). And I—all we were attempting to do was to find out so that we could decide about the grand jury meeting, whether the reports in regard to the quotations which said one thing, and then there was a statement that they were misquoted, and then the next day there was a clarification. We wanted to get the facts of this.

Now, both the reporters were cooperative; I didn't realize

they would be woken up at the time they were. The decision was made early in the evening, and I suppose making the connection, the FBI followed ahead, and I—and as I say, all the reporters except that of the *Wall Street Journal* were most cooperative. But the intention was not to disturb the reporters. The intention was to get the information as quickly as possible so we could determine what action we would take before the grand jury, and as always the FBI carried out its responsibilities immediately.

The fact is that the FBI was not used just that once. Hanson Baldwin, in the April, 1963, issue of the *Atlantic,* wrote "FBI agents have been employed in at least half a dozen separate instances in the past two years in investigations of the sources of news stories. The Eisenhower administration several times used the federal sleuths in attempts to detect the sources of stories published by various papers. But Mr. Kennedy has called upon the FBI far more frequently in cases of this sort than any prior president, and the methods used by the FBI in this administration, though sometimes repudiated or apologized for later, have smacked of totalitarianism rather than of democratic government."

Baldwin said federal agents have shadowed newsmen in corridors of the Pentagon and have visited them in their homes in attempts to question them about stories.

Among those reporting an FBI interest in their stories were columnist Joseph Alsop, *Newsweek*'s Lloyd Norman, and Richard Fryklund of the *Washington Star.* Philip L. Geyelin, when with the *Wall Street Journal,* reported that the Johnson administration continued the practice of using the FBI to explore news leaks. A Johnson press aide also told this author that the Secret Service, checking on one network reporter, wanted him barred from the White House because he was seen with members of the Soviet Embassy. Only press office intervention prevented an incident over the reporter's White House credentials being lifted.

Baldwin, writing in the *Atlantic,* told of FBI tapping of telephones, shadowing of reporters, investigating their acquaintances, etc. "In all cases," he wrote, "the newsmen concerned have told the FBI in effect that their sources were their business."

In the Nixon administration the practice continued, especially as far as government employees who might have been the source in leaking news. In September, 1971 it was revealed that FBI agents quizzed officials in State and it was even suggested that they take lie detector tests after leaks dealing with a U.S. offer in the Strategic Arms Limitations Talks and a second story dealing with U.S. arms being shipped to Pakistan. The threat of lie detector tests had a familiar ring. Richard Fryklund once wrote, during the Johnson administration, that one hundred and twenty Defense Department employees had been asked to take lie detector tests. The Fryklund article caused enough stir that Defense officials dropped the idea.

There was a flap at the end of 1971 when it was revealed that the FBI was checking the personal life of CBS Correspondent Daniel Schorr, allegedly because he was being considered for a high government post. After much press criticism for putting the FBI on a reporter's trail, the president announced that the matter had been handled in a "clumsy way" and that hereafter all potential appointees will be informed before the "customary" FBI check is made.

The *Washington Post* editorialized on "the Administration's propensity for confusing criticism with conspiracy" and asked the question: "Which would surprise you more: to learn that the Administration had named a well-known and highly respected critic, such as Daniel Schorr, to one of its top jobs or to learn that it had been hounding and harassing such a critic?" Schorr testified before a Senate hearing in February, 1972 that under the circumstances he, too, believed "it would have been an extraordinarily open-minded thing for them to have done."

At about the same time there were published reports that the FBI had also been checking into the private records and the bank accounts of Neil Sheehan, the *New York Times* reporter chiefly involved in their publication of the Pentagon Papers. It was said that his wife's private records were being checked as well.

Newsmen have long resented the practice of the FBI and other police authorities to have their men pose as newsmen while gathering information, frequently in connection with protest movements such as the anti-Vietnam and pro–civil-rights campaigns. In reply to this author's complaint in mid-1968, Attorney General Ramsey Clark agreed that the practice was bad and said instructions had gone out by the FBI director "that under no circumstances are they ever to pose as members of the news media in connection with any future investigations." Clark left office and when the John Mitchell administration came in, the practice was resumed.

One incident was reported when Rep. William Anderson of Tennessee held a news conference to discuss the case of the Berrigan brothers, two priests arrested for their anti-Vietnam activity. Reporters noticed a stout, balding man jotting notes and recognized him as an FBI agent they had seen before. He denied it but rushed out of the room. An aide to Rep. Anderson followed him and took down the license number of the cruising auto which picked him up. Police said the license plate is listed to the FBI.

In Saigon in early 1970, four agents of the U.S. Government had masqueraded as newsmen in an apparent attempt to find out how newsmen got information from military sources. When legitimate newsmen unmasked the impostors, the army said it was an isolated incident, "Somebody goofed" and that it was not the policy of the military to pose as newsmen.

In 1968, army security agents used a phony television remote unit to film protesters at the Democratic National Convention. An army agent posed as a reporter from a Richmond newspaper to obtain information on a civil rights group, the Southern Christian Leadership Conference.

Police authorities were spotted posing as reporters in the District of Columbia, Wichita, Chicago, Nassau County in New York, Detroit, Albuquerque, and San Juan among other places. Police issued press passes to army intelligence agents in New York to permit them close access to militant black leaders H. Rap Brown and Stokely Carmichael during the summer riots of 1967.

Another of the police-newsman charades was conducted by the Illinois Bureau of Investigation, which sent two men with portable TV equipment (marked station WJJO-TV) to record a peace demonstration at the college town of DeKalb, Illinois. When the Illinois News Broadcasters and others complained angrily about it, the Bureau of Investigation promised to discontinue the practice.

In Madison, Wisconsin—another college community—so widespread was the use of press credentials by government investigators that members of the Madison Newspaper Guild unanimously voted to destroy their own press cards. The president of the guild said, "We take this step not lightly but in response to repeated police use in this country of undercover agents using press cards."

The credibility of the news media is seriously crimped if news sources consider that their confidence will be betrayed. It is severely damaged if the news source isn't sure when the reporter himself is legitimate but rather an FBI agent in disguise. Considering the FBI's proud record of achievement, publicized so prominently by the FBI itself, it would seem that supercops would not have to lower themselves to parading as newsmen to gather information.

It was revealed during the riot-conspiracy trial of the "Chicago 7" following the Democratic National Convention of 1968 that the FBI also hired paid informers in the press. A photographer for *El Tiempo,* Louis Salzberg, and a television reporter-cameraman in San Diego, Carl Gilman of KFMB-TV, both appeared as witnesses and revealed that while working as newsmen covering the defendants, they were on the FBI payroll. Gilman had received between seven and eight thousand dollars plus two thousand more for expenses. Salzberg was paid a hundred dollars a month while on the Spanish language paper and six hundred a month after that, his principal source of income in 1969.

When the Twentieth Century Fund's Task Force on Governmental Power and Press Freedom inquired about the FBI's use of paid informers in the press, it received a Justice Department reply "prepared by" FBI Director J. Edgar Hoover which said: "The FBI accepts from any person information which may be of value in the course of an FBI investigation. The FBI does not now, and never has actively recruited journalists as informants. However, there is no policy against accepting information from a journalist or any news media representative if it is volunteered, which was the case with Mr. Louis Salzberg and Mr. Carl Gilman. Both of these individuals furnished information to the FBI on a voluntary basis. They were paid for their services and expenses."

As for FBI agents posing as newsmen, Hoover simply reported that "FBI agents are not permitted to pose as reporters or press photographers in the course of their investigations."

Presidents, by the way, are very protective of the FBI. Franklin Roosevelt had the U.S. attorney bring action against the *New York*

Post when it announced a series by a former FBI agent exposing spy actions. As the injunction was being sought, the paper defended its rights but agreed to stop publication. Roosevelt telegraphed the publisher to express his appreciation.

Presidential interference to stop a story is rare, possibly because they rarely know of it in advance, but in late 1964, two of President Johnson's closest friends tried to bottle up a story involving one of his closest aides in the White House. Presidential Assistant Walter Jenkins was arrested on October 7, 1964 in the men's room of a YMCA near the White House on a morals charge. The place was a notorious hangout for homosexuals and Jenkins and a second man were charged with "disorderly conduct (pervert)" and released after paying fifty dollars collateral which, in the manner of such cases, precluded court appearance when it was forfeited.

On the night of October 13, the Washington *Evening Star* received a tip and the next morning reporters checked the police blotter. The White House press office was called. Liz Carpenter, who was filling in for the press secretary (Reedy was *en route* to New York with the president for a campaign appearance) thought it a joke. Jenkins told her to deny the story and he immediately called Abe Fortas, one of Washington's leading lawyers, a close friend of Lyndon Johnson whom the President would one day name to the Supreme Court.

The *Star* got a call from Fortas saying he was on his way to the newspaper's offices. Accompanied by Clark Clifford, an equally distinguished lawyer and Johnson confidant, Fortas appealed to Newbold Noyes, editor of the *Star,* on the basis of charity and decency, asking that he not print this story about a married man who had six children. Noyes agreed to hold off as long as other papers did not publish since it was not the *Star's* policy to publish such stories anyway (there had been an average of twenty arrests for perversion every month in Washington and they were generally not reported in the *Star*).

Clifford and Fortas then went to the editor of the *Washington Daily News* with a similar plea and similar results. Finally, the pair went to the *Washington Post* with their appeal for compassion. While the Johnson friends were so engaged, however, staff members of the Republican National Committee had been calling other news organizations. CBS prepared a story on the Jenkins matter, withholding his name from its early reports until it could confirm the story fully. Republican National Chairman Dean Burch at 6 P.M. that night put out a cryptic statement that "the White House is desperately trying to suppress a major news story affecting the national security."

At 8:25 P.M. UPI ran the story and it was on radio and television. Morning papers—including the *Washington Post*—scrambled to include it. The president, in New York, sent word to Fortas to go to Jenkins, now hospitalized under heavy sedation, and get his resignation. First Mrs. Johnson and later the President issued statements regretting Jenkins' great personal tragedy. Mrs. Johnson said it quickly, simply, and with a dignity that touched the hearts of all who read her statement. "He is my friend," she said.

Republican spokesmen however, said it raised grave questions about national security, Chairman Burch noting "the vulnerability of morals offenders to blackmail," but if they had hopes of exploiting the case in the campaign against Johnson, the Republicans never had a chance—thanks to what they called "Lyndon's luck." At that moment, the Chinese touched off an atom bomb test and the gravity of that event pushed the Jenkins case off the front pages.

It is rare that friends of a president should try to intervene to prevent publication of an embarrassing story. There were extenuating circumstances in the unique nature of the Jenkins case. There is some evidence that the president learned about it fairly late, hours after Fortas and Clifford acted. But he did not stop them and the fact remains that men closely associated with the White House almost succeeded in having a story suppressed.

VI

WHEN POLITICIANS SEEK TO SEDUCE, ANTICIPATE, OR INTIMIDATE

In the day-to-day battle between the press and the politicians, events are rarely dramatic. The bag of tricks that political figures have at their disposal rarely includes direct moves to stop publication. The methods of news manipulation are usually more subtle, more adroit, and more successful.

One means of getting the story across is the protective cloak of anonymity offered by that often-used device, the backgrounder. Though copied elsewhere, the backgrounder was born and bred in Washington. It has proliferated to the point that hundreds of times a year, officials from the president down to civil servants deep in the bowels of the bureaucracy fill-in reporters while they themselves bask in warm, comfortable anonymity.

Though it existed through much of the twentieth century and FDR used it extensively, the backgrounder truly grew in the Washington of the Eisenhower Cold War years and continued throughout the Vietnam War as a prime means for floating ideas without standing behind them. An examination of some that surfaced in recent decades shows the scope of the backgrounder as an influence.

In 1953, Secretary of State John Foster Dulles was the anonymous source for a story that a Korean boundary settlement was
being considered along a line through the narrow waist of Korea.
Reaction from Capitol Hill was very negative. Another anonymous
story emerged from the White House denying that the original idea
was ever under consideration. The unnamed source for this: Dulles.

In 1954, Vice-President Nixon made a background appearance
before the American Society of Newspaper Editors and put forth
the idea, supported by Dulles and the hawkish chairman of the
Joint Chiefs of Staff, Admiral Arthur Radford, that U.S. troops
might be needed in Indochina to prevent a French defeat. The
editors reacted strongly and negatively. So did President Eisenhower, who rejected the advice. To the general public, however,
the identity of the vice-president as the author of the proposal was
not known.

Dulles, a skilled and frequent user of backgrounders, once called
in reporters in London just before an international meeting to discuss a Japanese peace treaty. On a background basis, he said that
unless the British made concessions, the negotiations would fail.
The subsequent publicity and the British knowledge, if not that of
newspaper readers, that Dulles was the author of the warning,
brought them around. Dulles had used the press to force the concessions he sought and the public remained ignorant of his role.

In 1955, the chief of naval operations, Admiral Robert Carney,
spoke to a group of columnists and correspondents at a background
session in which he predicted a Chinese invasion of the offshore
islands of Quemoy and Matsu in the Formosa Straits. He even predicted a date for the invasion. All of this supported a contention
he shared with Admiral Radford that the time might be near for
a military confrontation with China. The White House was shocked
and angry; Jim Hagerty called a news briefing—on a background
basis—to deny the story and to belittle talkative admirals. Called
before a Senate committee, Admiral Carney said, "I never made
such a statement." Before the year was out, he retired from the
navy.

In 1956, one backgrounder—that of Dulles—floated the idea
that monetary aid might be given to help shore up England and
France after their economies suffered from the closing of the Suez
Canal. Another backgrounder—that of Treasury Secretary Hum-

phrey—said that high officials saw no need for such grants. The device of the backgrounder was used here in ideological debate and the press went along as the willing conspirator, publicizing the conflict without identifying the debaters by name.

In the Kennedy administration, Secretary Robert McNamara of Defense and Secretary Dean Rusk of State were among the most prolific of backgrounders. McNamara would have reporters in on Thursday afternoon and a spate of military stories would frequently appear on Friday, insiders in Washington knowing the source. Similarly, Rusk's sessions over drinks late on Friday provided a similar rash of weekend stories with an anonymous State Department twist. Ben Bradlee of the *Post* observed that "everyone in Washington knows Max Frankel is quoting Dean Rusk—including the Soviet ambassador and the Red Chinese spies. Everyone, that is, except the readers. Who the hell is conning whom?"

McNamara, in his early days in office, told reporters that there was no "missile gap" between the United States and the USSR. He considered that view not for publication at all and was considerably embarrassed when it appeared in print. His boss, President Kennedy, had used "missile gap" as a key item in his election campaign.

On April 30, 1965 the State Department leaked to reporters the white paper describing "Communist participation" in the Dominican rebellion. As mentioned earlier, it was cloaked in anonymity. Printed on plain white paper, it was accompanied with a note that read: "The ground rules on this: The information is being given you on a BACKGROUND basis. It may be attributable to the U.S. Government or U.S. official sources. There should be no direct quoting of it, meaning you can use the language that appears in front of you but it should not be put in quotes. It is not to be called a document. It is not an official paper and should not be regarded as such. You should not use the word 'document.' " The "nondocument" document was later proved to be full of errors.

In 1966 in Saigon, Marine Corps General Wallace M. Greene, Jr., held a backgrounder which resulted in stories that the war might last another five years even with twice the number of American troops then in Vietnam. A defense official later said he thought Greene was trying to pressure the administration into increasing troop strength in Vietnam. In any case, the story caused such a stir that Greene, returning to Washington, called in reporters to admit he had conducted a backgrounder and to deny he said what they said he said.

In 1967, Walt W. Rostow was the source for a backgrounder that decried a Senate Foreign Relations Committee rejection of the administration's proposal for Latin American aid. The committee's alternative, said Rostow anonymously, was "worse than useless." The Senate knew who said it but neither the White House nor State would embrace the words; reporters attributed them to "American authorities" on Latin affairs.

There was, in 1967, one of those few cases where the insiders in Washington were fooled as to the source of a backgrounder. Newspaper reporters crediting a "high government official" told of another fifty thousand troops going to Vietnam and a rise in war costs along with that. Many considered the source to be State, Defense, or White House. It actually was from a backgrounder with William McChesney Martin, then chairman of the Federal Reserve Board.

Defense Secretary McNamara was chief guest at a background dinner in which he said that the possibility of using nuclear weapons in Vietnam always existed, he was not willing to rule out anything. It was said that he meant to warn China that the use of nuclear weaponry was not impossible. The headlines were sobering however and the American public more than the Chinese seemed frightened. McNamara emerged from anonymity and denied this story vigorously. He never revealed, of course, that the "official spokesman" for the original story was McNamara himself.

In early 1968, "a reliable administration source" said troop increases would be "moderate" and not the two hundred thousand mentioned in press speculation. About the same time, "a well-informed administration source" said the president seemed willing to go along with congressional cuts in appropriations in return for action on the income-tax surcharge. Columnists Robert Novak and Rowland Evans revealed, a few days later, that the source for both speculations as to what President Johnson might do was President Johnson himself.

The *Washington Post* once ran an editorial bemoaning the fact that a Justice Department story was credited to "it was learned" and offered a reader's guide to the euphemisms of backgrounders.

"For the edification of readers who may be unaware of the etymology, the family tree so to speak, of the wellsprings of news, it goes something like this: Walter and Ann Source (neé Rumor) had four daughters (Highly-Placed, Authoritative, Unimpeachable and Well-informed). The first married a diplomat named U.S. Officials, and the second, a Government public relations man named Reliable Informant. (The Informant brothers are widely known and quoted here; among the best known are White House, State Department, and Congressional). Walter Speculation's brother-in-law, Ian Rumor, married Alexandra Conjecture, from which there were two sons, It Was Understood and It Was Learned. It Was Learned went to work yesterday in the Justice Department, where he will be gainfully employed for four long years."

During the Nixon administration, "T.R.B." (Richard L. Strout) wrote in the *New Republic* about a backgrounder given by William Scranton, chairman of the President's Commission on Campus Unrest. "Well, an odd thing happened," he declared, "first Governor Scranton was there and then, presto, in the same chair sat a spectral 'Commission source.' We get used to that sort of hide-and-seek, of course, in Washington, but it's a bit confusing at first, like Alice interviewing the disappearing cat."

Early in the Nixon years there was a CIA rebuttal to charges that the intelligence agency had taken part in the killing of a South Vietnamese who had double-crossed the army's special forces, the Green Berets. Eight Green Berets including their commander were facing possible court-martial. The head of the CIA met with a select group of wire service, broadcast, and newspaper correspondents to refute the charge that his agency was involved. Unfortunately the *New York Times* was not invited and shortly afterwards reported the story, stating flatly that the CIA had held the backgrounder—something that reporters in attendance were forbidden to do by the rules of backgrounders.

No reporters felt more handcuffed by the rules of the game than nine reporters who had a background session with Vice-President Agnew in April, 1971 at the Republican Governors Conference in Williamsburg, Virginia. It was just after China surprised the world by inviting an American ping-pong team and a few reporters to visit Peking, the first friendly gesture towards the United States since the late 1940s. Agnew was concerned about the great press attention to the event. He feared the result would be an undercutting of U.S. support for Nationalist China.

At 12:30 A.M., Agnew's press secretary Vic Gold went through the hotel lobby inviting reporters to have a drink with the vice-president in his suite. One reporter, already in bed, was awakened; some of the nine were not on the original list but happened to be with some of the chosen as Gold approached them in the lobby. The meeting was to be off-the-record, nothing to be written about the conversations by those present. It lasted till 3:30 A.M. As they left, Agnew laughingly predicted he would probably see something about this in print in "six months" or so. He was to see it a lot quicker than that.

Agnew's apparent difference with the president on China, Nixon having received the ping-pong gesture approvingly, was too big a story to be buried. Other reporters and editors began to learn details of the postmidnight session. The *St. Louis Post-Dispatch* and the *Los Angeles Times* ferreted out the details and published the story. The AP picked it up out of St. Louis. Under the ground rules of the off-the-record session, the AP man who had attended in Williamsburg had his hands tied and could not report the story.

Their editors began demanding that the nine attending the Agnew briefing report the story. The reporters went to Press Secretary Gold to ask if the ground rules could be lifted now that the story was public. Vice-President Agnew, embarrassed and angry, refused. Some of the reporters then sought out Republican governors until they found those who had heard similar opinions from Mr. Agnew and got the story that way. One reporter later wore a sardonic press badge which read "Free the Williamsburg Nine." It was predicted that Agnew would hold few backgrounders in the future.

About three months later there was another backgrounder relating to China, this one held by Presidential Advisor Henry Kissinger after he returned from his secret meeting with Chou En-lai. Dr. Kissinger was to give details of the agreement for the president to visit China. Mr. Nixon was in San Clemente, California, at the time and after reporting to him, Kissinger went to the San Clemente Inn to background the press. He was filmed coming and going and even photographed standing next to the president's press secretary in the press room yet the rules of the backgrounder forbade the use of his name as a source. Everything had to be credited to a "White House source" or "White House officials."

The result was the strange double-think of backgrounders as they appear in print. The UPI report told us that "newsmen at the Western White House were briefed for an hour by a ranking administration official familiar with all details of the trip. The rules of the briefing prohibited him from being identified. He said Dr. Henry Kissinger, who made a secret visit to Peking last weekend to arrange the president's trip, discussed their plans in the Lincoln sitting room in the residence portion of the White House. The official said the preparations for the trip were so secret that the president did not work on the preparations in his oval office for fear of leaving papers in view."

The *New York Times* engaged in similar trick-step by telling that "the officials (at the White House) also disclosed some details of Henry A. Kissinger's forty-nine hour visit to Peking July 9 to 11 during which, in intensive discussion with Premier Chou, he worked out the final agreement for the visit."

The television networks similarly quoted anonymous sources at the White House but did so over pictures of Kissinger arriving for the briefing, standing in the room with reporters, and leaving. There was no doubt in the minds of TV viewers, for once, as to the author of remarks at the briefing.

Reporters failed to get the White House to put Kissinger on the record, even when they pointed to his constant references to "I" in the briefing (the White House suggested they simply change first person pronouns to third person) and the fact that no one other than the man who made the trip to Peking himself could give the kind of details now being reported as coming from a White House source. The background status of the briefing was not lifted.

Kissinger, by the way, was himself amused by the strictures of background rules. He speaks with a trace of a German accent and once suggested to reporters that they credit his remarks to a "White House official with an accent."

Dr. Kissinger was the central figure in two other incidents involving backgrounders in the closing days of 1971. Senator Barry Goldwater asked for Kissinger's December 7th backgrounder on Pakistan and later in the week inserted it in the *Congressional*

Record revealing the source of the remarks. Said the senator, "To
me there was no marking to indicate 'secret' or 'off-the-record.'
Besides I don't work that way. Occasionally I'm invited to a secret
briefing. I say the hell with it."

Earlier in the week Kissinger's remarks were reported by newsmen but attributed to "White House officials." By week's end, anyone reading pages S21012 to S21015 of the *Congressional Record*
would learn not only that Kissinger gave the briefing but could also
read Press Secretary Ron Ziegler's introduction and explanation of
the ground rules for reporting the Kissinger comments.

Later in the month, as the president's airplane returned from a
meeting with French President Pompidou in the Azores, Kissinger
gave a pool of reporters another background briefing. This one
included the suggestion that Russia's actions in the India-Pakistan
war over East Pakistan might lead to a cancellation of Mr. Nixon's
proposed summit meeting with Soviet leaders in May of 1972. The
story was front-page news everywhere and attributed to "high administration sources." The *Washington Post,* however, identified
Dr. Kissinger as the source.

There was a great deal of controversy over the *Post*'s move. The
pool report was written by David Kraslow, Washington bureau
chief of the *Los Angeles Times* who called the *Post* action "unprofessional and unethical" and "cheap journalism." The White
House also expressed its displeasure. The *Post*'s executive editor,
Benjamin Bradlee, announced a new policy of "fullest possible attribution" and said its staff would do everything possible to identify sources. The *New York Times* managing editor, Abe Rosenthal, said his reporters and editors would be "a lot more selective"
about attending background briefings.

The reporting of remarks by officials at backgrounders follows a
variety of ground rules, the best known being the so-called Lindley
rule named after Ernest K. Lindley, former *New York Herald
Tribune* and later *Newsweek* correspondent. The Lindley rule,
sometimes called a "deep backgrounder," forbids any reference to
the government source at all, his information appearing as the observations of the reporter. Lindley called it "a system of compulsory plagiarism." It was created by Lindley when he served as
president of the Overseas Writers Club in Washington just as the
Cold War was beginning after World War II. The participants

were less reporters than columnists, editors, editorial writers who did not look for news, for scoops, but rather an understanding to help them write intelligently.

In the years that followed, the number of backgrounders increased and the interests of the participants varied and soon it was a major source for news rather than a device to background pundits. The compulsory plagiarism was modified as reporters sought to peg some identification to their sources, some form of blurred attribution. Thus "high officials" and "government sources" and "administration expert" and all the other euphemisms were brought into play. In some cases it was authentic Lindley with no attribution at all, with true compulsory plagiarism, but most of the time stories are pegged to a government ghost.

Problems arise in the many variations in ground rules and wise bureaucrats make sure that they or their press aides spell them out before any background meeting with newsmen. There is the "pure off-the-record" session in which no information is to be reported at all although a reporter may inform his editor. There is the Lindley rule in which the story must appear to come from the reporter himself without attribution. There is the "modified Lindley" which permits very vague attribution or partial attribution if the official agrees during the backgrounder to permit a limited amount of his comment to be attributed to "government sources." There is the "not-for-attribution backgrounder" in which administration or congressional sources can be the author of quotes and opinions as long as they are not too clearly identifiable. There is the "blurred briefing," practiced largely at the White House, where the source is obviously one of several regular briefers but is credited to the institution (ie: "The White House said today . . .") rather than the individual.

Unfortunately there are variations of all classifications. Some reporters, primarily at the State Department, talk of backgrounders, deep backgrounders, and even deep, deep backgrounders (which has the flavor of a meeting in a darkened basement in the dead of night in which the Secretary of State whispers so quietly no one hears). The same terms mean different things to different news sources and one set of ground rules in the executive area take on different flavor on Capitol Hill. The result is occasional embarrassment as the results of backgrounders shift from the source's original intent. There is even occasional confusion among old hands. At least one president has told a reporter something off-the-record and, when the poor reporter complained that he wasn't sure he knew why he was being given such confidential information, was told "to print it, of course."

Despite the occasional lapses, the backgrounder has thrived in Washington and is embraced warmly by both reporters and their sources. Reporters have the opportunity, they feel, to get closer to real information than any other method permits, information that is not easily available otherwise. Julius Frandsen, the UPI bureau chief in Washington, once said, "A lot of skulduggery in government and in Congress would never come to light if everything had to be attributed. Employees often can't afford to risk their jobs by talking for attribution."

Those engaged in interpretive writing like backgrounders even more than those who expose skulduggery. Official views, even in a quasi-official and nonattributable setting, are the heart of much interpretive comment today.

Backgrounders, as the *Wall Street Journal*'s Al Otten once warned, present "constant pitfalls for the reporter. He has little time to check the facts independently and frequently can't alert his readers to the source's bias or motivation. Thus, he may find himself being used or may be left out on a limb if a story goes sour; the reporter himself may appear to have misled or misinformed the public."

Many of these pitfalls are the result of group briefings and professional competition. When a backgrounder is held for a number of reporters they face all the pitfalls that Otten foresees, since they must respond quickly or it will appear elsewhere, in print or on the air, before they can use the information. While Otten sees the backgrounder as "probably the most important thing we have going for us" in interpretive reporting, he recognizes that when there are twenty or thirty reporters at a mass background briefing, "each reporter knows that sitting across the room is his competitor from the other paper in his city, and he knows he's going to run out and get the story in the next edition, so each reporter runs out to do the same without taking the time to check the story."

A private session between a single reporter or two and a government official under any of the backgrounder rules can be very productive. There is time for the reporter to check his information, to chase down leads, and most important of all—to question the information he has received. In a group setting there is little time for anything other than getting the story out before the other fellow scoops you.

Among Washington news chiefs who have been most disturbed by the abuses of backgrounders over the years was Benjamin Bradlee, then managing editor of the *Washington Post*. In 1967, after consultation with his own people and some on the *New York Times,* Bradlee proposed guidelines for the *Post*. Its reporters were to "fight like hell: to get everything on the record and failing that, insist that the minimum attribution must be to the agency involved. The published story should say why it is background news. Finally, said Bradlee, a reporter is free on his discretion to leave a background session (A few days later, *Post* reporter Eric Wentworth did just that when Secretary of Agriculture Freeman refused to go on the record).

Days after the guidelines were issued, a White House backgrounder on the Common Market was interrupted by *Post* reporter Carroll Kilpatrick's insistence that there be an explanation as to why it was for "background only." Max Frankel of the *Times* then said, "I'm sorry but if you're going to give me information on that basis, I'm authorized by my editors to say that the White House has no comment on this." The White House backed down, the briefing was put on the record.

Unfortunately the opposition to backgrounders in 1967 was short-lived. The *Post* and the *Times* did not make a habit of such protests. They slid back into traditional acceptance of background ground rules. Bradlee, who once said "Ninety percent of the information given by background could be on the record," continued to attack the "system" but his paper continued to be a party to it.

Reaching agreement among reporters to fight the background system is nearly impossible. When a number of newsmen, in November of 1970, protested a backgrounder with Assistant Attorney General Jerris Leonard, then the civil rights chief at Justice, they walked out rather than accept his remarks on an off-the-record basis. It was Leonard's first appearance before the press in months and they felt he should not hide behind a cloak of nonattribution. He held his briefing for those reporters who did not walk out.

The temptation to stay, to participate in the nonattribution game is great. It is an easy way to get "news," a rare opportunity to be close to important sources, and a chance to probe top officials when they are, in theory, a little more relaxed, a little looser. The hot breath of competition hangs over the proceedings, however. The result is inevitably what Bill Moyers, a press secretary under Lyndon Johnson and later an editor, called "delayed-action Greek chorus." That, he adds, is just what the public officials want— "Anonymity is fearless, and if a public official wants to do so and can find a journalist willing to cooperate, he can hide behind that anonymity to grind an axe or to float a balloon."

Moyers, who confesses that his criticism of backgrounders "may appear hypocritical, coming as it does from someone who made his living by 'backgrounding' the press," has proposed a number of steps to improve the system. The first is simply to limit all backgrounders to explaining rather than announcing policy thus keeping them in the area of "soft" rather than "hard news." He would restrict them largely to matters of national security and foreign policy. He would put a one-hour embargo on reporting the contents of a "backgrounder" to permit at least limited cross-checking of the facts. He would tie the source closer to his agency —instead of attributing content to a "high U.S. Official," it would be a "State Department spokesman" or a "Defense Department source"—and would add "whose name is withheld at his insistence."

The problem is twofold, however. The source—not the reporter —usually sets the terms for backgrounders. He is not likely to prefer soft to hard news, foreign to domestic policy, delayed reporting to immediate acceptance, or close proximity to a more vague identification. The other part of the problem is that, while such guidelines help legitimize the use of backgrounders, they fail to identify the source to the public, the backgrounder remains open to inside Washington and closed to the public at large. As Senator Robert Kennedy observed, it has the unfortunate consequence of making it difficult for "an informed reader to make his own evaluation of the reliability, authority, and special interests of the official spokesman, forcing a reader to discount the news altogether or to accept it on faith."

McGeorge Bundy, a top adviser to Lyndon Johnson, complained that when he left office, he had trouble reading the morning news. In office, he knew who was briefing whom on what. Now away from the White House, he said he needed more help and was getting less. As Bundy once told editors, the rules are for the press and the public official and "the public very seldom knows what is going on."

There are times when anonymity is defensible. As Frandsen of UPI has noted, lower level officials with their jobs in jeopardy are unlikely to talk unless protected. Highly sensitive material is often available no other way though it has been noted that participants in what Bundy has called "the greatest guessing game on earth" usually are adroit at spotting the source of a backgrounder. Sometimes a reporter can be pointed in the right direction only on an off-the-record basis.

Backgrounders are far less defensible when they extend to large groups, however. Otten of the *Wall Street Journal* says the backgrounder is "a perfectly legitimate device" when used on an individual basis, but "the mass backgrounder, which is the device most subject to abuse and to manipulation by the government, is the one that comes earliest for the lazy reporter. . . . He just has to wander down to sit and listen for an hour."

Many distinguished reporters in Washington would take issue with this. They find mass backgrounders useful and practical. After all, how could a secretary of state find time to background every reporter individually? How could a secretary of defense deal with intimate matters, confidential matters of our national defenses except on a background basis? Reporters are reluctant to give up their membership in the intimate breakfast and luncheon groups which hold frequent background sessions—there is prestige as well as intimacy to membership. It is, they argue, a good chance to measure the man "close up."

The arguments illustrate the appeal and thus the popularity of mass backgrounders but they are less persuasive in terms of actual results. Public officials using the device can manipuate the news in the way they desire at the time they desire. The reporter arrives with a blank notebook but the official arrives with a set objective—a story he wants to push. While questioning may make his task more difficult than simply handing out a printed statement, it rarely trips up an experienced briefer. The advantage is his, the accomplice is the reporter, and the unwitting gull is the public.

More forthright than the backgrounder is, of course, the open, one-the-record news conference. Examination of that device, however, shows that it too can be a weapon in the artillery of news manipulation.

News conferences, on the surface, seem the opportunity to really grill a public official out in the glare of the public spotlight. Actually, the conference is called at the official's convenience to serve his purpose. Its timing has special significance to him; reporters don't call the news conference. Its opening announcements, which sometimes set the direction of much of the content, are his. Its pattern results from his handling of questions and cutting off of other questions. Its choice of questioners are his and the experienced official knows how to find a friendly questioner, a reporter given to soft or irrelevant inquiry.

In other words, far from being the ordeal that some paint it, the news conference is an opportunity for the official to make the news. He holds most of the cards.

To begin with, even before a news conference, the official has a great opportunity to prepare. A president, for example, will call upon advisors in every major branch of government to funnel in ideas of what might be asked and how the questions might be answered. Under Kennedy, Press Secretary Salinger would hold a conference in his office with the major press information officers of government, each producing the "hot issues of his department" until there was a list of about one hundred potential questions. On the morning of the news conference, the president would breakfast with Salinger, the vice-president, the secretaries of state and defense, and several top White House advisors. They would go through the one hundred questions quickly, the president noting those which called for more information than he had at his finger tips. This was provided and a review would take place just before the news conference.

Presidents not only have the vast resources of government to help them prepare for any question, they also have the opportunity to "plant" certain questions they want asked. Salinger used to call in favorite reporters and say that if a certain question were asked, "you will receive a most interesting answer." The question was always asked. Salinger defended the practice by noting that a president often comes prepared to answer a question of major significance and reporters who "don't do as much homework for the press conference as the president" aren't always prepared to ask that question. Salinger made sure it was asked.

Throughout the Johnson administration, the practice of the planted question continued—a syndicated column noting that one news conference had so many planted questions it "was very nearly as carefully staged as a Broadway play." On television, Paul Niven once asked Bill Moyers about this and was told, "You never can tell what's going to happen in one of these press conferences, and I wanted to be certain that the questions that the president did have on his mind, and for which he was prepared to deal in a substantive way, did get asked. Any number of questions could have come up which would not have given him this chance to make a statement that was newsworthy, and I felt it justified simply to provide insurance against someone not getting to what that day was very much on the president's mind."

When interviewer Niven pressed and asked Moyers why there had to be any planted questions at all, he received a pretty good description of how the news conference is viewed from the other side, the president's side. Said the press secretary, "It is the prerogative of the president to decide how he's going to make himself available to the press and how and when he makes certain information known to the press. It's to serve the convenience of the president, not the convenience of the press that presidential press conferences are held. There is no right—I mean the president has no statutory obligation to hold press conferences. His job is to make information known to the public. The press conference is a convenient device for doing that—for achieving that purpose. But there is no law, and in fact there's no inherent procedure that says he must do it in this way or that way. There's no law."

As Herb Klein, President Nixon's director of communications puts it—"The conference is the president's: this is undisputed."

Reporters would not agree. While the president, as Klein notes, chooses "when to hold it and in what form," it remains one of the few chances for interrogation of the chief executive in public forum. It is sometimes mistakenly compared with the question hour in the British Parliament where the opposition interrogates and debates a prime minister. It is not that. It is much more polite, far less argumentative, and represents not political opposition but reportorial inquiry.

Many White House reporters are unhappy with the pattern of news conferences. Not enough follow-up questions when the president gives insufficient answers, not enough tough questions and, they feel, not enough news conferences *per se*. After Richard Nixon announced one in December of 1970, a group of twenty-eight White House reporters met in the Hotel Washington to discuss the waning quality and number of news conferences. Nixon had gone nineteen weeks without a formal news conference, had held only eight in his first year of office, and this was to be only the fourth in 1970. The meeting primarily called for more follow-up questions and tougher questioning. The White House was then informed of the meeting, as reporters attending did not want to give the appearance of a conspiracy or news management in reverse.

Mr. Nixon came to his December 10 news conference prepared for tough questioning and aware of the committee of twenty-eight. For several days he had studied the two black, loose-leaf notebooks prepared by staff for this news conference. As one aide privately said with pride later, every question asked had been anticipated by material in those books. When Herbert Kaplow of NBC asked about news conferences as such, the president said formal sessions with the press were just one method of presidential communication to the public and perhaps others would be tried, perhaps more nontelevised conferences in his office, perhaps different kinds of approaches to television.

In the months that followed, the president did try different approaches—he gave exclusive interviews to Cyrus Sulzberger of the *New York Times,* columnist Victor Lasky, UPI's Helen Thomas, and Barbara Walters of NBC. He was interviewed on television by correspondents from the three commercial networks and public television. He called in nine, largely sympathetic and conservative, columnists. He held a briefing on "personal" matters with nine women writers (a mistake perhaps as the uninvited women reporters who cover the East Side, the family side, of the

White House marched on Press Secretary Ziegler with a fury never seen before in the press office). Nixon appeared before the April, 1971 convention of ASNE and took questions from four of its editor-members and two White House correspondents. He held a one-hour television conversation with Howard K. Smith. The following January he did the same with Dan Rather of CBS.

In terms of regular, formal news conferences however, President Nixon held comparatively few, far less than the average of any other modern president going back to Hoover. In 1972 the Washington News Committee of the Associated Press Managing Editors' Association angrily reported that "President Nixon has come close to killing off the presidential press conferences as a public institution during his term of office." The APME Committee noted that he held only nine news conferences in the entire previous year. FDR, Ike, Kennedy, Johnson—all held more. Johnson regretted publicly, on leaving office, that he had not conducted still more televised, formal news conferences. In retrospect, he said, while he much preferred the "more comfortable meeting with reporters around my desk," he recognized the formal news conference as one that "should be widely used by national leaders."

While the president has the advantages of the place and time of such sessions, the chance to prepare carefully with the knowledge that his staff can anticipate almost every question and can plant any he really wants, the news conference still retains enough spontaneity that it can serve public and press well. George Reedy, an ex-press secretary, noted in the *New York Times* that it is "the only occasion in which a President has an opportunity for brushing up against reality with some regularity. There is no group except the press that will confront him on a face-to-face basis with open skepticism." He suggests that it makes a president uncomfortable perhaps but it is good for a president as well as public and press. It is the rare opportunity to escape the sycophants who inevitably surround men of tremendous power.

The White House correspondents who met over crullers and coffee in the Hotel Washington failed to markedly change the news conference that followed in December, 1970 but their colleagues joined them in increasing concern over the pattern of news conference questioning. The head of the White House Correspondents Association wrote the president, suggesting ways to improve news conferences. A meeting of representatives of seven major journalistic organizations was held at the White House with Klein and Ronald Ziegler and it was discussed there. There was general agreement that one basic need was more follow-up questions.

On June 2, 1971 there was an unusual display of how effective follow-up questions could be. There occurred a rare pattern of reportorial insistence that the president fully answer a question. The original question, posed by Herbert Kaplow of NBC dealt with the mass arrests following the so-called Mayday anti-Vietnam demonstrations in Washington, demonstrations designed to "shut down the Federal Government." Did the president think the police handled it properly since charges against over two thousand of those arrested were dropped for lack of evidence? The president replied that he recognized the right to protest peacefully but this demonstration included vandals, hoodlums, and lawbreakers and that they would not be permitted to stop the government from operating.

Forrest Boyd of Mutual followed up by asking if keeping the government running warranted suspending constitutional rights. The president called this an exaggeration and praised the police for showing a great deal more concern for the demonstrators' rights than the demonstrators showed for the rights of residents of Washington.

Jerry terHorst of the *Detroit News* popped up and asked, "If that is true, then why are the courts releasing so many of the cases?" The president, uncomfortable, said, "The arrest does not mean that an individual is guilty. The whole constitutional system is one that provides that after an arrest an individual has an opportunity for a trial."

Jim Deakin of the *St. Louis Post-Dispatch* then said, "But they're not being released on the ground that they (are guilty). . . . they're being released on the grounds that they weren't properly arrested." The president retreated into another defense of police handling of "a very difficult crisis" and said he approved of what they did and hoped other cities would do as well "so that we do not have to resort to violence."

The next question changed the subject but on June 1, 1971, for the first time since televised news conferences began and for one of the few times ever, a president had been subjected to a series of related, pertinent questions. The follow-up pattern was most impressive. It produced a fuller picture of the president's views on one subject, uncomfortable as that might have been to him, than had any other similar questions in any previous news conferences.

If Mr. Nixon or his successors are troubled by aggressive questioning, they might have considered the words of Harry Truman at his very last news conference: "This kind of news conference where reporters can ask any question they can dream up—directly of the president of the United States—illustrates how strong and how vital our democracy is. There is no other country in the world where the chief of state submits to such unlimited questioning; I know, too, from experience that it is not easy to stand up here and try to answer off-the-cuff and all kinds of questions without any advance notice.

"Perhaps succeeding presidents will be able to figure out improvements and safeguards in the procedure. I hope they will never cut out the direct line of communication between themselves and the people."

Below the presidential level, of course, many news conferences are held by Cabinet members, agency heads, and others. An administration can control the flow of these and use them to help orchestrate its press relations. It also can stop such conferences when it finds them troublesome. This is exactly what happened during the Nixon administration when some career people in the Labor Department became a problem.

For years, when consumer-price index and employment figures were issued each month, a press briefing was held by professionals at the Bureau of Labor Statistics to explain the reports. For years, that is, until an upturn in unemployment was termed significant by the secretary of labor and statistically insignificant by the BLS. It happened at a period of rising unemployment which concerned the Nixon administration and a period when economic writers and even television cameras were giving extensive play to the usually dry bureau experts.

The administration ordered the BLS briefings stopped, the monthly material was to be handed out on paper without accompanying news conferences. Herb Klein speaking for the administration said too many people were interpreting the statistics, that job "basically is the task of the secretary of labor."

Politics, however, permits the opposition to counter some news management methods. Democrat William Proxmire, senator from Wisconsin and chairman of the Joint Economic Committee, found a simple way to veto the "muzzling" of the Bureau of Labor Statistics. The same men who gave BLS briefings were now called before Proxmire's committee when new statistics came out and were questioned by Proxmire and others to give their interpretation—as cameras rolled and reporters took notes.

It should be noted that Congress, generally, is perhaps the reporter's most powerful ally in combating White House news management. Congressmen hear a lot—an administration must keep Congress clued in on what's happening—and congressmen talk a lot. The Congress, as reporters have noted, is "the leakiest ship in town." Frequently the stories that can't be dragged out of Defense or State or the White House are leaked out by congressmen who know.

Political partisans thus are able to control some news at the source but, if congressmen are informed, have little control over other news. In another area, if they see a story coming, they can attempt to pressure news organizations to mold the news as they would have it. Here congressional friends will join an administration or *vice-versa* in news management.

One example of overt, heavy-handed and somewhat ominous pressure was directed against the CBS News broadcast "Face the Nation" in May of 1970 when it scheduled two youth leaders— Charles Palmer, president of the National Student Association, and Toby Moffett, who had just resigned as head of the Office of Youth and Student Affairs for the Commissioner of Education. Moffett, in particular, rankled the administration for his resignation was a sign of division between it and young people.

In quick order, the producers of "Face the Nation" received a call from an aide to Herb Klein suggesting that CBS add a third guest to their list, the president of the very conservative Young Americans for Freedom, to give "balance" to the broadcast. Individual broadcasts of Sunday interview programs are not required to be balanced (they are exempt from equal time legislation, for example) and it was noted that just the previous Sunday, Vice-

President Agnew had been on "Face the Nation." A similar request for the YAF president to join Palmer and Moffett came by telephone from a conservative publicist, prominent in GOP circles.

Another Republican publicist, who represented several conservative senators, called to warn that Republican Chairman Robert Dole was going to attack the choice of guests. A member of the staff of the Republican National Committee called and argued for fifteen minutes that the producers must add a conservative youth leader for balance. Meanwhile, a staff member of the Department of Health, Education and Welfare called to suggest that Moffett was a very low level employee in the Department of Education, had nothing to do with policy, and was certainly no spokesman. On the other hand, Moffett's boss, the commissioner of education, commended him highly at the time, said he was "sorry to see him go," and felt that they were losing an important link to "the concerns that are deeply troubling young people today." In time, the commissioner would speak critically of the Vietnam War and would himself be leaving the Nixon administration.

From Senator Dole, finally, came a strong telegram charging that CBS "has apparently set out to inflame passions and further polarize our nation." It demanded that the network clearly point out that Moffett was "a very junior civil servant, a Democrat and a holdover from the Johnson administration." Dole concluded, "Most viewers are aware of the strong antiadministration bias on CBS programs, but should CBS go this far in efforts to polarize America's youth and discredit President Nixon?"

Producers Prentiss Childs and Sylvia Westerman did not collapse under the pressures of the recurring calls and the Dole telegram. Palmer and Moffett appeared. The administration was not brought to a standstill nor did the nation's youth rise as one and march on Washington. It was a fairly ordinary broadcast which attracted ordinary attention from its audience despite the extraordinary attention from angry administration supporters who feared what they saw coming.

Political figures can't resist trying to influence a story when they know it is coming. Fortunately, in the nature of news, they rarely have that advantage; they usually know about the story after it is published or broadcast. In 1963, then-Attorney General Robert

F. Kennedy learned from a Justice Department staffer in Nashville that the *Nashville Banner* was about to do a story relating to the Tennessee trial of Jimmy Hoffa, the Teamsters Union chief. Kennedy personally called Publisher James G. Stahlman to note that such a story might cause a mistrial. The administration defended the action as simply an attempt to avoid prejudicing a very important trial. V. M. Newton, Jr., chairman of the Sigma Delta Chi Freedom of Information Committee, damned it as an "improper move" carrying with it all the power of the U.S. Attorney's office and the administration. He said that the press cannot concede the right of the executive branch to intervene in news coverage even though, in this case, the executive sought to persuade a publisher not to print and failed.

It is comparatively rare that political moves to stop stories become general knowledge. There is no way of knowing how often such pressures are exerted and succeed. The successes are not publicized; it is a silent censorship. Those are the times when the journalists are quiet about "the people's right to know." Those are the times when the public needs freedom from the press more than freedom of the press.

Sometimes concessions to politicians involve little things but they can accumulate into a record of acquiescence to the news molding by political image makers. In all modern administrations, for example, the image makers have control over a simple, little thing—the placement of cameramen at public events. Generally this is meaningless, but there is no question that they place photographers where they think the results will favor their man.

Lyndon Johnson, for example, was convinced that his left profile was better than his right profile and photographers were assigned angles accordingly. Once a camera stand was moved to accommodate this problem and blocked out much of the president's audience to preserve the proper profile. On May 21, 1967, the Washington *Sunday Star* merrily recounted how a press assistant ordered cameramen over from the "wrong side" of the hall before a presidential appearance. The newspaper published a picture of the president's right profile and entitled it "The Wrong Lyndon."

Modern presidents engage in another form of photographic management. They have their own staff photographers who not only take the expected photos of the president handshaking White House guests, to be inscribed later and sent out to the flattered visitor, but also take candid photos of the president in action. Dozens, hundreds of these are carefully studied by staff members, and even the president himself on occasion, and then handed out to the press. It is to their eternal shame that many publications fail to identify the source of these photos which, of course, are generally dramatic and impressive views of the president. In July, 1966 for example, a series of very dramatic candids of President Johnson during an airline strike crisis were taken by his personal photographer, Hoichi Okamoto, and published in newspapers and news magazines with no identification of their source. Needless to say, a poor picture of a president is never released by the White House.

So-called sweetheart deals are made with publishers and private photographers, permitting them to have exclusive access to the president at various times in return for a White House veto on which pictures are made public. Poor pictures of the president are never released outside the White House either. Only occasional candid shots in public can ever go contrary to White House wishes.

Planting flattering pictures in the press is a run of the mill contrivance. In the lexicon of news management, it is not a very daring device. Ranking high, however, in an inventory is that most blatant expedient: the outright lie.

Governments don't get caught lying often but often enough to make a press and the public wonder how much of it goes on. The nature of the governmental surrounding is such, especially in sensitive areas, that it is easy to float the lie. Jefferson once warned that "he who permits himself to tell a lie once, finds it much easier to do it a second and third time, till at length it becomes habitual; he tells lies without attending to it, and truths without the world's believing him." And so it can be with governments that lie.

Governments engage in falsehood with the knowledge that they can cover up when false seams in the fabric show through. They can always deny part or all of a story; they can amend it or turn it away with other facts. A government can keep from being caught. It can. Most of the time.

One of the few times that all the devices known to a government to patch up or cover up failed came during the Eisenhower administration. On May 1, 1960 the Soviets shot down an American spy plane, a Lockheed U-2 high altitude jet used for photographic reconnaissance.

Spy planes have the ability of self-destruction and their pilots the instructions to do just that. When that U-2 didn't return, the U.S government assumed it was destroyed and simply said a plane on a weather flight had gone down. As the president's press secretary James Hagerty was later to note, "If there was any mistake in the U-2 affair, it was that we moved too fast on our cover story. The pilot of that plane, with a simple movement of his hand or even finger, could have pushed a button and would have ceased to exist. We thought at first the Russians were bluffing and that the plane and the pilot were just dust in the air."

The first U.S. comment on the missing U-2 came not from Defense or State or the White House. It came from NASA, the National Aeronautics and Space Administration. The plane, claimed NASA, was missing on a "meteorological observation flight" over Turkey, and probably went down due to mechanical failure. It was conceivable, continued the lie from NASA, that the pilot had blacked out from lack of oxygen and had drifted on into Russia. The State Department added a footnote: "There was no deliberate attempt to violate Soviet airspace, and never had been."

Unfortunately for the deceivers in Washington, the Soviets had the plane, had the pilot. As late as May 6, State was still denying spy flights. On May 7, Nikita Khrushchev told the Supreme Soviet that the pilot, Francis Gary Powers, was alive and had fully confessed flying a spy plane. A few hours later, a lame comment came from State saying "an unarmed civilian U-2 plane" had "probably" made such a flight over the Soviet Union.

President Eisenhower had once noted that "in the diplomatic field it was routine practice to deny responsibility for an embarrassing occurrence when there is even one percent chance of being believed, but when the world can entertain not the slightest doubt of the facts there is no point in trying to evade the issue."

Eisenhower did not in this case. He took full responsibility for the spy flights (doubly embarrassing since he told a news conference one year earlier that he personally had prohibited any provocative flights over the Soviet Union). It was an unprecedented admission of espionage activity by a head of state. Walter Lippmann said that while he had a vested journalistic prejudice against official deception, he still felt "the head of a great state must always disown his spies. If he does not do that, it makes it impossibly difficult for his adversaries, who also use spies, to shrug off the incident."

Eisenhower was heading for Paris and a Summit Conference with Khrushchev. There were published reports that the U-2 flights were suspended but Hagerty denied this strongly on the eve of the president's departure. Three days later, however, the president told the Soviet premier that the flights were indeed suspended and were not to be resumed.

Khrushchev used the U-2 as a means to denounce Eisenhower and the United States, putting an end to any hopes of a successful summit conference. Later that year, he appeared before the United Nations with similar denunciations of the United States. He said any summit negotiations would have to wait for Eisenhower to leave office and it was the following New Year, after Kennedy's election, before Khrushchev declared that the USSR was dropping its complaint against the United States over the U-2 matter.

As for Eisenhower, he later said, "The big error we made was, of course, in the issuance of a premature and erroneous cover story. Allowing myself to be persuaded on this score is my principal regret—except for the U-2 failure itself—regarding the whole affair." Ike also talked of "falsehood and hypocrisy, which would be promptly exposed by a free press." That, it should be noted, after the falsehood was exposed.

Public officials rarely have to deal with the U-2 kind of lie. More often they do a little dance around the truth to mislead reporters, what Wilson's adviser Colonel Edward M. House used to call "grazing the truth." As a reporter of that day noted about President Wilson, "He took such an intellectual pleasure in stating a thing so as to give an opposite impression to fact, though he kept strictly to the truth, that one had to be constantly on the alert to keep from being misled." The distance between misleading and outright prevarication is a short distance, however. Furthermore, according to some historians, and Colonel House himself, Wilson considered lying itself justified and practiced it when sensitive matters of state were involved.

Half a century later, presidents were still "grazing the truth." Lyndon Johnson, for example, complained that a Washington newspaper was in error when it reported he would ask for a three percent pay increase for government workers in 1964. A short time later he did just that. In early 1966, the White House denied a story that it was asking for a $4 billion cut in the excise tax. A few months later, the president asked Congress to cut excise taxes by $3.964 billion.

One White House press aide in that administration, Robert Fleming, told a student audience that the government was opposed to lying but that "hiding the full truth is sometimes in the interest of national policy." At about the same time, the United States denied that an American guard at the Guantanamo Naval Base had shot a Cuban infiltrator. Some days later, the Pentagon confessed that this had in fact happened. Also at about the same time, the United States denied China's charge that Americans had shot down a Communist plane over China, insisting that it had gone down over North Vietnam. Days later a State Department spokesman, confronted with reports to the contrary, implied that the Chinese claim was true. In both cases, the U.S. public learned about it first from Communist sources and, as the *Los Angeles Times* noted, "When the American government did speak up, its initial response was what the charitable might call misinformation."

In August, 1965 Singapore's Prime Minister Lee Kuan Yew claimed a CIA agent had offered him a $3.3 million bribe five years earlier. The State Department strongly denied the story. Lee then produced a letter sent to him by a secretary of state apologizing for the incident. Now the State Department admitted it. The denial, it said, was "a bureaucratic error," a denial made by a man who hadn't known all the facts.

Earlier in 1965, President Johnson made a conciliatory speech on the war at Johns Hopkins University in Baltimore. He tried to convince his old friend Walter Lippmann that the Vietnam effort was going in another direction. Wrote Lippmann, "The day before making his Baltimore speech, Johnson told me that he agreed with me that the war had to be won on the nonmilitary side. But a short time later, I found that he was telling other people other things. He was either lying to me or to the others. I resolved at that point never to go back to the White House again. I have not been there since."

Each administration had its collection of lies to the press. Under Nixon, it was said that all U.S. ground troops would be removed from Cambodia after the original thrust. CBS Correspondent Don Webster sent back film of embarrassed U.S. troops —dressed as civilians—at the Phnom Phen airport long after the order to be out had been issued.

When the Pentagon sent in a dramatic, though unsuccessful, team to try to rescue prisoners of war at the Son Tay prison in North Vietnam, it denied that it had engaged in any bombing raids to distract the enemy. Later it admitted the raids.

After approving a deep raid into Laos by ground forces, Defense Secretary Melvin Laird attended a press briefing by a lieutenant general espousing the importance of cutting across the enemy's supply lines through Laos. The general produced a piece of pipe to indicate that they had cut a gasoline pipeline, itself an indication of how settled-in the enemy was in Laos. Unfortunately, as the press revealed later, the famous piece of pipe had not been captured by the invading troops at all—it actually had been brought out of Laos the previous year.

Perhaps the most famous "flap" over lies in government came in the Kennedy administration when Arthur Sylvester went forth to defend the right to lie. Sylvester, the assistant secretary of state for public affairs, was speaking in the wake of the Cuban Missile Crisis.

There had been a series of deceptions beginning with President Kennedy's cover story that a cold had caused him to break off campaigning in Chicago when in reality he was hurrying back to make the decision to order the naval blockade around Cuba. Newsmen were misled before, during, and even after the crisis. David Kraslow told how false information from Pentagon news officers resulted in his and other newspapers being "suckered by a lie." Both State and Defense led reporters astray before the president's revelation that the Soviets had placed missiles on the island of Cuba and both distorted numerous reports during the crisis.

When the crisis ended, Sylvester issued a statement in which he said that "News generated by actions of the government, as to content and timing, are a part of the arsenal of weaponry that a president has" in dealing with crisis. He added, "In the kind of world we live in, the generation of news by actions taken by the government becomes one weapon in a strained situation. The results in my opinion, justify the methods we used."

Secretary Sylvester said it a little blunter when he appeared before the New York chapter of *Sigma Delta Chi* on December 6, 1962. He declared "It would seem to me, basic, all through history . . . that it's inherent in the government's right, if necessary to lie to save itself when it's going up into a nuclear war. This seems to me basic."

It was also candid and, to journalists, infuriating. There was a flood of angry comment from newsmen and from editorial pages. Senators wanted to quiz Sylvester about it and friends advised him to find a hundred ways to avoid using the word "lie"; if he meant to say "lie down," he should use the word "recline." The secretary was asked by congressional committees and he said he never said "right to lie." Unfortunately, officers of that *Sigma Delta Chi* chapter reported that ABC had made a tape recording of it and they produced a transcript. Sylvester continued through his remaining years in office and later to deny the "right to lie" assertion.

If Sylvester was too blunt and too candid, it must be reported he also was courageous. President Kennedy himself asked that a letter be drafted for Sylvester to sign, a letter which apologized for the choice of words which "should have been more carefully phrased and considered." Sylvester refused. He would sign nothing to appease his accusers. The president was said to admire this "show of spunk" and withdrew the suggestion. Sylvester remained to serve seven years in office, the longest any man has held that post.

The impact of his remarks, however, remains long after their author departed his position of power. The "right to lie" statement was the embodiment of government's private thinking. The pious proclamation that government tells the truth is always issued but the private conviction is that the means justifies the end. J. Russell Wiggins, when editor of the *Washington Post,* was to observe that "a government that too readily rationalizes its right to lie in a crisis will never lack for either lies or crises."

Arthur Sylvester's contribution to news management was not limited to his observations on generating news as part of the "arsenal of weaponry." He was also father of a Pentagon directive dated October 27, 1962 that forbade anyone in the Pentagon from talking to newsmen in person or on the phone unless the substance of that conversation were reported to the public information office by day's end. The alternative to such a report was simply to invite a public information officer to sit in and monitor the interview as it took place.

Secretary McNamara, approving of the directive, said it was simply to make information available in "an expeditious and equitable manner." Veteran reporters at the Pentagon called it a "Gestapo tactic."

A similar directive was issued at the State Department but the protest from reporters and staff was such that it was withdrawn within a month. Pierre Salinger at the White House insisted that there was no such policy there and he had personally removed a similar restriction imposed by the previous administration, one that had all White House staff people clear with the press office before granting interviews to newsmen. The White House, however, made no move to compel Sylvester or McNamara to change the directive at Defense.

It was in 1967, after the retirement of Sylvester, that his successor Phil Goulding announced that Secretary McNamara was rescinding the order that interviews be monitored or reported. "Over the past six years a number of steps have been taken to increase the flow of unbiased information," proclaimed McNamara, "The memorandum of October 27, 1962 is no longer necessary." A year later, reporters there were to note that even with the absence of the directive, cautious Pentagon officers would still invite a monitor to be present when they granted interviews.

In the Nixon administration, the Office of International Security Affairs in the Pentagon revived the practice of monitoring conversations with newsmen. When reporters asked for a copy of ISA's monitoring rules, they were told that it was an internal matter.

The Pentagon remained one of the toughest areas for reporters to operate in freely. No outpost of government, not even the White House itself, could so easily and did so readily invoke "national security" to help mold the news. The interservice rivalry, much cursed by civilian secretaries, certain congressmen, and many editorial writers was one of the few ways to crack the military lines surrounding news. Advocates of competing views would often provide reporters with their freest glimpses at what makes the monster military machine operate. McNamara called it "parochial salesmanship," but for reporters, it opened the door just a little bit more.

The military headquarters kept a close eye on reporters. A number of newsmen reported that telephones were tapped including their own phones in the press room. Defense denied this. Security agents have conducted investigations of news reports to find the source of leaks. Reporters have been called in for questioning by FBI agents or Pentagon investigators. Such interrogation is rare, always low key and friendly, the security people not prying very deeply. With Pentagon personnel, they can be tougher and lie-detector tests are threatened or used.

Even a reporter's desk at the Pentagon is not sacrosanct. Occasionally he will find a small, yellow card reading "No violations of security regulations were detected during a security inspection of this office." It is signed "Pentagon Counterintelligence Force."

The Defense establishment professes innocence and insists that it simply takes prudent measures to assure security of the nation's military secrets. Its dealings with the news media are not to manage the news but to provide information to the American people. Did not Secretary McNamara issue a directive in 1967 stating flatly that "news management and meddling with the news will not be tolerated"?

The Pentagon not only manages and meddles with its vast public relations empire but it also can, and occasionally does, seek to discredit stories it does not like. A most glaring example of this occurred in the spring of 1970 when the Pentagon and the White House combined in what Walter Cronkite called an "undercover campaign" to discredit CBS News because of a report, on

November 3, 1969 by Correspondent Don Webster. The story
from Vietnam dealt with the treatment of prisoners by South
Vietnam soldiers and the film reached a climax with the stabbing
of one prisoner.

The Pentagon asked CBS to provide the name of its cameraman
and all outtakes (film shot but not used in the story as aired).
CBS News refused, noted that it was contrary to its policy to turn
over outtakes, and stated that the cameraman, a Vietnamese national, feared for his life if his name were known.

Subsequently there were those in the military in Vietnam and
in the Pentagon who spread rumors that the news story was
staged. They claimed that some of the footage was from a training
exercise not a battle, that American observers were not present,
that the helicopters shown were Australian not American, and
that the Vietnamese sergeant had stabbed a dead body (implying
that the incident was staged for the TV cameras). Clark Mollenhoff, special counsel to the president, went to the Pentagon and
received a full briefing on these allegations which he subsequently
put in a memorandum.

In April, the *Des Moines Register and Tribune,* Mollenhoff's
former employer, published stories about the Pentagon's questioning of the CBS report. Richard Wilson, Washington bureau
chief for the newspaper, repeated them in his syndicated column
which is carried in sixty newspapers. He also wrote of White
House interest in the matter.

CBS News determined that Mollenhoff's information was being
shared by others. He admitted talking to reporters about the
matter. Jack Anderson repeated the charges in his column which
reaches 620 newspapers.

On May 21, in a most unusual newscast, Cronkite cited this
past history and then offered a point-by-point rebuttal of the allegations. He noted that atrocities occur from time to time, on
both sides, in any war but "for reasons not entirely clear, the
White House has engaged in an undercover campaign to discredit
CBS News by alleging the story was faked." With Correspondent
Don Webster narrating, the rebuttal was shown. The battle scenes
were replayed to show they were real, not a training exercise.
With stop-frame technique the helicopters were clearly shown to
be not Australian but of the U.S. 187th Assault Helicopter Squad-

don. The American observer's shoulder patch—when the film was stopped—was clearly First Air Cavalry.

Then an interview with the Vietnamese sergeant—Nguyen Van Mot—was included. Mot said he thought his prisoner was reaching for a rifle in the grass and so he stabbed him; he said he had personally killed thirty-nine enemy soldiers. Mot, it was revealed, was named Soldier of the Year for the entire III Corps regional forces in 1969. Concluded Webster, "The Pentagon may wish to believe this story never happened. But it did."

White House Press Secretary Ronald Ziegler announced publicly that there was no campaign to discredit CBS News. Defense Secretary Laird was quoted as saying he in no way challenged the integrity of CBS News.

A short while later, Mollenhoff resigned from the White House staff. He noted that Richard Wilson was stepping down as bureau chief of the Des Moines newspaper and this presented him with an opportunity to fulfill a long-held ambition to succeed to that position.

Cronkite, in his lengthy rebuttal to the allegations, ended his report with this observation: "We broadcast the original story in the belief it told something about the nature of the war in Vietnam. What has happened since then tells something about the government and its relations with news media which carry stories the government finds disagreeable."

Relations between Pentagon and the press reached new lows during the 1971 invasion of Laos. In the past, military commanders had placed brief embargoes on news to keep the enemy from knowing about maneuvers but in the case of South Vietnamese troops going into Laos, the lid on news was extreme. An embargo on any news of any kind was imposed, one which lasted six days. Further, there was an embargo on the embargo—reporters were not even to tell that they were forbidden to tell.

Unable to report or to report the blackout on reporting, news executives protested strongly but vainly. They were compelled to publish stories emanating from third countries, many of them unfriendly towards the United States. The maneuvers inside Laos were supported by the United States but conducted by South Vietnamese forces, and news reporters were told that access to the battle area depended on the latter. The South Vietnamese had no enthusiasm for cooperation. Truck drivers, under orders, refused rides to newsmen, shouting "No Bao Chi, No Bao Chi (no journalists, no journalists)". An NBC cameraman somehow got on a U.S. helicopter ferrying South Vietnamese rangers into Laos only to have one of them snatch away his movie camera and throw it out the door.

Herbert Klein, the president's chief of communications, came to the defense of the military, saying embargoes had been imposed before and this one was essential to protect troop movements. As for the complaint that foreign sources were reporting the story while Americans were in the dark (ironically the story was being carried in Saigon papers but could not be sent out of country by Americans), Klein said if one examined the foreign reports, he would find they were largely speculation, "a fishing expedition" by foreign newsmen. He expressed doubts "whether it is really important to know what is happening in Laos every minute."

Journalists had no doubts. They felt it important. In its Freedom of Information report, the American Society of Newspaper Editors, was to note that embargoes lead to misunderstandings, misconceptions, doubts, and hard feelings. The failure to let correspondents get to the battle scene "was raw censorship." The handling of the press at the start of the Laos engagement led to "destructive rumors—as the absence of first-hand, hard facts always does."

President Nixon, in his March 22nd interview with Howard K. Smith on ABC, was to complain about the reporting that finally came out of Laos. He cited the U.S. commander in Vietnam, General Creighton Abrams, as saying that eighteen out of twenty-two South Vietnamese battalions were doing fine but news coverage only dealt with the four "that were in trouble." Complained the president, "They haven't shown the people in the other eighteen battalions."

Of course, as the beginning of the Laos invasion showed, the military has tight control over the movement of newsmen. If there were eighteen successful battalions, General Abrams who has the key to those helicopters could easily have moved newsmen to those areas. Further, much of the news out of Laos came second-hand when reporters interviewed returning U.S. helicopter pilots. One would presume that these Americans would not hide the fact that so many battalions are doing so well. The president, however, offered a different explanation. He told Smith that the "good" battalions were being ignored and the others reported "because those make news."

Reporting was most difficult in the Laos action, which the administration called an "incursion" rather than an invasion (there is a study to be made of image makers and their tampering with the language—bombing raids into North Vietnam are called "protective retaliation" raids, or "air interdiction," retreats are "mobile maneuvering," U.S. "advisors" became "delivery team auditors"). Reporting was difficult but when viewed later, pretty accurate under the most trying of circumstances. Newsmen are not looking for good or bad battalions, for victories or defeats. They are looking for the story, no matter which way it turns. A major South Vietnamese victory is worth headlines as big and film as prominent as any defeat. Newsmen were killed in Cambodia and Laos, not while trying to discredit the efforts of United States or South Vietnamese forces "because those make news" but while trying to bring back a difficult story.

Five days after the president's criticism on ABC, the head of ABC News, Elmer Lower, spoke in Chicago in defense of field correspondents and camera crews in Laos. He had asked four ABC correspondents and the ABC Saigon bureau chief to respond to the president's criticisms.

On the question of casualties (Nixon had told Smith, "Pictures have not shown all that has happened to the enemy, and their losses by conservative estimates are five times as large"), Bureau Chief Nick George responded that the South Vietnamese claimed 13,688 killed and over 40,000 wounded. High U.S. sources said the enemy had only about 33,000 men in Laos. The claimed casualties were 20,000 more than the assumed total of all enemy there.

As for the president's information that newsmen covered four battalions in trouble and ignored the other eighteen, George said the South Vietnamese reported that only four to six of twenty battalions in Laos saw heavy combat but "neither the South Vietnamese nor U.S. people here know which four battalions President Nixon is talking about." He noted that ABC had reported that two battalions were badly mauled but "fought like tigers," one of them returning with less than a hundred men but convinced they had beaten a North Vietnamese regiment.

ABC corrspondent Don Farmer cabled Lower that "the president may be confusing poor performance with heavy losses" and while four battalions lost so many men they became ineffective, it is not necessarily proof of poor performance. "To my knowledge," reported Farmer, "no Western newsman ever was allowed to film any South Vietnamese unit in heavy combat or during a retreat inside Laos. So we cannot personally judge the quality of their fighting."

ABC correspondent Jim Giggans said when press helicopters were finally permitted over Laos, they were limited to "safe" areas not where the fighting was actually going on despite newsmen's protests. Steve Bell noted that the South Vietnamese "have seldom passed up an opportunity to take newsmen to the scene of 'good news.' We used to be led to formal displays of captured weapons and dead enemy bodies, even on the remotest battlefields. If there were so many victories in Laos, why were we never taken to view them? We were ready and willing. . . . We saw and heard the worst from those who went and came back. We were never once given the opportunity to see the best that was claimed to be there." Farmer noted, "Not once were Western newsmen shown any of the caches claimed captured by (the South Vietnamese) inside Laos."

ABC correspondent Howard Tuckner told Lower, "The correspondent doesn't have a vested interest; the briefing officer does," and concluded by noting that battle reporters "have no axe to grind. They have no cause to push. They play no favorites. They are professional journalists; men willing to risk their lives to gather information. It is a distinct disservice to the public— and an insult to the correspondents—to suggest that they embarked on a campaign to undermine the Laotian incursion through their coverage. They told us what they saw and heard. If what they saw and heard wasn't what some people wanted them to see, the fault does not lie with the field correspondents."

President Nixon's criticism, while more muted than the strident attacks of his vice-president, served some of the same functions.

One, it raises doubts as to how much the public should trust the journalist, and two, it serves to warn journalists that the product of their efforts is being carefully watched.

Supporters of presidents often find less reason to be subtle. If he uses a scalpel, they are free to use an axe. Their purpose is to help him achieve his. The Laos matter offered a fresh example of how powerful supporters of the president might axe the uncooperative press.

Early in March of 1971, Senator Clifford Hansen invited all members of Congress and the Washington press to view video-tapes of network war coverage in Laos. The Wyoming Republican took the floor of the Senate to urge his colleagues to view the tapes and witness "some obvious manifestations and clear evidences of unfairness and distortions in order to project a particular point of view, or a particular philosophy."

The tapes came from a videotape project associated with Vanderbilt University which had been taping the major network news and documentary broadcasts nightly. These tapes covered nine days of newscasts following the invasion of Laos, from February 25 through March 5 on two networks, NBC and CBS. According to published reports, Hansen was asked to arrange the viewings by Senator Robert Dole of Kansas, the Republican National Chairman. Hansen, however, told reporters only that Dole, who had been to Vanderbilt and was aware of the taping, had helped him procure them.

Only a few congressmen and a number of congressional assistants showed up at Room 457 of the Old Senate Office Building for the viewings which, in their entirety, ran for several hours. Hansen claimed that over one hundred persons watched on the first day alone. He, himself, he told the Senate, was astounded at what the tapes revealed—"I had felt some newscasts had been slanted, but frankly, I was astonished at just how slanted the presentations were when I got to see them run in chronological order with no commercials and no news of other subjects interspliced."

He was joined on the Senate floor by Brock of Tennessee who said he shared Hansen's shock—"It is one thing to see network bias demonstrated on a night by night basis; it is entirely different to see the cumulative effect of unfair reporting." Dole of

Kansas rose to agree and called it "a heavy-handed and thoroughly consistent attack on the administration's policies in Indochina." Scott of Pennsylvania said some news reports "unfortunately have misled the American people" and urged the news media to reserve judgement on Laos until all the results were in.

Chariman Dole, in the days that followed, made a number of speeches and held several news conferences and discussed the videotapes which he said proved that the networks were guilty of biased news reporting. He referred to a "Vanderbilt University survey" of the content of the tapes which indicated that one network alone (CBS) had made 107 statements about Indochina in the nine-day period on tape and "only 16 did not state or imply criticism of the conduct of the war."

When CBS in Washington asked to look at the Vanderbilt survey, it was told that Chairman Dole had erred, he really meant a Republican National Committee staff analysis of the Vanderbilt tapes. A list of the 107 statements was provided and the explanation that the 91 "unfavorable" items included any that referred to weakness in the South Vietnamese or strength of the North Vietnamese, low troop morale, any threat of a widening war, references to credibility gaps or news control, drug usage or race problems among troops, and danger to troops (and/or horror of war). Any reference to any of this was considered anti-Nixon. The sixteen pro-administration items included an interview with Dr. Henry Kissinger ("although," said the GOP analysis, "Kissinger did not project well"), an interview with the president after the bombing of the Capitol (but the same story was also counted as anti-Nixon because there was a reference to the bombing as perhaps a protest against the involvement in Laos), reports showing South Vietnamese strength, and the time Eric Sevareid said the chances were slight that China would enter the war.

And so it was that the chairman of the Republican Party was quoting a "Vanderbilt survey" showing evidence of network bias and proclaiming that only 16 of 107 statements were proadministration. It was antiadministration to report that the Soviets called Laos an "escalation of U.S. aggression" or, apparently, to quote President Thieu of South Vietnam saying that it was only a matter of time before his armies would invade North Vietnam. It was antiadministration to quote its own officials saying they under-estimated North Vietnamese strength in Laos or even to note that U.S. jets were giving air support to the South Vietnamese.

The "proadministration" sixteen were themselves questionable. The Kissinger interview was in the "pro" group but Kissinger did not dismiss the possibility that Red China might enter the war (when this was reported by others elsewhere, it counted as an "anti" statement). Also considered "pro" were announcements that Nixon was to hold a news conference, that "showdown" battles were near, that more troops were preparing to enter Laos, that South Vietnam claimed victory.

All in all, it was hardly a scientific survey. Network newsmen viewing the tapes found them to be, interspliced on a single reel or not, no different than they had been as isolated stories on the evening newscasts. They were little different than TV war report-ing from the start; they were not biased or part of any plan to reflect a particular philosophy—they were more of the same, war reporting like that which had been going on for seven or eight years.

It was recalled that the sponsor of the showings, Senator Han-sen, while stating that his objective was to help the news media do a better, an unbiased job, was the same Senator Hansen who the previous June had urged executives of the gas and oil indus-try to use their advertising expenditures to influence newspapers in their handling of news about the industry. Speaking to a luncheon of the Gas Men's Roundtable in Washington, Hansen said "oil is a dirty word" in "most of the eastern press" and urged his audience to convince publishers they should print the achieve-ments of the industry rather than news about oil spills, oil pollu-tion, and oil depletion allowances. If the publishers are not per-suaded, he suggested, "then your advertising agency might get the message through more effectively."

In New York, the networks viewed copies of the Vanderbilt videotapes and concluded that the Hansen charges had no basis, the Dole "survey" notwithstanding. NBC and CBS were not ready to join the Clifford Hansen School of Journalism. In a most un-usual move, on March 24, Julian Goodman as president of NBC sent a letter to every single member of the Senate and the House or Representatives noting that Hansen and several other senators claim the tapes prove bias and distortion.

The news material itself does not support these charges. It includes film shot in the field; interviews with men who have been engaged in combat; reports from Washington officials describing the military operations; and the reporting of views, both favorable and unfavorable to the administration's war policy and its effectiveness. Anyone who viewed this material fairly would consider it valuable in the information it offered as straightforward actuality reporting and would not read into it the bias charged by the Senator.

The charges of bias are not only unsupported, but dangerous, because they seek to interfere with the free flow of information essential to the public. The standard for news coverage is accuracy and fairness, not whether the news presentation serves the purpose of those who would like to see it reported in a way that would support their own views.

This latest incident, taken with other equally groundless attacks on television journalism, for partisan purposes appears to be part of a continuing effort to discredit and intimidate the networks news organizations so that they will not be effective or independent in presenting the facts the public must have to examine the course and soundness of government policy.

I ask you to consider the very fundamental point of principle involved here—the need of a free people to have the facts and the developments on issues realistically reported even though the facts are unpleasant.

Television journalism—together with the rest of the press—deserves the support of all who recognize that the very nature of our democratic system rests on the independence of the press to report events and issues free of political pressure. This is a right that belongs to the public and needs careful and constant protection.

Hansen took to the floor of the Senate to express disappointment with the Goodman letter. He said it was markedly different than a letter received from Goodman one year earlier in which the NBC president welcomed "responsible criticism." Said Hansen, "The welcome mat is no longer out." He inserted a letter of reply to Goodman in which he said it was Goodman's opinion that the tapes didn't support the Hansen charges but that the public had the same right to make its own judgment as Hansen had to make his. In Hansen's judgment NBC failed "to measure up to the standards we expect of it."

Hansen had those remarks, earlier Senate speeches on the subject, and a pro-Hansen column by conservative columnist Victor Lasky ("Laos Reports Distorted") reproduced and sent to various newspaper editors. A covering letter simply invited the editor to read the material enclosed which they would find of interest. He then made another speech on the Senate floor attacking a journalism "so slanted as to be alarming" and expressed the hope that the American people won't be fooled.

Senators Hansen and Dole had demonstrated in the case of the Vanderbilt tapes, how much power U.S. senators have. Hansen offered no specifics, Dole offered a highly questionable "analysis," yet both had influence on their colleagues—especially supporters of the president's war policies who were eager to believe adverse news was a product of the reporting not the event. Both had influence on the public at large. Both made a significant contribution toward shaking the credibility of current journalism.

In attacking television, they were after the one form of journalism which is subject to federal licensing. On April 15, one of the elders of the Senate establishment, Senator Stuart Symington of Missouri, rose to criticize the criticism. He said, "Such charges by federal officials against the only federally licensed medium of journalism could prejudice the very function the press is supposed to have in our society. It could reflect a calculated effort to pressure the broadcast media into presenting only those views of events with which the government agreed, rather than the information and background to which the public is entitled; for the public has the right to participate in any broad discussion that is pertinent to what priorities should be allocated our increasingly limited resources."

Symington noted that military briefings and executive branch testimony before the Senate Foreign Relations Committee had explained the purpose of the Laos invasion in an articulate manner. Subsequent briefings made it clear that the goals had not been achieved. "This would come as no surprise to any American citizen who had read, looked at, or listened to reports by a variety of news correspondents." Why, then, were some senators charging bias in the reporting?

When government officials criticize any segment of the press, they should be specific, and should support their charges by particulars. If facts are misrepresented, or issues misstated, the errors should be called to public attention. If an official disagrees with the point of view presented in an editorial or a documentary, he can challenge the substance of the opinion expressed.

When an attack is general, and partisan, and defensive of a particular course of action, however, the suspicion grows that this is an exercise in effort to transfer a credibility gap from the makers of government policy to those who report and analyze it; and neither the press nor the government is strengthened by such a maneuver.

What makes this concerted attack even more questionable is the fact that, in its reporting, broadcasting has not presented a single fact, or stated a single issue that has not been covered at least as extensively by newspapers and news magazines.

That observation refers particularly to Laos, one of the causes of the present uproar. Television was not responsible for the abandonment of a single South Vietnamese position or the shooting down of a single American helicopter. But positions were abandoned and helicopters were shot down.

Would any responsible person suggest that this should not have been reported to the American people; or that it should have been reported as a victory?

The function of the press is to bear witness to all the acts of government—its accomplishments as well as its shortcomings, its failures as well as its successes. By and large broadcasting and other media have done so—honestly, fairly and professionally.

"The function of the press is to bear witness to all the acts of government." In many ways the government has opportunities to affect the way in which the press bears witness and the way in which it bares its findings. There are powers to restrain, hinder,

inhibit, impede, obstruct, and check the flow of news. There are
ways to manage, guide, regulate, manipulate the material available to newsmen. There are opportunities to mold, and bend, and
delay, and distort, and leak, and prevent leaks of raw material.

There is also one powerful tool which government has used
rarely in the past but dramatically and with chilling effect beginning in the late 1960s. It is the tool that legally forces the journalist to tell what he knows, how he got to know it, and who he
learned it from—the power of the subpoena.

The subpoena has been used in various ways but in the post-
1968 period following the riotous Democratic National Convention, was used extensively to find out more about dissident,
militant, radical protest groups and their leaders. In mid-1971
two networks, CBS and NBC, revealed that between them and
their owned stations something like 123 subpoenas had been
issued in an eighteen month period, fifty-two of them by government. After the military Weatherman group had conducted wild
demonstrations in Chicago in October, 1969 subpoenas were issued to newspapers, broadcast stations, and magazines in Chicago. The four-day rampage, the "wargasm" of the Weathermen,
resulted in subpoenas asking broadly for films, photos, files, reporters' notes, and memories of what had happened. Similar subpoenas were issued in San Francisco, New York, and Chicago in
relation to the Black Panthers, a militant group which also troubled authorities greatly.

Time, Inc. and CBS issued statements early in 1970 saying
they would resist the attempts of government to commandeer their
files and films. Hedley Donovan, editor-in-chief of *Time,* promised that "appropriate legal action" will be taken to combat subpoenas which are "fishing expeditions" for information. Richard
Salant, president of CBS News, said much the same and added,
"This can't become a dragnet operation in which law-enforcement
people are relying on us to do their police work. (People) are
going to duck when we come around because they'll think we are
arms of government. Our sources will dry up. We have trouble
now covering the activities of militants because they regard us
as part of the government."

CBS, by the way, provided early evidence of the quickness
with which militant groups anger at news organizations used by

law enforcement agencies. When federal authorities tried to get film outtakes and reporters' memories of an interview with Black Panther leader Eldridge Cleaver, the network resisted. At one point, however, an internal mixup at CBS permitted Justice Department representatives to view some of the filmed outtakes. CBS executives, who had decided to stand firm against the subpoena, were embarrassed. Radical groups immediately called it "capitulation" and the Black Panther Party appeared in front of all three network office buildings in New York passing out pamphlets which said "Employees of CBS and other media corporations can no longer ignore the fact that their executives have turned them into police agents."

The most famous case of the period, and the one which became the symbol of government resolve to use the legal power and the newsman's resolve to resist, involved the Black Panthers and a black reporter for the *New York Times,* Earl Caldwell. The thirty-two-year old Caldwell had good lines into the militant black group and on December 14, 1969 did a story quoting David Hilliard, national chief of staff of the Panther party, as saying, "We are special. We advocate the very direct overthrow of the government by ways of force and violence." For Caldwell and other students of the Panthers, it was the usual militant rhetoric designed to shock. For the Justice Department lawyers, it was pertinent to grand jury proceedings they were planning against Hilliard and the Panthers.

Caldwell was subpoenaed to appear before a grand jury in San Francisco. He refused on the grounds that he could never report the radical group's activities again if he betrayed their confidence. He hired lawyers, as did the *Times,* to fight the subpoena. At first they discussed the possibility of his appearing to confirm the matter in his published stories *if* the Justice Department would guarantee that the questioning would be limited to that. The government lawyers said that was all they really wanted but could not agree in advance to so limit the questioning.

Caldwell's personal position was firm and clear. "I don't have any nonconfidential information. Everything I could print has been printed. If I go before a grand jury, my credibility with the black community is gone."

In April of 1970, Judge Alfonso J. Zirpoli of the Federal District Court in San Francisco ruled that a "compelled appearance of Mr. Caldwell before the grand jury will have a drastic chilling and repressive effect on First Amendment freedoms." The judge noted that the issue goes "to the very core" of the First Amendment and enters sensitive areas never fully explored by the U.S. Supreme Court. His decision: Caldwell must appear before the grand jury but only to confirm nonconfidential material that he had written, "that he need not reveal confidential association that impinge upon the effective exercise of his First Amendment right to gather news . . . until such time as a compelling and overriding national interest which cannot alternatively be served has been established to the satisfaction of the court."

The government was distressed but before it could seek an appeal of the Zirpoli ruling, Earl Caldwell saved them the trouble. He now refused to go before the grand jury even under these terms. "I knew I wasn't going to go in there no matter what. . . . I was prepared to go to jail and stay."

When cited for contempt, he won the support of many organizations—civil liberty groups and news organizations—but for a while at least, lost the support of his employer. *Times'* managing editor A. M. Rosenthal wrote, "We are not joining the appeal because we feel that when a reporter refuses to authenticate his story, the *Times* must, in a formal sense, step aside. Otherwise, some doubt may be cast on the integrity of *Times* news stories." The *Times* chief counsel James Goodale was to say, "We didn't want to risk throwing away the whole Zirpoli opinion. It carried the privilege of a reporter many steps further than any court decision before."

Caldwell's stubbornness, however, prevailed. On November 17, 1970 the U.S. Court of Appeals for the Ninth Circuit overturned the contempt citation and ruled that the government must show a pressing need before they could compel a reporter to testify in secret grand jury proceedings. The three-judge court bluntly noted that "to convert newsgatherers into Department of Justice investigators is to invade the autonomy of the press by imposing a governmental function upon them. To do so where the result is to diminish their future capacity as newsgatherers is destructive of their public function."

The court made note of the special nature of the times, the

special role of militant and radical groups in contemporary society. "The need for an untrammeled press takes on special urgency in times of widespread protest and dissent. In such times the First Amendment protections exist to maintain communication with dissenting groups and to provide the public with a wide range of information about the nature of protest and heterodoxy."

Some months earlier, the chief legal officer of the United States —Attorney General John Mitchell—had addressed the American Bar Association on "Free Press and Fair Trial: the Subpoena Controversy." It was a conciliatory speech which even admitted that "some of the subpoenas were issued in haste with little awareness of their burden on the press." Mitchell noted that there was no Supreme Court guidance on the matter—"a bitter dispute which has already produced seeds of suspicion and bad faith."

He then issued guidelines on the issuance of subpoenas which began with the declaration that the Justice Department did not consider the press "an investigative arm of government." He outlined a pattern of negotiations with the press when a subpoena is contemplated and, should negotiations fail, a subpoena still was not to be issued without the express authorization of the attorney general himself. His own decision would then be based on whether the government has unsuccessfully sought the information from nonpress sources, whether the subpoenas be narrow and not broad fishing nets, whether there be adequate time to provide material, whether there is sufficient reason to believe a crime has occurred rather than "utilizing the press as a spring board for investigations," and whether it was clear that the "subpoena should not be used to obtain peripheral, nonessential, or speculative information." He reserved the right, in emergencies, to depart from the guidelines.

On the whole the Mitchell guidelines resulted in a sharp decline in the issuance of subpoenas by the federal government. A full year later, one Justice Department official said that only two had been issued since the guidelines were proposed, both involving radical publications which apparently deserved protection somewhat less than powerful, more establishment-oriented news organizations. One subpoena was issued against Michael Myerson who wrote an article in the January, 1971 issue of *Ramparts* about David R. Poindexter, accused and subsequently acquitted of charges that he harbored black militant Angela Davis when she was a fugitive. The other subpoena was issued to Mark Knops, editor of an underground newspaper at the University of Wisconsin in connection with the bombing of a building on campus.

The entire question of newsman's information and a court's right to know is a thorny one. There is the traditional contention of the courts that "the public has a right to every man's evidence." In libel suits, the aggrieved can ask that all evidence be brought out. Courts have consistently rejected any contention that the news media has similar privilege to that of a lawyer and his client or a doctor and his patient. While it is a prideful tradition of journalists not to reveal their confidential sources of information, it is a tradition which has had little standing in law.

In 1857, J. W. Simonton of the *New York Times* refused to reveal his sources for a story about members of the House of Representatives taking bribes from a group of land speculators. He was cited for contempt and held by the sergeant of arms for nineteen days before being discharged. In 1871, Zeb White and Hiram Ramsdell of the *New York Herald Tribune* published a secret copy of the "Treaty of Washington" then under consideration by the Senate in executive session. They, too, were held in custody to be released at the end of the session.

In 1911, a reporter for the Augusta, Georgia, *Herald* tried to avoid testifying by saying that if he revealed his source, a policeman in a murder case, he would forfeit his ability as a reporter and would lose his means of earning a livelihood. He was fined and imprisoned for contempt, the Georgia Supreme Court refusing his claim since "To sustain such a doctrine (that the wishes of employers be allowed to outweigh the commands of the law) would render courts impotent and the effort to administer justice oftentimes a mockery." On the other hand, a 1933 case in the Dauphin, Pennsylvania county court ruled that Frank Toughill of the Philadelphia *Record* did not have to reveal his sources because, as he argued, he would lose his job if he did so.

One of the most publicized cases was the action of Judy Garland against CBS after a newspaper columnist, Marie Torre, quoted an unnamed CBS executive as indicating the singer's unfitness for television. Miss Torre was called in to name her source. She refused and with great fanfare was placed behind bars. Judge Potter Stewart, then circuit justice for the second court, ruled that freedom of the press "is not an absolute" and that it must "give place under the Constitution to a paramount public interest in the fair administration of justice."

In 1967, a student reporter in Oregon, Annette Buchanan was fined for her refusal to name seven persons she interviewed about marijuana usage on campus. She appealed saying that disclosure abridges a protected freedom. The court took the position that "freedom of the press is a right which belongs to the public; it is not the private preserve of those who possess the implements of publishing," therefore the public had a right to Miss Buchanan's seven names. It said press privileges are extended by government to the news media, privileges not necessarily conferred by the Constitution.

The Caldwell case, and two comparable cases—that of a television reporter in Massachusetts who also had confidential access to Black Panthers and that of a Louisville newspaperman writing about marijuana usage—were brought before the U.S. Supreme Court in late 1971. They came, as the record indicates, with little guidance from the lower courts. There was the decision in a 1970 Illinois case in which Criminal Court Judge Louis Garippo struck down state law on the issuance of subpoenas to newsmen without (a) the show of relevance, (b) proof that there is no other way to obtain the evidence, and (c) proof that the absence of the evidence is sufficient to cause a miscarriage of justice. Garippo said police have the function of gathering information for the court, not the press.

Illinois, one year later, became the eighteenth state to pass "shield" legislation to help newsmen protect their sources. The first such legislation was passed in Maryland in 1898 and at the time was dismissed by one legal authority as "detestable in substance as it is crude in form" with the prediction that it would remain unique. It did until New Jersey passed similar legislation in 1931. Other states came along with like law in 1935, the late forties, and the late sixties. The laws vary widely in the kinds of protections they offer and to whom they are given, some protect newspapers but not broadcasters.

Attempts to pass a federal shield law have met with no success.

In the early 1970s, the hostility of many members of Congress against news media formed a built-in bloc of opposition to such legislation. Further, more members of Congress are lawyers by profession than any other occupation. Lawyers are reluctant to grant broad protective powers to journalists, though they have it themselves in their lawyer-client relationships. They note that confidences protected by law involve persons more carefully screened by society than are newsmen, namely doctors, lawyers, psychologists, accountants, and priests.

The abuse of the subpoena privilege by government resulted in what the courts have called the constriction of the necessary "breathing space" that a free press needs, what the courts called a "chilling effect" on First Amendment rights. But there were other ways to constrict, to chill. At virtually the same moment, in 1971, two major news organizations were challenged by government in frontal attacks matching anything in U.S. history. The *New York Times,* in a throwback to the Alien and Sedition Acts, was forced to suspend publication for several days in the matter of the Pentagon Papers. The CBS network was challenged by a House committee as to whether its rights were the same as newspapers and cited for contempt by that committee for failing to produce film outtakes under demand of subpoena.

These two case studies of the government versus the journalist reveal all one needs to know about each in times of dramatic confrontation. Neither case fully cleared the air and the battle for absolute First Amendment protection of newspapers and networks continues. Both cases, however, tell us much about how politicians wield their power. We know them better as a result.

VII

THE PENTAGON PAPERS
How to Stop the
New York Times

The handsome, distinguished general—a veteran of the very top posts his government could offer in both military and diplomatic areas—sat up straight in his chair in the television studio and deplored what he called "a deliberate betrayal of government secrets."

Three days earlier, the *New York Times* had started publication of the "Pentagon Papers" and now General Maxwell Taylor, once chairman of the Joint Chiefs of Staff and later ambassador to South Vietnam, was the first principal involved to comment publicly on the publication. He was opposed to it. "I think it's most regrettable that they were ever published in the first place." He supported the government action to stop publication.

"Well, what do you make, General," asked Bernard Kalb of CBS, "of the people's right to know when decisions of this dimension are taken?"

"I don't believe in that as a general principle," said General Taylor. "You have to talk about cases. What is a citizen going to do after reading these—these documents that he wouldn't have done otherwise? A citizen should know those things he needs to know to be a good citizen and discharge his functions—not to get in on the secrets which simply damage his government and indirectly damage the citizen himself."

A citizen should know what he needs to know to be a good citizen—the candor of phrase openly expressed was rare. Believed by those in power, yes—but never, never spoken for it had the flavor of élitist arrogance that would irritate "the good citizen" and intellectuals not in power. Yet, there was General Taylor saying what most leaders believe: that the citizen know no more than he needs to perform his patriotic function as good citizen.

It was shocking to leaders, past and present, to find the *New York Times* telling so much more about the years of the Vietnam War. It was shocking to discover that the raw material was a top-secret Pentagon study, never declassified. It was frightening to speculate on what the *Times* might still find in those documents, discoveries affecting not only past reputations but also current security, since Vietnam was far from a war ended.

The *Times* began its publication on Sunday, June 13, 1971. The mammoth Sunday edition of the paper arrived, 486 pages long, with a dry page One headline reading "Vietnam Archive: Pentagon Study Traces 3 Decades of Growing U.S. Involvement." It was hardly a catchy title. The six pages of deliberately low-keyed prose and column after column of official memoranda were hardly designed to pique reader interest.

Many simply laid it aside with the assumption that it was obviously important or the *Times* would not give it that much space but certainly could wait another day. The previous day had seen the marriage of President Nixon's older daughter and many a Washington newspaper and broadcast bureau was tired from the effort of the wedding coverage and not quite alert to what the *Times* had. The wire services underplayed it. The AP ran almost nothing until Monday; UPI ran a short item of a few hundred words Sunday afternoon. On CBS, Defense Secretary Laird appeared on "Face the Nation" that Sunday and was never even asked about it. To the chagrin of reporters, he afterwards suggested that it might have been important to raise the question. Hubert Humphrey—on ABC's "Issues and Answers"—was similarly spared. With the exception of NBC Sunday, evening news broadcasts were terribly slow in catching on to the significance of what was happening. So were Monday morning newspapers with a few exceptions like *The Louisville Courier Journal.*

All that changed later on Monday. A second "chapter" was published by the *Times.* Other newspapers and the networks began reacting to the importance of the series. So had the government. The *Times* received a telegram from the Justice Department asking it to stop printing and start returning classified source material before doing "irreparable injury" to the nation. The *Times* refused and published a third installment. The government went to court and stopped publication.

Two themes were to emerge from the government's side during the ensuing debate, two questions about the role of news in a democratic society. First, was there no recourse by government to protect itself from damaging publication? Secondly, where was the patriotism of the news people, have they no love of country?

Questioning the patriotism of news reporters and editors is not new. It has been around for a very long time. It generally pops up when there is extreme official agitation over press reporting or speculation. Example—the press clearly saw, and reported, the growing differences between President Harry Truman and General Douglas MacArthur, following their meeting at Wake Island.

Harry Truman, at his October 19, 1950 news conference, snapped angrily at a questioner who suggested that he and his general disagreed. "Let me tell you something that will be good for your soul," the president said. "It's a pity that you columnists and reporters that represent a certain press service can't understand the ideas of two intellectually honest men when they meet. General MacArthur is the commander in chief of the Far East. He is a member of the government of the United States. He is loyal to that government. He is loyal to the president in his foreign policy, which I hope a lot of your papers were—*wish* a lot of your papers were."

A patriotic press would, of course, have reported harmony between such loyal American, intellectually honest men. Not very many months later, Truman removed MacArthur from command.

Several decades later, Secretary of State Dean Rusk was to berate reporters with the suggestion that, in search of Pulitzer Prizes, they are probing "for things one can bitch about when there are two thousand stories on the same day about things more constructive in character." Rusk warned that "none of your papers or your broadcasting apparatuses are worth a damn unless the United States succeeds. They are trivial compared to that question."

Finally, Rusk posed the question that bureaucrats, great and petty, and their fellows in all branches of government often think but rarely speak: "There gets to be a point where the question is, whose side are you on? I'm the secretary of state, and I'm on our side."

Rusk presided during the most important years of the Vietnam War—1960–1968—and throughout that period his fellows in government frequently felt the press was remiss in failing to rally to the flag, to be on "our side." During the "Pueblo" incident when an American ship was seized by the North Koreans, a reporter asked the White House press office if he could hear a "Pueblo" tape recording quoted at the United Nations by Ambassador Arthur Goldberg. The angry response was, "Why is so much fuss made about this. . . . Why do you all question everything we do and nothing, or very little, the Communists do?" When the reporter protested, the official continued, "I just don't understand this constant carping on minor details with us compared to the willingness to take almost everything at face value from the other side."

Over at the Pentagon, it was much the same. A veteran reporter there, who later served as an assistant to the secretary for public affairs—Richard Fryklund—wrote, "I know of no other beat where officials appeal to patriotism to suppress a legitimate news story." The Pentagon has no monopoly on waving the flag but no other beat sees it more often.

A common complaint from many official sources, finally expressed by the Defense Department's Arthur Sylvester was, "I can't understand how you fellows can write what you do while American boys are dying out there." He, and others, complained of a reluctance on the part of American reporters to make America look good.

The underlying theme of such commentary is that the news media is somehow working to undermine the government, to engage in a form of sedition. Indeed, from the earliest days of the nation this was a question under consideration by those in high places and generally rejected by the public at large. The most flagrant excursion into actually punishing the press for its carping at government came as the eighteenth century came to a close —in the administration of John Adams—and the Sedition Acts, passed at that time, provide an interesting and proper background for any examination of the Pentagon Papers which emerged 273 years later.

Secret papers were part of the Sedition Act story, too. Benjamin Franklin Bache, a grandson of Benjamin Franklin and the publisher of the Philadelphia *Aurora,* was a thorn in the side of the Federalist establishment. In 1795, he received a copy of the Jay Treaty with Great Britain which the Senate had voted to keep secret. His source was said to have been a member of the Senate. Bache published it in full and the president, the Senate, and the partisan supporters of the Federalist parties were furious. The public was also unhappy but for a different reason. They viewed it as proof that government was sacrificing American interests to England which only too recently had been the oppressor of the colonists. The government was more than a little embarrassed.

Three years later, Benjamin Bache did it again—this time with even more telling effect. At a time when the John Adams administration and the nation were jumpy over the possibility of war with France, Bache published secret diplomatic memoranda dealing with our French policy. He and Vice-President Thomas Jefferson were advocates of peace with France. The correspondence he published, between the French government and our envoys there, indicated a conciliatory attitude on the part of the French. The letter from Talleyrand appeared in *Aurora* before the secretary of state had even shown it to President Adams.

Bache was accused by some of being an agent of the French. By this time, there had been the attacks on American ships by the French to enforce their embargo on trade with England. A state of near-war existed and was being encouraged by many Federalists. The publication of still another secret document by Bache was considered near treasonous and they sought to bring action against him.

The government moved with a common-law prosecution for seditious libel in June of 1798. By definition, the charge accused Bache of attempting to arouse disrespect for the government and/or resistance to lawful authority. At the same time, Bache's example was used as a justification for passage of a formal Sedition Act.

There were four acts passed in as many weeks by a Congress and administration feeding on national hysteria over France. On June 18, the Naturalization Act was changed to require a fourteen-year instead of five-year residency for citizenship. On June 25, the Alien Act was passed to authorize the president to expel from the United States any and all aliens regarded as dangerous to public safety or even suspected of "treasonable or secret" inclinations. On July 6, the Alien Enemies Act was passed and authorized the jailing or expulsion of aliens subject to an enemy power during a time of declared war. The last of the four acts was the Sedition Act aimed at oppressing political opposition, particularly in the area of free speech.

The Federalists were irritated at many in their midst, men like Albert Gallatin of Geneva, Minority Leader in the Congress at the time; Dr. Joseph Priestley, who fled to America after being nearly mobbed in England for his pro-French sentiments; and Thomas Cooper, founder of a Republican newspaper. The Federal press lumped Gallatin with Jefferson and Madison as an "American Directory" in the service of France.

Gallatin fought the Alien Acts on the House floor. He said that they meant a president could remove, restrict, or confine anyone—aliens or citizens whom he declared "suspect"—a blatant violation of the Constitution's insistence on "due process of law." With strange logic, Rep. William Gordon replied that since no crime is charged, due process does not apply. The Alien Acts passed with a six-vote margin.

Defenders of John Adams have noted that he never availed himself of the privilege of expelling aliens. Sometimes he didn't have to since many departed on their own, at least two shiploads of Frenchmen leaving in anticipation.

The Sedition Act, which was introduced to compliment the Alien Acts, would make it a high misdemeanor for anyone conspiring to oppose execution of national laws, to keep federal officers from their duties, or to aid in an insurrection or otherwise unlawful gathering. Penalties could run up to five years in prison and a five-thousand dollar fine. In addition, anyone convicted of publishing "any false, scandalous, and malicious writing" reflecting badly on the government, the Congress or the president could be imprisoned up to two years and fined up to two-thousand dollars. On the 4th of July, 1798 the Senate passed the Sedition Act and sent it on to the House. That night, at an Independence Day dinner in Orange Courthouse, Virginia, a defiant James Madison offered a toast to "The Freedom of the Press—The Scourge of the Guilty, and the Support of Virtuous Government." It was a cynical salute to a freedom lost, a free press about to be scourged itself.

There is no recorded debate of what happened in the Senate, sessions were secret then. The roll call vote was sixteen to six (both Virginia Senators and one each from Tennessee, Kentucky, New Hampshire, and Maryland).

There is a record of the debate in the House, the first major discussion of the Bill of Rights in the generation of its adoption. Free press in America was the subject. The object of the anti-French Federalist supporters and others who heard the mounting calls for war was to stop an irritating press.

John Allen of Connecticut led the battle to pass the Sedition Act and referring to Bache's newspaper, the *Aurora,* said, "If ever there was a nation which required a law of this kind, it is this. Let gentlemen look at certain papers printed in this city and elsewhere, and ask themselves whether an unwarrantable and dangerous combination does not exist to overturn and ruin the government by publishing the most shameless falsehoods." He could have been a Justice Department lawyer using the same argument in 1971 against publication of the Pentagon Papers.

South Carolina's Robert Goodloe Harper joined Allen and complained about hearing "harangues on the liberty of the press, as if it were to swallow up all other liberties." Harper contended that the Constitution gave men the right to print what they want as long as they did not offend existing laws. It never said no law could be passed to regulate this liberty nor to bring the press to trial, providing it was a fair trial by jury. Liberty of the press for those who would overturn society, he said, "ought not to be allowed, either in speaking or writing, in any country."

Harrison G. Otis of Massachusetts joined Allen and Harper to proclaim that government had the right to protect itself "against injuries and outrages which endanger its existence." All of this was heard again two centuries later in the Pentagon controversy.

Rep. John Nicholas of Virginia rose in opposition. He said that Allen, Harper, and Otis, unable to silence opposition congressmen, sought to "prevent the publication of their sentiments to their constituents and the World." The much-hated Albert Gallatin spoke. He said the backers of the bill were proclaiming that there would be liberty of the press while saying at the same time that if the press published anything against them, it would be punished. He charged that the supporters of the bill were saying the Constitution "had given Congress a power to seal the mouths or to cut the tongues of the citizens of the Union."

His arguments did not prevail. The House passed the bill forty-seven to thirty-seven. On July 14, 1798 President Adams signed it into law.

The Federalist eagerness to pass the act did President Adams no favor. He had not sought it and though he signed it, he was signing the death warrant for his own presidency and his party as well. Even Alexander Hamilton, who headed the prowar faction of the Federalists and was hated and feared by Jeffersonian Republicans, felt the law unnecessary and opposed it.

As for Benjamin Bache, he was spared the opportunity to be tried by the new act. He died late that summer in the yellow fever epidemic that had spread across Philadelphia.

There was a general revulsion across the country to the Sedition Act during the next eighteen months as Federalist judges and district attorneys sought to enforce it. In November, the Kentucky Resolutions—authored by Thomas Jefferson—were passed in that state and a month later, the similar Virginia Resolutions were passed there. Usually lumped together and called the Kentucky and Virginia Resolutions, they declared the Alien and Sedition Acts illegal and held that when the federal government took on powers not specifically delegated to it, state governments had a right to reject these acts. They spoke of the right "to interpose for arresting the progress of the evil." Many other states rejected the concept, stating that only the federal judiciary could rule on questions involving the Constitution.

This "states' rights" concept of "interposition" was to haunt the nation for almost two hundred years. From their formulation in 1798 until the Civil War, public figures would embrace these resolves whenever their constituents felt oppressed and would reject them when in power. Even after the Civil War allegedly put the propositions to rest, they continued to have a life of their own. In the 1960s they were defiantly quoted to prevent any carrying out of the Supreme Court school desegregation rulings. In late summer 1971 when President Nixon imposed a ninety-day wage-price freeze, the governor of Texas rejected his right to do so, saying a president could not wipe out pay raises voted by his state's legislature.

Brushing aside the resolutions, the Adams administration engaged in an extraordinary campaign to silence its critics and supporters of Jefferson. Secretary of State Timothy Pickering and Supreme Court Justice Samuel Chase led the campaign. Pickering was said to pore over newspapers every day in search of sedition. He ordered all U.S. district attorneys to do the same in their districts and to keep him informed. As for Justice Chase, he said, "There is nothing more dread than the licentiousness of the press" and used his court to prove it.

Bache's death did not stop action against the *Aurora*. A Federalist paper, *Russell's Gazette* of Boston, wrote, "The Jacobins are all whining at the exit of the vile Benjamin Franklin Bache. So they would do if one of their gang was hung for stealing. The memory of this scoundrel cannot be too highly execrated." Bache's widow, Margaret, married his print shop foreman, William Duane. The Irish printer, an alien himself, took over the editorship and began attacking the Alien and Sedition Acts.

In July, 1799 Duane published a charge that the British minister in Philadelphia had spent eight hundred thousand dollars in the 1798 election and had even bribed members of Congress. By the end of the month, he was brought before the authorities under the Sedition Act but the charges were dropped.

He continued to criticize the administration. The *Aurora* attacked a proposed election bill pending in the Congress as a Federalist plot to steal the election from Jefferson.

Duane was then brought before the Senate to be questioned. He published a letter from Thomas Cooper, the Philadelphia lawyer, who declined to act as his counsel because the rules of the Senate made a fair defense impossible. Wrote Cooper, "Where rights are undefined and power is unlimited—where freedom of the press is actually attacked, under whatever intention of curbing its licentiousness, the melancholy period cannot be far distant when the citizen will be converted into a Subject."

The Senate was split even on whether to arrest Duane for contempt. Jefferson, as president of the Senate, broke the tie and voted for Duane's arrest. He was arrested but later released and not prosecuted for contempt by the Senate. He was then indicted under the Sedition Law for the same acts. However, he again was not tried though Secretary Pickering was to complain to President Adams that *Aurora* was "an uninterrupted stream of slander of the American government."

Others were not as lucky. All told, twenty-five persons were prosecuted and ten convicted of violating the Sedition Act.

Justice Chase was the most notorious of the prosecutors. One of his trials was the case of James Callender, a Virginian whose crime was the book *The Prospect Before Us,* a bitter attack on the Federalist regime. Chase refused Callender's lawyer the right to challenge the law's constitutionality and openly boasted that he would teach Virginians the difference between the liberty and licentiousness of the press. Chase warned, "If a man attempts to destroy the confidence of the people in their officers, their supreme magistrate, and their legislature, he effectually saps the foundation of government."

Callender was fined two hundred dollars, jailed for nine months, and put under bail for good behavior for the two years after his release. Callender, not one bit repentant, spent his jail time composing a second edition of *The Prospect Before Us.*

In time, he was pardoned by President Jefferson. A few years later Callender fell off a ferryboat while drunk and died. It should be noted that this Scottish journalist was hardly restrained in his attacks on presidents (he called John Adams a "contemptible outcast") or judges (he called the federal judges who carried out the Sedition Act "abandoned pimps of usurpation") nor was he particularly loyal to Jefferson, whom he supported when criticizing Washington and Adams, but attacked viciously during Jefferson's own administration.

Perhaps the most notable victim of the Sedition Act was Duane's friend, Dr. Thomas Cooper. A prominent Republican leader, Cooper was tried for a series of criticisms of Adams which he published in Northumberland, Pennsylvania. At his trial he asked, "Is it a crime to doubt the capacity of the president? . . . Have we advanced so far on the road to despotism in this republican country, that we dare not say our president may be mistaken?"

Presiding was Justice Chase, whose treatment of Cooper was so biased and unbending that it became a factor in impeachment proceedings later brought against Chase himself. Cooper was fined four hundred dollars and sentenced to four months in jail.

Not all victims of the Sedition Act were guilty of publishing seditious libel, some were tried for speaking it. A man in a Newark, New Jersey saloon was arrested and jailed for saying he hoped the wadding of the cannon fired in honor of John Adams might hit the president in his backside.

Even congressmen were not immune. Rep. Matthew Lyon of Vermont was given four months in jail for articles attacking the government's war policy. He wrote, from his cell, "It is quite a new kind of jargon to call a Representative of the People an Opposer of the Government, because he does not, as a Legislator, advocate and acquiesce in every proposition that comes from the Executive." Lyon, a hero to his constituents, was re-elected from jail. He emerged as a national hero.

Anthony Hoswell, editor of the *Vermont Gazette,* published an advertisement in support of Lyon and asking for contributions to pay his fine. Hoswell was fined two hundred dollars and jailed for two months. When he was released on July 9, 1800 he discovered that the citizens of Bennington were out in force, greeting him with a band and word that they had postponed their Fourth of July celebration five days to coincide with his release.

There were other cases. John Daly Burk, a part-owner of *Time Piece,* published in New York, avoided punishment by hiding out in Virginia which welcomed refugees from the Sedition Act (he was killed ten years later in a duel occasioned by attacks on the very French whose cause he had defended so strongly in *Time Piece*). The eagerness to punish Boston's *Independent Chronicle* extended beyond the inconvenient death of its editor, Thomas Adams. His brother and bookkeeper, Abijah Adams, was indicted, fined, imprisoned. His paper was sold while he was in jail.

Jeffersonians put a label to all of this persecution—"The Federalist Reign of Terror." Some historians disagreed. The phrase has been called "mere humbug. Nobody was drowned, hanged or tortured, nobody went before a firing squad. A few scurrilous journalists were silenced, a few received terms in jail."

That was not the feeling of the country, however. There was increasing apprehension over the Federalist actions. It was said that there were not enough prisons to hold all the newspaper writers and politicians violating the Sedition Act.

Though there had been naval encounters with the French, there was also diplomatic action to end differences. Despite the capture of the *Retaliation* by the French off Guadaloupe and the capture of the French ship *L'Insurgente* by the *Constellation* (which also fought a drawn battle with *La Vengeance* in early 1800), President Adams conducted negotiations culminating in the "Convention of 1800." He also moved against his prowar Cabinet members and dismissed Pickering as secretary of state. His party was split, the anti-French segment furious at the president's diplomatic moves.

The schism in the Federalist Party and the bad taste of the Alien and Sedition acts led to the election of Thomas Jefferson in 1800. Jeffersonian Republicans also won control of both houses of Congress.

In 1802, the Naturalization Act was repealed and the 1795 version, requiring only five-years residency to be a citizen, was restored. The Alien Act which permitted expulsion of "dangerous" aliens by presidential edict was allowed to expire unused in 1802. The Sedition Act also expired, early in 1801, and Jefferson on becoming president pardoned all those convicted and still in jail. Congress restored their fines with interest.

The trend across the nation was for more popular participation in government. The élitists of the Federalist Party were ousted.

They never regained power. Self-government, it was shown, could be compatible with a free press, with free discussion.

The rejection of government's heavy hand on the eighteenth century press had its echo in the twentieth century when government moved against the *New York Times,* ultimately three other newspapers in court, and still others by threat of court, to prevent publication of the so-called Pentagon Papers.

The parallels are many. Secret documents were involved in 1798 and again in 1971. A country troubled by war, with strong feelings pro and con, provided the common atmosphere of both periods. The use of the courts to inhibit and prevent publication was true in both cases. The basic meaning of the First Amendment and its relationship to governmental prerogative were at issue both during the Sedition Act and Pentagon Paper controversies.

The repugnance expressed by newspapers and many citizens to any government intrusion into publishing; the demand of public leaders that they be allowed to conduct the nation's affairs without private discussion of state matters being made public; the suggestion that suppression was an instrument of hiding embarrassing revelations rather than protecting the proper privacy of decision making—all these were evident in 1798 and again in the closing years of the Vietnam War.

There was one important and major difference. John Adams and his followers were punishing after the fact of publication. John Mitchell, the Nixon attorney general, and his supporters were seeking to prevent the very publication itself. Even in the worst of the anti-French hysteria that led to the Sedition Acts, no supporter of the Federalist position argued in favor of prior restraint of publication. They held, as English common law had before them, that newspapers can publish and must, thereafter, face the consequences of that publication. In 1971, that was not the argument.

The father of the Pentagon Papers was Robert McNamara, secretary of defense for seven years under both John F. Kennedy and Lyndon B. Johnson. He commissioned a study in 1967 of the history of the Vietnam War to date. He left office early in 1968 before the study was completed.

It was said that Secretary McNamara had been impressed with a similar study conducted by Richard Neustadt for the Kennedy administration, a study of the Skybolt missile controversy. Mr. McNamara called for a major and careful examination of how and why the United States became so deeply involved in Vietnam, a study that would be both "encyclopedic and objective." It was to be a "management audit" and McNamara made clear that he wanted it a thorough reflection of the Pentagon's involvement, regardless of whether it might show him personally in a poor light.

Six middle-level officials, later to grow to three dozen in all, started on the survey. About half the researchers were military, half civilian. They were given full access to all papers in the Pentagon but were directed to interview no one, to stick to the matter in the files. Critics of the study were later to label this the major weakness. The researchers did not have access to many White House or State Department papers, they did not have the opportunity to question decision makers and delve into motives and the essence of decision-making.

The head of the Vietnam history task force was Leslie H. Gelb, head of the Office of Policy Planning in the Pentagon's Office of International Security Affairs. His fellow authors were experienced State Department and Defense Department career men and defense-oriented experts from so-called think tanks, the government-financed research institutes. They were promised anonymity as a protection for their careers should judgments later displease higher authority.

Eighteen months later, McNamara now gone, the study was completed. It was forty-seven volumes long, running to more than seven thousand pages and one and a half-million words of historical narrative plus another million words in government documents. The official title was "History of U.S. Decision-Making Process on Vietnam Policy" but in the public mind, the title of "Pentagon Papers" was firmly and quickly affixed to it. Republican partisans and Defense Department officials—now reporting to a Republican president—tried to call them the "McNamara Papers" but that title did not stick.

The forty-seven volumes covered U.S. involvement in Indochina from World War II until May, 1968, when peace talks began in Paris. Fifteen copies were made, three of them hand delivered to McNamara, now president of the World Bank, by Mr. Gelb. Others went to President Johnson, the State Department, President Nixon's staff (it was completed after his election but before his inaugural), and to the Pentagon itself.

In a letter to Secretary of Defense Clark Clifford, Mr. Gelb wrote, "We had a sense of doing something important and of the need to do it right. Of course, we all had our prejudices and axes to grind and these shine through clearly at all times, but we tried, we think, to suppress or compensate for them." He warned that the history was based on documents that were sometimes contradictory, not immediately self-revealing nor self-explanatory, and thus were checked and rechecked "with antlike diligence."

"Writing history, especially where it blends into current events, especially where the current event is Vietnam, is a treacherous exercise," wrote Gelb to Clifford.

The thirty-six authors assumed from the start that their anonymity would be protected and their product confined to private examination by government alone. They were wrong. Much of the study became public. One of the authors was responsible for making them so, and ultimately confessed his participation.

He was Daniel Ellsberg.

A brilliant student at Harvard, Daniel Ellsberg had written his PH.D. thesis on "Risk, Ambiguity, and Decision." He was third in his class ('52) and spent one year at a British university and three years in the marines before returning to postgraduate work in economics.

On graduation, he joined the Rand Corporation and became a consultant to the White House during the Bay of Pigs and Cuban missile crisis. In 1964, Ellsberg went to the Pentagon and became an assistant to John McNaughton, assistant secretary of defense for international security affairs. An outspoken hawk on the war, Ellsberg contributed to speeches for both McNaughton and Robert McNamara.

The transformation of Daniel Ellsberg on Vietnam began when he was sent there in 1965 to work on pacification studies for the famed Edward Lansdale. General Lansdale was later to evaluate him as "independent and brilliant but lacking in security discipline." Ellsberg was fully exposed to the political and civil sides of the war as well as the military. He was particularly expert on the political rivalries in Saigon.

When hospitalized in Bangkok with a severe case of hepatitis, he started to have a change of heart on the war. In 1967, he returned to the Rand Corporation in Santa Monica, California and began to openly voice doubts about the government's policy in Vietnam. After the Tet offensive in early 1968, he became particularly disturbed at the course of the war and his own role in it. At the time, he had already put in months on the Pentagon Papers study.

Rand officials were disturbed when Ellsberg and five associates joined in a bitter denunciation of the war sent to both the *New York Times* and the *Washington Post.* For the *New York Review of Books* he wrote a scathing attack on Nixon's decision to go into Laos. In November of 1969 he was appearing at antiwar meetings.

In May of 1970 Ellsberg appeared as a witness before the Senate Foreign Relations Committee and attacked American actions in Vietnam. He said the Nixon administration, as its predecessors, cited "self-determination" for Vietnam as its goal—"That statement has never been true in the past. It is not true today." He said American policy is actually to prevent self-determination if it comes in forms unacceptable to the U.S.

By early 1971 he was appearing on college campuses telling student audiences, "I come before you as a war criminal."

Daniel Ellsberg was believed to have gotten his copy of the Pentagon Papers late in 1969. He rented a Xerox copier from a friend, Lynda R. Sinay, who ran a small advertising agency in Los Angeles, and began the laborious task of copying the immense report. It was said that he even enlisted the aid of his teen-age son and twelve-year old daughter to help in the arduous copying and paid Miss Sinay a hundred and fifty dollars.

Early in 1971 the papers went from the ex-adviser to the Pentagon to Neil Sheehan of the *New York Times*—the *Times,* because it was America's most important paper and one of the few that would devote sufficient space to reporting the Papers, Sheehan, probably because of an acquaintanceship that went back to the years in Vietnam.

Ellsberg was not alone in all of this but he sought to take full responsibility alone. Other copies, later in the spring of 1971, found their way to other newspapers. Some of it was done in the best cloak-and-dagger manner of paperback spy thrillers. One thousand pages of the document reached the Knight newspapers with the "Top Secret" stamp blotted out when the Xeroxing was done. On a few pages, however, the words "Top-Sensitive" remained. The *Boston Globe,* recipient of some two thousand pages, found the pick-up arrangements so melodramatic that the editors were convinced that it was a hoax. Examination of the bag of documents, however, made it clear it was not.

Ellsberg, now a M.I.T. Fellow, was quickly traced as the main source after the *New York Times* began publication. He ultimately turned himself in to authorities saying, "I took this action on my own initiative, and I am prepared for all the consequences." Reminded that the consequences could include, under the Federal Espionage Act, a fine of ten thousand dollars and ten years in prison, he said, "Ten years in prison is very cheap if that would contribute to ending this war."

The forty-year-old, curly-haired scholar said that not all forty-seven volumes were turned over to newspapers. Four of them, dealing with secret negotiations between Washington and Hanoi, Moscow, and other world capitols were kept by Ellsberg and given to the Senate Foreign Relations Committee. It was revealed that Chairman J. William Fulbright had been trying for eighteen months to get the Pentagon to release the full study to his committee but Defense Secretary Melvin Laird had refused on grounds that national interests would be jeopardized.

Indicted and facing trial in 1972, Ellsberg may have set the tone for his defense on that day in July of '71 when he turned himself in. "Obviously, I don't think there is a single page," he said, "that would do grave damage to the national interest, or I wouldn't have released them." The Espionage Act states that the violation in transmitting secret matter to others comes when "the possessor has reason to believe (the information) could be used to the injury of the United States or to the advantage of any foreign nation."

Mr. Ellsberg surfaced about four months or so after the *Times* had received the product of that Los Angeles Xerox machine. Sheehan, on April 5th, left the Washington bureau of the *Times* and went to the Jefferson Hotel, less than one mile from the White House. There he joined Assistant Foreign Editor Gerald Gold who had been told of a special, hush-hush project in Washington just a short while earlier. In Gold's two-room suite, the two men spent two weeks working out the dimensions of the project. They also gathered a library of books and magazines dealing with Vietnam to separate that which was new from that already published about decision-making in Vietnam.

At about that same time, Sheehan had completed an extremely long article for the newspaper's book review magazine, nineteen columns on the literature dealing with the war. He had a remarkable grasp of what had and what had not yet been made public.

"Project X," as it was known to a handful of *Times* people, was under the direction of Foreign Editor James Greenfield and moved to New York after the two weeks work by Sheehan and Gold. Abe Rosenthal, managing editor of the newspaper, outlined the plans to the publisher and got the signal to go ahead.

The *Times* security was remarkable, something the Pentagon might have envied, but there was a "leak" in May. Nat Hentoff wrote in the *Village Voice* that the *Times* was working on a "breakthrough" story involving Vietnam and that there was a "fierce internal debate" on whether or not to carry it. Hentoff asked, "Is this story going to be published?" Others had also heard that some on the *Times* were unsure as to publication. One story said Publisher Arthur Ochs Sulzberger was opposed to the idea when first exposed to it but became an enthusiast after his editors convinced him that it must be run. Rosenthal admitted "a hell of a lot of discussion" but denied any battle over publication.

On Thursday, April 22, roommates Sheehan and Gold checked into a three-room suite in the New York Hilton, the hotel chosen because *Times* people felt its huge size would help protect anonymity. Electric typewriters, filing cabinets, desks, and chairs were moved into Suite 1107. The *Times* also brought in two safes.

Another assistant to Greenfield and a secretary joined the two men. In the weeks to come the crew continued to grow. From Washington, Hedrick Smith who was scheduled to go to the *Times* Moscow bureau disappeared, allegedly off somewhere to study Russian. E. W. "Ned" Kenworthy, veteran congressional and political writer and now the paper's environment expert, also showed up in Suite 1107. His cover story was a vacation. In time, Washington staffers, noting the prolonged absence of both Sheehan and Kenworthy, would ask about it and would be told "Don't ask."

Another reporter disappeared from his beat to join Project X. Fox Butterfield, suburban New Jersey reporter, joined the group at the Hilton as did more editors from the foreign desk. Butterfield had extensive reporting experience from both South and North Vietnam. He was to interrupt his tour with Project X at one point to appear before a Newark grand jury investigating an attack on him during a Newark school strike the previous winter.

Three secretaries and Linda Amster, chief newsroom researcher, left for Suite 1107. Everyone assigned to Project X was told to avoid the 43rd Street offices of the *Times*. Only Foreign Editor Greenfield shuttled back and forth between the Hilton and the newspaper.

Suite 1107 could not hold the growing team. Another three-room suite (1310) was rented and before the project ended, nine rooms in all were taken. All were in Gold's name to preserve the anonymity of the others. The rooms were rarely unused except at night or during an occasional meeting in Greenfield's apartment. On those occasions, security guards were dispatched from the *Times* to protect the contents of the Project X quarters.

Sheehan lived in Suite 1107. So did Gold, who returned home only five times in the ten weeks of preparation. He was the target of neighborhood gossip that divorce was pending in the Gold home since his rare appearances always ended with Gold leaving with a loaded suitcase.

In the way of mammoth, big city hotels, no one at the Hilton seemed to be puzzled by the goings-on in Suite 1107. Even room service seemed to take it in stride when they got as many as twelve orders for breakfast by Mr. Gold.

The four reporters, the foreign editors, and the others waded through thousands of pages of documents, cross-checking with their library of already published Vietnam material. Rosenthal had put down a very firm guideline: don't give a *New York Times* version of the war, just report what the Pentagon Papers have to say about U.S. decision making. Greenfield said the team would start with specific decisions and work back through the documents to find how each decision was made. "We threw out literally hundreds of documents—some that would have put your hair on end—because they didn't show how the decision was made."

In late May the work was almost complete. Rosenthal said, "As a professional journalistic accomplishment, I've never seen anything like it."

The amount of material was immense even after weeks of condensation. In addition, the *Times* people felt the need to publish many of the original documents in full. The next problem was how to set this massive result in type without outsiders discovering the project.

Production Manager John Werner was told about the project and told that it would run forty-two pages and had to be kept in absolute secrecy. How much advance notice would he need? Two days, said Werner.

On the ninth floor of the *Times* building an empty office was found and was stripped of furniture, drapes, built-in bookcases, and carpeting. Masonite was installed on floor and walls to protect against the heavy equipment being moved in; banks of fluorescent ceiling lights were installed to provide enough illumination for the typesetters. A page proof press was dismantled and moved into the office; next came six TTS perforators, a galley proof press, a page storage cabinet, desks for proof readers, and a paper shredder to destroy all extra proofs prior to publication.

On Thursday, June 10 the first batch of copy arrived and tapes were punched, carried to a corner of the composing room downstairs, where they were run through Linotypes and the type carried back upstairs, where proofs were pulled. The number of printers increased, fifty to sixty in all, that moved in and out of the ninth floor office in the round-the-clock typesetting. By this time, rumors spread throughout the building that something very big was afoot.

On Friday morning, Publisher Sulzberger who had been reading the material by Sheehan, Smith, Butterfield, and Kenworthy gave his final approval. It was not an easy decision to make. At one point he had consulted the law firm of Lord, Day and Lord which had been counsel to the *Times* for twenty-three years.

Senior Partner Louis Lieb was reported to have warned that publication would be improper and possibly illegal. Despite repeated warnings from outside counsel that the *Times* should not publish classified material, Sulzberger decided to go along with his editors. The *Times'* own general counsel James Goodale agreed. The law firm said it would not represent the newspaper in any resulting litigation because of "a conflict of interest." One of the firm's partners was Herbert Brownell, attorney general in the Eisenhower Administration, and a long-time associate of both President Nixon and Attorney General John Mitchell.

On Saturday afternoon, the Sunday staff was informed that there would be a special page one story which would continue through six full pages in the first news section. The type had already been set. As they laid out the Sunday paper, at the top of the page one dummy, a five inch deep, four column space was slugged "Neil." Secrecy was still the order of the day. Instead of the unlimited number of page one dummies run off on the Xerox, only ten were made—just enough for key editors and make-up men.

The man with the honor of having that large space marked with his name didn't have time to relish it. Neil Sheehan was still in Suite 1107. He was working on upcoming installments.

Galleys came down from the ninth floor. Just before closing time, the lead was dropped into the page as a complete unit. The page was locked up and at 6 P.M. the presses started rolling—the story was out.

On that Sunday, June 13 most newspapers in America had a fairly light news folio. The lead story in most was the marriage of President Nixon's daughter Tricia on the previous day. In the *New York Times,* there was that story headlined "Vietnam Archive: Pentagon Study Traced 3 Decades of Growing U.S. Involvement" by Neil Sheehan.

The first installment of the scheduled series dealt with how the United States got involved in Vietnam, explained the nature of the two and a half million-word Pentagon study, and included thirteen classified documents relating to events from late 1963 to the 1964 Tonkin Gulf resolution. Sheehan's lead read, "A massive study of how the United States went to war in Indochina, conducted by the Pentagon three years ago, demonstrates that four

Administrations progressively developed a sense of commitment to a non-Communist Vietnam, a readiness to fight the North to protect the South, and an ultimate frustration with this effort— to a much greater extent than their public statements acknowledged at the time."

There was not much impact. The wire services, other papers (including subscribers to the *Times* news service who had been warned that a major story could be expected), and the networks were slow to pick up the significance of what the *Times* had.

By the next morning, that lapse was corrected. All the nation's news media and certainly its political leaders were discussing only one story: the Pentagon Papers. A second installment now told of documents that discussed a "general consensus" on the decision to bomb North Vietnam that was made before the 1964 election. Senator Barry Goldwater, the defeated Republican in that election, said it proved that Lyndon Johnson had lied to the voters. Senator George McGovern, a leader in the antiwar movement, called it a record of "almost incredible deception."

Secretary of Defense Laird said it violated "security regulations of the United States." The White House said it was unfamiliar with the study but had a copy sent over from the Pentagon.

The Justice Department sent a telegram to the *Times* asking "respectfully" that it stop publishing the material voluntarily. The *Times* "respectfully" said no.

The third installment was on the streets in New York when a group of Justice Department lawyers met in the office of Robert Mardian, assistant attorney general in charge of the Internal Security Division. They met at 11 P.M. and spent the night improvising legal action against the *Times*. On the 7:30 A.M. flight to New York, Justice Department representatives were on their way to bring that suit before a federal judge.

In time they would bring similar suits against the *Washington Post,* the *Boston Globe,* and others for a number of newspapers were receiving copies of Pentagon Paper excerpts, thanks to the diligent work of Ellsberg and his colleagues and the invention of the Xerox machine. In the days that followed, the public enjoyed the dual spectacle—new revelations daily from the papers and new legal action involving the papers.

The revelations were not without their detractors. Some newspapers claimed that there was nothing really new in the Pentagon study. A prominent anti-war critic said while there was nothing new over what we knew or suspected, the Pentagon Papers filled in the names and the dates.

Newsweek magazine summed it up with, "The secret Vietnam study commissioned by Robert McNamara is a historian's dream and a statesman's nightmare."

Just what were the revelations emerging from the reports in the *New York Times,* the *Washington Post,* the *Boston Globe,* the *Chicago Sun-Times,* and others?

The Pentagon Papers blamed Truman's military aid to France against the Communist Vietminh as the move which "directly involved" the United States and "set" the course of American policy.

The Eisenhower administration's decision to rescue South Vietnam from a Communist take-over gave the United States a "direct role in the ultimate breakdown of the Geneva settlement" reached in 1954.

In 1954, John Foster Dulles fought to prevent the scheduling of Indochina elections in fear that the two Vietnams would be unified under Ho Chi Minh. Nevertheless, the Pentagon analysis says, "The U.S. did not—as is often alleged—connive with Diem to ignore the elections"; it simply deferred to Ngo Dinh Diem when he refused to hold them.

When Dulles failed to get support from America's allies, Eisenhower dropped contingency plans for American intervention in Laos and Vietnam.

The Pentagon Papers says this "limited-risk gamble" policy was changed by Kennedy into a "broad commitment." The president, the papers say, sent then-Vice-President Johnson to Vietnam in 1961 with a message to "encourage" Diem to ask for U.S. ground troops. He also authorized secret raids against North Vietnam.

During the Kennedy administration, in August, 1963 a State Department expert, Paul Kattenburg, urged complete U.S. withdrawal before defections to the Viet Cong reach a point where "we will be obliged to leave." Secretary of State Rusk, presiding over the National Security Council in the president's absence, said, "We will not pull out of Vietnam until the war is won."

The *Chicago-Sun Times* gave details of Kennedy's approval of covert action in Indochina including the infiltration of special forces into Laos and similar American agents into North Vietnam.

The *Times* wrote of 1964 when, it said, the United States was mounting a greater war in Vietnam and planning a congressional resolution as to the equivalent of a declaration of war. The ultimate resolution, the Bay of Tonkin Resolution, was "not improvised in the heat of the Tonkin crisis."

In this vein, the *Times* wrote of a "general consensus" to bomb North Vietnam that was reached during the '64 political campaign even as President Johnson was "presenting himself as the candidate of reason and restraint"—even as the president said he wouldn't send American boys to fight where Asian boys should. Supporters of Lyndon Johnson reacted strongly to the *Times* assertion, denying any such "general consensus." As one put it, "there was neither decision nor clear consensus during the election campaign," the decision to bomb was not made until February of the following year; anything suggesting something else in the Pentagon Papers was a contingency plan.

It was noted that Johnson vetoed military recommendations five different times in November and December of 1964 and January, 1965. In 1966, however, he told Charles Roberts of *Newsweek* that he had made the decision to bomb in October of 1964.

Many of the disclosures in the Pentagon Papers were dismissed as "contingency plans." There were even contingency plans to bomb Moscow but that doesn't mean they were seriously considered, said the critics of the Papers. The weight of evidence, the very mass of memoranda in the Papers suggests, however, that not very many of its assertions could be so airily dismissed.

The *Times* revealed that much of the administration action was taken against the advice of the intelligence community. The CIA, which looked very good to the Pentagon analysts, was often proper in its warnings. CIA director, John McCone, warned that gradual escalation was a foolish policy, the United States must try for a knockout blow or get out of Vietnam.

McCone also warned the president, in late 1964, that bombing the North would not work—"They'll turn their collars up around their ears, pull in their necks and ride it out." In April of the following year, after the bombing started, McCone wrote a memo which predicted events with uncanny accuracy and said, "With the passage of each day and each week, we can expect increasing pressure to stop the bombing. Therefore time will run against us in this operation and I think the North Vietnamese are counting on this. We can expect requirements for an ever-increasing commitment of U.S. personnel without materially improving the chances of victory. We will find ourselves mired down in combat in the jungle in a military effort that we cannot win."

Similarly, the Pentagon Papers reveal that an interagency task force headed by Under Secretary of State William H. Sullivan predicted that North Vietnam's resistance would stiffen under the bombing.

The Papers reported an effort to have the Soviet Union tell Hanoi that the United States would offer a bombing halt as a gesture but it would come with the warning that the United States would not accept further aggression from the North. Our ambassador in Moscow found that Soviet Deputy Foreign Minister Nikolai Firyubin would not relay that message to Ho Chi Minh. Said Firyubin, "I am not a postman."

With the "broad commitment" in Vietnam, Lyndon Johnson inherited the "domino theory" of his predecessors. In June of 1964, he asked the CIA to evaluate the theory. It responded that, "with the possible exception of Cambodia, it is likely that no nation in the area would quickly succumb to Communism as a result of the fall of Laos and South Vietnam." It added that the spread of Communism is not inevitable, future circumstances may even prove unfavorable to the Communists.

Throughout the Pentagon Papers one finds an arrogance of language in eager discussion of matters never or only reluctantly permitted before the public. When, in 1965, thirty-five hundred marines waded ashore near Da Nang and the president approved more troops for Vietnam, changing their mission from defense to offense, approving "search and destroy" missions, he was asked at a news conference if there were some new moves in Vietnam. He replied, "I know of no far-reaching strategy that is being suggested or promulgated." The new offensive posture was revealed about two months later.

In January of that year, Assistant Secretary of Defense John McNaughton offered a memorandum about U.S. purposes in Vietnam. He said they were "seventy percent—to avoid a humiliating U.S. defeat. Twenty percent—to keep SVN (South Vietnam) territory from Chinese hands. Ten percent—to permit the people of SVN to enjoy a better, freer way of life. Also—to emerge from crisis without unacceptable taint from methods used." As one news magazine later put it: hardly an idealistic statement. It also was at variance with the official administration posture that we were trying to help South Vietnam get strong enough for democratic, self-government and to keep it from falling into North Vietnamese hands.

The arrogance of McNaughton's evaluation was matched in other Pentagon Papers memoranda dealing with our allies. Souvanna Phouma and others were regarded as entities to be manipulated. Canada's J. Blair Seaborn, a member of the International Control Commission in Vietnam, could be "revved" up to carry secret messages to Hanoi. There is an account of General Maxwell Taylor dressing down several South Vietnamese generals, telling them Americans were tired of coups. After this was made public in the Pentagon Papers, General Nguyen Kanh said, "He was convoking me as if he were MacArthur on occupation in Japan."

In 1968 the administration was furious with the press for its treatment of the Tet offensive. They damned newspapers and networks for characterizing Tet as a defeat. They called it a major allied victory that left the Viet Cong crippled and ineffective after an obvious suicide mission. At the same time, the Pentagon Papers reveal, the chairman of the Joint Chiefs of Staff was privately reporting, "To a large extent, the V.C. (Viet Cong) now controls the countryside. His determination appears to be unshaken. His recovery is likely to be rapid; his supplies are adequate. He has the will and the capability to continue."

And so it went, one story after another contradicting the public postures of the administrations and the military in command.

Newsweek said, "None of it cut deeper than the implication that Lyndon Johnson and his war counselors—McNamara himself included—had planned the great escalations of 1964–65 long in advance and then had lied about their plans for political as well as military advantage."

Johnson men insisted it just wasn't that way. The Pentagon Papers, they noted, had a narrow focus—simply those items in the Pentagon files. This was true. Missing were the White House archives, the State Department papers, the records of National Security Council discussions, the intimate decision-making moments when a president is alone with his top advisors and no records are kept. Dean Rusk, for example, a major figure in the most important years of the study, is hardly evident in the Pentagon Papers because there was no access to State Department messages except those sent to the Defense Department, because Rusk wrote few memos himself, and because the heart of Rusk's influence was in private conversation with the president.

The *Times,* which apparently had more of the Pentagon Papers than any other newspaper, still lacked those four volumes dealing with the peace negotiations. The Papers themselves were unable to evaluate the actual impact of the hundreds of recommendations, to determine which really were simply contingency plans, or to measure what other suggestions from other sources were placed before presidents.

There was one other matter. For all the hundreds of column inches devoted to the story, the *Times* could publish only about five percent of the documents in its possession. Critics wondered what it left out.

Neil Sheehan recognized the many limitations but he also noted: "Whatever its limitations, the Pentagon's study discloses a vast amount of new information about the unfolding American commitment to South Vietnam and the way in which the United States engaged itself in that conflict. It is also rich in insights into the workings of government and the reasoning of the men who ran it."

His colleague Hedrick Smith added: "Although necessarily incomplete and inconsistent at points, the over-all effect of the history, however, is to provide the American public with a vast storehouse of new information—the most complete and informative central archive thus far on the Vietnam era."

Less interested in archives than in current diplomacy were a number of friendly countries, at least five of which—Canada, Germany, France, Thailand, and South Vietnam itself—made troubled, if not always official, inquiry of the State Department. One European diplomat said, "If diplomatic communications cannot be held in confidence, then we are in trouble."

The disclosures were not limited to communications between countries, of course. They were replete with embarrassing commentary on friendly nations by U.S. officials. One American diplomat called it "a disaster for the integrity of government."

The Canadians were particularly distressed. Their man on the ICC had been portrayed as a messenger boy for American escalation threats to Hanoi. The external affairs minister, Mitchell Sharp, protested the disclosures which he called inaccurate. "There were no messages in the sense that the United States instructed us to have any messages carried," Sharp said in Ottawa, "Mr. Seaborn at all times was acting for Canada."

Diplomats were disturbed by the undiplomatic language that surfaced in the Pentagon Papers (Walt Rostow writing McNamara that a certain action would "help pin our allies to the wall"). They also were bothered by the disclosure that the United States shared information in different degree with different countries. During December of 1964, in anticipation of the air war, the president was said to want "new, dramatic, effective" assistance from several allies, Australia, New Zealand, Canada, and the Philippines. The Papers state that Britain, Australia, and New Zealand were given "the full picture," Canada told "slightly less," and the Philippines, South Korea, and Nationalist China "briefed on Phase I only."

Foreign nations had further reason to be troubled. The publication indicated that certain governments had misled their own people to accommodate the United States. An Australian opposition leader demanded that the prime minister "come clean" with the truth. A newspaper in Sydney said that the Australian public had been "fooled" at a price of 470 dead and 3,000 Australian soldiers wounded in Vietnam.

The *Guardian* in London said, "The McNamara papers show that superpowers take decisions much the same way the world over—with scant concern for the opinions or the feelings of those they represent."

The expected foreign reaction and security were said to have been the major elements in the Nixon administration decision to seek court action to stop the *Times* from further publication. Vice-

President Agnew said the *Times* knew it had classified material but "proceeded to publish it in a secretive and clandestine fashion." He urged that any declassification be limited to experts in office—"The Nixon administration has a great deal more confidence in the judgment of elected officials than it does in the *New York Times.*"

Herbert Klein, Nixon's director of communications, said he did not think "a newspaper should take the law into its own hands. . . . I do not know of any editor who is qualified to decide what is or what is not a matter of military security if it involves top secret material."

The head of the Veterans of Foreign Wars, H. R. Rainwater, said the *Times* should be prosecuted to the full extent of the law. He called the newspaper's action very dangerous, "We are in the middle of a war. It's very close to the thin edge of treason, if not treasonable itself."

At one point, administration officials floated the story that the *Times* publication had threatened the U.S. code. Because the *Times* had published some documents in full (the *Post* and others quoted at length but had not printed full text of documents from the Pentagon Papers), enemies of the United States might be able to crack the code protecting other messages in the early 1960s. One official told reporters, "You may rest assured that no one is reading this series any more closely than the Soviet Embassy."

As cryptographers emerged to note that the U.S. code would not be a very sophisticated one if it could be cracked on receipt of a few messages, the issue started to fade. Ultimately there was official confirmation that the code was not threatened.

In the Soviet Union, the papers were interpreted as an indictment of current as well as past administrations. Said *Pravda,* "The uneasiness that has gripped official Washington in connection with the new exposé shows how fearful the United States Government is of Americans' learning the truth about its criminal aggression."

Soviet leaders generally assert there is no real freedom of the press in the United States and sought explanations for the publication of the Pentagon Papers. *Komsomolskaya Pravda* said the documents were published because of "contradictions within the ruling circles" in America. Later *Literaturnaya Gazeta* would see it as a reflection of the struggle between U.S. military and U.S. consumer-goods industries. Newspapers which published the story had "the closest relations" with the consumer industries and those strategic arms industries which were not benefiting from the war in Vietnam. It was the Soviet Union's most bizarre explanation on why the American press—which they are convinced is not free—could defy the government.

Fellow newspapers saluted the *Times* and damned the government's court action against it. The *Des Moines Register,* sympathetic to the Republicans in power, wrote: "The Nixon administration was foolish to keep the forty-seven volume Defense Department study secret after it came to office. It is still more foolish to try to enforce secrecy now." The *Minneapolis Tribune* added: "One answer stands out boldly in the part of the Pentagon study published until now. Those who made U.S. policy in Vietnam had great faith in their own judgement and little in the judgement of Congress and the public."

The *Arizona Republic* said the publication obviously fitted the *Times'* ideological passions, "But motives aside, we disagree with Government contentions that publication of the documents will cause irreparable injury to the defense interest of the United States. . . . The *Times's* revelations are in the public interest. Why shouldn't the American public, whose sons are fighting and dying in Vietnam, be allowed to know the origins of the war? Why should Congress be denied legitimate documents? Why should the Nixon administration cover up for the Johnson administration by perpetuating a cloak of secrecy?"

The *Charlotte Observer* said the documents show the executive branch "did not level" with the people. The *St. Louis Post-Dispatch* asked that, "No newspaper . . . be sued or threatened with prosecution for publishing stories involving the Government's action". The *Milwaukee Journal* reminded that, "The normal and proper procedure is to punish an illegal expression rather than to suppress it in advance."

Not all newspapers agreed. The *Nashville Banner* called publication "an act of recklessness unmatched in U.S. history." The *Tulsa World* asked, "Isn't it true that the secret processes of government—if they are sensitive enough to be classified—can be released only at the risk of embarrassing the nation and possibly harming its foreign relations?"

Among the most outspoken critics of the *Times* was the *Detroit*

News which on one occasion devoted two-fifths of its front page to an editorial attacking the *Times* decision to publish. It suggested that no individual, be he an editor, scientist or public official, should be permitted to substitute a personal definition of national interest as a basis for declassification. "In summary," the *News* said, it "does not want the freedom of the press so important to our existence stretched to justify this type of irresponsibility."

As for the public at large, it apparently was more approving of the *Times*. A Gallup poll showed that fifty-eight percent of those familiar with the controversy felt the paper had done right in publishing. Thirty percent thought it the wrong thing to do and twelve percent had no opinion.

Gallup's poll had one surprising note. Despite the tremendous publicity given the publication of the Pentagon Papers, only about fifty-five percent of those questioned were familiar with the articles.

By Tuesday, June 15 there was virtually no one in official Washington who was not familiar with the Papers and the controversy. The Justice Department lawyers went before U.S. District Judge Murray I. Gurfein in the Federal District Court House at Foley Square in New York. They were pressing a civil suit against the *Times* and twenty-two of its officers and employees, asking the court to permanently enjoin the newspaper from any further publication of the Papers.

For the first time in history, the government was before the courts trying to stop a newspaper from publication of material it found objectionable.

VIII

THE PENTAGON PAPERS
Days in Court

The *Times* was without a lawyer, its corporate counsel having —in the words of one *Times* official "backed out on us." There wasn't much time to shop for legal help. The *Times* was to be in court the next morning.

Vice-President James Goodale thought of Professor Alexander M. Bickel, a leading constitutional authority from Yale who had worked on the Earl Caldwell subpoena case. They also sought a former Bickel student, Floyd Abrams of Cahill, Gordon, Sonnett, Reindel, and Ohl. Abrams was found and agreed to take the case, his firm ultimately becoming permanent counsel to the *Times* replacing Lord, Day and Lord. Bickel, however, could not be found and it was approaching midnight.

The *Times* news desk finally found Mrs. Bickel in Palo Alto, California. She asked them to check the Yale Club. He wasn't there. They called her again. She suggested his mother's apartment on Riverside Drive. He was there and agreed to join the defense. At 2 A.M. in the Cahill law firm offices on Wall Street, Professor Bickel and Abrams met and researched arguments through the night and, bleary-eyed, arrived in court the next day to present their arguments.

Representing the government that day was Michael Hess, a thirty-year-old staff member of the U.S. attorney's office.

Presiding in Room 605 of the U.S. Court House was Murray Gurfein who had taken his oath of office just days earlier. A Nixon appointee, Judge Gurfein was virtually in his first day on the bench.

The government's argument was presented by Hess. The *Times,* he said, had violated the Espionage Act in its "unauthorized possession" of the documents; "serious injuries are being inflicted on our foreign relations, to the benefit of other nations opposed to our form of government." He asked that the *Times* be enjoined until Friday when the case could be heard, otherwise publication would make the matter moot.

Professor Bickel rose to call it a "classic case of censorship" and said a newspaper should not "submit its publishing schedule to the United States government." Bickel said that the Espionage Act cited by Hess was never intended to be used against the press, that to do so and bar publication "for the first time in the history of the republic" would be setting a most unfortunate precedent.

Judge Gurfein, in his chambers, heard brief statements from civil liberties groups in support of the *Times* and then asked the newspaper to accept a temporary restraining order that would expire at 1 P.M. Saturday and would permit a hearing on Friday. Bickel refused, calling such action an invitation for future government efforts to stop publication. Gurfein issued the order over Bickel's objections.

"In my opinion," the judge said, "any temporary harm that may result from not publishing during the pendency of the application for a permanent injunction is far outweighed by the irreparable harm that could be done to the interests of the U.S. government if it should ultimately prevail."

He added, "I believe that the matter is so important and so involved in the history of the relationship between the security of government and the free press that a more thorough briefing than the parties had an opportunity to do is required."

In Washington, Secretary of State Rogers held a news conference and condemned the publication of the paper which he said would cause him "a great deal of difficulty" in dealing with foreign governments. Up at the Hill, Senate Majority Leader Mike Mansfield expressed shock and surprise at the *Times* revelations. He promised a Senate hearing into the decision making in Vietnam.

The next morning, Wednesday, the *Times* issued a blistering editorial aimed at the "unprecedented example of censorship" and promised to continue to fight. "The documents in question," said the *Times,* "belong to history."

The *Wall Street Journal* also took to its editorial pages to condemn the Justice Department's actions. It said there is nothing in the published record of the "inside working of American policy before 1968" which could in any way injure current defense interests. "The flap over the Pentagon report might be an appropriate occasion for the present administration to reexamine its own attitudes toward secret formulation and conduct of national policy. Its reaction to the publication of the report suggests that some of the attitudes of the discredited Johnson regime have carried over into this administration.

"Except when national security actually could be endangered, it should be the function of a democratic government to make public the record of past policy decisions on its own and to make current policy abundantly clear. If it fails to do so, and the public has to rely on the ingenuity of the press for such information, the government has very little justification for complaint."

The Justice Department asked Judge Gurfein to order the *Times* to permit government inspection of their copy of the secret Pentagon Papers, having failed earlier on Wednesday to get the *Times* to voluntarily surrender the documents. The government said it needed the material to properly present its case. Gurfein told the *Times* to appear before him at 10 A.M. the next morning to give reasons why it should not be so ordered. The *Times* expressed several concerns, the main one being that the government would use the documents to trace them to the source that had provided them to the *Times* originally.

That night, in a broadcast interview on WMCA, the name of Daniel Ellsberg emerged publicly for the first time. Sidney Zion, a former *Times* reporter, said Ellsberg was the source. The *St. Louis Post-Dispatch* also reported that a high source had revealed that the search was "centering" on Mr. Ellsberg.

The next day, Thursday, the FBI was in Cambridge, Massachusetts looking for Ellsberg. He had disappeared.

Thursday morning, the *Times* and the government argued the

matter of Justice Department examination of the papers held by the *Times*. Judge Gurfein asked Michael Hess if this were not a fishing expedition by the government. The assistant U.S. attorney said it was not, that in order to prove its case on Friday the government had to know exactly what the *Times* had.

The *Times* lawyer (Floyd Abrams that day) expressed fear of tracing to the source and submitted an affidavit from James Greenfield, the foreign editor. Greenfield noted that on many of the Xerox pages are handwritten notations which could be traced to their authors. Hess said they could block out such notes.

Gurfein sought a compromise. He asked the *Times* to produce a list and description of the documents in its possession. Before nightfall that was done but the list was so skimpy that the government denounced it as useless.

In Congress that day, sixty-two members of the House appealed to Attorney General Mitchell and Defense Secretary Laird to declassify and release the Pentagon study. Representative Paul McCloskey, a California Republican and antiwar spokesman, revealed that Daniel Ellsberg had given him copies of Pentagon Papers the previous April. He said he was unable to tell, from the Xeroxed sheets now locked in his office safe, whether they were the same as those the *Times* had. He said his copies were not marked secret.

In Paris, the North Vietnamese spokesman at the peace talks said the Pentagon Papers proved that America was the aggressor in Indochina. As for efforts to stop further publication, Nguyen Than Le denounced them, saying, "Mr. Nixon fears the truth as an owl fears daylight."

The *Times* that day published excerpts of editorial comment, eight columns across under the heading "World Press Overwhelmingly Supports Publication by Times of Series on Vietnam." It quoted such U.S. publications as the *Washington Post* ("The Federal Government does not have a constitutional leg to stand on"), the *Boston Globe* ("The Government is saying . . . official conniving and duplicity or, perhaps, simple stupidity, are none of the American people's business"), the *Miami Herald* ("We trust . . . that the public now will better understand . . . 'the credibility gap.' What are those Government officials saying today who in the past have accused the press of inventing the gap?"), and in strong opposition to the *Times* publication, the *San Diego Union* ("There is no justifying the action of the *New York Times* . . . they are documents for which our enemies would pay a King's ransom—and they are getting them for nothing.").

As for press reaction overseas, the *Times* of London wrote, "All governments find that they have to be less than frank and all governments are divided by their own hopes, but to go to war on a lie is a different matter." *Die Welt* in West Germany said that while it is shocking to the United States, "Hanoi has no reason to be shocked." The *Daily Mirror* in Australia said the people of Australia had been fooled, "The Australian Government had a blindingly uncritical—even willing—role in President Johnson's hypocrisy."

These were harsh words pouring out of many newspapers, harsh in their indictment of what the Pentagon Papers revealed, harsh in their condemnation of efforts to stop further publication. Defenders of the government began to emerge.

The first was Maxwell Taylor. He appeared on several networks replying to the criticisms surfacing as a result of the Pentagon Papers. Some excerpts from his CBS interview by John Hart and Bernard Kalb give the flavor of his position. Asked "Who was more honest at that time—the media in reporting what was going on in Vietnam, or the American Embassy or the Johnson administration?" Taylor replied, "Obviously, because you can't wage war and you can't conduct a negotiation and you can't have a very, very weak ally who you're trying to support, and go before the public and tell everything you know. Disaster! And this country will be destroyed if that's the course of action we're going to follow in the future."

He offered three criticisms of the Papers and their publication: "One is it's laying a foundation for bad history. Secondly, it's initiating a practice, if it is a practice, of officals betraying their government's secrets and a distinguished newspaper printing them. And third, it's ruinous to relations within our government and our international relations abroad."

General Taylor also noted that while it is easier with hindsight, it is difficult to make the right decisions at the moment of crisis. "Unfortunately, presidents and governments don't have these crystal balls. And if you look at the evidence available to Eisenhower, to Kennedy, to Johnson at various points, I've always found it very difficult to fault the decisions they made at those times."

It was in this interview that General Taylor offered the observation that "A citizen should know those things he needs to know to be a good citizen and discharge his functions . . . not to get in on secrets which simply damage his government and indirectly damage the citizen himself." On the morning after that interview, Tom Wicker wrote in the *Times,* "The great lesson of the Pentagon record is that the ability to operate in secrecy breeds contempt for that very public in whose name and interest officials claim to act. It often is argued that government cannot function if its officers cannot deal with one another in confidence; but seldom if ever has it been so graphically demonstrated that when men are relieved of the burden of public scrutiny, uncomfortable as it may be, no other form of accountability takes its place."

On Friday, June 18 as all interested parties turned their attention to Judge Gurfein's courtroom in New York, there was a major event two hundred miles south of that. The *Washington Post* published the first in a series of articles based on its copies of the Pentagon Papers. The Xerox machine had struck again.

The Justice Department now raced into court to stop *Post* publication. They found little sympathy from District Court Judge Gerhard A. Gesell. He did try to get the *Post* to informally agree to delay publication for two or three days to give him more time but the *Post* refused.

At a few minutes after 8 P.M., the judge ruled in favor of publication. He noted that the Espionage Act cited by the government provided for criminal penalty but not for prior restraint of publication. He ruled, "The *Post* stands in serious jeopardy of criminal prosecution. This is the only remedy our Constitution has provided. The *Post* will be allowed to publish."

The newspapermen raced off to get the Saturday paper out with the second installment ("The Pentagon study discloses that some strategists planned to use unproductive bombing pauses as a justification for escalating the war."). The newspaper's lawyers trudged over to the U.S. Court of Appeals where the government lawyers sought to overturn Gesell's decision.

They succeeded.

Acting at 1:20 A.M. on Saturday, two appellate judges overruled Gesell and ordered the *Post* to stop publication after the second installment, the one now reaching the streets. The appellate court instructed Gesell to hold new hearings and reach a decision by 5 P.M. on Monday.

Back in New York, the Justice Department was equally busy as it presented the case against the *New York Times*. The U.S. attorney general in New York, Whitney North Seymour, Jr. argued the basic government case. He said the *Times* had violated the law by illegally declassifying government secrets. He said this had compromised current military and defense plans, intelligence operations, and had jeopardized foreign relations.

Seymour produced four witnesses for the government. Dennis J. Doolin, deputy assistant secretary of state for internal security affairs, testified that he had several times examined the forty-seven volumes because Chairman Fulbright of the Senate Foreign Relations Committee had asked to see them. Doolin said declassification was rejected even in part because the nonsensitive matter was entwined with the sensitive and the "universe" of security interests would be affected.

The vice-chief of naval operations, Vice-Admiral France J. Blouin, testified that other-nation intelligence operations have already derived "a great deal of benefit" from the three published articles. "It would be a disaster," said the admiral, to publish any more.

George MacLain, director of security classification management at the Pentagon, explained how classification is done and subsequently how declassification comes to be.

Deputy Under Secretary of State William B. Macomber testified that relations with other countries had already been damaged by the *Times* articles. He said the essence of diplomacy was the ability to deal in confidence and not to fear that communications will appear in the public prints. He called such communication "the life blood" of diplomacy.

Professor Bickel began the *Times* case by noting that the *Washington Post* had started publication of the Pentagon Papers, that the wire services were picking it up, and that by afternoon, the *New York Times* might be the only paper in America forbidden from carrying the story. There is nothing, he said, left to protect in the order restraining publication before 1 P.M. Saturday. He moved that the order be vacated.

Judge Gurfein asked the government if it planned to move against the *Post*. Michael Hess said that he didn't know yet but the government wanted to proceed here anyway. Gurfein asked for reaction to Bickel's point that all other newspaper readers except those of the *Times* could now read the Papers. Hess said that the *Times* put themselves in that "unique" position by being the first to publish and by agreeing to let the court decide the issue.

Bickel snapped back that the newspaper was not there to seek court approval but there because the government had brought action. The government had pleaded injury: the *Times* had been restrained because it would not mean further injury to hold up for a few days. "We suggest to Your Honor," said Alexander Bickel, "that the position has changed radically on both sides. There is now damage to the *Times* and from the government's point of view the security interest is not visible with the naked eye any longer."

Judge Gurfein said, "You pose a very difficult problem." He suggested that a newspaper might sit down with the Department of Justice and "as a matter of simple patriotism to determine whether the publication of any of them is or is not dangerous to national security." Failing that, the press and the government have an equal right to come to court. The court will make that decision.

Whitney North Seymour, Jr., said he would prove the government's case with his witnesses and documentary evidence. He asked that after preliminary testimony of a general nature by the career officers of State and Defense, that they proceed *in camera,* in court session closed to the public to maintain "appropriate protections" of the sensitive material. He said that since the *Times* had provided only the four-page list of what they had, the government would have to speculate—in private session—as to their holdings and the security implications associated with them.

Judge Gurfein agreed to the secret testimony, none of which was later revealed. The *Times* however, offered affidavits dealing with classification of government documents and the entire question of government secrets. These were made public.

The central *Times* presentation was an affidavit from Max Frankel, chief of the Washington bureau of the newspaper and once its White House correspondent. Frankel's arguments are worth special examination for his basic theme is that government, in partnership with the press, is constantly violating its own classification procedures to serve its own ends:

"The Government's unprecedented challenge to the *Times* in the case of the Pentagon papers, I am convinced, cannot be understood, or decided, without an appreciation of the manner in which a small and specialized corps of reporters and a few hundred American officials regularly make use of so-called classified, secret, and top-secret information and documentation. It is a cooperative, competitive, antagonistic and, arcane relationship . . .

"Presidents make 'secret' decisions only to reveal them for the purposes of frightening an adversary nation, wooing a friendly electorate, protecting their reputations. The military services conduct 'secret' research in weaponry only to reveal it for the purpose of enhancing their budgets, appearing superior or inferior to a foreign army, gaining the vote of a Congressman or the favor of a contractor. High officials of the Government reveal secrets in the search for support of their policies, or to help sabotage the plans and policies of rival departments. Middle-rank officials of government reveal secrets so as to attract the attention of their superiors or to lobby against the orders of those superiors. Though not the only vehicle for this traffic in secrets—the Congress is always eager to provide a forum—the press is probably the most important.

"In the field of foreign affairs, only rarely does our government give full public information to the press for the direct purpose of simply informing the people. For the most part, the press obtains significant information bearing on foreign policy only because it has managed to make itself a party to confidential materials, and of value in transmitting these materials from government to other branches of government as well as to the public at large. This is why the press has been wisely and correctly called The Fourth Branch of Government . . .

"The Government's complaint against the *Times* in the present case comes with ill-grace because Government itself has regularly and consistently, over the decades, violated the conditions it suddenly seeks to impose upon us—in three distinct ways:

"First, it is our regular partner in the informal but customary traffic in secret information, without even the pretense of legal or formal 'declassification.' Presumably, many of the 'secrets' I cited above, and all the 'secret' documents and pieces of information that form the basis of the many newspaper stories that are attached hereto, remain 'secret' in their official designation.

"Second, the Government and its officials regularly and customarily engage in a kind of ad hoc, de facto 'declassification' that normally has no bearing whatever on considerations of the national interest. To promote a political, personal, bureaucratic, or even commercial interest, incumbent officials and officials who return to civilian life are constantly revealing the secrets entrusted to them. They use them to barter with the Congress or the press, to curry favor with foreign governments and officials from whom they seek information in return. They use them freely, and with a startling record of impunity, in their memoirs and other writings . . .

"Third, the Government and its officials regularly and routinely misuse and abuse the 'classification' of information, either by imposing secrecy where none is justified or by retaining it long after the justification has become invalid, for simple reasons of political or bureaucratic convenience. To hide mistakes of judgment, to protect reputations of individuals, to cover up the loss and waste of funds, almost everything in Government is kept secret for a time and, in the foreign policy field, classified as 'secret' and 'sensitive' beyond any rule of law or reason. Every minor official can testify to this fact.

"Obviously, there is need for some secrecy in foreign and military affairs. Considerations of security and tactical flexibility require it, though usually for only brief periods of time.

"But for the vast majority of 'secrets,' there has developed between the Government and the press (and Congress) a rather simple *rule of thumb*: The Government hides what it can, pleading necessity as long as it can, and the press pries out what it can, pleading a need and right to know.

"Some of the best examples of the regular traffic I describe may be found in the Pentagon Papers that the Government asks us not to publish. The uses of top secret information by our Government in deliberate leaks to the press for the purpose of influencing public opinion are recorded, cited and commented upon in several places of the study. Also cited and analyzed are numerous examples of how the Government tried to control the release of such secret information so as to have it appear at a desired time, or in a desired publication, or in a deliberately loud or soft manner for maximum or minimum impact, as desired."

To the average American, Frankel's analysis comes as a surprise—this sharing of secrets between politicians and press. It is only when one examines the scope of classification, the ease with which it happens, the large number of government types who can classify, the strange abuses and ironies of classification—only when all of that is examined does Frankel's explanation become easy to accept.

Over thirty thousand people in the Pentagon alone have the right to classify documents as "confidential." Almost eight thousand of these can also call a matter "secret" and several hundred have the original authority to classify something as "top secret." Then there is the matter of "derivative classification authority" which extends classification rights to those reporting to the original classifiers.

William G. Florence, a retired air force civilian security classification expert, testified before a House subcommittee hearing on classification during the Pentagon Papers controversy. He said the derivative classification authority extends classification privileges to "any individual who can sign a document or who is in charge of doing something." Florence said, "Hundreds of thousands of individuals at all echelons in the Department of Defense practice classification as a way of life. . . . To them classifying a document is like putting a period at the end of a sentence."

Former U.N. Ambassador Arthur Goldberg told the same Foreign Operations and Government Information subcommittee, "I have read and prepared countless thousands of classified documents and participated in classifying some of them. In my experience, seventy-five percent of these never should have been classified in the first place; another fifteen percent quickly outlived the need for sercecy; and only about ten percent genuinely restricted access over any significant period of time."

Florence was not as generous. Of the twenty million documents held as classified by Defense, he estimated that less than one-half of one percent justify keeping them secret.

The other 99.5 percent, said this veteran of almost twenty-five years as a classification expert, "literally clogged" the defense classification system. The cost to the taxpayers was fifty million dollars a year.

An idea of the accumulation of "classified" material can be had by looking at the National Archives collection. A quarter of a century after the war's completion, 160 million pages of records of World War II remain classified, enough to fill 10,300 filing cabinets. Almost as much material, some 9,300 filing cabinets full, deals with the period of 1946 to 1950. Still another area of almost as many thousands of filing cabinets and millions of papers deal with the Korean War years. None of this is open to the public.

Florence said that while "the basic classification system was originally designed for the very narrow field of military information that could be used by some foreign nation against the United States . . . it's become a way of life, and it's used as a cover-up for all sorts of governmental inadequacy and failure, and these rightly should be made public." He noted that in addition to the tens of thousands of people in Defense who could classify anything, there were another six thousand in the State Department and thousands more in the fifty-seven other government agencies which have security information systems.

Some of the classification was laughable. Florence testified about one air force division which used a rubber stamp marked "Although material in this publication is unclassified, it is assigned an overall classification of confidential." He also testified that one service chief of staff wrote a memo to his colleagues proposing that they cut down on classifying documents "top secret." His memo was promptly marked "top secret." By the way, the Air Force Systems Command in correspondence with Mr. Florence objected to declassifying anything unless declassification could be proved to "actually benefit the air force."

The mania for classification has had truly absurd moments. Years ago a senator revealed that the army had classified as a military secret the use of the bow and arrow. The navy classified a report on attacks by sharks on seamen in New York Harbor, a study done in 1916. There have been numerous reports of newspaper clippings being classified as secret and only when this finally became public and embarrassing, the Defense Department issued an order permitting newspapers to remain in public domain. Once

Queen Frederika of Greece visited an army post during an official tour of the United States and a thoughtful officer stamped "classified" on her dinner menu, apparently to avoid any comment on what Her Highness had to eat.

The record shows, however, that there are many incidents of classification designed to prevent embarrassment or to cover up error. The Justice Department classified material relating to expense-paid trips by border-patrol inspectors to shooting matches. The air force classified pictures of transport planes remodeled with plush quarters for traveling generals. Defense won't make public a list of military posts where liquor is sold to servicemen by the bottle. Civil Service Commission classifiers have bottled up an investigation of abuses in rural mail-carrier examinations.

The gist of Max Frankel's affidavit was, of course, to show that those in authority play fast and loose with the quick and casual classification system when it serves their ends. Presidents, cabinet members, congressmen, military officers, administrative aides, agency chiefs, and almost anyone in Washington with some degree of power, some access to confidential material, and some theme he wants to push in the press will share his secrets with a reporter.

Benjamin Bradlee, executive editor of the *Washington Post* at the time it published the Pentagon Papers material, told of President Kennedy revealing top secret material to him upstairs at the White House. Bradlee was the *Newsweek* Washington bureau chief at the time and says, "I can testify that President John F. Kennedy once read to me portions of a highly classified memorandum of conversations between him and Nikita Khrushchev in Vienna in 1961. I received his permission to use this material, which is still highly classified, and it appeared in *Newsweek*. His stated purpose was to convince the American public that the Soviet Union was taking an extremely hard, belligerent line on Berlin."

Richard Nixon, when vice-president, was himself party to sharing state secrets on an off-the-record basis before hundreds of newspaper editors. As Robert U. Brown recalled it in *Editor and Publisher* years later:

It is interesting to note that in April of 1954 then Vice-President Nixon was in the possible position of having violated the Espionage Act and Executive Order 10501, both of them fairly new on the books, when he addressed the American Society of Newspaper Editors off-the-record in Washington.

The Vice-President at that time gave the editors an hour-long background analysis of the Indo-China situation and, in answer to a question from the floor, commented on the possibility of American troops going to that area. The U.S. editors did not violate the off-the-record stipulation. What he said was widely quoted as coming from an administrative source.

His name was linked to it in reports abroad which came back to the U.S.

In the Eisenhower administration officials leaked the classified Yalta Papers to the *New York Times.* Democrats howled at the move, calling it an attempt to discredit Democratic administrations.

Sometimes congressmen, who routinely have access to much classified material, just as routinely pass it on to reporters. Ben Bradlee told of visiting a congressman in the late '50s and receiving a "secret" State Department document dealing with foreign aid. Just before the document changed hands, the congressman took a scissors from his desk and carefully removed the "secret" stamp from each page. His stated purpose in requesting the document from State was to help in drafting legislation. His purpose in giving the document to Bradlee was to help in killing the pending foreign aid bill.

Sometimes the leaking of secret documents can backfire. Reporters still independently evaluate confidential material. Murray Marder, the senior State Department man for the *Washington Post,* was recipient of classified diplomatic cables dealing with the 1965 intervention in the Dominican Republic. The secret cables were meant to sustain the administration contention that the use of U.S. troops there was to "save American lives." Marder managed to get other cables, also classified, from other sources which showed a conflicting story. His article, rather than sustaining government contentions, actually deepened the impression of government duplicity.

Max Frankel while the *Times* man at the White House, received classified material dealing with the United States-Soviet summit talks in 1967 simply by standing in a swimming pool and listening. This source in the pool with him was President Johnson.

Sometimes newspapers wax editorially indignant over classified leakage. The *Washington Post* called it "unconscionable" that Otto Otepka, a State Department officer, leaked classified material to a Senate subcommittee in 1963.

The *Times* itself engaged in editorial anguish when a *Saturday Evening Post* article by Stewart Alsop and Charles Bartlett gave an account of decision making during the Cuban Missile Crisis. Under the heading of "Breach of Security," the *Times* insisted that views of National Security Council members remain confidential else "how can there be any real freedom of discussion or dissent; how can anyone be expected to advance positions that may be politically unpopular or unprofitable?" Said the *Times*, "The secrecy of one of the highest organs of the United States has been seriously breached."

It was during the Pentagon Papers controversy that Alsop resurrected that editorial and revealed that the reporters' source was President Kennedy. Further, Kennedy had read the article in advance and, Alsop recalled, "rather badly" edited it. Unable to resist twitting the newspaper, Alsop concluded, "The *Times* series, by the *Times'* own standards, is the most serious 'breach of security' in modern history. Yet those who wait for the *Times* to denounce this particular breach will have a long wait."

One publication which did have serious security implications took place early in World War II, the second of two controversial stories published by the *Chicago Tribune*. Debate about those stories surfaced again during the public debate over the Pentagon Papers.

On December 4, 1941—just three days before the attack at Pearl Harbor—the *Tribune's* Chesly Manly filed a story from Washington which told of secret war plans during the Roosevelt administration. His source was Senator Burton K. Wheeler, an outspoken isolationist, who had actually referred to the plans in a little-noticed Senate speech one month earlier. An anti-Roosevelt employee of the War Department leaked it to the senator who leaked it to the reporter.

Actually, the plan was—as critics have described Pentagon Paper plans—a contingency measure, one of several drafted by the Department of the Army. The *Tribune* published them as proof of a secret plot to go to war; Publisher Robert R. McCormick rather sanctimoniously explaining he was doing his duty as a patriot.

The administration took no action. Presidential Press Secretary Stephen T. Early simply told reporters, "Your right to print the news is, I think, unchallenged and unquestioned. It depends entirely on the decision of the publisher and editor whether publication is patriotic or treasonable."

The government reacted far more strongly, however, when the *Tribune* engaged in a more serious breach of security on June 7, 1942. Stanley Johnston, the veteran war correspondent, had returned to Chicago to devote more time to a description of the Battle of the Coral Sea which he had just covered. Johnston while writing on the actions of Japanese ships in the Battle of Midway used remarkable detail. To the expert eye, it was clear from his report that the United States had surely broken the Japanese naval code.

The Bureau of Censorship notified the *Trib*'s Washington bureau chief that censorship had been violated. After receiving a reply, the bureau said, "it had no further quarrel with the *Tribune* in this matter."

On August 7, however, Attorney General Francis Biddle announced that a federal grand jury in Chicago would investigate. Johnston and others from the newspaper testified. According to Clayton Kilpatrick, who became editor of the paper years later, "The *Tribune* has never wavered in its conviction that the controversial stories violated no law and publication was consistent with a newspaper's privileges under the First Amendment." He said the jury, on August 20, refused to indict.

Columnist Joseph Alsop, however, in a now-it-can-be-told report during the Pentagon Papers matter, said a sealed indictment actually was handed down. The government never used it, however, for a very good reason. The Japanese apparently never read the *Chicago Tribune*. They continued to use their secret code. The government decided, wisely, that dropping the matter would improve chances that the Japanese would continue their coded way, oblivious to the great revelation of a newspaper in Chicago. It was only after U.S. planes ambushed Admiral Yamamoto a year later that the Japanese realized their code had been broken and proceeded to change it.

Early in 1971, five months before the Pentagon Papers were published, President Nixon ordered a high-level interagency review of declassification. He said it was "to enlarge the American people's right to know by making more information available, not less." Some weeks after the Papers were published, the president stepped up the campaign and asked Congress for a six-million dollar, five-year program to declassify World War II secrets. The White House said the program would continue then to declassification of secrets of the Korean War, the U.S. landing in Lebanon in 1958, the Bay of Pigs, and the Cuban Missile Crisis.

Presidential Assistant John Erlichman announced the declassification proposals saying the administration hoped to be "classifying fewer documents in the future, but classifying them better." He said the Pentagon Papers publication had demonstrably affected negotiations with foreign powers. He was asked of this is why the administration had gone to court with the *Times,* if this were a demonstration to other nations of the good faith of the Nixon administration. "Yes," he replied.

A reporter from the *Times* asked Erlichman if his reference to reporters "innocently" publishing troublesome material meant that he thought reporters doing the Pentagon Papers series were innocent. Erlichman said he couldn't comment since the matter might come before the courts but he added, looking at the reporter, "Deep in the questioner's heart must lie the answer to that question."

But there was another question to be answered and it was deep in the conscience of Murray Irwin Gurfein who had sworn in some new citizens and had done little else from his new post on the federal bench before receiving this historic case. Gray-haired, stocky, mustached, Judge Gurfein had been a key assistant to Thomas E. Dewey during Dewey's racket-busting days as district attorney. He had been a Lt. Colonel in Army Intelligence during the war and afterwards served as an assistant to the U.S. chief counsel at the Nuremberg war crime trials. On June 19, 1971 he was a federal judge and at noon, the lawyers were to come to his chambers to hear his verdict.

Ninety minutes after they arrived, the judge ruled. He told the lawyers "I am not going to grant an injunction." He had ruled for the *Times.*

His sixteen-page opinion was then released. Judge Gurfein wrote that there had never been a case like this one, never a claim that national security permits restraint of publication. On the other hand, the government had shown that there never was an attempt to publish such a massive compilation of documents, something the judge termed "unique" in the history of "leaks."

He said the government was acting in good faith in protecting security and not trying to suppress dissent or unpopular political opinion. But, he added, "The issue is narrower—as to whether and to what degree the alleged security of the United States may 'chill' the right of newspapers to publish."

Judge Gurfein dismissed the suggestion that there was a violation of the Espionage Act. Congress, he noted never intended that the act be used against newspapers. The government is then left with the premise that, without statutory authority, it has a right to protect national security. Nothing said in private, "in camera," said the judge, convinced him that the Pentagon Papers violated national security. These were historic documents. The *Times* had acted "to vindicate the right of the public to know." He dismissed the "jitters" of security people and foreign governments.

Near the end of his ruling, Judge Gurfein said, "If there be some embarrassment to the government in security aspects as remote as the general embarrassment that flows from any security breach, we must learn to live with it."

He continued, "The security of the nation is not at the ramparts alone. Security lies in the value of our free institutions. A cantankerous press, an obstinate press, a ubiquitous press must be suffered by those in authority in order to preserve the even greater values of freedom of expression and the right of the people to know."

In continued eloquence, the judge also wrote: "These are troubled times. There is no greater safety valve for discontent and cynicism about the affairs of government than freedom of expression in any form. This has been the genius of our institutions throughout our history. It has been the credo of all our presidents. It is one of the marked traits of our national life that distinguish us from other nations under different forms of government."

U.S. Attorney Seymour immediately walked upstairs to the offices of Court of Appeals Judge Irving R. Kaufman and filed an appeal. Within the hour, Judge Kaufman extended the restraining order against publication until noon Monday to permit a three-judge panel to now hear the case.

At Key Biscayne, Florida a presidential spokesman defended the government's pursuit of a judgment to stop publication. Presidential

Press Secretary Ron Ziegler said the government "cannot operate its foreign policy in the best interest of the American people if it cannot deal with foreign powers in a confidential way."

Republican National Chairman Robert Dole, the highly partisan senator from Kansas, was having it both ways in a Saturday speech in Hot Springs, Arkansas. He said the Pentagon Papers showed the Democrats guilty of "eight years of deception and escalation." At the same time, Dole attacked their publication calling it irresponsible journalism which left heads of state "at the mercy of sensation-seeking newspapers."

On Sunday, the newsmagazines came out and both *TIME* and *Newsweek* reported the views of the key figure of the Vietnam War, Lyndon Johnson. *Newsweek* said Johnson saw "the ghostly hand of Robert Kennedy" in the preparation of the Pentagon history, the senator desiring Vietnam as the issue in his intended challenge against Johnson in 1968 (McNamara was close to the Kennedys and originally named to his post by Robert's brother). *Newsweek* also reported that Johnson felt the circumstance surrounding the leak to the *Times* "comes close to treason." *TIME* said Johnson felt the Pentagon Papers "do not tell the true story because they are mostly contingency plans."

On Monday, the *Times* lawyers went before the three-judge panel and were told that the case was so important restraint of publication was to be extended again to permit all eight judges in the appeals court to hear it. In Washington, Judge Gerhard Gesell (son of the famous pediatrician, Dr. Arnold Gesell) rejected the government's case against the *Post* but the nine-member U.S. Court of Appeals extended the ban on publication another twenty-four hours to permit further appeal.

Three things happened on Tuesday—the *Times* did poorly before the circuit court of appeals, the *Post* saw the U.S. Court of Appeals extend its ban indefinitely until it could rule, and the *Boston Globe* got into the act.

The *Globe* began a series on the Papers with special reference to the Kennedy years, especially that president's role in approving "covert actions" in North Vietnam and Laos. The Justice Department asked it to stop. The *Globe* refused. In a now familiar routine, Justice went to court and U.S. District Court Judge Anthony Julian issued an order enjoining it from further publication of its series.

The *Post,* after a three-hour hearing in which the U.S. solicitor general himself argued the government's case, was told that there was to be no further publication until the court rules. There was no indication as to when it would do so. Solicitor General Erwin Griswold offered to have the State and Defense Departments appoint a special task force to expedite reclassification of the Pentagon Papers within forty-five days. The *Post's* lawyer, William Glendon, rejected the offer calling it "government by handout" and adding, "We're not willing to leave it up to them. Where do we go if we don't agree with them?"

The *Times* found the appeals court unsympathetic. U.S. Attorney Whitney North Seymour, Jr. argued that the case was important enough to warrant an exception to the First Amendment. He said that he realized the government's position was unpopular "but great constitutional issues are not decided by catchwords like 'freedom of the press' and 'the people's right to know.' "

On Wednesday, the appeals panel sent the case back to Judge Gurfein and asked him to hold more secret hearings. It extended the stay on publication for several more days. In Washington, the *Post* fared better. The U.S. Court of Appeals ruled seven to two in support of Judge Gesell. The *Post* however was told not to publish; the restraining order was continued to permit the Justice Department to take the case to the U.S. Supreme Court. The *Times* decided that it, too, would go to the nation's highest court.

On that day, in Chicago, still another newspaper came out with fresh revelations. The *Chicago Sun-Times* spelled out the U.S. intimacy with plans to overthrow South Vietnamese President Diem in 1963.

On that day, the *Los Angeles Times* published still another Pentagon Papers story. Eleven Knight newspapers on that day published theirs. The purloined papers were being published faster than the government lawyers could stop them in the courts.

On that day, too, Daniel Ellsberg surfaced.

On the CBS Evening News with Walter Cronkite, with no advance notice, there was Ellsberg saying, "The fact here is that, in the seven to ten thousand pages of this study, I don't think there was a line in them that contains an estimate of the likely impact of our policy on the overall casualties among the Vietnamese, or the refugees to be caused, the effects of defoliation in an ecological sense. There is neither an estimate nor a calculation of past effects, ever."

Cronkite explained that "perhaps because of his clearly delicate legal position, he (Ellsberg) will not talk right now of whatever part he played in the release of the secret documents." Cronkite then led to the long interview emphasizing Ellsberg's views on "official cold-heartedness" toward the civilian casualties of the war:

> The war has been an American war. And there's certainly realism to the way that it's reflecting the actual attitudes of the people making the decisions. Never in those cables or estimates, I think, outside of memos by a few people, General Lansdale being one, I think will the public find when they read these, a Vietnamese leader described with concern, friendship, respect, or evaluated in any terms other than as an instrument of American policy. . . .
>
> By '68, I had read most of the study, written a draft for one volume of it. And, well, can you imagine yourself what you'd feel like to have read those seven thousand pages, judging from the thousand or so you've seen summaries of so far? . . .
>
> I've read all of it. I've read it several times. I think it obviously led me to kinds of activity against the war, publicly. But it was simply very baffling to my colleagues, none of whom had read the study. Almost none of whom knew of its existence or the fact that I had read it.
>
> I think maybe they'll understand there are some strange things about my intensity that they described, a month from now. I hope we'll see some more intense involvement in ending this war. I'm sure this story is more painful for many people at this moment than for me because, of course, it is familiar to me, having read it several times. But it must be painful for the American people now to read these papers, and there's a lot more to come, and to discover that the men who they gave so much respect and trust, as well as power, regarded them as contemptuously as they regarded our Vietnamese allies.

How had Daniel Ellsberg come to be on nationwide television on that Wednesday evening? All journalists were, of course, eager to interview the man who supplied the Pentagon Papers to the *Times*. Walter Cronkite, a long-time friend of the family of Mrs. Ellsberg, called everyone he knew suggesting such an interview be done on television. Word came back that Ellsberg would talk to a representative of Cronkite.

Gordon Manning, the energetic vice-president of CBS News, immediately flew to Boston and checked into a hotel awaiting contact. The next days were full of intrigue comparable to any that newspapers endured in dealing with those who leaked the papers. Manning would be asked to call his wife back home in Connecticut. She in turn would tell him about a call from Ellsberg's representative suggesting the next step. Manning was sent to a hotel in nearby Cambridge and literally expected his contact to step from behind a potted palm. In time he was driven around the darkened streets of Cambridge in a manner designed to make it difficult to know where he was going.

When Manning finally reached the Ellsbergs and their friends, he found them more interested in having CBS reveal more of the documents than in doing an interview. Manning, whose particular genius is unbending persistence when tracking down a story or an interview, argued that the real value of television is the opportunity for Ellsberg to tell his story his own way. Besides, many newspapers were now publishing the Papers. At first it appeared that his doggedness would not prevail. He was given a sample chapter of the Papers to examine and was returned to Boston. Manning walked through the streets in the middle of the night, the Papers under his arm. When dawn arose, he went to an army surplus store and bought a knapsack to keep them in.

The next day was spent in the hotel room with phone calls from the Ellsberg contacts and back and forth to New York. Manning continued to argue for the interview, his contact ("Just call me Mr. Boston") for CBS to "publish" the chapter. Finally a messenger came to pick up the Papers in Manning's possession. Manning continued to urge the interview with Ellsberg.

Word finally came back—"Yes, Ellsberg would be interviewed." Walter Cronkite flew up towards Boston. The city was weathered-in and he landed in Providence, raced by auto to Boston. There he met Manning and the camera crews, then went to a private home in Cambridge where the interview was filmed. It was rushed back to Boston for processing. Due to the plane delay, the film was barely edited in time for transmission to New York. A longer, in-depth

version was then fed to New York for a special half-hour broadcast that night at 10:30 P.M.

In it, Cronkite began with a discussion of the publication and its
importance, Ellsberg noting:

> I was struck, in fact, by President Johnson's reaction to these
> revelations as 'close to treason,' because it reflected to me this
> sense of—that what was damaging to the reputation of a particu-
> lar individual, was in effect treason, which is very close to saying
> 'I am the state.' And I think that quite sincerely many presidents,
> not only Lyndon Johnson, have come to feel that. What these
> studies tell me is we must remember this is a self-governing
> country. We are the government. And in terms of institutions,
> the Constitution provides for separation of powers, for Congress,
> for the courts, informally for the press, protected by the First
> Amendment. Well, we've seen all of those branches, if we call
> them branches, of the government, alive and functioning, I think,
> very well this last week. That hasn't always been the case. I think
> we can not at all let the officials of the executive branch deter-
> mine for us what it is that the public needs to know about how
> well and how they are discharging their functions.

CRONKITE: Speaking of Mr. Johnson's words, that this is
treasonous, or whatever that exact quote was, there is a question here, though, isn't there, of an individual setting up his own
moral judgment over that of the law in—in the question of revealing these documents, for instance. I mean, when we talk
about public responsibility, and private morality, and government responsibility, there—there's a crossroads there, and what
about this question of individual moral responsibility and the
law?

ELLSBERG: I think you're right in describing it as a moral
choice, a very difficult one. It's very similar, I would take it, to
the responsibility, the choice that the *New York Times* and the
Washington Post, and now the *Globe,* the *Sun-Times* I believe,
have faced. Having been informed by the Justice Department
that in the interpretation of the law by the Justice Department,
James Reston, Sulzberger, Bradlee, Katharine Graham would be
in violation, they went ahead, at their jeopardy, like in feeling
that their obligations to the people of the country, and their

rights under the First Amendment, came above the interpretation by the Justice Department, or the Defense Department. That's, basically, an analogy.

Cronkite dealt at length with basic criticism of administration supporters that the Papers really dealt with contingency plans:

CRONKITE: Well, then, is it possible to draw conclusions, Mr. Ellsberg, from what we have read so far in this documentation, and I ask that with a couple of specifics in mind. I mean, let's just take some cases. Assistant Secretary of Defense McNaughton, I think in 1964, I believe it was, came up with a paper, it was in there, suggesting possible provocation of North Vietnam as an excuse for escalation, bombing. There is really no evidence at all that President Johnson approved such a—such a program, or a thought, or would have entertained it if it had been brought to him, is there?

ELLSBERG: When you say there's no evidence on President Johnson, you are—you're correct. The record, the documentary record available for this study is fairly complete on the record of presidential decisions, but not on the thinking that the president may have brought to bear on those decisions, and not on the internal memoranda that I'm sure flowed within the White House. As a matter of fact, my impression is that presidential opinion on such matters is less committed to paper than that of almost any other official. It's more on the telephone, more in private conversation. It doesn't leave a documentary trail. So it would certainly be right, from a historical point of view, to say that conclusions about presidential motives are least accessible from this particular documentary record.

CRONKITE: So all we really do have here, except where the presidential documentary trail, as you say, crosses the Pentagon area, what we have here then is the thinking of lower echelons on the contingency planning basis primarily, isn't it?

ELLSBERG: Far more than contingency planning. That is a quite deceptive description being given to this by former officials, and current ones. We're talking, in most cases, about plans that were called for by the president because of a recommendation by a high official, one or another, that they might well be used in the future. They were done in most cases, in the period you're talking about, with the expectation that one of several, of a small group of plans, would be used. In many cases, we're talking about a plan that was used, or a plan that was recommended. The fact that it was recommended, the fact that it had the character that it did and the kind of argument that it did, is information that I would say is very much needed to know by the public. The quality of thinking, the kinds of alternatives that are presented to the public—to the president.

Before the interview was over, Cronkite raised the question of why the Pentagon Papers were released at this time. He asked . . .

Why now? Why today, when President Nixon has a policy of withdrawal from Vietnam, and seems to be proceeding along on that plan, should—should this be thrown up to the—before the American people? Wouldn't it be better to let this war get over with, and—and then take a look at how decisions were made, and see how we can improve that process in the future?

Ellsberg replied that he envisioned a "replay of '64" with elections coming up and the public being kept from plans to escalate the war.

ELLSBERG: Now, I came to believe, in late '69, on the basis of information from the administration, that again we had an administration at least—of which at least the two high officials, President Nixon and Henry Kissinger, believed that it was essential to their purposes, their understanding of American interests, that the president have again a credible threat of bombing. This came in conflict, of course, with the cutoff of bombing in November 1968. In effect we had set conditions in which we would restore bombing, and could not really make a threat credible unless those conditions were violated. Apparently it seemed essential that the president, in his eyes, I am told, you understand, again be ready to threaten bombing, and he understood that to do this would require demonstrations, would require the actual practice of bombing, to achieve again either an acceptable settlement—acceptable to him, in terms defined very similarly to those of the past, or an acceptable stalemate, which by now would have to mean one with less U.S. ground troops involved.

The evidence, as time went on in '69 and then Cambodia, and in '70, Son Tay, and the bombing of North Vietnam in the fall of 1970, the bombing, almost very frequently after that, and the operation into Laos, all convinced me, and I think ultimately began to suggest to a larger number of the public that this is the direction we were going, the direction in which the threat of escalation and the practice of escalation was once again part of U.S. policy. In this sense, it did come to seem to me, especially in the spring of 1970, after Laos, that suddenly the history of 1964–65 had become of extremely urgent relevance to the people of this country, to the Congress, and to the officials."

On the following morning, the Justice Department having lost its case against the Washington paper, filed before the U.S. Supreme Court on appeal. The New York paper, having lost its court battle with the Justice Department, similarly appealed to the Supreme Court. They were labeled cases No. 1873 and 1885 but were handled together.

There was little breathing time for anyone involved. The Supreme Court term ended on the following Monday and here it was Thursday. There was no certainty that the Court would even hear the case, but on Friday it agreed to hear the matter on Saturday. The Court also voted five to four to continue the restraint on publication by the two papers involved.

At the Justice Department, meanwhile, it was announced that the articles in the *Los Angeles Times* and the Knight newspapers did not reveal secret information. Justice, however, was not done with outbreaks of Pentagon Papers—the *Baltimore Sun* offered some new revelations and, on Friday, the *St. Louis Post-Dispatch* reported extensive excerpts dealing with McNamara's growing pessimism in 1966. Within twenty-four hours the St. Louis paper would be restrained from further publication by the U.S. district judge there, Judge James H. Meredith.

On Saturday, June 26, the Supreme Court was prepared to hear the arguments. The *Chicago Sun-Times* was offering still new revelations on that Saturday, Ellsberg's lawyers announced that he would give himself up the following Monday, and in Phoenix, Vice-President Agnew called publication of the Papers a "cheap, common, fencing operation," adding that the people responsible "are the same people who are firmly controlling American opinion through a biased and slanted and an oversighted viewpoint of what is taking place around the world."

A long line of Americans formed outside the handsome marble building that housed the Supreme Court, east of the Capitol and north of the Library of Congress. They were there to witness the climactic chapter in a story just two weeks old with shadows that stretched far into years ahead.

The spectators lined up in very early morning. The courtroom's 165 public seats quickly filled. The arguments were low-key and very business like with an hour set aside for the government's case, thirty minutes each for the *Times* and the *Post* beginning at 11 A.M.

Chief Justice Warren Burger opened with the simple announcement, "We will hear arguments in numbers 1873 and 1885, the *New York Times* against the United States and the United States against the *Washington Post* Company."

He gave the decision on the government's petition for "in camera" proceedings, declaring the request denied. He reported that the vote was six to three with Justices Harlan, Blackmun, and himself voting in the minority. He added that the parties could submit writings under seal in lieu of "in camera" oral arguments and then invited Solicitor General Griswold to proceed.

In the two hours and fifteen minutes of argument that followed, the government repeated its basic case involving national security. It also included other arguments, including the possibility of a copyright violation in the newspapers' publication of other men's words. Griswold said, "In the court of Appeals I gave the example of a manuscript written by Ernest Hemingway, let us assume while he was still living, unpublished, perhaps incomplete subject to revision. In some way the press gets hold of it. Perhaps it is stolen. Perhaps it is bought from a secretary through breach of fiduciary responsibility, or perhaps it is found on the sidewalk. If the *New York Times* sought to print that, I have no doubt that Mr. Hemingway or now his heirs, next of kin, could obtain from the court an injunction against the press printing it."

Justice Harlan expressed concern over the speed with which the matter had raced through lower courts and Griswold responded by citing one example of why he thought things were moving too fast: "It is perfectly true that there was a trial before Judge Gesell in the district court of the United States. I referred to it in my closed brief as 'hastily conducted' and have said that there was no trace of criticism in that. Judge Gesell started the trial at 8 o'clock last Monday morning, and was under orders from the court of appeals to have his decision made by 5 P.M., and there are forty-seven volumes of material, and millions of words."

Griswold offered property right, unauthorized possession, and the "top secret" classification as reasons for restraining publication, but he didn't press those points. The heart of his argument was that the printing of some of the documents—and he concentrated on a list of ten items, one of those items including four of the forty-seven volumes—would pose a grave and immediate danger to the security of the United States. That brought a question from Justice Stewart.

STEWART: "Your case depends upon the claim, as I understand it, that the disclosure of this information would result in an immediate grave threat to the security of the United States of America."

GRISWOLD: "Yes, Mr. Justice."

STEWART: "However it was acquired and however it was classified?"

GRISWOLD: "Yes, Mr. Justice. But I think the fact that it was obviously acquired improperly is not irrelevant in the consideration of that question. I repeat, obviously acquired improperly."

Responding to Justice Harlan, the solicitor general warned of specific consequences of publication.

GRISWOLD: "I think the heart of our case is that the publication of the material specified in my closed brief will materially affect the security of the United States. It will affect lives; it will affect the process of the termination of the war; it will affect the process of recovering prisoners of war."

Later Professor Bickel speaking for the *Times* was asked about this very question. The inquiry came from the chief justice.

BURGER: "Can anyone know in any certain sense the consequences of disclosure of sources of information, for example, the upsetting of negotiations, if that were hypothetically true, in

Paris or possible negotiations that we don't know anything about in the release of war prisoners, and that sort of thing? How does a government meet the burden of proof in the sense that Judge Gesell laid it down? That does not bring any battleships to the outer limits of New York Harbor, or set off any missiles, but would you say that it is not a very grave matter?

BICKEL: "Your Honor, I think if we are to place possibilities or conjecture against suspension or abridgment of the First Amendment, the answer is obvious. The fact, the possibility, the conjecture, or the hypothesis that diplomatic negotiations would be made more difficult or embarrassed does not justify, and this is what we have in this case, I think, and is all we have, does not justify, suspending the First Amendment. Yet this is what has happened here."

Addressing the government, Justice Thurgood Marshall asked about the future, about other Pentagon Papers dealing with other questions. He was concerned about the court having to deal with similar problems again and again.

MARSHALL: "Mr. Solicitor General, what particularly worries me at this point is that I assume that if there are studies not now being made, in the future there will be studies made about Cambodia, Laos, you name it. If you prevail in this case, then in any instance that anybody comes by any of those studies, a temporary restraining order will automatically be issued. Am I correct?"

GRISWOLD: "It is hard for me to answer the question in such broad terms. I think that if properly classified materials are improperly acquired, and that it can be shown that they do have an immediate or current impact on the security of the United States, that there ought to be an injuction."

MARSHALL: "Wouldn't we then—the federal courts—be a censorship board, as to whether this does? . . ."

GRISWOLD: "That is a pejorative way to put it, Mr. Justice. I do not know what the alternative is."

BLACK: "The First Amendment might be.

GRISWOLD: "Yes, Mr. Justice, and we are, of course, fully supporting the First Amendment. We do not claim or suggest any exception to the First Amendment."

STEWART: "Of course, as you know, Mr. Solicitor General,

that unless the constitutional law, as it now exists, is changed, a prior restraint of publication by a newspaper is presumptively unconstitutional."

GRISWOLD: "It is a very serious matter. There is no doubt about it, and so is the security of the United States a very serious matter. We have two important constitutional objectives here which have to be weighed and balanced, and made as harmonious as they can be."

The solicitor general chided the newspapers on their position that they must protect news sources while here the government was not able to protect its sources. Chief Justice Burger picked up that theme in an exchange with the *Post* lawyer, William R. Glendon.

BURGER: "This is an equity proceeding, and there are certain standards about people coming into equity with clean hands, which is one of them, and prepared to do equity."

GLENDON: "We did not come into equity. The government came into equity.

BURGER: "You were brought in.

GLENDON: "We were brought in kicking and screaming, I guess.

BURGER: "You are now in the position of making demands on the First Amendment. You say the newspaper has a right to protect its sources, but the government does not.

GLENDON: "I see no conflict, Your Honor. We are in the position of asking that there not be a prior restraint in violation of the Constitution imposed on us, and that equity should not do that. We are also in the position of saying that under the First Amendment we are entitled to protect our sources, and frankly I just do not find any conflict bearing on it."

Justice White posed a question concerning the circumstances under which prior restraint on publishing might be considered necessary. He asked Bickel, "Professor, your standard, that you are contending for, is grave and immediate, or is it not? Is that too general for you?"

In his reply, Bickel said, "The standard, in general, that I would have in mind, would at one end, have a grave event—danger to the nation. Some of the things described in the description of 'top secret' classification, in the executive order that the solicitor general read off, I think, would fit that end of the standard. At the other end would be the fact of publication. And I would demand, and this would be my second element, that the link between the fact of publication and the feared danger—the feared event—be direct, immediate, and visible."

Justice Stewart was still dissatisfied. He framed a hypothetical question. "What if the disclosure did not pose a grave threat to the nation, but did pose a danger to only a few men—perhaps a hundred soldiers?" He asked a direct question. "You would say the Constitution requires that it be published and that these men die. Is that it?"

BICKEL: "No. I am afraid that my inclination to humanity overcomes a somewhat more abstract devotion to the First Amendment, in a case of that sort. I would wish that Congress took a look to the seldom-used, and not in very good shape, Espionage Acts, and clean them up some, so that we can have statutes that are clearly applicable."

Justice Douglas had been scribbling notes on a tablet, as he often does during arguments. But he looked up with a question interrupting Bickel.

DOUGLAS: "Why would this statute make a difference? Because the First Amendment provides that Congress shall make no law abridging freedom of the press. Do you read that to mean that Congress could make some laws abridging freedom of the press?"

BICKEL: "No, sir. Only in that I have conceded, for purposes of this argument, that some limitations, some impairment of the absoluteness of that prohibition, is possible. And I argue that, whatever that may be, it is surely its very least when the president acts without statutory authority, because that inserts into it as well."

Douglas interrupting, said, "That is a very strange argument for the *Times* to be making . . . that Congress can make all of this illegal by passing laws."

The hypothetical question of Stewart was sobering: what if publication meant a death sentence for soldiers? As he put it, "Let us assume that when the members of the court go back and open up this sealed record we find something there that absolutely convinces us that its disclosure would result in the sentencing to death of a hundred young men whose only offense had been that they were nineteen years old and had low draft numbers. What should we do?"

Bickel said he was sure that they would not find that but he could only fall back on those humanitarian grounds. Douglas demanded the purity of the First Amendment. There was another argument possible: a revelation that might result in some deaths might also prevent many more. John F. Kennedy admitted that exposure in the case of the Bay of Pigs preparation would have saved a disaster. Is it not possible, one might ask, that exposure of clandestine military activity at other times might not—in the long run—prevent national error and subsequent deaths rather than simply endanger a few or a hundred men?

After the arguments ended, the supreme court retired to deliberate, taking with them mountains of secret evidence and three very fat briefs from the government, the *Times* and the *Post*. At 6 P.M. they left without announcing a decision.

An examination of the three briefs shows how the government's case and that of the newspapers was presented.

The *Post* quoted at length from the opinion of the district court, which ruled in the newspaper's favor earlier. The *Post* concluded, "One, the Government failed to prove that publication of material from the Vietnam history would lead to any break in diplomatic relations, any armed attack on the United States, or any of its allies, the revelation of any information respecting current troop movements, or any compromise in military or defense plans, intelligence operations, or scientific and technological materials. Two, the Government failed to demonstrate that publication of such material would result in any immediate grave threat to the national security. And three, that there was no likelihood that the Government would succeed on its merits."

The government brief said, "The issue before the Court, although of great importance, is narrow. There is no question here of any blanket attempt by the Government to enjoin the publication of a newspaper, or any attempt to impose a generalized prohibition upon the publication of broad categories of material. The only issue is whether, in a suit by the United States, the First Amendment bars the Court from prohibiting a newspaper from publishing material whose disclosure would pose a grave and immediate danger to the security of the United States."

The *New York Times* case stated, "In the public testimony of the Government witnesses, there was a total absence of a single specific piece of evidence indicating that publication of the Vietnam volumes could damage the national security interests of the United States in any particular area. None of the three witnesses for the United States referred to a single document in his open testimony, nor a single instance of prejudicing such defense interests. None in his open testimony suggested that *The Times* had published shipping dates, future military maneuvers, plans, weapons systems, data, or the like."

The government said, "In this subtle and difficult world of diplomacy, things are often said in confidence that will prove so embarrassing if disclosed that the mere threat of disclosure is enough to leave them unsaid. Sensitive negotiations often are carried on through people, who, if they knew their identity might be disclosed, would be unwilling to participate. The publication of material relating to confidential discussions and negotiations between this country and both friendly and unfriendly powers would have the gravest consequences because it could dry up vital sources of information and thwart, if not sometimes destroy, meaningful communication."

To that point, the *Washington Post* said that a previous Supreme Court case held that the president had no such inherent powers. The *Post* also contended that the president in his role as the executor of foreign policy could not deprive American citizens, whether here or abroad, of the rights guaranteed them under the Bill of Rights.

The government contended, "The only case in which this Court has considered whether the First Amendment bars an injunction against the publication of a periodical was *Near vs. Minnesota.* The Court there struck down as violating the prohibition in the First Amendment, a part of the press made applicable to the states by the Fourteenth Amendment. It concerned an anti-Semitic periodical under a Minnesota statute permitting the suppression of newspapers or periodicals as public nuisances. Although the Court held that this statute sanctioning suppression of the offending newspaper or periodical was unconstitutional, as a previous restraint upon publication, the Court recognized that under the First Amendment, 'the protection even as to previous restraint is not absolutely unlimited. No one would question but that a Government might prevent actual obstruction to its recruiting service, or the publication of the sailing dates of transports, or number and location of troops.' "

"These examples," says the government, "were merely illustrative, and obviously there are other items of information so vital to the security of the United States that their publication may be enjoined. The exception to the prohibition upon prior restraint recognized in *Near vs. Minnesota,* surely covers material whose publication would pose, 'a grave and immediate danger to the security of the United States.' "

The *Post* regarding the Near case, said, "That case speaks of actual obstruction to the Government's recruiting services, the publication of the sailing dates of transports and the number and location of troops. It seems obvious," said the *Post,* "that the exception to the prohibition against prior restraint was conceived as embracing only the most serious, immediate, and substantial threats to the Government's ability to wage war, imminent risk of death to its military personnel, grave breaches of the national security and the like. No such injury was established here."

Over and over again, the *Times* brief returned to its main point about prior restraint. It said, "Prior restraints on publication are peculiarly disfavored by the First Amendment. Whatever difficult conceptual issues may yet be presented with respect to the First Amendment, the bar on prior restraints is at the core of the theory of that Amendment. As such, the Government bears an extremely heavy burden to demonstrate that the prior restraints sought in this case could possibly be justified."

The *Times* also noted, "The violation of a prior restraint may be assured of being held in contempt. The violator of a statute punishing speech criminally knows that he will have to go before a jury and may be willing to take a chance, counting on a possible acquittal. A prior restraint therefore, stops more speech, more effectively. A criminal statute chills. The prior restraint freezes."

The United States emphasized the question of classification. In its brief, the government explained, "The determination of the particular classification that is appropriate for national defense purposes, and whether and when that classification should be changed are matters of the highest sensitivity and difficulty. They require judgments based on wide knowledge of and familiarity with many interrelated factors. Whether a particular document requires a 'top secret' classification, or whether that classification should be removed, cannot be decided on the basis of a simple reading of the documents. Material that seems relatively innocuous to the casual observer may to one more familiar with the intricacies and intimate details of the situation, be revealed to have an entirely different significance."

The *Times* response came when it said, "Max Frankel, the Washington Bureau Chief and Washington Correspondent of the *New York Times,* attested to the practice of officials in Government regarding disclosure of secrets to the press. Mr. Frankel's affidavit is replete with instances of Government officials, from the President and the Secretary of State on down to lower ranking officials, leaking classified information to himself, with knowledge that this information would be published in news stories appearing in the *New York Times.*"

The *Times* then went on, "the *Times* has also submitted affidavits of James MacGregor Burns, Eric F. Goldman, and Barbara W. Tuchman, each of whom is a well-known historian of great repute. Each of these affiants attested to the importance to the historians of the type of material published by the *New York Times,* and to the essentially historical nature of that material. Professor Burns, in addition, from past experience in Government service, particularly in Army Intelligence and as a military historian, avers that Governments, both United States and foreign, tend to take an excessively self-protective and parochial view of the 'security problem.' This results in a failure to make frank and clear disclosure of historical events and thus reduces the ability of the public and Governments to learn from mistakes of the past."

In a sense, the government's case in the end hinged on a quotation from Alexander Hamilton in "The Federalist." He had written, "The circumstances that endanger the safety of nations are infinite, and for this reason, no constitutional shackles can wisely be imposed on the power to which the care of it is committed. This power ought to be coextensive with all the possible combinations of such circumstances. It ought to be under the direction of the same councils which are appointed to preside over the common defence."

Having thus quoted "The Federalist," the government said, "Obviously, in circumstances like those here, the only effective means of protecting the nation against the improper disclosure of military secrets is to enjoin their impending publication. To limit the President's power in this regard, solely to punishment of those who disclose secret information, would render the power meaningless. The harm sought to be prevented would have been irreparably accomplished."

The *Times* closed its case by talking about censorship and the relation of government to press. "This country's experience with censorship of political speech is happily almost nonexistent. Through wars and other turbulence, we have avoided it. Given a choice of risks, we have chosen to risk freedom as the First Amendment enjoins us to do. As our affidavits show, press and government have a curious interlocking, both cooperative and adversary relationship. This has been the case, more or less, in this country, since the extension of manhood suffrage and the rise of an independent, rather than party-connected or faction-connected, press. It is not a tidy relationship. It is unruly, or to the extent that it operates under rules, these are unwritten and even tacit ones. Unquestionably, every so often, it malfunctions from the point of view of one or the other partners to it.

"The greater power within it lies with the government. The press wields the countervailing power conferred upon it by the First Amendment. If there is something near a balance, it is an uneasy one. Any redressing of it at the expense of the press, as this case demonstrates, can come only at the cost of incursions into the First Amendment."

The *Times* then concludes, "In effect in this case, the Court is asked, without benefit of statute, to redress the balance, to readjust the uneasy arrangement which has, after all, served us well."

This was the matter that the highest court of the land took to its private conference. The second-guessers on the sidelines noted that the newspapers seemed to have four sure votes—Black, Brennan,

Douglas, and Marshall. The government was confident of support from Burger, Blackmun, and Harlan. The case hinged on the
deliberations of Stewart and White. As the hours wore on, the
second-guessers offered third and fourth guesses. No one was sure
how the court would rule. On each side, everyone was convinced
that the lengthening hours were ominous.

Across the green lawn that separates the home of the judiciary
from the home of the legislative, congressional committees were in
session that Saturday. The pro-Pentagon House Armed Services
Committee voted twenty-five to two to reject the resolution of inquiry, introduced by Rep. Bella Abzug, dealing with the Pentagon
documents.

Seven members of the House Government Operations Committee, on the other hand, asked Defense Secretary Laird to deliver
a set of the documents to that committee by the end of June. The
group's investigation of the top secret classification problem in the
Pentagon Papers was chaired by Pennsylvania's William Moorhead.
The hearing had given him insight into the classification process,
Moorhead saying he knew why the practice was so widespread—
"First, I think it's the fact that a bureaucrat doesn't get in trouble
for classifying. He might get in trouble if he didn't classify. So we've
got to devise some sort of discipline on the bureaucrat. The second
thing, the old thing, it makes the fellow seem big. If the document
he's working on can be classified 'Top Secret,' that makes him and
his boss just a little more important. And some even said that it's
a way of getting attention of people that you want to have read the
document."

With the Supreme Court exploration of the question, Representative Moorhead saw more classified matter coming to members of
Congress and less being buried in the federal bureaucracy. When
asked if he saw the possibility of a similar constitutional confrontation over classified material between the legislative and executive
branches, the chairman said, "I have a feeling that a confrontation of
this type is actually overdue. I believe that over the years the executive has whittled away at the powers of the Congress, and that each
one didn't seem important enough to make a stand on it at the
time, and that we've got to reverse that process. I welcome that
confrontation. Not as a confrontation. I think that out of it will

come a compromise which will make our democracy more a democracy. That is with more power in the people's representatives in Congress, and correspondingly, a slight diminution of the power of the executive branch, with only two elected offices. The rest, the millions of government employees don't have to face the electorate, so are not as responsive to the electorate. So I think it's for the benefit of the people that the power of the people's representatives be increased."

On Sunday, George W. Ball, former under secretary of state, appeared on "Face The Nation" and defended his former chief. Ball, identified by the papers as the chief opponent to escalation in Vietnam—a confirmation of his reputation during the Johnson years as the president's devil's advocate—insisted that Lyndon Johnson did not stifle dissent but was "grateful" for all advice. He described the president as "deeply troubled" by the war and rejected any suggestion of duplicity or deceit on the part of the Johnson administration.

On the same day, Walt W. Rostow—former advisor to the president and among the most hawkish of policy planners according to the Pentagon study—also defended the Johnson years. He strongly asserted that President Johnson "did not deceive the people."

The *Christian Science Monitor* joined the long list of newspapers publishing excerpts from the Pentagon Papers. In a cautious editorial on "Why We Print," the *Monitor* was to explain that it carefully examined all the material in its possession to be sure that there was no breach of security, no danger to the welfare of American or allied forces in Vietnam. It explained that "it is in the nature of governments to tell less than the whole truth to their people. Special pleading, unwatched and unchecked, leads to arbitrary government and deprives people of a chance to give or withhold their consent on the basis of full and balanced information. The proper role of a responsible press is to do its best at all times to tell those things which the public should know but governments would prefer to withhold."

On Monday, June 28 Daniel Ellsberg surrendered in Boston. In Los Angeles, a federal grand jury indicted him on charges of violating the Espionage Act and stealing government property.

The Congress that day received two copies of the Pentagon Papers. One set went to the Senate, the other to the House. Only members of Congress were permitted to read them.

At the Supreme Court, no decision was announced. The term, scheduled to end that day, was extended.

On Tuesday, hints came from the Supreme Court. The decision would come within a matter of days. On Tuesday, the justice department asked the *Christian Science Monitor* to stop publishing its series. The paper refused.

In the Senate, a strange event took place. The junior senator from Alaska, Mike Gravel, announced that he was the holder of a set of the Pentagon Papers and planned to read them on the Senate floor as long as he was physically able to continue. His prepared introduction, released to the press, said, "The greatest representative democracy the world has ever known, the nation of Washington and Jefferson and Lincoln, has had its nose rubbed in the swamp by petty war lords, jealous Vietnamese generals, black marketeers and grandscale dope pushers."

Gravel never got the Senate floor. Minority Whip Robert P. Griffin prevented that by a parliamentary maneuver in the absence of a quorum. Gravel sought for three hours to have the necessary fifty-one senators summoned to such a quorum. At 9:28 P.M. he gave up and acceded to adjournment of the Senate but fifteen minutes later called a "meeting" of his little known Public Works Subcommittee on Buildings and Grounds. A friendly colleague, Rep. John G. Dow of New York, appeared as a hearing "witness." Chairman Gravel began to read from the Pentagon Papers.

As Gravel plodded through the estimated forty-four hundred pages in his possession, his staff began giving newsmen parcels of the papers. They would be taken to Washington news bureaus, Xeroxed, and returned for more parcels of the Papers. This went on for hours, an estimated twenty-five hundred papers suddenly finding new circulation among Washington journalists.

Gravel, overcome by emotion and fatigue, began crying as he read on and on. Finally he could continue no longer and at 1 A.M. called the strange hearing to an end. His staff continued to circulate the papers.

The next day, an angry Hugh Scott, Republican leader in the Senate, condemned Gravel's action. Senator Scott said it appeared to be in violation of the Senate rule prohibiting members from divulging confidential communications from the executive branch. Scott said Gravel was liable to expulsion should his colleagues vote to censure him and he asked Majority Leader Mike Mansfield to make a determination. The Montana Democrat said Gravel broke no rule; there would be no action to discipline him.

The fuss over Gravel was forgotten before the day ended for on that Wednesday, June 30 the Supreme Court of the United States issued its decision.

By a vote of six to three, the High Court upheld the right of the *Times* and the *Post* to publish. Chief Justice Burger was joined by Associate Justices Blackmun and Harlan in dissent. Both of the so-called swing votes, White and Stewart, swung to the side of Black, Douglas, Marshall, Brennan, and two noted American newspapers. Each of the nine justices issued an opinion.

Justice Hugo Black, the oldest man on the Court and the member with the longest service, wrote the strongest comments. In words as clear as those in the First Amendment itself, Black said, "I believe that every moment's continuance of the injunctions against these newspapers amounts to a flagrant, indefensible, and continuing violation of the First Amendment." There was no question where he and Justice Douglas, who concurred in that opinion, stood on the issue at hand.

Black charged that "The Executive Branch seems to have forgotten the essential purpose and history of the First Amendment.

He made no attempt to conceal his anger at the government's case: "The Bill of Rights changed the original Constitution into a new charter under which no branch of government could abridge the people's freedoms of press, speech, religion, and assembly. Yet the Solicitor General argues and some members of the Court appear to agree that the general powers of the Government adopted in the original Constitution should be interpreted to limit and restrict the specific and emphatic guarantees of the Bill of Rights adopted later. I can imagine no greater perversion of history. Madison and the other Framers of the First Amendment, able men that they were, wrote in language they earnestly believed could never be misunderstood: 'Congress shall make no law . . . abridging the freedom of the press.' Both the history and language of the First Amendment support the view that the press must be left free to publish news, whatever the source, without censorship, injunctions, or prior restraints."

In contrast, Chief Justice Warren Burger decried the "unseemly haste" in which the cases were conducted and said, "When judges are pressured as in these cases the result is a parody of judicial process."

The chief justice was particularly critical of the *Times:* "It is not disputed that the *Times* has had unauthorized possession of the documents for three to four months, during which it has had its expert analysts studying them, presumably digesting them and preparing the material for publication. During all of this time, the *Times,* presumably in its capacity as trustee of the public's 'right to know,' has held up publication for purposes it considered proper and thus public knowledge was delayed. No doubt this was for a good reason; the analysis of seven thousand pages of complex material drawn from a vastly greater volume of material would inevitably take time and the writing of good news stories takes time. But why should the United States Government, from whom this information was illegally acquired by someone, along with all the counsel, trial judges, and appellate judges be placed under needless pressure? After these months of deferral, the alleged right-to-know has somehow and suddenly become a right that must be vindicated instantly.

"Would it have been unreasonable, since the newspaper could anticipate the government's objections to release of secret material, to give the government an opportunity to review the entire collection and determine whether agreement could be reached on publication?"

Mr. Chief Justice Burger expressed the belief that agreement could be reached on declassifying much of the material. Justice Potter Stewart, on the other hand, talked of the danger of "secrecy for its own sake." He noted the dangers: "For when everything is classified, then nothing is classified, and the system becomes one to be disregarded by the cynical or the careless, and to be manipulated by those intent on self-protection or self-promotion. I should suppose, in short, that the hallmark of a truly effective internal security system would be the maximum possible disclosure, recognizing that secrecy can best be preserved only when credibility is truly maintained."

Mr. Burger saw the case as involving colliding constitutional privileges and said only his brothers on the bench who were absolutists found the course clear. "In this case, the imperative of a free and unfettered press comes into collision with another imperative, the effective functioning of a complex modern government and specifically the effective exercise of certain constitutional powers of the Executive. Only those who view the First Amendment as an absolute in all circumstances—a view I respect, but reject—can find such a case as this to be simple or easy."

He found support from Justice Blackmun: "The First Amendment, after all, is only one part of an entire Constitution. Article II of the great document vests in the Executive Branch primary power over the conduct of foreign affairs and places in that branch the responsibility for the Nation's safety. Each provision of the Constitution is important, and I cannot subscribe to a doctrine of unlimited absolutism for the First Amendment at the cost of downgrading other provisions."

In contrast, Justice Stewart, with White concurring, expressed concern over the growing concentration of power in the presidency and noted the role of the press in serving as a check to this trend: "In the governmental structure created by our Constitution, the Executive is endowed with enormous power in the two related areas of national defense and international relations. This power, largely unchecked by the Legislative and Judicial branches, has been pressed to the very hilt since the advent of the nuclear missile age. For better or for worse, the simple fact is that a President of the United States possesses vastly greater constitutional independence in these two vital areas of power than does, say, a prime minister of a country with a parliamentary form of government.

"In the absence of the governmental checks and balances present in other areas of our national life, the only effective restraint upon executive policy and power in the areas of national defense and international affairs may lie in an enlightened citizenry—in an informed and critical public opinion which alone can here protect the values of democratic government. For this reason, it is perhaps here that a press that is alert, aware, and free most vitally serves the basic purpose of the First Amendment. For without an informed and free press there cannot be an enlightened people."

While this was pleasing to the press, the tenor of many of the opinions made it clear that this six to three vote was not absolute; that conditions could change. Justice Byron White, with Stewart concurring, said it bluntly: "I concur in today's judgments, but only because of the concededly extraordinary protection against prior restraints enjoyed by the press under our constitutional system. I do not say that in no circumstances would the First Amendment permit an injunction against publishing information about government plans or operations."

If this were the warning to the press that tomorrow's Pentagon Papers might be treated differently by the court, Mr. Justice Brennan issued a comparable warning to government that tomorrow's attempt to suppress publication is subject to similar treatment as today's, White and Stewart notwithstanding. "The First Amendment," he wrote, "stands as an absolute bar to the imposition of judicial restraints in circumstances of the kind presented by these cases."

It remained for the blunt words of Hugo Black to pay the newspapers their greatest compliment. He wrote, "Only a free and unrestrained press can effectively expose deception in government. And paramount among the responsibilities of a free press is the duty to prevent any part of the government from deceiving the people and sending them off to distant lands to die of foreign fevers and foreign shot and shell. In my view, far from deserving condemnation for their courageous reporting, the *New York Times,* the *Washington Post,* and other newspapers should be commended for serving the purpose that the Founding Fathers saw so clearly. In revealing the workings of government that led to the Viet-Nam war, the newspapers nobly did precisely that which the Founders hoped and trusted they would do."

And so it was done: 2:40 P.M., Wednesday, June 30, 1971.

There was jubilation in the offices of the *New York Times* and the *Washington Post.* Executives held news conferences as TV reporters and cameramen invaded the wild, celebrating newsrooms. "This is a joyous day for the press—and for American society," declared Managing Editor Abe Rosenthal of the *Times.* Said the *Post's* Executive Editor Benjamin Bradlee, "It's beautiful."

Of course, Attorney General John Mitchell was less enthusiastic. He warned that the government would now pursue the prosecution of "all those who have violated federal criminal laws in connection with this matter," including—it was presumed—newspapermen.

TIME magazine saw trouble in the pattern of the court's decision. It said, "The court's public brevity and restraint only masked intense personal differences among the Justices over the grave issues. These divisions emerged in the rare determination of all nine Justices to write their own, sometimes emotional, opinions."

Paul Freund, of Harvard, one of the nation's leading constitutional experts, hailed the Supreme Court decision as a "landmark, not in the sense of making new law, but in the sense of underscoring old law in very difficult circumstances." He was asked if he agreed with those who felt the decision quivered because there was not one but nine separate opinions. Freund didn't read any special significance in this: "I don't think there's any great puzzlement about the judgment of the Court because it was announced by the chief justice very succinctly. I think it's a case of what Cicero said: 'If I had more time, I would write you a shorter letter.' They didn't have time to consult, to collaborate, to coalesce, and accommodate their opinions, so in the brief time available, each went his own way."

A former director of public information for the Justice Department, Jack C. Landau of the Newhouse National News Service, did his own analysis of what nine opinions meant and was far from pleased with the results. In the August, 1971 issue of *Quill,* the *Sigma Delta Chi* magazine, he said:

Perhaps a more helpful way to understand the diverse opinions in the case is to synthesize the nine separate opinions by issues:

Did the government present enough evidence on June 15th to justify the initial ban against the *Times?* yes, 4–to–4 (1 unsure).

Did the government present enough evidence after hearings in the District Courts and Courts of Appeals to justify a long-term ban against the *Times* and the *Post?* no, 6–to–3.

Could Congress pass legislation giving the courts the power to censor newspapers, at least temporarily, under circumstances similar to the *Times/Post* case? yes, 6–to–2 (1 unsure).

Could the Court, in the *Times/Post* case, permanently ban the Pentagon Papers if the government had presented enough evidence to show a "grave," "immediate," and "direct" threat to the national security? yes, 7–to–2.

In a similar analysis for the *Wall Street Journal,* Louis Kohlmeier wrote that his examination indicated "the individual opinions that were handed down gave a majority of at least five Justices an opportunity to say two things that the Supreme Court has never before in history said: first, that the Constitution would not prevent the Jusitce Department from bringing criminal prosecutions against newspapers for publishing vital national defense secrets and, second, that Congress could pass a law allowing the President to censor newspapers, even though the 6–to–3 decision . . . held the Executive Branch can't restrain the press by relying simply on a claim of the 'inherent' powers of the Presidency."

There was another matter that came before the courts—the commercialization of the journalistic "scoops." Both the *Times* and the *Post* had their material copyrighted and served client newspapers across the country. In addition on July 8, just four days after the *Times* articles resumed, the Pentagon Papers series appeared as a Bantam Books paperback. It was a sentational best seller. In a single day, much of the first printing of 500,000 copies of the 677 page book was sold out. But the end of July, 1,400,000 were in print.

Kohlmeier noted that Chief Justice Burger "rather sneeringly" referred to the *Times'* claim to "sole trusteeship . . . of its journalistic scoop." Kohlmeier wrote "in future cases it would be surprising if the Government did not develop a line of reasoning that takes into consideration not only copyright privileges but such items as the *Times'* . . . paperback book . . . and the newspaper industry's successful campaign to win from Congress . . . antitrust protection other industries don't enjoy."

Landau, in his examination of the decision, was particularly harsh with the *Times* for its failure "to publish anyway and ultimately risk being held in contempt of court—a risk taken by one of the *Times'* own reporters, Earl Caldwell, when he refused to turn over his notes to a federal grand jury in San Francisco; and by CBS President Frank Stanton when he refused to give the House

Interstate and Foreign Commerce Committee outtakes of 'The Selling of the Pentagon.' "

Landau suggests that the *Times* could have engaged in other forms of protest—printing a thousand test-run copies of the paper including the Pentagon series and then burning them each night the court barred publication. It might also have permitted U.S. Marshals to seize those thousand copies.

The damage was done, said Landau, when the *Times* agreed to a four-day ban. In Washington, the courts imposed a three-day stay, in Boston a week, and in St. Louis ten days. "So next time a court enjoins your newspaper for a week or so and you complain," he warned editors, "don't be surprised if the judge tells you to calm down. After all, how can your First Amendment rights be damaged by a temporary restraining order when a similar order did not pose an 'irreparable injury' to the *New York Times*—that is, not until the *Post* got hold of the story." Landau suggests that the *Times* really stood tough in Judge Gurfein's courtroom only after the competition started putting out the same story, something the government—as Kohlmeier warned—was quick to spot.

Sardonically viewing the *Times* agreement to give the government the "opportunity" to study the evidence, Landau says Justice Brennan was "being more protective of the right to publish than the *Times*' own lawyer" when he wrote, "Every restraint issued in this case, whatever its form, has violated the First Amendment—and none the less so because that restraint was justified as necessary to afford the court an opportunity to examine the claim more thoroughly."

The pressure of the clock that nagged at government lawyers also plagued newspaper counsel. While it is easy to become distressed over the failure to stand firm from the first moment, to challenge the court, and even invite contempt, it was not as easy when viewed from the *Times*' offices that Monday midnight when the paper was without a lawyer and facing action in the morning.

The Pentagon Papers have now become part of the historic record. They would be amended and expanded with growing knowledge of other events from other sources. The Court decision on their publication became part of the precedent for press battles still to be fought, not solid enough to avoid future confrontations but sturdy enough to buttress the tradition of a free press in America.

What purpose had the publication served? The dialogue on the way modern democracies go to war was greatly expanded; the insights enlarged by this lengthy look at high level decision making in the most crucial moments of history. The London *Economist* saw this as evidence that perhaps, only through secret maneuvers and public deception could modern democracies go to war. If true, then maybe more publication of this sort was badly needed.

In a brilliant essay on the Papers, published by the *Times* on July 6, 1971, Max Frankel said, "The Pentagon Papers on how the United States went to war in Indochina probably mark the end of an era in American foreign policy—a quarter of a century of virtually unchallenged Presidential management and manipulation of war and the diplomacy bearing on war."

Frankel observed that there was a consistency in the flow from Truman to Eisenhower to Kennedy to Johnson, each president passing the problem of Vietnam on to the next in worse shape than he received it. All the presidents were reared in memory of a Congress which destroyed the League of Nations and hampered Roosevelt's search for alliances against Japan and Germany, all in memory of two world wars that might have been avoided if America had mustered its power soon enough to prevent foreign aggression, all remembering the curse of appeasement, and all recognizing the fact that the next major war would be a nuclear war unless it were deterred early enough.

The *Times*' Washington bureau chief did not see the papers offering clear evidence to support charges of deception by Lyndon Johnson either when the decision to escalate was made or when American troops were authorized to switch to a combat role. The Papers showed Johnson "moving and being moved toward war, but reluctant and hesitant to act until the end." On the other hand Johnson knew that his principal advisors saw escalation as inevitable. The forces that moved each president deeper into Vietnam themselves escalated. Said Frankel, "Neither on the way in nor on the way out, it is now clear, was the American hand ever 'free.' "

The Papers, he wrote, are a major contribution to understanding no matter what their flaws; they are "massive but incomplete, comprehensive but by no means exhaustive, remarkably honest but undoubtedly warped by perspective and experience."

He noted that they offer more than histories because they show development in a prolonged period of crisis—"Unlike diary, which can never escape the moment, and unlike history, which must distill at a remote future, the Pentagon study was able to re-enact a fateful progression of attitudes and decisions while simultaneously viewing them from a perspective greater than that of any of the participants."

The *Times,* the *Post,* the *Globe,* the others had finished their task. The publication was completed. Book versions would reveal more of, and some sets all of, the forty-seven volumes called the Pentagon Papers. Public opinion polls would show public uneasiness with the publication, some indicating three out of four persons opposed to newspapers printing state secrets. The attacks on the press, duly reported in that press, had turned many in the general public against the very newspapers which proclaimed their defense of that public's right to know.

Head-on confrontations with powerful forces, with the government itself, always leave their mark. The newspapers had won—but it seemed one battle, not a war. The history of the First Amendment seemed to be a history of such skirmishes, none quite like this and few as pronounced or bitter, but a history nevertheless of journalists fighting to remain what Thomas Jefferson called the only safeguard of public liberty, the only censors of their governors.

In the words of Judge Murray Gurfein, "The security of the nation is not at the ramparts alone."

IX

THE SELLING OF THE PENTAGON

How to Go After a Network

In 1971, the First Amendment was to be tested twice in two weeks. On June 30, the Supreme Court handed down its ruling on newspapers publishing the Pentagon Papers. On July 13, the House of Representatives was handed an opportunity to deal with broadcasters and the First Amendment.

On that sunny summer afternoon the House gathered in unusually good attendance to decide whether or not CBS's president, Dr. Frank Stanton, had committed contempt of Congress. Dr. Stanton had refused certain requests of the House Commerce Committee in its investigation of a CBS documentary. As with the Supreme Court matter, the subject of attention was the Pentagon. The broadcast, much acclaimed and much damned, was "The Selling of the Pentagon," an examination of the military's public relations activities.

Stanton refused to cooperate with congressional investigators who subpoenaed the "outtakes," film shot for but not used in the documentary. The investigating group, the Special Subcommittee on Investigations of the Committee on Interstate and Foreign Commerce, was chaired by Representative Harley Staggers, a West Virginia Democrat who was also chairman of the full Commerce Committee. It was Staggers who asked the full committee to vote Stanton in contempt. They did. It then went to the full House for a similar vote.

Throughout the controversy Chairman Staggers insisted that the First Amendment was not at issue. Indeed, his fellow committee members raised serious questions as to whether broadcasting, a licensed medium, should have First Amendment shelter in any manner approximating that of newspapers.

The events relating to that July 13th vote of the House are important because they say a great deal about the impact of television, the enemies that tough television reporting can quickly arouse, the nature of broadcasting's problems with government, and the amount of freedom that broadcasting should or does have.

Washington's bureaucrats and congressmen have long been nervous about television. It is too powerful. It was capable, someone once said, of making a national celebrity in just fifteen minutes. Was it not equally capable of shaking up an institution in one hour?

Television news had kidnapped the attention of America. Studies showed that most people were getting most of their news from television, not newspapers. Some were getting all their news that way. It was disturbing to the power élite in Washington.

There were some, including the ranking Republican on the Commerce Committee, who felt that television was not journalism, was not the press. Congressman William Springer, in a colloquy with Dr. Stanton during the subcommittee hearings, went after the differences in the media.

MR. SPRINGER: Do you have the same power as the press?

DR. STANTON: Under the First Amendment, yes.

MR. SPRINGER: All right. Now let's just go at it for a second. Does the newspaper apply for a license to the Federal Communications Commission?

DR. STANTON: No, sir.

MR. SPRINGER: Do You?

DR. STANTON: Yes, sir.

MR. SPRINGER: Do you say yes, sir?

DR. STANTON: I did.

MR. SPRINGER: Does a newspaper comply with the Fairness Doctrine?

DR. STANTON: Do you mean is there a rule from the government that says they shall?

MR. SPRINGER: Is there anything in the Constitution or law, either one?

DR. STANTON: There is not.

MR. SPRINGER: Do you have a rule of fairness at the FCC with which you comply?

DR. STANTON: We do, and we had it before the FCC had its Fairness Doctrine.

MR. SPRINGER: Right. Now does the newspaper supply equal time to candidates for public offices?

DR. STANTON: Not by law.

MR. SPRINGER: Do you by law?

DR. STANTON: We do.

MR. SPRINGER: All right. Then you are not the press, are you?

DR. STANTON: I think we are the press, sir.

The white-haired Illinois Republican had been fingering a book. He now lifted it to open pages and said, "You have mentioned here, Dr. Stanton, what you call TV. Let me please just go a little further because I think we ought to stay with what we are talking about. I read from Webster's *New Collegiate Dictionary* and it says as follows, and this is the press: 'the publishing establishment and also its personnel; newspapers and periodicals collectively.' Are you the press?"

Stanton tersely replied, "We are."

Springer looking down from the tier of Congressmen to the witness table: "You say you fall within that definition?"

Dr. Stanton confesses, "I do not" and then has an inspiration—"What is the date on that?"

Springer fiddles with pages and finds the copyright. "This is 1956."

Stanton, remaining carefully polite, responds. "Mr. Springer, I am not here to be contentious, I am here to try to be as helpful as I possibly can, but I think one thing that we have got to recognize is that in the quarter century that television has grown to the position it is today, I think the public looks to the broadcast media as the press as well as the print journalist as the press."

Springer quickly asks, "Is that what the dictionary says?"

Stanton grimly replies, "That is what the Supreme Court says."

The congressman repeats, "I said is that what the dictionary says?"

The CBS president, in reference to the fifteen-year-old dictionary being quoted, answers "I don't have all the dictionaries." The congressman goes on to define journalism from his dictionary ("the business of managing edition or writing for journals or newspapers") and then in strong, deliberate, ominous tones continues, "Now, Dr. Stanton, you are using some things very liberally here and when you are talking about a chilling effect you are giving me a very chilling effect when you start using words here which you don't define and when I go to the dictionary and don't find any resemblance to any words that you have used. I go back to the beginning because I think we have to start at the beginning of this in order to get an understanding of what you people are."

Stanton simply replies, "If you went back far enough, I don't suppose you would find print."

"An understanding of what you people are"—that is what the congressman wanted. Who were these broadcast upstarts who operate with stations licensed by the government, who must go before the FCC every three years to renew that license, who are compelled by FCC edict to observe the Fairness Doctrine, who are compelled by law to grant equal time to political candidates, who are limited by law to five television, seven AM and seven FM stations? Most important, who are these men who are susceptible to congressional investigations of their practices while newspapers are not?

It did not matter that the congressmen had an old dictionary and newer ones defined both the press and journalism as including broadcasting. What mattered was that broadcasting came under the purview of the Congress, newspapers did not.

The broadcast, which brought a network president before this hostile committee and ultimately the full House, had its beginnings on a rival network in January of 1970. Richard Salant, president of CBS News, was watching NBC's "First Tuesday" broadcast and saw an excerpt from a polished film produced by the Atomic

Energy Commission. Salant wondered, "What is the government doing in this business, making these elaborate, expensive-looking films?" He asked his producers to look into the possibility of a documentary on government public relations.

Assigned to the task was a bright, young producer named Peter Davis. The thirty-four-year-old son of a Hollywood screen writer, Frank Davis, and veteran of some earlier CBS documentaries of note including participation in the highly acclaimed, highly controversial "Hunger in America," Davis spent ten weeks exploring the subject. He found it too broad.

He recommended concentration on a single branch of government public relations, that of the Department of Defense. As he wrote, "Although all of the agencies do a lot of self-serving publicity, the one that has the most influence over the country's mind, and the one that is the most conspicuous is, of course, the Department of Defense."

CBS News executives examined the recommendation and agreed. It would be the Pentagon.

Narrowing the focus to this area was still chewing off quite a bite. A former assistant secretary of defense for public affairs, Phil Goulding, has called it "the biggest public affairs kingdom on earth."

Senator J. William Fulbright, chairman of the Foreign Relations Committee, did a study of this kingdom in his book *The Pentagon Propaganda Machine*. He noted that "In November 1969, Vice-President Spiro T. Agnew in his speech castigating television commentators gave us his views of a 'small group of men' who help shape public opinion by deciding what forty to fifty million Americans will learn of the day's events in the nation and the world. There is another group of people much larger than that attacked by the vice-president—numbering approximately twenty-eight hundred—working to shape public opinion. This group is even less known to the public since its members are never seen or heard directly. It is made up of government employees and military men on active duty whose job is selling the public on the Department of Defense, individual military services, and their appropriations."

Fulbright continued, "This vast apparatus has grown quietly since World War II, obediently serving the aims of successive Administrations and its own ends at the same time. Apparently its activities do not disturb the Vice President, whose quest for objectivity is directed at Administration critics rather than supporters."

In fact, the vice-president became disturbed—not at the military's public relations but at the CBS broadcast about it. He became one of the first and loudest to attack the network for its documentary.

It took Peter Davis ten months to put his broadcast together. During that period, film crews went to the Pentagon itself, to Army posts, to retired members of the publicity apparatus. On Tuesday, February 23rd, 1971 the finished product was broadcast over 165 stations on the CBS network line.

Roger Mudd, the veteran Washington correspondent for CBS News, opened the broadcast over film of a Marine maneuver in North Carolina with invited civilians in the audience. This battle, Mudd noted, was not only a military exercise "but it was also an exercise in salesmanship—the selling of the Pentagon."

Appearing on camera, Mudd notes: "Nothing is more essential to a democracy than the free flow of information. Misinformation, distortion, propaganda all interrupt that flow. They make it impossible for people to know what their government is doing, which, in a democracy, is crucial." The largest agency in government is the Department of Defense, and he cites their thirty-million dollar budget for the current year but notes that while it is ten times as large as it was twelve years ago, it is only the tip of the iceberg—"a special, still unpublished report for the prestigious Twentieth Century Fund estimates the real total at $190 million."

Mudd moves on to an Armed Forces Day at Fort Jackson, South Carolina, where civilian audiences watch a demonstration of military hardware. At the end of the demonstration, children swarm over the weapons "so they can get the heft and feel of the genuine article."

The film abruptly takes us to a Colonel MacNeil saying, "In the Chinese view only one country has been liberated from colonialism, and that is North Vietnam. The others will not be considered liberated, in the Chinese viewpoint, until each and every one has a Communist government."

Mudd explains that there is a Pentagon "team of colonels" touring the country to lecture on foreign policy. "We found them in Peoria, Illinois" where they spoke to a mixed audience of civilians and military reservists. He notes that the invitation was arranged by Caterpillar Tractor of Peoria which does a thirty-nine million dollar business with the Defense Department.

Mudd quotes the army regulation forbidding discussion of the foreign policy implications of the Vietnam war and we immediately hear the colonel say, "Well, now we're coming to the heart of the problem—Vietnam. Now the Chinese have clearly and repeatedly stated that Thailand is next on their list after Vietnam. If South Vietnam becomes Communist it will be difficult for Laos to exist. The same goes for Cambodia, and the other countries of Southeast Asia. I think if the Communists were to win in South Vietnam, the record in the North—what happened in Tet of '68—makes it clear there would be a blood bath in store for a lot of the population of the South. The United States is still going to remain an Asian power."

Mudd notes that the colonels have spoken to a hundred and eighty thousand people in 163 cities over the years. Another colonel talks of a "bloodbath," noting the killing at Hue during the Tet offensive; a third notes that protesting college students are sincere but haven't studied history, and Colonel MacNeil returns to conclude "I feel when we put a million men in there, at least we placed national interest at stake when we did that."

We see the children at Fort Jackson again and then Mudd shows us army displays in a St. Paul shopping center. "The Army Exhibit Unit has been to 239 cities in forty-six states and has been seen by over twenty million people. The cost to taxpayers: $906,000 a year."

Pentagon speakers, six to ten every night, are addressing public audiences and we see General Lewis Walt of the marines saying, "We fought them up on the DMZ, we fought them across the Laos border, we fought them south across the Cambodian border. But they're trying to keep the war going on—why? Because they think we're going to give up and pull out before the job is done. That's what they've been told, that's what they read in our newspapers and our magazines."

Correspondent Mudd then tells us that each year, the Pentagon runs special guided tours for three thousand influential citizens. The Joint Civilian Orientation Conference is the "aristocrat" of these tours. For eight days, sixty-four prominent citizens visit key military installations all over the country.

We see the group in North Carolina, Mudd noting that they paid part of their own costs and the official price of the tour is only $12,000. This does not include the expenses of the several thousand servicemen who performed for the civilians.

We see them watching war games, meeting Marine Commandant General Leonard Chapman, sitting in a military boat. We do not—Mudd notes—see them firing weapons, something CBS was not permitted to film. But they are not shy in talking about it: "We fired the rifles and were told what excellent shots we were. . . . We fired grenade launchers and drove their tanks and so on." Says one, "There is no substitute for hands-on experience." Says another, "I think that one part of this tour is that you won't find a George Romney statement about being brainwashed."

After a commercial (it is, after all, commercial television), the broadcast goes into the question of military-produced films. Over three hundred a year are produced by the Pentagon. While most are meant for troop information, a large number are later released for public showing. Cost: over $12 million a year.

The army's "The Big Picture" series cost $900,000 alone. In the decade of the '60s, fifty-two million Americans saw these movies at 45,000 public gatherings and on at least 356 commercial and educational television stations.

Movie stars like Jack Webb, Robert Stack, and John Wayne are shown in films. The Webb excerpt talks about "our finest young men" fighting in Vietnam while "other young men and women, safe at home, openly advocate abandonment of Vietnam to Communism. Perhaps they really don't know what this war is all about." Mudd notes that scenes of war protestors are "tinted red for emphasis."

The CBS documentary also tells of well-known journalists participating in the film. This sequence caused much internal discussion at CBS News in the preparation. One of the military film narrators was Walter Cronkite, the leading figure on-air for CBS News, anchorman of its major evening news and many special broadcasts. The decision was made to include this, too, no matter how it reflected on CBS. Cronkite is shown in a 1962 film stating that "our army is face to face with Communism around the world."

Chet Huntley of NBC is shown narrating a film on the Navy's role in Vietnam. The films remain in distribution "even though Walter Cronkite and Chet Huntley may now disagree with the intent of the films they narrated."

Mudd notes that while the Pentagon "says it has discarded the rhetoric of confrontation" these films, with the language and symbols of the early '60s, continue. An excerpt is shown from "Road to the Wall" with Jimmy Cagney as narrator, then "Red Nightmare" with Jack Webb, which presents a Russian scheme to crush American freedom. Nine hundred prints of the latter are still in circulation. Says "The Selling of the Pentagon": "Although the Pentagon labels them informational, these films contain a high proportion of propaganda, as well as an obsession with monolithic Communism. . . . It has been more than a decade since the national policy of peaceful coexistence replaced the harsher rhetoric of early Cold War years."

After another commercial, the broadcast looks at a Pentagon news briefing conducted by Deputy Assistant Secretary of Defense Jerry Friedheim who "does not, of course, tell all he knows; he wouldn't have his job long if he did." From this we go to a former public information officer, Jack Tolbert, who served as an air force major in public information for twelve years and tells us "The Department of Defense has so many avenues of getting its story across, around, and over and under the media, that I'm not sure even if every reporter who covered the Pentagon was a hard-nosed reporter, that we still wouldn't get the story through."

The assistant secretary of defense, Daniel Z. Henkin, is asked if he thought the press covering the Pentagon did a good job:

> HENKIN: I believe that it does. From time to time of course it gives me some headaches and I give the press some headaches. We understand that—we act professionally, as a professional relationship, not only with the Pentagon press and other members of the Washington news corps, but with newsmen who cover military activities around the world.
>
> MUDD: What about your public display of military equipment at state fairs and shopping centers—what purpose does that serve?

HENKIN: Well, I think it serves the purpose of informing the public about their armed forces. I believe that the American public has a right to request information about the armed forces, to have speakers come before them, to ask questions, and to understand the need for our armed forces, why we ask for the funds that we do ask for, how we spend these funds, what are we doing about such problems as drugs—and we do have a drug problem in the armed forces; what are we doing about the racial problem in the armed forces—ar d we do have a racial problem. I think the public has a valid right to ask us these questions.

MUDD: Well, is that sort of information about the drug problem you have and the racial problem you have and the budget problems you have, is that the sort of information that gets passed out at state fairs, by sergeants who are standing next to rockets?

HENKIN: No, I wouldn't limit that to sergeants standing next to any kind of exhibit. Now there are those who contend that this is propaganda. I don't—do not agree with this.

The documentary discusses the problem of press coverage at the Pentagon in an interview with the *Washington Post* military specialist, George Wilson. It moves to Kansas City and demonstrates the army's Hometown News Center which sends out twelve thousand radio and television tapes and over two million printed releases annually.

The next few minutes deal with military relations at Capitol Hill and a congressional film for hometown distribution is featured as follows:

REPRESENTATIVE EDWARD HEBERT: I'm one of those who believes that the most vicious instrument in America today is network television.

MUDD: Using sympathetic congressmen, the Pentagon tries to counter what it regards as the antimilitary tilt of network reporting. War heroes are made available for the taped home district TV reports from pro-Pentagon politicians. Here Representative F. Edward Hebert of Louisiana asks Major James Rowe, a Green Beret and former POW, what keeps the Viet Cong fighting.

MAJOR ROWE: The support that the VC receives from the United States is the only thing that keeps them fighting.

MUDD: Later, Congressman Hebert, who is the new chairman of the House Armed Services Committee, asks Major Rowe for his reaction to a peace rally.

ROWE: I walked up and I heard one of the speakers yelling, "Down with imperialism, down with capitalism, down with the oppressive leadership in Washington. Power to the people." I heard the same thing from the Viet Cong, except there it was in Vietnamese and here it was in English. I looked around the crowd—I walked through the crowd, and I saw some VC flags flying from the flagpole of the Washington Monument, I saw American flags with VC flags flying over the top of them. I saw American flags with the stars removed and a peace symbol superimposed. I saw the red flag with a black peace symbol on it, and then I heard one of my senators say that "We are here because we cherish our flag." And the only thing I could think of in answer is what flag does he cherish?

HEBERT: Let me congratulate you, please, sir. It's an honor to have you on this program with me, and I only wish to God we could have more people wearing the uniform privileged to speak as you've spoken, because the silent majority will and must be heard.

"The Selling of the Pentagon" moves rapidly on to look at the Pentagon's own film crews in Vietnam which provide footage for DOD releases to television stations back home. The networks, by the way, are among the prime users of these handout films. Though they follow a policy of visual identification of them as "Department of Defense film," the nicety can be lost on the viewer. Further, each network provides a "syndication" service to member stations in late afternoon, a service to give them additional film stories for local use. Many DOD releases find their way into this service and get wide local usage. Generally network usage is limited to particularly sensational footage or film that the networks cannot get themselves in Vietnam such as aerials from American planes.

There were charges that the Pentagon crews in Vietnam staged some of its footage and we are introduced to former Air Force

Sergeant Thomas Demitor, a sixteen-year veteran of the service and one of the DOD cameramen. He tells us that a number of stories were staged. He cites one story, "U.S. and South Vietnamese Forces Patrol Enemy Infiltration Routes," which featured a Vietnamese noncombat action, ending up in a release that "would leave someone to believe that the Vietnamese were doing the majority of the work" of subduing the enemy when actually they had encountered none, had simply performed for Demitor's camera.

Immediately we see Henkin again on the matter of staging:

HENKIN: We are trying our best to provide information. There undoubtedly have been times when certain actions have been staged. I think this is true of all TV news coverage; after all this interview here is being staged.

MUDD: How so?

HENKIN: Well, props were set up, arrangements were made. You and I did not just walk into this room cold. Arrangements were made for it.

MUDD: Well, we wanted to film in your office but your people said, "Let's go into the studio", so—we didn't stage it.

The broadcast moves on to the so-called Five o'Clock Follies, the news briefings in Saigon which have been heavily criticized for their failure to provide much information.

Former Information Officer Tolbert reappears and tells how, when he was in Vietnam, he handled a network crew coming over to do a documentary on the air war. They were exposed to the most articulate, best-looking, well-briefed pilots. The result? "Frankly, it was just great. It represented the pilots, it represented the way we conceived the air war in the North was being fought by very professional people, and it was as good as if we had done it ourselves."

MUDD: Well, I'm duty-bound to ask, I've got to ask you which network it was. Will you tell me?

TOLBERT: Yes, yes, I will.

MUDD: Which one was it?

TOLBERT: It was CBS.

Mudd concludes the broadcast with a summation which says, in part:

"On this broadcast we have seen violence made glamorous, expensive weapons advertised as if they were automobiles, biased opinions presented as straight facts. Defending the country not just with arms but also with ideology, Pentagon propaganda insists on America's role as the cop on every beat in the world. Not only the public but the press as well has been beguiled, including at times ourselves at CBS News. This propaganda barrage is the creation of a runaway bureaucracy that frustrates attempts to control it.

"Last November 6, President Nixon sent this memorandum [shown for television viewers at that moment] to executive agencies, criticizing what he called self-serving and wasteful public relations efforts. He directed an end to what he described as 'inappropriate promotional activities.' The president specifically ordered, in his words, a curtailment of 'broadcasting, advertising, exhibits, and films.'

"Just since the memo was written the army's Golden Knights, a parachute team, have performed for the public in Nevada, California, and North Carolina. Other army exhibits have travelled to fifty-nine different locations. Air force displays, like this Hound Dog-Quail missile, have appeared in at least thirty-six shopping malls and municipal centers since the memo was written.

"We went back to the Pentagon and asked what effect the presidential directive would have. We were told there will be cuts in personnel, not activities. There may be some disagreement, of course, over just what constitutes an 'inappropriate promotional activity,' but to date not a single activity shown on this broadcast has been eliminated. Tomorrow morning, according to Defense Department schedules, there will be an army show pushing the ABM in Mountain View, California; an air force missile will turn up in Houston on Friday; the Pentagon's traveling colonels will be in Hampton, Virginia, March 8; and next week fifth graders at the Hill Elementary School in Davidson, Michigan, will get to see the navy's propaganda film on Vietnam.

"This is Roger Mudd for 'CBS Reports.' "

The broadcast was still on the air when CBS started getting phone calls. Most of the early ones were angry. Typical of these were some received at the CBS Washington news bureau. The broadcast was only fourteen minutes in progress before a caller angrily termed Mudd the "agent of a foreign power." Seven minutes later, a caller said it was rotten and inciting to riot. Just after that another called it "very biased."

An air force colonel called as the second half began to say, "Next time I see Mudd, I'm going to take the nose off his face." Someone called to congratulate "Comrade Mudd." All of this while the broadcast was still on the air.

After 11 P.M., phones continued to be busy but there were now many callers who offered compliments as well as those who attacked it strongly. The mail that followed was much the same. The broadcast had stirred up strong reaction, pro and con.

Reaction by television critics was largely favorable. *Newsweek* called it "a landmark of sorts. For a long time, it has been commonplace for public officials to claim that the media in general and network television in particular made a habit of 'perverting' the news. In Peter Davis's program, CBS News—with a courage rarely displayed by television—counterattacked with a convincing demonstration that when it comes to stage-managing the news, no one tries harder or succeeds better than the government itself."

The *Washington Post* critic called it "a gutty and intelligent show" in "the finest tradition of muckraking TV documentary." The *Boston Herald-Traveler* said it was "a hard-hitting, no-punches-pulled exposé" which "should make every citizen burn with rage." The *Denver Post* said it was "a model of that all too rare quality—journalistic guts."

Frank Getlein, writing in the *Washington Star,* called it "the most important television program to come out of the tube in years. . . . The program did exactly what television can do without compare—and does it rarely—that is, it gave an intelligent, orderly, eyewitness account of many aspects of a complex and important phenomenon as shown by events taking place at widely separated points in time and space."

In the *Chicago Sun-Times,* Ron Powers wrote, "No wonder the public-relations people at the Pentagon got all green and fuzzy in the mouth when they saw the documentary. They would have been pinching at the cotton swabs in their pill bottles if it had been only one-tenth as reproachful as it actually was. . . . It is the touchy function of public-relations people to at once guide the news and stay away from it. The fact that 'The Selling of the Pentagon' caused so many Administration vocal chords to warble reminds us of two things: how used to the soothing darkness these public-relations eyes had become and how highly into government the public-relations mentality had crept."

The *Los Angeles Times* had an article by Lance V. Stalker who had spent twelve years in the U.S. Navy as a public relations specialist. He wrote, "I saw nothing in the documentary that did not parallel my own experiences as a military PR man."

The text of the broadcast was promptly placed in the *Congressional Record* three times by three different congressmen, a waste of taxpayers' funds in the printing but quite a tribute to the documentary. Congressman Michael J. Harrington of Massachusetts preceded his submission with the observation, "In one hour, this outstanding example of journalism bared before this nation the razzmatazz public relations programs of the military establishment. I congratulate everyone connected with the production."

Senator William Proxmire of Wisconsin placed it in the *Record* with the observation that it was "a devastating critique from the mouths of the Pentagon spokesmen and the Pentagon propaganda films themselves".

Senator Thomas Eagleton of Missouri placed it in the *Record* also. He called it "reporting at its best" and admonished, "Congress, not the press, must bear the responsibility of carefully scrutinizing the moneys it authorizes and appropriates. And 'The Selling of the Pentagon' shows how much work we must do."

Eagleton proved to be a poor prophet. Congress showed no interest in probing the public relations effort of the Pentagon. It showed great enthusiasm, however, for investigating the producers of the broadcast.

While congressional reviews and those of other newspapers were welcome, the most important organ of television reviews was the *New York Times* and the most important reviewer in the short history of television was the *Times* TV critic, Jack Gould. He loved it.

Gould opened the review with the observation that CBS News "packed its old-time wallop last night in a brilliant documentary." He accurately noted that "the fur seems certain to fly in Washington" and approved of the "frank admission that CBS and its nightly anchorman, Walter Cronkite, had either been duped or had know-

ingly cooperated in shows not under their independent supervision."
He called Richard Salant, the CBS News chief, "a man known for
his guts," and said the broadcast was "one of the best on TV in a
great many years."

Gould also noted, "The Pentagon seems certain to wince under
the exposé, but the hour was like the proverbial fresh breeze in
electronic journalism. An institution supposed to be untouchable
was roughed up by some hard-nosed digging that not once impinged
on national security. Inevitably, there may be screaming from sincere patriots, but this will not negate the program's main point: In
the vast sprawl of the Pentagon there is a lot of Madison Avenue."

If CBS was basking in the light of such glowing reviews, it was
not to enjoy unbroken praise for long. The very next day, in the
halls of Congress, the broadcast was called "the most misleading,
damaging attacks on our people over there that I have ever heard
of . . . antimilitary, anti-Pentagon, antiuniform." The speaker
was one of the most powerful men in the House of Representatives,
Louisiana's F. Edward Hebert, chairman of the House Armed
Services Committee.

He had read Gould's review. He had not seen the broadcast.

Hebert didn't have to wait for any rebroadcast. The Pentagon,
which frequently tapes broadcasts off air had already made copies
of "Selling" to show any congressman who had missed the attack on
their integrity. One was shown to Hebert.

If hell hath no fury like a woman scorned, Washington has none
like Mr. Hebert angered. Typical of his reaction were some of the
notes he struck in a CBS "Morning News" interview after the
broadcast. He called it "the most horrible thing I've seen in years.
The most—the greatest disservice to the military I've seen on
television. And I've seen some pretty bad stuff . . . a splendid
professional hatchet job." As to the description of him as a "pro-
Pentagon politician," Hebert termed it "the damndest lie and the
damndest misrepresentation of a fact that I've ever seen on the
screen."

A few days after the broadcast, on March 3rd, he issued a press
release entitled "False Allegations Concerning Congressman F.
Edward Hebert in the Television Program, 'The Selling of the
Pentagon.' " In it, Hebert complained of the manner "in which I

am presented in opprobrious tones." Congressman Springer's dictionary would tell us that "opprobrious" means "attaching disgrace, reproachful, scurrilous . . . infamous."

"It may be," Congressman Hebert wrote, "that falsehood runs like a hare and truth moves like a tortoise. It may be that I may never be able to get the truth to catch up with all of the false innuendos in this case, but I am going to try."

Hebert states that there are four inferences "obviously intended" by the broadcast: 1. That Hebert was used by the Pentagon because he was sympathetic, 2. Therefore, the hometown TV program, his interview with Rowe, was the Pentagon's idea, 3. That the Pentagon used it to counter network TV reporting, and 4. That the Pentagon provided Rowe. All, said Hebert, are "very clearly and very categorically" false.

He said the Pentagon did not "use" him to make the taped interview, that it was his idea not theirs, that it was not planned to counter network reporting but meant for his home district, and lastly that Rowe was not supplied by the Pentagon—"I asked him to appear. No one in the Defense Department hierarchy, to my knowledge, even knew that Rowe was going to be on the program with me prior to his appearance."

Whether or not the chairman was being "used" was indeed inference—not stated as such in the broadcast nor did it even speculate as to whose idea the Rowe interview was. If there is an inference that such broadcasts "counter network reporting," it comes from Hebert's own comments in the Rowe interview ("I'm one of those who believes that the most vicious instrument in America today is network television").

But was Rowe appearing at Hebert's request? With no one in the Defense Department hierarchy knowing? Elsewhere in the Rowe interview, in a portion not broadcast in the CBS documentary, Representative Hebert says, "I want to pause momentarily now to express my deep appreciation to our mutual friend, Colonel Scooter Burke, a Congressional Medal winner, and we are very proud of him on the Hill, for bringing you to me and allowing you to come down to talk with us." Colonel Lloyd "Scooter" Burke is a Pentagon liaison to the House Armed Services Committee which Hebert chairs.

The interview was conducted in late 1969 and Bernard Nossiter wrote in the *Washington Post* on November 23 of that year that Rowe had filmed at least twenty television interviews and had recorded six radio tapes with congressmen. These, he says, were then sent to home stations of the congressmen or used in army information programs. In addition, according to this report, Major Rowe filmed a thirty minute show for the Republican National Congressional Campaign Committee. "This performance, however, is more muted" than the others in which Rowe attacked "anti-war legislators and certain newspapers and magazines."

The article describes Colonel Burke as "an Army legislative liaison officer and Rowe's immediate sponsor". Burke told the *Post* that Army Chief of Staff General William Westmoreland "knows of all his (Rowe's) activity on the Hill and approves of it." According to this report then, someone in the Defense hierarchy knew about Rowe's filming activity.

Someone else knew. Nossiter asked the army's chief of information, Brig. Gen. Winant Sidle, if Rowe were violating army policy after Colonel Burke said "We slipped on one show, I think" in mentioning legislators that Rowe disliked (He said the enemy had quoted Senators Fulbright, Mansfield, Morse, and McGovern). Sidle said soldiers must restrict themselves to matters they know of through their personal knowledge, "they are not supposed to speak on foreign policy or the implications of the U.S. involvement in Vietnam." General Sidle would not say whether Rowe had breached such guidelines.

Major Rowe, in the 1969 *Post* report, is said to have told Rep. Page Belcher of Oklahoma that the Paris peace talks were stalled in the belief that Americans will yield—"Concessions are a sign of weakness." He told Rep. Ed Foreman of New Mexico that "precipitate withdrawal . . . would mean total victory for Communists" and that Thailand, Laos, the Philippines, and Indonesia would all be threatened. He told Rep. Larry Winn of Kansas that he was shocked by peace demonstrations here, "to see Senator McGovern say we cherish our flag . . . I question what flag. . . . Our flag was degraded."

The *Post* article notes that while others might be uneasy about these matters, Rowe was not: "We are entering into an ideological conflict . . . where the political and military are married into one. If someone says you can't speak and stay in the military, I would resign. . . . The thing is, you're going to have to choose sides."

Hebert's March 3 press release also charges that CBS received the copy of his interview with Rowe under false pretenses. He claimed, and supplied memoranda from his press aide, that CBS had indicated they were doing a documentary on prisoners of war and were interested in Rowe because he was an ex-POW.

CBS denied this. There were a number of exchanges between the congressman's office and CBS in what a subsequent Hebert press release called "a heated controversy." CBS would offer the denials by Producer Peter Davis and those who worked for him. Hebert produced memos from five congressional offices suggesting that CBS had similarly contacted them for interviews with Rowe. The memos said they understood CBS was doing a documentary on POWs. CBS would respond that if there was confusion, it was because Rowe was an ex-POW, but that they had clearly told these congressional offices and the many others they contacted that it was to be a broadcast "on how the Pentagon presents its message to the American people."

On the day of the March 3rd release, Representative Hebert also inserted into the *Congressional Record* and released to the press at the some time a letter from Dan Henkin, the assistant secretary of defense for public affairs assessing "The Selling of the Pentagon."

Henkin first nailed a factual error. The broadcast had talked of thirty thousand offices in the Pentagon—there are only five thousand.

He wrote of the colonel in Peoria and said that, when talking policy, he was really quoting the prime minister of Laos. "I think you will agree that this distortion misinformed the viewers of that program who were led to believe they were hearing one U.S. military officer's personal view rather than a quotation from Souvanna Phouma of Laos."

Henkin said of the old films that they could not be suppressed because of the Freedom of Information Act (which prohibits government agencies from withholding nonclassified information but seems markedly lax in any details dealing with supplying motion picture film for public or television presentation). Henkin then revealed, that CBS failed to identify one of the old films, "Road to the Wall," as having been produced by CBS Films in 1962 (he attached a CBS Films press release on it). Wrote Henkin, after noting that CBS was paid for the troop information documentary, "I wish to emphasize, Mr. Chairman, that I do not think CBS is in the business of propaganda. Neither is the Department of Defense."

CBS officials were puzzled by the triumphant revelation that CBS Films had made one of the DOD productions. If Henkin were trying to show CBS covering up its involvement with DOD, it was strange since the broadcast mentioned the participation of Walter Cronkite and Ed Murrow in DOD films in the past and showed a former information officer telling how he tricked a CBS documentary producer. If *mea culpa* were needed, it was there enough. This added "confession" hardly seemed important enough to warrant comment.

Henkin's letter to Hebert talks about that former air force information officer, by the way, expressing surprise that CBS should use an individual who had fooled them in the past. He also took issue with the CBS description of his assistant, Jerry Friedheim, as one who "does not, of course, tell all he knows. He wouldn't have his job long if he did." Henkin notes that to answer some of the questions would have been a violation of national security.

The secretary's most serious charge was rearranging of the interview with him. He was to elaborate greatly on this in another letter to Hebert a few days later.

Twice in his letter, Dan Henkin—much admired and liked by many at CBS News—said, "I have never questioned the integrity of CBS News, and I do not do so now." He would all, "However, I do question the integrity of this particular show."

So did Chairman Hebert. He fired off fifteen questions to Melvin Laird, the secretary of defense. Back came a reply from Henkin noting that Laird had asked him to reply. Some old Washington hands, including many at CBS, wondered if DOD had been the composer of the questions as well as the answers since Hebert wrote Laird on March 2 and the lengthy Henkin reply was dated March 4, remarkable speed for such great detail. Such suspicion had no fact to support it but was indicative of the CBS News reaction to what they saw as the beginning of a long ugly battle with a shaken establishment. It was clear that powerful foes, in the Congress and at the Pentagon, would pull out all stops to discredit the broadcast.

In his fifteen answers to Chairman Hebert's inquiries, Henkin made the definitive attack on the editing of Mudd's interview with him. It became very important in the months that followed for it was to be the heart of the congressional attack on CBS. Because DOD had an audio tape of the original interview, Henkin could easily see exactly how it was edited from forty minutes down to two minutes and four seconds.

Henkin said that he was edited out of context and cited four instances. The first was his evaluation of how good a job the Pentagon press does in its coverage. He noted that only half his answer was used but admitted "The meaning and intent were not changed substantially."

The second incident involved his response to a question about military displays at state fairs. Henkin's first sentence of reply was used as were several sentences from a later answer to a similar question.

It should be noted that the latter answers were in response to a continuation of the first question, a series of questions on the displays at state fairs and other civilian gatherings. Examination of the full text of the original interview, as submitted into the *Congressional Record,* shows the questions were of a single theme.

It should also be noted that Henkin in the original interview made a reference to the "ancillary benefit, I would hope, of stimulating interest in recruiting," which was dropped from the air version. Henkin said the omission "alters the tenor of the response." However, the response, as broadcast, did deal with the right of the public "to understand the need for our armed forces."

The third incident cited by Henkin became the most controversial. In his answer to the previous question about state fair exhibits, Henkin referred to the right of the American public to know about the armed forces including "what we are doing about such problems as drugs—and we do have a drug problem in the armed forces; what we are doing about the racial problem—and we do have a racial problem."

On film, Mudd's next question logically followed: "Well, is that the sort of information—about the drug problem you have and the racial problem you have—is that the sort of information that gets passed out at state fairs by sergeants who are standing next to rockets?"

Henkin's reply, as seen in the documentary—and in the original text, begins, "No, I wouldn't limit that to sergeants standing next to any kind of exhibit." The next line on the documentary ("Now, there are those who contend this is propaganda. I do not agree with this.") was from the previous answer. Henkin's letter to Hebert says this was a comment that actually referred to the "increasing Soviet threat."

In his earlier comments about drug and racial problems, he had talked of these problems, then had added, "And also I believe that we have an obligation to inform, discuss with the American public the problems that we confront, problems such as the increasing Soviet threat." He then went on, "Now, there are those who contend this is propaganda . . . ," etc.

CBS was remiss, perhaps, in omitting the reference to the "increasing Soviet threat" but it seems clear—in the original text—that he was talking of *all* these items: drugs, racial problems, increasing Soviet threat. The DOD contention that it referred *only* to the increasing Soviet threat is hard to accept.

Clearly CBS had taken two sentences from an earlier reply and had tagged them to a later question. They might be on the same subject but these two sentences would haunt the network in the months to come, give rise to much discussion of cut-and-paste editing, and would be at the heart of congressional attacks.

Henkin's fourth citation seemed to bother him the most. In a colloquy with Mudd on television "staging," Henkin said, "After all, this interview is being staged." Mudd asks, "How so?" and Henkin talks about props being set up, arrangements made, and not walking into the room "cold." In the original he said, "After all, this interview is being staged" and added four words "as one might say."

Dan Henkin contends that it changed the flavor of that dialogue and made "a statement into an accusation." The producers said the four words were mumbled and it seemed a cleaner way to do it, dropping them. Few could see how deleting "as one might say" really made that much difference. It was still an accusation of a sort, no matter how good-humored. Perhaps it softened the accusation enough to satisfy Henkin. In any case, it bothered Secretary Henkin enough that he made a point of it, time and again. Dan Henkin, exnewspaperman and a strong defender of newsmen's rights, didn't want to appear to be accusing people of staging.

Ironically, in the Henkin interview, is another comment never used on the air which could well have served as the best three sentence explanation of CBS editing and its presentation of this broadcast. He said, when asked about TV coverage in Vietnam, "Television news presentation requires condensation. That is just a reality. But it has brought—in my view, television has brought to the American public more information about defense activities than ever before."

He is quite right, television news does require condensation. All news does but television in particular has strictures of time that exceed anything most newspapers have in terms of space restrictions. An hour cannot be stretched. If an hour documentary covers much ground, it must condense, condense, condense. It cannot include every nuance.

Remarks about recruiting may be dropped. Reference to propagandizing or not propagandizing the Soviet threat may fall by the wayside. Three days of filming the colonels in Peoria must be condensed to a matter of minutes on the air.

Condense, condense, condense. There is, however, a vital partner to condensation—condense but do not distort. Every professional editor, television or otherwise, knows this. Fewer tasks are more difficult but none more necessary.

This examination of "The Selling of the Pentagon" and the criticisms attaching to it may seem prolonged and tedious but it is necessary. No television broadcast in history was ever scrutinized more carefully by its critics than was "The Selling of the Pentagon." Few broadcasts could withstand such inspection unmarred. "Selling" did not. Errors were found.

One can contend that any broadcast, any article, any history—under similar fine-comb examination with the immense resources behind the examiners—would reveal some flaws. Finding them makes the documentary and its producers no more "opprobrious" than did this broadcast make Representative Hebert.

There is a difference between finding fault and doing fatal injury. The critics of "Selling" were determined to do the latter. They were not in search of apology for error; they were eager for full confession and capitulation.

The massive effort to raise doubts about this broadcast, emerging from the great power centers in Washington, showed how power can be used to discredit a broadcaster. Ultimately, it tested the ability of broadcasting to remain in the field of investigative reporting at all.

To supplement the lengthy Henkin critique, two weeks later Chairman Hebert placed in the *Congressional Record* more questions, thirty-seven more. They lead with an interesting innuendo aimed at Roger Mudd. Question One asks if any CBS official ever asked for the favor of a military unit at any event in the last five years? Why, yes, came the reply—Roger Mudd, in 1969, when he was chairman of the Radio and Television Correspondents Association dinner, asked for and received the participation of the U.S. Marine Band at the dinner.

No mention was made of the fact that every other chairman had made similar requests though it was noted that "Traditionally, media associations have requested and have received the same support granted to other national organizations and groups." No mention that military bands had made 4,800 appearances in Washington during fiscal year 1969. Military choral groups made another 262 appearances in that period.

The thirty-seven new answers offer no great revelations nor startling flaws in the broadcast. Question sixteen does deal with the accusation by former Sergeant Demitor that he had filmed staged events for DOD release. The answer: "First Lieutenant John Beeler was in charge of the film team. The fact sheet received with the footage did not say that the film was 'staged.' "!

There is a touch of twenty-year-old irony in the fact that Representative Hebert should be the first and among the most vociferous to attack this broadcast. True, as he often noted throughout the controversy, he was once a newspaperman of highest reputation in New Orleans. It was also true that in 1952 he was the most outspoken critic of the Pentagon's public relations effort and attacked them with phrases far harsher than any in "The Selling of the Pentagon."

On February 26, 1952—almost nineteen years earlier to the day—Hebert was the subject of the following article in the *New York Times*. "Representative F. Edward Hebert, Democrat of Louisiana, chairman of the Armed Services subcommittee on military waste, disclosed meantime that he had asked the Defense Department to supply him with a list of all public relations personnel on duty at the Pentagon. 'It is about time the American public be informed as to the identity of the individuals and what it costs the taxpayers to maintain and support this gigantic and colossal propaganda machine on the banks of the Potomac,' he said. 'Since the exposé of waste in the military and its effect on the taxpayers' pocketbook has been so vividly brought to the attention of the American people by the committee which I head,' he added, 'all the faucets have been turned on by the Pentagon propagandists, alibi artists and apologists.' "

On March 9, 1952 the *Times* reported this: "Mr. Hebert also has the military payroll under scrutiny. He has asserted that he found 395 'press agents' among the workers at the Pentagon and accused the Defense Department of 'concealing' others. He predicted a further study would show at least 500. The Representative said he would take a look at the entire 161,000-man military payroll in the Washington area."

Later in the spring, the *Saturday Evening Post* (May 10, 1952) reported in similar vein: "Hebert brushes aside most explanations as 'efforts prepared by Pentagon alibi artists and propagandists to confuse the issue.' At one point in the hearings he demanded to know the names and salaries of the 'Potomac Pitchmen' writing the explanations. Not satisfied with the list furnished him, Hebert accused the Defense Department of holding out on him and announced that his committee would investigate the military payroll for the entire Washington area."

While Defense Secretary Laird urged Henkin to speak for the defense establishment throughout the controversy, he did deal with the subject himself on March 16 when interviewed on the CBS "Morning News." When asked if he would join those who called the broadcast disreputable and un-American, Laird replied, "Well, I believe that there probably could have been a little more professionalism shown in putting the show together."

Laird urged listeners to write the Pentagon for a detailed and factual account. At the Pentagon a six-page "white paper" with questions and answers (literally on white paper without Defense Department letterhead) plus the lengthy Henkin replies to Hebert, as published in the *Congressional Record,* were sent to anyone writing in about the broadcast. Pentagon reporters in Washington were mailed copies of the collected works.

Secretary Laird did question whether some of the old films ("produced by CBS or by anyone else" he pointedly noted) are adequate today. He noted that the skirts on the women were too long.

What was the effect of the broadcast? Said the Secretary of Defense: "We've had tremendous response from it and we've had great support. It's increased our support in the Congress many times, we don't look for any close votes this year."

Chairman Hebert had riddled away at the broadcast with machine-gun bullets. Secretary Laird had brushed it once over lightly. Now the biggest cannon of all was about to boom. The warning came from Hebert's home country in a little-noticed news conference.

On March 9 in New Orleans, Vice-President Spiro T. Agnew told local reporters he would like to commend Hebert for "his astute and very athletic endeavors to point out to the people of the country some of the real facts concerning that particular issue."

Agnew said it would be interesting for the average citizen to be in the cutting room and see how a documentary is put together, how some interviews are used and others rejected "all to accomplish a given thesis compatible to the interest of that particular network." He then said, "I might digress here to say that, thank heaven we had the Pentagon during a couple of crucial times in our history. I think they defended the country a lot better than CBS is doing at the present time."

He said he didn't think the Pentagon guilty of trying to mislead people. Of the broadcast: "I thought it was a disreputable program."

Nine days later, on March 18, Agnew spoke to the issue again. This time, the vice-president made lots of news. His office distributed the speech in advance and as he rose before the Middlesex Republican Club in Boston, he, himself, called it "perhaps the most important I will deliver in my term as vice-president."

The vice-president's speaking style includes a touch of either alliteration or rarely used, multisyllabic words or both. He did not fail this audience of fifteen hundred faithful as he described his lot and explained why he is so outspoken. "I found it an onerous choice between the ennui of easy chair existence and pointless verbosity. And so, quick constitutional research revealing no authoritative reason why a vice-president is required to choose between catalepsy and garrulity, I forsook the comfortable code of many of my predecessors, abandoned the unwritten rules—and said something."

He gaily mixed sports metaphors to the crowd's delight. "Everywhere big media referees were flinging down their handkerchiefs and calling foul. The *Washington Post* stepped off fifteen yards for un-vice-presidential-like conduct. *Time* magazine waved me to the penalty box. And Eric Sevareid took two free throws at the line—both rolling around the rim and, as usual, dropping out."

Turning serious, he said the "widening credibility gap that exists between the national news media and the American people . . . has simply been reported, not created by this . . . vice-president." He talked of the average citizen's frustration in trying to complain about inaccurate or biased news reporting while any extremist "is treated with the utmost deference."

Finally, he seemed to turn to CBS and its "vicious broadside" against the Pentagon. "However," said Mr. Agnew, "considering the serious charges leveled recently by the CBS television news organization against the public affairs activities of the Department of Defense, the matter of the network's own record in the field of documentary-making can no longer be brushed under the rug of national media indifference."

The vice-president then launched into a prolonged attack on CBS News but never touched on details of "The Selling of the Pentagon." He attacked CBS for the opening scene in the 1968 documentary "Hunger in America," in which a baby is seen dying, the script said, of "starvation." Agnew said not, quoted an FCC report that the baby had died of other causes. Why bring that up now? Because, said the vice-president, the same CBS employee who wrote that script (Peter Davis) wrote "The Selling of the Pentagon."

Next target: "Project Nassau." In 1966, CBS News had filmed a group of men who planned to invade Haiti—the project called Operation Nassau. In time the entire matter was dropped when it was evident that the group was not to be taken seriously. None of it was ever broadcast. Agnew, however, had the benefit of a strongly critical report by the Commerce Committee's Special Subcommittee on Investigations.

The report, as quoted by the vice-president, talked about a possible "crisis for American foreign policy in the sensitive Caribbean area," about payments by CBS to the leader of the conspiracy ("If these acts did not actually involve the network in the conspiracy to violate the U.S. Neutrality Act, they came dangerously close to doing so"), and concluded with the subcommittee's observation "that the CBS News organization, having become elated at the prospect of a sensational news first—a complete documentary of the forcible overthrow of a foreign government—proceeded in a reckless attempt to capture the hoped-for film, and that it did so with no great regard for either accuracy or legality."

"The executive producer of the aborted documentary, 'Project Nassau,' " crowed the vice-president, "also served as executive producer of 'The Selling of the Pentagon'—a documentary, keep in mind, that sought to indict the Department of Defense for 'misinformation, distortion' and the alleged staging of event." The executive producer in question, not named by Agnew, was Perry Wolff, one of television's most distinguished and honored producers.

For the benefit of the audience, Mr. Agnew—as he has in the past—gratuitously noted, "I have grave doubts about how much of my criticism tonight will be carried in the national media." As in the past, much of it was carried.

The following morning, in Boston still, the vice-president was more specific about "The Selling of the Pentagon," repeating some of his New Orleans remarks. He did inject a new note, asserting that the Defense Department had sought air time to refute allegations and had been refused by CBS.

Both CBS and DOD denied any such request for time. CBS noted that it had carried much of the criticism against it including a long interview with Hebert, an excerpt from Agnew's own news conference in New Orleans, the interview with Laird, and—of course—excerpts of Agnew's speech the previous night.

One result of the distribution of the vice-president's speech in advance was that CBS could see it and respond. Dr. Frank Stanton did. The president of CBS pointed out that the charges against "Hunger in America" were extensively examined by the FCC and, in a report issued after the Commerce Subcommittee report, the FCC "found no wrong-doing by CBS News." He enclosed an excerpt of an October, 1969 FCC memorandum which said, "We conclude that no further action is warranted here with respect to the issue of slanting the news—the issue which was presented in the complaints."

Stanton also included a February, 1969 quote of President Nixon in a talk to Department of Agriculture employees. The president had praised "Hunger in America" as being responsible for that moment "when the public conscience finally became aroused—really aroused about the problem of hunger in the United States."

As for "Project Nassau," Stanton noted that it was abandoned and never resulted in a broadcast. He produced a lengthy letter from CBS News President Richard Salant denying the subcommittee allegations and asking that the subcommittee make public testimony from the CBS producer, testimony made in executive sessions and only quoted in part in the subcommittee report.

Stanton's statement in response to Agnew closed with a strong affirmation of his faith in his news organization. "CBS stands behind 'Hunger in America,' 'The Selling of the Pentagon,' and the integrity of CBS News. I am confident that impartial, professional observers will agree that these documentaries are important contributions to 'the people's right to know.' "

The vice-president responded with a statement for release in the Sunday newspapers. He called Stanton's response "a typical nonrejoinder." He said Stanton "cleverly avoids an encounter with the direct evidence of CBS error and propagandistic manipulation."

The baby in "Hunger in America" did not die of starvation, said Agnew. "Why won't CBS admit its error?" The reason that Project Nassau was never broadcast, said Agnew, is that "the CBS-stimulated invasion of Haiti" never occurred because a CBS cameraman reported the plot to the government.

He then attacked the "Selling" use of the traveling colonels, quoting them out of context and showing Souvanna Phouma's words as if they were those of the colonel quoting them. CBS, he accused, had "cut and paste the widely separated statements of military spokesmen to create a false impression." He concluded, "I believe the American public is entitled to have these serious accusations either admitted or denied by the network. They will not be satisfied with another nonresponse from Mr. Stanton."

That dispatched to the press for Sunday consumption (and Saturday night network news broadcasts), the vice-president's office awaited the next step. It was a short wait. CBS, in a bold show of faith in a broadcast so controversial, announced that it was rebroadcasting "The Selling of the Pentagon" Tuesday night at ten, CBS would follow this with a quarter-hour compilation of some of the criticisms by Agnew and others.

An angry press release rocketed out of the vice-president's office. "I have seen what CBS film editors have in the past done to my own remarks, as well as those of other critics of their network editorial position." CBS News, which has no editorial position, responded to Mr. Agnew's request that he and others be permitted to edit their own remarks. It rejected the suggestion.

At the Pentagon, Dan Henkin warned, "let the viewer beware" in watching the repeat. He also said, rather ominously, "I also hope that CBS News has now complied fully with certain legal requirements concerning the use of some of the material provided at their request." What did that mean? The *New York Times* suggested that the Pentagon was trying to block the rebroadcast. Henkin strongly denied that, stating it would be "abhorrent" to do so. He explained that the legal requirements dealt with the use of certain people in Pentagon films shown in "The Selling of the Pentagon."

There were a number of complaints about the pending rebroadcast reflecting the strong feelings about it. A few days before the repeat was scheduled, an anonymous phone caller asked the CBS News desk in New York when there would be a repeat broadcast. Told it was set for Tuesday night at ten, he asked, "Is that Communist bastard Mudd going to narrate it again?" The answer was "yes" and the caller said, "We're going to blow your ass off, you Communist bastards." When? "Tuesday at 10 P.M." Are you serious? "You bet your sweet ass. I'm going to blow up CBS."

On the night of the broadcast, guards were placed at CBS studios in both New York and Washington.

At 10 P.M. up popped the marines in North Carolina and "The Selling of the Pentagon" was repeated. At its conclusion, Roger Mudd explained that there would be a twenty-minute postscript. Television broadcasts are usually held firmly to their time, be it thirty minutes or an hour. On March 23rd, the stations of the CBS network ran this special broadcast one hour and twenty minutes (except for WTOP in Washington which had earlier repeated the broadcast because they thought it that important and now, not wanting to give it a third showing, simply carried the twenty minute postscript).

Mudd explained that phone calls, mail, and telegrams responding to the showing four weeks earlier were unusually high in number and predominantly favorable. Because of the adverse criticism, "much of it sharp and angry—and some of it from high places," CBS has decided to rebroadcast some of the criticism as well as the documentary. In addition, CBS would offer a brief response to that criticism.

The critics appeared. First there was the interview with Chairman Hebert of the Armed Services Committee. "Professional hatchet job," he said and talked of subtleties and innuendoes ("vicious, devious things") in the editing, charged again that the Rowe interview was received under false pretenses, that the Pentagon didn't know of his interview with Rowe, and that he was no "patsy" for the Pentagon. He referred to the sentence in the script dealing with the "pro-Pentagon politicians" as "the damndest lie and the damndest misrepresentation I've ever seen."

Next came a replay of the interview with Defense Secretary Laird. He gave his evaluation ("could have shown a little more professionalism"), his invitation to the viewers to write in for the facts, and his charge that a colonel was quoted out of context— "He was using a quotation and the words were put in his mouth."

Finally—Agnew. From the Boston speech, the attacks on "Hunger in America" and "Project Nassau." From his news conference the next day, his noting that "a bit of cut and paste" was done on the colonel's speech, his charge that the Defense Department was not given air time to challenge the documentary, and his assertion that he had no intention of intimidating networks nor seeking stronger laws, but simply to show the people "through uncontroverted evidence that they cannot rely on CBS documentaries for facts."

After fifteen minutes of criticism, the president of CBS News— in a rare television appearance—put a postscript to the postscript. Richard Salant defended the documentary.

He opened with the flat statement, "No one has refuted the essential accuracy of 'The Selling of the Pentagon.' " None of the critics, he noted, questioned the manipulation of news by the Pentagon, the staging of events, and the selling to the public of the Pentagon's points of view.

Each criticism that was raised, he said, can be answered but he would deal with only a few charges. First Salant denied getting the Hebert-Rowe interview under false pretenses, further noting that dozens of people on Capitol Hill as well as the Pentagon knew about the documentary as it was being prepared, it was no secret. As to editing the colonel so that he appeared to be the author of words that were really a Souvanna Phouma quote, Salant said the colonel never made it clear that it was part of a quotation and further, "he embraced it and simply used Souvanna Phouma" as his authority "to make a Pentagon point."

On Project Nassau, Salant said, "We did *not* finance the planned invasion. We did *nothing* illegal. . . . the Department of Justice found *no* unlawful activities on the part of CBS News." Salant called it "a journalistic investigation that never became a broadcast about an invasion that never took place."

He spoke of "Hunger in America" and Mr. Agnew's charge that the baby in the opening scene did not die of malnutrition. "We have checked and rechecked this fact," said Salant. "At the time, we were told by a hospital official that the baby *did* die of hunger. Later, *after* the broadcast, she changed her story somewhat; and new evidence came to light. There is no way, however, that the fact can be proven with certainty at this point."

Salant concluded, "We are proud of 'The Selling of the Pentagon' and CBS News stands behind it. We are confident that when the passions die down, it well be recognized as a vital contribution to the people's right to know."

Agnew did not agree. In St. Louis the next day, he said, "I am totally dissatisfied with what they characterized as a rebuttal on the part of administration officials, who include myself." (CBS had not called it a rebuttal but simply adverse criticism which it felt appropriate to rerun following the documentary's rebroadcast). Agnew said, "It's rather unusual to give you the right of rebuttal and not allow you to decide what you're going to say in rebuttal."

After charging that CBS edited him to show only those remarks they wanted shown, he complained that "they insisted on a right of rebuttal to my rebuttal." Agnew characterized Salant's remarks as "a very, very clever confession and avoidance, if I can use a legal term. There was a half confession and avoidance and sort of a half a subtle disclaimer that he conducted."

The vice-president's attacks on the rebroadcast a few days earlier were considered instrumental in building an audience. For one of the few times in television history, a rebroadcast commanded a larger audience than the original showing. On February 23rd, something over nine and a half million viewers saw "Selling." The rebroadcast on March 23rd commanded an audience of over fourteen million.

Royce Brier, in the *San Francisco Chronicle,* gave the credit to Agnew, "An ace press agent. . . . It was probably the most dazzling feat since P. T. Barnum. Moreover, this ace press agent didn't get a dime from CBS." He wrote, "This baby was sleeping peacefully until last week, when Mr. Agnew journeyed to Boston to give it the shaft."

CBS switchboards were flooded with phone calls and most of the views expressed were expressed strongly. Almost three thousand calls were received at the five CBS-owned television stations, 2,064 recorded in favor af the broadcast and 890 critical of it. To CBS's chagrin, a press release got these figures backwards and many newspapers published the error indicating more critics than friends of the broadcast. On the other hand, while the calls on the West and East coasts were heavily pro-CBS, they were only marginally so in Chicago and two-to-one critical in St. Louis.

Said the *New York Times,* in an editorial following the rebroadcast: "The bill of irrelevancies invoked by Vice President Agnew and Defense Secretary Laird . . . missed the central issue. . . . The heart of the matter is the flagrant violation of traditional rules —unmistakably spelled out in Defense Department regulations— which prohibit the military from engaging in political propaganda activities."

In Charlotte, North Carolina the local CBS station was offering one hour of prime time to the administration because they felt CBS had not been fair. Charles Crutchfield, president of the Jefferson Standard Broadcasting Company, offered the hour on WBTV to either the administration or Chairman Hebert. "In our opinion," he said, "CBS News did not give government officials an adequate opportunity to express their criticism."

In a twist of usual roles, it was the newspaper in Charlotte that defended the network. In its article headlined " 'Selling of the Pentagon' Has Yet To Be Discredited," the *Charlotte Observer* called the criticisms of the broadcast "weak" and concluded: "Most disappointing in this whole business is the 'you're one, too!' response of Agnew, Laird, and Hebert. They have not spoken to the facts presented and the thesis projected by CBS News. They have chosen instead to impugn the network's motives and assault its character. 'Dishonest!' says Agnew. 'Unprofessional! cries Laird. 'Un-American!' says Hebert. There may be things wrong with CBS News. No news organization is perfect in its selection of facts and opinion. But one thing that is not wrong with CBS News is its documentary, 'The Selling of the Pentagon.' "

At week's end Jack Anderson, the syndicated columnist, reported that the vice-president's attack on "Hunger in America" "during his recent Boston tea party" brought immediate results: "The Office of Economic Opportunity, which had been using the film for two years to dramatize the nation's hunger problem, abruptly blacklisted it."

Associate OEO Director Leo Churchville confirmed that the documentary was no longer being shown by his organization but it "had nothing to do with Agnew, strangely enough." Churchville said that some days before the Agnew speech, a staff member complained that the CBS documentary showed "too much of the negative aspects of the hunger problem and not enough of what OEO was doing with the taxpayers' money." Churchville concurred and the film was no longer shown.

"Hunger" found one friend in the administration: Dr. Jean Mayer, the famed Harvard professor of nutrition, member of the president's Consumer Advisory Council and chairman of the White House Conference on Food, Nutrition, and Health. Dr. Mayer wrote the *Washington Post* that he felt compelled to defend "Hunger in America" which he called "a watershed in the social history of the United States." He credits it with building up public pressure for action to which President Nixon responded by calling the White House Conference, pledging to eliminate hunger in America, and by launching new food programs.

The nutritionist wrote, "At this late date, the point raised by the vice-president that a malnourished child was reported on hospital records as having died of a disease other than malnutrition may be correct. I do not know the facts of this particular case" but death in starving individuals is commonly ascribed to whatever other disease the patient has. "To quote but one example, measles, usually a very innocuous disease in well-nourished populations, can kill up to fifty percent of children affected in a starving population. All are then reported to have died of measles. So what?"

So Mr. Agnew also wrote the *Post,* that's what. He bluntly stated that Dr. Mayer, having admitted he did not have the facts in this particular case, should disqualify himself—"The FCC investigation determined the baby shown by CBS was born prematurely as the result of a fall taken by the mother." Saying Mayer was guilty of "an obfuscatory generalization of such magnitude that, if I had uttered it, the *Post,* the *Times,* all three national networks, and the ACLU would now be driven into a state of ideological frenzy," the vice-president concluded, "that others suffered from malnutrition; that the film won an award; that CBS inaccuracies in the documentary were not determined to be actionable in terms of the FCC's mandate to regulate—none of this is responsive to the factual charge made, not by me, but by the FCC field investigator." *Sic semper* Spiro.

The furious nature of Mr. Agnew's feelings about CBS gave President Nixon a chance to joke at the May dinner of the White House Correspondents Association. "The vice-president," he said, "has three television sets in his bedroom. The first is turned to ABC. The second is turned to NBC. The third one he has standing in the corner."

Mr. Nixon never spoke of "The Selling of the Pentagon" publicly but apparently an opportunity was missed in the spring of '71. He was interviewed for an hour on ABC by Howard K. Smith. After the broadcast, according to reports, Smith asked him what he would say if asked about the CBS broadcast. Mr. Nixon was said to have replied, "I would have given them hell. . . . I would have defended the Pentagon."

In print, others did give them hell. The *Detroit News* said the pot was calling the kettle black when CBS pictured DOD as a secretive, runaway, unethical bureaucracy. "CBS, where the late

Edward R. Murrow once nailed Senator Joseph McCarthy to the mast, now employs the techniques of McCarthyism in the making and defending of its documentaries." The *San Diego Union* agreed, saying the indictment of the armed forces turned out to be an indictment of CBS standards.

Barron's weekly, a financial publication, was nearly hysterical, devoting its full front page and long columns inside to an attack on CBS with the headline, "CBS Has Forfeited Access to the Nation's Airwaves." It repeated every criticism against CBS over a period of at least eight years including some novel ones: taking the network to task because "Face The Nation" devoted a broadcast to Tom Hayden, founder of the Students for a Democratic Society (CBS let him "get away with intellectual murder"); and noting that in covering the story of a hijacker who forced a plane to go to Rome, the CBS reporter quoted the editor of a Communist paper who called the hijacker "Robin Hood."

Barron's concluded that Vice-President Agnew didn't go far enough, Dr. Stanton should resign, citizens should challenge CBS license renewals, the FCC should respond—"CBS, in our view, has forfeited its access to the nation's airwaves. The time has come to turn it off."

Not everyone quite wanted to put CBS out of business. Hugh Lucas, in *Aerospace Daily,* complained about the editing and concluded, "The salient point about Pentagon public relations is that DOD lies and spies and sometimes it even lies about spying. CBS never once touched on this. One wonders what the critics and the public would think had CBS done even a passable job."

Orr Kelly in the *Washington Star* approvingly repeated paragraphs from Lucas under the title, "CBS Missed The Pentagon Mark." Concluded Kelly, "CBS didn't come very close." Quite a contrast from Frank Getlein, in the same newspaper some weeks earlier, who wrote, "There was just a monumental and magnificent job of assembling the pieces that have been lying around in plain view for some years now."

Reading Lucas ("TV had a chance to give the taxpayer a glimpse of how little he is actually told by the military and how suspect the 'facts' are when released by the Pentagon. It failed miserably") and Kelly ("The program seemed not so much to distort reality as simply to miss it almost altogether"), one is troubled by a haunting question. If the small, professional publication or the immense Washington daily, knew so much that "Selling" has missed, why haven't they published it? One can understand the reluctance of *Aerospace Daily,* which Kelly calls "a journal servicing a part of the military-industrial complex," but Kelly's own paper—it would seem—had some obligation to seek that "large target" that the network missed.

Robert Manning, editor of the *Atlantic Monthly* and once assistant secretary of state for public affairs, had quite a different view though he too felt there was more to be reported. In a letter to the *Boston Globe,* he wrote, "To one who has enjoyed more than a passing acquaintance with the way Washington works, 'The Selling of the Pentagon' rings true from start to finish; and if it were to be faulted, it should be for the reason that in the time at hand, CBS could throw the light on only a part of the story of the Defense Department's mighty propaganda engine."

Of all the printed criticism of "Selling of the Pentagon," none was more detailed than an article by Claude Witze, senior editor of *Air Force* magazine in its April issue. It was to become sort of a bible for critics of the broadcast and copies of it were distributed to the Washington press corps in advance of publication. A veteran military writer, Witze was quoted by UPI as saying of the broadcast, "It is the kind of journalistic dishonesty that a reputable newspaper would not tolerate. Many reporters have been fired for lesser indiscretions."

While Witze made only one inquiry of CBS (he asked for a photograph of Roger Mudd for the article), he did a very thorough digging job at the Pentagon. He offered a mild apology that "this magazine has neither the space nor the desire to do a detailed critique" of the documentary, but proceeded in six full pages to do one of the most detailed examinations of all. There is repetition of the charges dealing with the editing of Henkin and Friedheim's briefing, with the Hebert charges that he had been deceived, and with the fact that CBS Films had produced one of the cited DOD films eight years earlier.

Witze reported that Henkin's office told him that it expended 640 man-hours assisting CBS in the production of "Selling" and "CBS reimbursed the government for the cost of one guard and one electrician" during one day of shooting. CBS did indeed use many man-hours of DOD help but when offers to pay were made, they were rejected with the comment that they were just doing their job. Henkin, in a letter to Hebert said, "It was completely appropriate to provide this assistance." (Bob Schieffer, CBS Pentagon correspondent, mischievously requested a count on how many man-hours DOD expended in answering queries from congressmen. The response: the amount of time necessary to carry out their responsibilities to Congress and the public. He resubmitted the query asking for details. The answer: "We do not care to elaborate.")

Air Force magazine devoted most of its critique to the question of the "traveling colonels" in Peoria. It objected to Mudd's narration; that CBS "found" the colonels in Peoria. Witze noted that they weren't found there; they were scheduled to be there as CBS well knew. Further, he noted, that they weren't all colonels, one was a navy captain—only four were colonels. Witze said a State Department foreign service officer was part of the team. They weren't "touring the country"—they simply gave seven briefings on national security policy. (The seven, of course, are in different parts of the country. The Industrial College of the Armed Forces, which prepared these briefings, differed slightly on number—it said there were eight seminars in 1968–69, nine in 1969–70, and eight in 1970–71.)

There is more, but the heart of Mr. Witze's concern in Peoria deals with the remarks of Colonel John MacNeil. Since the editing of them, along with the editing of Henkin, became the heart of the case against CBS, it would be well here to repeat Witze's remarks about MacNeil in full.

In the CBS show, the camera moves from Mr. Mudd, following his recitation of the above inaccuracies, to one of the lecturers at Peoria. CBS does not identify the speaker in this paste-together of film clips, but he is Col. John A. MacNeil of the U.S. Marines, a veteran of World War II and Vietnam. If the TV audience sensed that the next five sentences, out of the mouth of Colonel MacNeil, sounded somewhat disjointed, there was good reason for it. They came from four different spots in the camera record, and the sequence was rearranged to suit the somewhat warped taste of producer Davis. Sentence by sentence, the quotes go like this:

MACNEIL: "Well, now we're coming to the heart of the problem, Vietnam."

This appears on page fifty-five of the prepared, and approved, text of the briefing. Next sentence:

MACNEIL: "Now, the Chinese have clearly and repeatedly stated that Thailand is next on their list after Vietnam."

That one was cut out of what the Colonel was saying back when he was on page thirty-six and discussing an entirely different aspect of the presentation. Then:

MACNEIL: "If South Vietnam becomes Communist, it will be difficult for Laos to exist. The same goes for Cambodia and the other countries of Southeast Asia."

This is found on page forty-eight of the script. What is most important is that the statement was not original with Colonel MacNeil or the drafters of the briefing. It is a quotation. The CBS scissors-and-paste wizard deleted the attribution. Colonel MacNeil made it clear, in the words immediately preceding the above sentences, that he was quoting Souvanna Phouma, the Prime Minister of Laos. In other word, Souvanna Phouma said it; CBS distorted the film to make its viewers think Colonel MacNeil said it. It is the kind of journalistic dishonesty that a reputable newspaper would not tolerate. Many reporters have been fired for lesser indiscretions.

MACNEIL: "So, I think if the Communists were to win in South Vietnam, the record in the North, what happened in Tet of '68 makes it clear that there would be a bloodbath in store for a lot of the population of the South."

To get this one, the CBS film clipper searched deeper into his filmed record. In the prepared script of the ICAF team, it appears on page seventy-three.

Let us examine this "paste-together." Is it jumbled all out of sequence to suit the warped taste of Peter Davis? Not really. The first sentence ("Well, now we're coming to the heart of the problem, Vietnam") is indeed from page 55 but it is also innocuous, simply an introduction. The other four sentences (Witze somehow dropped the last: "The United States is still going to remain an Asian power") are sequential though separated in the colonel's lengthy presentation.

There was much discussion in the long speech of many other items, historical and social, many of them dealing with other Asian countries. It did not appear improper that Davis should condense, as all writers and editors must.

The problem in television is that there is no opportunity to indicate disparate quotes as the newspapers do when they use three dots (. . .) to show a break in text. Television uses "cutaways," shots of the audience listening but this is often too subtle for the general public. The appearance is one of a continuous quote.

The dilemma of television in this regard is very real. Only the sophisticated recognize the cutaway as a sign of an edit. Even then, it need not be but may simply be a device to show audience reaction. Yet, edited or not, the important thing is fidelity to what actually was said. CBS in its five-sentence run of Colonel MacNeil sought to be faithful to his comments on the domino theory and the bloodbath that will follow if the Communists win in South Vietnam.

Witze declared that the network was not faithful for it had the colonel saying, "If South Vietnam becomes Communist it will be difficult for Laos to exist. The same goes for Cambodia, and the other countries of Southeast Asia." That statement, he noted, was not MacNeil but was a quote of Souvanna Phouma.

Indeed, an examination of Colonel MacNeil's prepared script as later provided by the Industrial College of the Armed Forces, showed that this was the second part of a two-paragraph quote from Souvanna. But in actual presentation, the colonel never made clear where the quote ended. It was clear in the first paragraph because there are references to "we" and "us"—"we can count" and "by what right, what moral do they assume the right to liberate us." That is clear. But it is followed by the paragraph used in the film in which there are no personal pronouns. To the film editor as to the audience, it is not clear where Souvanna ended and the colonel began.

As for the sentiment expressed in that sentence—the domino theory—there is little question that Colonel MacNeil's prepared remarks embrace it. Prior to the Souvanna portion, he noted "still another domino" in referring to Malaysia's prince and added, "It is of interest that the Soviet Union is a strong believer in the domino theory as a result of the Sino-Soviet split. The Soviets want neither China nor a Chinese-style communism dominating Southeast Asia." Near the end of his long speech, *not* quoting Souvanna, the Colonel said: "The loss of Vietnam to the free world could start the fall of the domino countries adjacent to it and to Red China, and then we shall face a threat from a hostile Asia quite similar to the threat we perceived in Europe nearly thirty years ago as the dominos adjacent to and around Germany fell into the grasp of the Third Reich.

"No one should be confused as to what is at stake—it is our national security."

Colonel MacNeil took his case to court to sue CBS and the *Washington Post* Company (owners of WTOP-TV, the CBS affiliate in Washington) for twelve million dollars. The suit accused the documentary of making him "the object of public ridicule, odium, shame, and contempt," causing him mental anguish and humiliation, and damaging his military career.

Chet Huntley, retired NBC correspondent who appeared in "Selling" as narrator of one of the Pentagon films, had apparently been encouraged to bring legal action against CBS. Huntley, who would have none of this, gave a speech in Midland, Michigan in which he said he had made recruiting films for the military—"Now, I am disturbed, however, by the use the Pentagon frequently will put these films and other efforts to. They put them into another context and try to indicate that Walter Cronkite or David Brinkley or I have given an unlimited and unreserved endorsement to everything that the Pentagon may be doing or may be planning and such is not the case." He added that the military is engaging in "a hard sell piece of advertising—or I suppose you could say propaganda. Much too much money is being spent on this whole enterprise. We just don't need the military coming on so strongly engaging in that hard sell."

There was a second legal action along with that of Colonel MacNeil. Actor Robert Stack, shown in "Selling" in a clip from an air force training film, named CBS in a twenty-five-million-dollar damage suit, contending that he was depicted as a hawk on the Vietnam war. Stack said he always has opposed U.S. involvement in Vietnam.

For the record, the Stack excerpt, in its entirety, went, "Hi, I'm Bob Stack. As you may know one of my hobbies is collecting guns. I've hunted on and off all my life from California to Mexico to safaris in Africa. Speaking of guns and faraway places, I've just come back from a trip to Vietnam where guns are used for an entirely different purpose."

Returning to *Air Force* magazine, Mr. Witze's lengthy effort ended with the admonition that the broadcast industry must carry responsibility for public misunderstanding. "The incredible thing is that the camera is not to blame. It's scissors, paste, and a collection of calloused consciences."

The *Air Force* article enjoyed enormous popularity at the Pentagon and many military officers, past and present, wrote in praise of Mr. Witze's effort. Elsewhere, one past officer, retired Marine Corps Commandant General David M. Shoup, had a somewhat caustic view of that magazine's credentials. Long before this controversy arose, General Shoup described *Air Force* as "the official mouthpiece of the U.S. Air Force doctrine, 'party line,' and propaganda." He added that "The thick mixture of defense conously repeated in this publication provides its readers and writers with a form of intellectual hypnosis, and they are prone to believe their own propaganda because they read it in *Air Force.*"

Far more serious than an attack from a promilitary publication, no matter how thorough or nettlesome, was a brief letter from Congressman Harley Staggers to CBS President Frank Stanton on March 9, 1971. It cited newspaper reports that told of Henkin's charges concerning the editing of his interview and the colonel's speech. It said these allegations were also made in a letter to Representative Hebert. It asked for "the benefit of your observations on the accuracy of Mr. Henkin's observations" and for CBS policy on editing and filming interviews.

A copy went to the Honorable Dean Burch, Chairman, Federal Communications Commission.

X

THE SELLING OF THE PENTAGON

Confrontation in the Congress

Richard Salant, the head of CBS News, replied to Harley Staggers in a letter which spelled out CBS News policy and declared that "The Selling of the Pentagon" was produced in accordance with that policy. Henkin's allegations, he said, were not justified. "CBS achieved what it set out to do," he wrote, to broadcast material fairly representing the views of both Henkin and Colonel MacNeil.

At that moment in history, Salant found himself being attacked from another source, a most unexpected one: the *Washington Post*. It was not the best moment for CBS to receive such an attack.

On March 26, the *Post* ran an editorial, "Mr. Agnew versus CBS versus the DOD," which offered a plague on all houses. It chastised the vice-president for quoting the FCC about questionable CBS practices while giving "not the merest hint that this and other evidence of wrongdoing had been dismissed by the FCC in the same document." It proceeded to charge CBS with distortion in its editing, saying that the mechanical elements of TV introduce one element of distortion and the need to boil down the material introduces the danger of another.

The *Post* offered this advice: "Given these built-in problems, the TV producers, it seems to us, should go out of their way to preserve intact and in sequence the response of those they interview, or, at the very least, indicate that something in the sequence has been dropped and/or give the subject of the interview an opportunity to see and approve his revised or altered remarks."

On March 30, the *Post* printed a strong response from Salant. He noted that the question of editing is precisely as important for TV as for print but "you question not only our right to do the same thing, but also the methods by which we edit and even our motives ('innocent or not'). You do not in other words grant us the right to do precisely what you do and must do if you are journalists as distinguished from transmission belts. . . . Except in verbatim transcripts, neither medium preserves intact or in sequence everything it presents."

He noted that "most astonishing of all" was the suggestion that the interviewee see and approve his revised remarks. "Is that now the policy of the *Washington Post?* Of course not. You know and I know that this strikes at the very core of independent and free journalism. . . . I almost wrote—'tell you what, we'll do it if you'll do it.' Then I had a second thought: No, we won't even if you should do it."

Across the page, the *Post* editorialized ("Mr. Salant's Letter") that he was off the point. What he and others in television regard as "editing" seems to "take an excess of unacknowledged liberties with the direct quotations of the principals involved." The *Post* cited Henkin's interview, ran excerpts, and concluded, "Surely, something different from and less cosmic than a challenge to CBS's First Amendment rights is involved in the question of whether or not the subject of such a rearranged interview should not be given a chance to see and approve what he will be demonstrated to have said."

On Friday of that week there was more. Reuven Frank, president of NBC News, wrote to protest the original editorial which he termed "admirable arrogance." To deny reporters and editors the right to choose the "interesting and important" is to deny that reporters and editors are needed. Further, Frank called it "fright-

ening" that the lead editorial in an important American newspaper should suggest that another medium delegate this "choosing
process" to the most narrowly interested party, the man who made
the speech.

In the same edition, Fred W. Friendly offered similar comment
noting that "editing, 'foreshortening and rearranging,' in journalism
is as evident to viewers of 'The Selling of the Pentagon' as it is
to readers of the *Washington Post.* Indeed, there may be even
more editing and distillation in a single issue of the *Post* as in half
a dozen documentaries or a month of Walter Cronkite news
shows." As for allowing news sources to review the editing: "It
has always been my understanding that one of the major points of
newspaper independence has been never to permit a news source
to review and/or edit what is to appear in the newspaper."

Once again—across the page—an editorial comment ("F.Y.I.")
by the *Post.* It termed Frank's letter "singularly strident" and repeated its position, that it ought to be easy for TV to identify
"disjointed" excerpts. "Nor does it seem to us to be too large a
surrender of rights, when there has been serious rearranging of the
original material, to allow the subject to at least look at the
product before it is printed or aired and to argue about it."

This author once asked a reporter on the *Post* whether they
ran interviews past interviewees. "Only," he said, "if it involves
our publisher."

Critics of CBS were delighted with their unexpected ally. Several put the *Post* editorials in the *Congressional Record* including
Senator Robert Dole of Kansas, the Republican National Chairman, who accused CBS of "dubious practices involving both the
manufacturing and the editing of so-called news." For good
measure, Dole also inserted the lengthy polemic against the network that had appeared in *Barron's.*

Among those disagreeing with the *Post* was its own television
station, WTOP. In a March 31st editorial, it noted that "Even the
Washington Post, which previously had applauded the documentary's air, lapsed editorially this week into a technical, one-up-
manship debate with CBS over editing techniques." The WTOP
editorial continued with a very perceptive point: "All this has
taken the heat off the Pentagon, but it has not dispelled the spectre
of a Pentagon working feverishly to sell itself."

Indeed, there was no interest in Congress in probing the Pentagon publicity machine. There was growing interest in investigating CBS. Editorial and critical comment shifted attention from the thrust of the broadcast. The new issue was the making of the "Selling."

Time magazine weighed in on April 12, raising the issue of the editing of the colonel. It noted that CBS, with some support from a tape of the speech, maintains that the Souvanna quote was confusingly interwoven with the colonel's own remarks but *Time* said there is "a vital difference between print and television journalism. Newspaper and magazine readers as well as their editors understand that what is printed is a comprehensible reordering of reality; written stories normally can and do make that clear, through both words and punctuation, where significant reordering has occurred. By its immediacy, TV creates the illusion of verisimilitude." *Time* recommended superimposing "Edited Excerpts" over the film.

Time reported that Salant would "have the near-unanimous support of all journalists in rejecting one (Washington) *Post* proposal—that the subject of a film interview be granted approval rights over the final cut."

The magazine's article, "The Art of 'Cut and Paste' " ends by suggesting that "transposition of sequence, as in the Colonel's speech on the *Pentagon* show, is against standing orders at all networks. David Buksbaum, ABC News producer, who learned his trade under Ed Murrow and Fred Friendly at CBS, says: 'When we edit, it never gets out of sequence. And if someone would edit out of sequence, the guy ought to be fired.' "

This surprised many of Mr. Buksbaum's friends. They could not conceive, for example, of editing a presidential news conference in which a major pronouncement was made in a sequential manner resulting in that "lead" item waiting until lesser presidential comments were broadcast in the order they were given.

What David's friends did not know was that—ironically—he was taken out of context. In a note to the "Letter to the Editor" section of *Time,* Buksbaum said, "I was quoted as saying, 'When we edit, we never take quotes out of sequence so as to change their context. And if anybody did it, he ought to be fired.' I think the essential word is *context.* It should be obvious from all of this

that quotes, whether in print or on film, demand loving editorial
care to keep their context correct—especially quotes about
quotes."

The reply from *Time* said, "Our correspondent did not hear
you correctly and therefore, we quoted you incorrectly. . . . We
entirely agree with you that the word "context" changes the meaning of what you said." Perhaps if *Time* had the quote on tape or
film, the error would not have been made. The *Time* reply came
to Buksbaum six or seven weeks after his letter and added, "We're
only sorry that we couldn't publish your letter in our column in
order to set the matter right."

CBS was not without friends in this period. The Peabody Prize
Award, one of the most coveted in broadcasting, was given to
"The Selling of the Pentagon" on April 21st. A special award, announced eight days earlier, it was considered an industry testi-
monial of faith in CBS. Paul Porter, a former chairman of the
FCC and long a member of the Peabody Prize committee, quipped,
"We nominated 'The Selling of the Pentagon' even before Vice-
President Spiro T. Agnew did." The award was unusual in that
it broke from its thirty-one year history of not considering programs after the calendar year ending December 31st; the exception was made for "Selling" because many felt it necessary to
salute it while it was under fire. The *New York Times* noted Porter
had denied reports that the DOD or congressmen sought to thwart
the award.

The Peabody citation called the documentary "historic" and
"great." It offered "a special salute" to Salant for his support of it.
A sardonic Spiro Agnew said such an honor for "Selling" was like
giving an award for costume design to the Broadway production
of "Oh, Calcutta"—a play known for its nudity.

Some weeks later, the *Saturday Review* also honored "Selling"
with its award, calling it "courageous, terse, and revealing." The
citation noted that two of its five judges registered demurs that the
editing techniques were unfair but "all of the judges were unanimous in their agreement that Peter Davis's memorable documentary was superbly effective in its visual and verbal contrasts and
in the dramatic simplicity in which it made its points. The Selling
of the Pentagon demonstrated that the time has not yet come in

this country when a single institution is possessed of such great power that no voices in network television will be found to challenge it."

On May 7, the National Academy of Television Arts and Sciences announced its "Emmy" awards in news. For "outstanding achievement in news documentary," they honored "Selling" and its producers.

Perhaps the biggest salute to the broadcast was a reluctant admission, at an April 9 regular Pentagon news briefing, that the Department of Defense was making changes as a result of the broadcast. A review was being made of DOD films and efforts made to withdraw those which no longer reflect U.S. policy. Specifically, in reference to the film "Red Nightmare," the admission that "Obviously it no longer represents U.S. policy." The spokesman, Jerry Friedheim, said the Pentagon is continuing to work with the Industrial College of the Armed Forces to make sure that remarks made by traveling colonels are in line with U.S. policy. As for Armed Forces Day displays, local commanders were asked to review all public displays and programs to insure that they are appropriate for viewing by children.

Of the last, the worry about impressionable children at military displays, apparently word didn't get out quick enough for all local commanders. An Ohio congressman sent CBS News a copy of an invitation to "Family Day" at a military base in his district. "Family Day" would include participation "in a Vietnam-type infantry patrol" ambushed by enemy forces and a chance to "try your hand at throwing dummy hand grenades." The invitation was to all members of the family, "especially the children."

Assuming that they would ultimately catch on in Cleveland, it appeared that Friedheim's remarks on April 9 were evidence that "The Selling of the Pentagon" had made a major impact on the Pentagon. "Times do change," he said, "and we try to learn from them." DOD was not going to concede much to the broadcast. He said the warning to base commanders about children at inappropriate displays was really prompted by Representative Hebert's question to Henkin. He quoted Laird on "girls wearing long skirts" when talking about film review.

"The Selling of the Pentagon" would win no popularity prizes in the Defense establishment. Most viewed it as a "cheap shot," a stab in the back. The bitterness remained for a very long time and hostility towards CBS was prolonged.

It should be noted that an hour of television can hardly exhaust a subject. "Selling" was hardly a definitive work on military publicity efforts. There were many things it barely touched on, others it missed completely, and much that it went over once lightly.

It did not explore—as Senator Fulbright did in his book, *The Pentagon Propaganda Machine,* the Magazine and Book Branch which acts as a literary agent to place material written by the military; the Organizations Division which has liaison to five hundred defense-oriented private groups and regularly mails material to two hundred eighty-seven of them; the report of the Air University in Alabama which reported 1,574 speeches, radio broadcasts, and TV appearances by its personnel in its semiannual report; the 39,000 still photos, 49 news films for TV, and 55 TV "news featurettes" for TV put out by the Navy alone; or the Air Force's "Pro Sports Report" which is carried on 150 radio stations, its "Serenade in Blue" which goes to 4,000 radio stations, and a thirty-minute Christmas television show sent to 204 stations (He wrote that "It is hard to put one's finger on the cost of the Air Force's film production for public consumption". . . . The costs are "buried among the funds of the Military Air Transport Command").

"The Selling of the Pentagon" did not explore those matters nor, as the Twentieth Century Fund's "The Military Establishment" did, the question of press trips, junkets. Such free trips for newsmen, it said, continue to be a popular practice by both the Pentagon and defense contractors.

Nor did the broadcast get into military magazines as did a report by Bernardine Kopec in *Armed Forces Journal.* She writes of the publication of about 371 magazines by the military, eight times as many as the nation's largest publisher of consumer magazines. The cost is estimated at $57 million a year which, if she was accurate, is almost twice the amount budgeted for all public affairs and is one more indication of how military publicity costs can be hidden and spread around.

Nor did the broadcast go into the question of the Pentagon's lobbying effort on the Hill which CBS News itself did months

earlier in Bob Schieffer's report on the "Evening News." There
are over 300 such lobbyists who "don't like to be called that; they
say they are 'legislative liaison.' " They operate from a series of
offices in the Pentagon and on Capitol Hill itself, are assigned to
work with pertinent congressional committees, collect information
for and about Congress, plan congressional junkets overseas, and
offer advice wherever needed. Schieffer reported that the cost of
legislative liaison is three million dollars a year. It is not registered
with Congress as a "lobbyist" activity but registered lobbyists
groups, some 269 of them at that time, spent only $5.1 million
and the largest of the civilian lobbyists reported expenditures coming to only one-tenth of the cost of military legislative liaison.

But, as indicated earlier, attention shifted from Pentagon publicity to the nefarious network which had produced the offending
documentary. Chairman Staggers had his investigators look into
the broadcast and started hearings on "The Selling of the Pentagon." Some lawyers made appearances but basically there were
two witnesses, Dan Henkin and Frank Stanton.

Henkin appeared on May 12. He was to complain about his
interview and go over its editing with the committee but Henkin
also said, "I am certain that the members of this committee share
with me an unswerving belief in the sanctity of the First Amendment for all information media" (They did not). Henkin said, as
a former newsman, if pressed by the committee, he would not produce his notes or source material. Asked if he considered producing the outtakes of the interview with him "doing any violence to
the First Amendment," Henkin said, "no, but there is a matter of
principle here."

The reason for the question was simple. Stanton, some weeks
earlier, had been asked for the outtakes of film relating to the
broadcast. He had refused. In response to the April 8 subpoena
asking for "all film, workprints, outtakes, sound tape recordings,
written scripts and/or transcripts" related to the broadcast, Dr.
Stanton said, "We will comply with that part of the subpoena
which calls for a film copy and written transcript of the material
actually broadcast." No other part of the press, he said, would
turn over material gathered by reporters and not published; CBS
would be no different.

There is irony in asking for outtakes relating to the Henkin interview. It is the custom of DOD to tape record every radio or television interview done in the Pentagon for its own files. It does not do so for newspaper interviews and when tape recorders showed up in late summer, 1971, during interviews for the print media, reporters complained mightily. However, television interviews done in the Pentagon studios, are easily recorded. This one was. Henkin could give the committee a full transcript of the original. DOD also provided a text of Colonel MacNeil's Peoria speech.

Some weeks after the CBS refusal to provide outtakes, and after extensive press criticism of the Staggers subpoena, the Investigations Subcommittee issued a revised subpoena on May 26—this asking for outtakes relating only to interviews and events covered by the broadcast and dropping the request for films of interviews not broadcast. The net tightened but the fishing continued. CBS refused again.

Representative Staggers insisted that the First Amendment was not at stake, "all we're interested in is the fraudulent practices." He also drew a distinction between broadcasters and newspapermen. In an exchange with *Television Digest*'s reporter, Staggers was asked if a print reporter's notes are different from TV's outtakes.

STAGGERS: I've always believed they were different. You know that.

QUESTION: Do you have power to subpoena my notes from this interview?

STAGGERS: No.

QUESTION: What if I were a reporter for TV talking to you on the phone?

STAGGERS: Well, then that would be different. The committee could subpoena your notes.

QUESTION: Why?

STAGGERS: TV is different. It's very important that the networks be accurate.

QUESTION: Is a congressional committee qualified to determine what's accurate?

STAGGERS: Yes. By using the outtakes, then we can determine if what was aired was fair and accurate.

The prospect of congressional subpoena of newsman material brought swift and almost unanimous reaction from the press. Staggers was almost universally condemned. Even newspapers which disliked the broadcast, now came to the defense of CBS in its refusal to honor the subpoena fully.

The *Washington Post,* whose cutting criticism earlier had sent tremors through the nerwork hierarchy and perhaps had done more to stain the reputation of "Selling" than anything else, came out in ringing support of CBS. The action of Staggers "is . . . unwarranted and a substantial threat to the news media of this country." Continued the *Post:* "In essence, what Mr. Staggers now wants to do is to sit in judgement, not of the program, but of how CBS operates as a collector and disseminator of information. That, to put it bluntly, is none of his or Congress's business."

The *St. Louis Post-Dispatch* asked, "Who defines truth?"

Editor and Publisher editorialized: "The worst fears of those who have constantly reminded others that federal licensing of broadcasting stations might someday be used against them by government threaten to be a reality. For the first time since broadcasting of radio and teievision began in this country a network is threatened with punishment—at the least, investigation—either for being painfully right, or painfully wrong, in something it has aired. . . . Let the Pentagon prove error, if it can, but what this country does not need is legislative surveillance of the news judgments of any news medium."

The *Cleveland Press* wrote, "To give government the power to poke around in a journalist's notes and second-guess him on his interpretations—and in the end to intimidate a reporter in this fashion—is to relinquish one of the basic freedoms in a democracy." The *Washington Star* said, "The congressman's right to second-guess all the editorial decisions that went into the documentary—that's one we'll bet the Founding Fathers would have laughed out of Independence Hall, as it would be laughed out of any (newspaper) city room."

The *Omaha World-Herald,* which hated the original broadcast and called it "The Smearing of the Pentagon," reacted strongly to the subpoena question. It wrote that "criticism is one thing, and congressional meddling is another. The subcommittee's initiative could open a can of worms that would never be closed until government had imposed a form of official censorship on the broadcast media." The *Los Angeles Herald-Examiner* which also disliked the broadcast ("a biased attack on the military") disliked the subpoena even more—"Poking through the private files and wastebaskets of TV editors—or of any others in the communications media—is not a proper function of democratic government."

CBS's competitors offered support. Julian Goodman, president of NBC, said, "CBS is absolutely correct in resisting this invasion of a basic, journalistic right." Reuven Frank, president of NBC News, wrote, "If the people we film or interview believe their words and actions will be a happy hunting ground for even the highest-minded investigators, the flow of news will dry up, and the public itself will be the ultimate victim." Elmer Lower, president of ABC News, issued a statement of opposition to "congress or any other legislative body subpoenaing untelevised material . . . reporters' notes and sources of information."

The Nixon administration found itself in an interesting dilemma. Many were blaming it for the congressional investigation. The heavy attack by Agnew earlier had associated the White House with an anti-CBS position. Senator Edmund Muskie, the leading Democratic candidate for the presidential nomination at the time, in a Delaware speech attacked the White House criticism of news, "Whether the Nixon administration acts with the velvet glove of (presidential communications director) Herbert Klein or the mailed fist of Spiro Agnew, the intent is the same. The intent is to limit access to information. . . . We must say to this administration as clearly as we can: Stop trying to manage the news. Stop trying to limit the American people to one side of the story. . . . I hold no special brief for CBS. Nor do I argue that its documentary was flawless. Charges of unfair editing certainly merit review and corrections where appropriate. Newsmen make mistakes as do politicians, and both should be criticized when it happens. But what is important is not this network or that documentary. What is important is our right as a free people to the continuing flow of information, including facts and opinions from sources the public can compare. When this administration tries to undermine that opportunity, it undermines public trust in this administration."

Muskie spoke those words on March 31, a week before the subpoena but his and other equally strong responses to Agnew put the administration in a guilt-by-association position once the subpoena was issued. Many thought the White House responsible. Communications Director Herb Klein moved to disassociate the administration from the subpoena, calling it a danger to a free press. He told interviewers, "I believe that in going beyond what was broadcast and asking to get, in effect, notes of programs that they infringe on the ability of broadcasters or print media to develop a story."

Nixon's news secretary, Ronald Ziegler, made similar remarks at a regional meeting of *Sigma Delta Chi* in Chapel Hill, North Carolina, on April 25. Ziegler observed that it was not the Republicans but a Democratic majority in the committee and the entire House and that a Democratic chairman had called for the subpoena.

The president himself was asked about the matter on May 1 in San Clemente, California. He said network commentators and newspaper reporters are not above criticism but "when you go, however, to the question of subpoenaing the notes of reporters, when you go to the question of government action which requires the revealing of sources, then I take a very jaundiced view of that kind of action."

At about the same time, the FCC released *its* report of "The Selling of the Pentagon" declaring that any further action by it would be inappropriate. "Lacking extrinsic evidence of documents that on their face reflect deliberate distortion, we believe that this government licensing agency cannot properly intervene. It would be unwise and probably impossible for the Commission to lay down some precise line of factual accuracy—dependent always on journalistic judgment—across which broadcasters must not stray."

The Staggers subcommittee suffered from no such inhibition. On June 24 in Room 2123 of the Rayburn House Office Building, Dr. Frank Stanton appeared before the Investigations Subcommittee in what *Variety* called "Stanton's High Noon on News."

It wasn't truly high noon with two cowboys walking towards each other on a dusty, Hollywood set. It was two quite disparate men, each with tremendous influence in broadcasting, meeting in that antiseptic hearing room at 10 A.M.; going past noon, four hours in all, through a vital debate over broadcast rights and prerogatives. With Staggers were three like-minded members of his subcommittee and Counsel Daniel Manelli. With Stanton, several lawyers in the first row of seats and at his side, Special Counsel Lloyd Cutler.

Harley O. Staggers first came to the Congress in 1948 after a career that began as a high school coach and teacher and included being sheriff and a right-of-way agent. There is not a single television station in his district. His home and place of birth sixty-four years earlier was Kaiser, West Virginia—a tiny B & O Railroad town with a populatian of six thousand. Cherubic looking, the white-haired, rosy-cheeked Staggers had been Commerce chairman since 1966 and had led investigations in the WBBM–TV "pot party" story and the CBS involvement in the proposed invasion of Haiti.

In this case, his views were strong. What was at stake was deception. The First Amendment, he said, had "nothing to do with it." If broadcaster freedom to edit as they choose is unchecked, Staggers had warned, then "Big Brother has arrived."

There were reports that Staggers' friend, Chairman Hebert, had encouraged him in the probe. One columnist, Milton Viorst in the *Washington Evening Star* flatly stated so—"Staggers, normally a decent and moderate man, had been put up to nettling Stanton by Chairman Edward Hebert." There was no real evidence of this, however, and despite the normal proclivity of House chairmen to protect and defend each other, Staggers' prior interests in the area would indicate he needed no special prodding from friends.

Frank Stanton, the 63-year-old president of CBS—a post he had held for the last twenty-five years—was the broadcast industry's premier witness in matters of national significance. He had led the fight for reforms in the political use of television, had taken strong steps to clean up practices after the 1959 quiz show scandals; he was credited with bringing about the Kennedy-Nixon debates in 1960, and was generally recognized as a key figure in all network battles for news freedoms. Blond hair stylishly long, blue eyes carefully evaluating his adversaries, Frank Stanton was a strong witness.

THE CHAIRMAN: Have you brought the materials with you which were called for by the subpoena of May 26?

DR. STANTON: No, sir, Mr. Chairman; I have not.

THE CHAIRMAN: Since you are the president of CBS, are the materials requested in the subpoena subject to your control so that if you wished you could have brought them here today?

DR. STANTON: Yes; they are.

THE CHAIRMAN: Is there any physical or practical reason why these materials have not been provided?

DR. STANTON: No; there is not.

THE CHAIRMAN: Is your decision not to bring with you these materials made with full knowledge of the possible action that may be taken against you for your refusal?

DR. STANTON: Yes.

THE CHAIRMAN: Do you realize that as a result of your refusal to comply with the subpoena you may be found to be in contempt of the House of Representatives with all the consequences that flow from such contempt?

DR. STANTON: Yes; I do.

THE CHAIRMAN: Knowing this, do you persist in your refusal to provide the subpoenaed materials?

DR. STANTON: Yes; I do.

THE CHAIRMAN: Does the decision not to provide the subpoenaed materials reflect a decision of the management of CBS?

DR. STANTON: Yes; it does.

THE CHAIRMAN: So that the record may be clear on this point, speaking as the chairman of this subcommittee, I hereby order and direct you to comply with the subcommittee subpoena and to provide forthwith the materials therein described. What is your response?

DR. STANTON: I respectfully decline.

THE CHAIRMAN: At this point, Dr. Stanton, it is my duty to advise you that we are going to take under serious consideration your willful refusal today to honor our subpoena. In my opinion you are now in contempt.

Staggers having already confirmed the outcome of the hearing, the inquiry began. Again and again Stanton refused to answer questions about the editing of "The Selling of the Pentagon."

Again and again they pushed. He freely discussed editing principles and policies and other broadcasts but each time Counsel Manelli or subcommittee members pressed to relate them to "Selling," Stanton refused.

Manelli noted that outtakes of "Project Nassau" had been turned over to the committee. Stanton said that case involved a possible violation of law, this did not. Manelli pressed on the Haitian film and said, "You will concede that should the same events have occurred today and you were to maintain your position it would be impossible for the Congress to get any information on how it happened." Stanton replied that he must say "in candor" that "we have learned a little bit more about the surveillance of broadcast material. The accumulated experience to this point would lead me to tell you that I might give you a different decision today than we gave at the time we supplied the materials."

Manelli introduced the *Time* article and quoted Buksbaum on editing out of sequence. Stanton said Buksbaum was quoted incorrectly and later supplied the letters exchanged between the ABC producer and the magazine.

The subcommittee's ranking Republican, Springer of Illinois, bore in on Stanton concerning "Hunger in America." He said the FCC ruled that certain things, namely the death of a baby due to starvation, never took place—"You are willing to concede that are you not?" Stanton said that was not what the FCC said.

Chairman Staggers was to read a section of the FCC report which stated that the infant involved had died of causes other than malnutrition. Stanton asked if there was objection to including the rest of the material in that FCC report. The rest included, "There is a conflict with the memory of the CBS witnesses differing from that of hospital personnel. In these circumstances, it is, we believe, inappropriate to hold an evidentiary hearing. . . . The 'truth' would always remain open to some question."

He might have also produced the article by FCC Commissioner Nicholas Johnson which had appeared some weeks earlier in the *Washington Post*. Johnson, taking issue with Agnew's treatment of the same subject, wrote—[his] "text quotes from an FCC order regarding 'Hunger in America.' What they fail to quote— from the commission's unanimous October, 1969, order—is even more relevant: 'We commend CBS for undertaking this documentary on one of the tragic problems of today. . . . [In] this democracy, no government agency can authenticate the news or should try to do so. We will therefore eschew the censor's role, including efforts to establish news distortion in situations where government intervention would constitute a worse danger than the possible rigging itself."

Springer of Illinois went into praise of public broadcasting and talk programs that present representatives of both sides of an issue. "I would hope you people in TV would give this some thought about trying these balanced programs as an experiment and see if you cannot make just as interesting a program out of it as you can with this one-sided stuff."

Stanton ignored the reference to "one-sided stuff" and tried to explain that fairness and balance is achieved in a number of ways in the broadcast schedule. He also asked whether balance is possible in investigative reporting, especially when corruption or crime is exposed.

Rep. J. J. Pickle of Texas spoke: "Is it your contention now that we are trying to set up some kind of government control of the press?"

Stanton replied, "I think that is where you come out if you persist in this investigation."

Moments later, Jake Pickle quoted Stanton as talking earlier of "government standards of truth" and asked, "Now who else is going to pass judgments on these matters if it is not the government of the people. We are representing the people."

A patient Stanton noted, "You are the government and this was a broadcast about government activity" but before he could explore the propriety of the government investigating the investigation about government, the chairman interrupted saying, "I think this has all gotten out of context. I think, Dr. Stanton, you and Mr. Cutler know why you are here, not to have anything to do with the First Amendment at all."

Springer returned to the editing of the Henkin interview, noting that Henkin had testified that in thirty-two years in the newspaper business, he knew of no journalist that considers it allowable or commendable to edit as CBS did in this case. Springer pressed Stanton for the name of a single journalist who considered it allowable or commendable to edit out of sequence.

Stanton later supplied the names of the incoming president of the American Society of Newspaper Editors, Edward J. Murray, and a past president of *Sigma Delta Chi,* William Arthur, the editor of *Look Magazine* but he noted that enumerating names simply would obscure the central issue—no journalist subscribes to editing which results in a deception but all must compress. This example was cited:

QUESTION: Do you know Mr. Smith?
ANSWER: Yes.
QUESTION: How long have you known Mr. Smith?
ANSWER: I have known Mr. Smith for twenty years.

Stanton contended that there is nothing wrong with editing that resulted in the following:

QUESTION: Do you know Mr. Smith?
ANSWER: Yes, I have known Mr. Smith for twenty years.

Such techniques, he noted, are used by responsible journalists without question. Practices can be abused, of course, but responsible men do not do so.

Near the end of the four-hour hearing, Chairman Staggers said he had known Stanton for twenty years and "I respect you as a man. I don't blame you, I blame your organization."

Stanton said, "Please, Mr. Staggers, don't separate me from the organization because the men in the organization are the men that I put in that organization."

Staggers proclaimed, "But Jesus picked twelve disciples and one sold him for thirty pieces of silver, another denied him on the night that he was crucified, and another doubted him when he came back. Now that is the kind of men we have today and that we had then."

The until-then cool witness snapped back with anger in his voice. Said Stanton, "I think that is most unfair to refer to our news organization that way." Staggers: "Being prophets and disciples of Christ?" Stanton: "No; as being traitors." Staggers backed off—"I didn't call them traitors or anything like that; no, sir, I would not do that."

Springer changed the subject and returned to the mail the subcommittee members had been receiving. Staggers earlier complained about the lobbying effort. He cited a letter from a CBS vice-president urging journalism school professors to write in support of CBS. He demanded to know how many letters had been mailed—"One thousand, two thousand?" Stanton said he would get the exact figure (176) for the record but added, "Is there anything wrong with trying to get a point of view to the committee? We didn't tell these people they had to write you, we simply said if [they share our view]."

The subcommittee was uncomfortable over the massive editorial support given CBS in the subpoena matter, the word from broadcasters back home and from the growing mail. One letter to Staggers was from the president of Notre Dame, the Rev. Theodore M. Hesburgh, who noted "In our democratic society, the press is an auditor of government, not the other way around."

The chairman, disturbed when Stanton said newspaper editors would hardly do something for a competing medium unless they believed in it, declared that one could hardly exaggerate television's influence. In a loud voice, nearly shouting across the crowded hearing room, he said, "This is the most powerful media we have in America today, and you talk about chilling effects. This runs chills up and down the spine of every person in America. When there is untruth put over these networks they can control the land, and you know they can if we allow this to go on. Anything I say or you say can be distorted and made to be a fact and they can ruin every president, every member of this Congress, or anybody else if we allow this to go on. WE MUST HAVE THOSE OUTTAKES."

On June 29, the subcommittee voted 5 to 0 to seek a contempt citation against Stanton.

The next day the full Commerce Committee met on the matter. There was a bit of lobbying for the votes. From Staggers' office came a press release and a copy of a letter to him from Dean Burch, Chairman of the FCC who wrote "We cannot conclude that CBS has failed to comply with the requirements of the Fairness Doctrine" (somehow, in the press release, "Cannot" became "are unable to conclude"). The Staggers' press release said the issue was not fairness but deliberate distortion; the Congress had to act where the FCC was unable to act.

From CBS's office to the committee chambers came a letter from Stanton to Staggers on editing guidelines and the enclosure of a new memo (dated just two days earlier) on CBS operating standards for news and public affairs. The seven page, single-spaced memo was a compilation of existing news policy statements, some of them going back many years. But under documentaries, there were three new items, (1) if answers are responding to questions other than the immediate one, the broadcast must so indicate in narration; (2) if excerpts from speeches are used out of their original sequence, this must be indicated; and, (3) transcripts of the entire interview will be made available to the interviewee on request.

These new standards were available to every member of the Commerce Committee on the morning they met. With less deliberate speed they reached members of the CBS News organization, some of whom were greatly disturbed. One, they felt that new guidelines weakened the very arguments on editing that Stanton had made to the subcommittee. Secondly, they felt that the issuance was a reflection on their professional integrity, that they had nothing to apologize for, that the broadcasts they do— including "The Selling of the Pentagon"—were proud efforts. Thirdly, they speculated (correctly) that many critics of CBS—in and out of the Congress—would view this as a partial capitulation, a confession of guilt.

Why the new standards at this moment? The best guess was that it was the pressure from CBS lawyers who, in the way of all lawyers, felt that this might be just enough to win their case, that a little compromise is not a bad thing.

The full committee voted 25 to 13. Against CBS.

For those who knew the Congress best, it seemed obvious that CBS and Stanton were sure to be voted in contempt when the full House dealt with the matter. Committee recommendations on contempt citations are not overturned. It had happened only once in the remembered history of the House, in February, 1879, when a member of Congress offered a contempt citation against George Seward, minister to China. The matter was referred to the Judiciary Committee to see if Seward might be forced into self-incrimination (he faced impeachment). Congress adjourned before there was any action taken on contempt or impeachment.

On July 9th, every employee at CBS received a message from the Chairman of the Board, William S. Paley. An unprecedented gesture, the note was attached to a CBS fact sheet on the controversy and simply said that if the House of Representatives does not act favorably, CBS will go to the courts. "To lose this fight," said Mr. Paley, "would be a serious setback to free speech in this country. It would also go against every principle that CBS has stood for and fought for since its founding. The issue is as grave as that."

CBS attorneys asked a number of correspondents, producers, and news exceutives to write affidavits on the effect that the Staggers subpoena and potential examination of outtakes would have. For the CBS News people, it was a familiar routine. They had written similar affidavits in behalf of Earl Caldwell of the *New York Times* as he fought his subpoena. They had entered other affidavits in similar cases where CBS was a friend in court. This time it was for CBS itself.

As the CBS lawyers began thinking beyond an upcoming defeat in Congress, there was a first sign that perhaps the Staggers' forces were not as certain of their position as one would expect. The incident also serves as an example of how congressional power is used to influence broadcasters.

Daniel Manelli, acting chief counsel of the subcommittee, called each of the network bureau chiefs in Washington to discuss a possible filmed statement by Chairman Staggers—this less than a week before the vote. In his conversation with CBS, Manelli said the network might want to consider carrying the statement in keeping with the Fairness Doctrine. He was asked if he was suggesting that CBS had not been fair in its treatment of the story. Manelli said he was not suggesting that but simply calling to alert CBS to the Staggers statement.

Staggers had been invited to appear on "Face the Nation" that Sunday and had declined. Manelli said he didn't know about that. He was asked if Staggers would be interviewed on the statement. He said no, it was to be on film done in the House studio and handed out.

Manelli again made vague reference to the Fairness Doctrine and said the filmed statement was, of course, something different than interviewing Staggers as he emerged from a hearing (the chairman did not permit television cameras in any of his hearings but crews were stationed outside to interview him and witnesses as they emerged).

The counsel asked for advice: how long should the Staggers statement be as far as television was concerned? The answer: CBS News in Washington doesn't give advice of this nature to news sources. He said he simply didn't want it to be too long to be practical for television. He was told that if the statement was too long, and it were used, he could be happy in the knowledge that when CBS engaged in the editing, he would have a full transcript of the outtakes.

The film statement was never issued.

Staggers, by the way, for a crusader against rigging in broadcast news once engaged in what *Broadcasting* magazine called "deception and staging" in an editorial entitled "The Expert." It happened prior to his previous campaign for re-election in the fall of 1970. According to the magazine, he sent tape recordings to fifteen radio stations in his district with his answers to questions on prayers in the public schools, federal highway funds, and the situation in the Middle East. The packet with the tapes included cueing information, a script of his answers and suggested questions, plus a covering letter suggesting a live-taped format be followed. It went out in envelopes mailed free under the Congressional frank with similar envelopes, also franked, to provide for return of the tapes.

Broadcasting asked a Staggers aide if listeners wouldn't be misled into thinking that the program was live. He replied that the American public was sophisticated enough to recognize live and taped programming.

CBS picked up another bit of support on the weekend before the vote. Congressman Henry Reuss of Wisconsin charged that Secretary Henkin, when he placed the cost of the public relations tour shown in "selling" at fourteen thousand dollars, was considerably short of the mark. The real cost, according to a General Accounting Office report to Reuss was about eighty thousand dollars to the government. Reuss found it an expensive price to take Methodist bishops, savings and loan executives, and others on a tour of army posts.

The *Washington Post* that Sunday worried editorially that "Mr.

Staggers is apparently making some headway in the House—working assiduously to invoke support on the floor in his capacity as a committee chairman." It urged that Speaker Carl Albert take the lead "to turn this vindictive campaign around."

The *Post* also had fun by noting that the "most altered, revised, rearranged, cut-and-pasted version of 'reality' that exists among public documents" is the *Congressional Record*. Because congressmen can "revise and extend" their remarks, the *Post* noted, "Perhaps you won't believe it, but in the *Congressional Record sentences may be cut in half, qualifying words removed and the sentence put together without the least indication that this occurred*. Members of Congress, in fact, remake their remarks in such a way as to *mislead the public into believing that they are reading what really happened, when they actually are often reading a fiction created not by a film editor but an anxious, second thought-laden Congressman*. Make no mistake, as Mr. Staggers might put it—and has, in fact—*we have clear evidence of deceit —men's words altered to change their very meaning*."

On the day before the vote, Tom Wicker was writing for the *New York Times* edition of the next morning and observed, "Two well-established operating rules of legislative life are at work against CBS News in its struggle against Chairman Harley Staggers and the Commerce Committee: 1. Legislators are reluctant to offend or oppose powerful leaders whose favor they may later need, 2. Those who think they have the votes always want to vote as soon as possible." He noted that "never in contemporary history—not even to forestall some of the worst excesses of the Communist-hunters of the 1950s—has the House failed to uphold one of its committees and its chairman when they have recommended a contempt citation."

Still there seemed a glimmer of hope on that last day. CBS asked the news people who had submitted affidavits if these could now be distributed to certain key members of the House. The answer was yes.

Late that afternoon, supporters of CBS asked for and received permission to state their case on the floor of the House. Rep. Brock Adams of Washington spoke and said if editing is to be reviewed by government, then television news "will cease to be an energetic seeker of truth but instead becomes a pallid conduit for that propaganda which is palatable to the majority of Congress or the administration of the moment."

Rep. Bob Eckhardt, a Texas Democrat, reported on his own careful examination of the documentary. He took issue with Henkin's criticism that CBS had dropped remarks about recruiting saying that politicians would love to pick which two minutes TV uses out of each fifteen minute speech they give, "But he (Henkin) never contended that anything which was stated in the broadcast was something other than something he had said." As for Colonel MacNeil, Representative Eckhardt noted that it was difficult to spot where the Souvanna quote ended, "I defy anyone to tell exactly where the quotes ended and the colonel's speech began." The congressman also said, "But let me point out another thing about that speech. I have checked the whole speech through and I find in the speech a couple of paragraphs in which almost precisely the same thing is said in Colonel MacNeil's own statement."

Rep. Lionel Van Deerlin of California, an ex-television newsman and a frequent defender of television's journalistic rights, rose to reflect the *Washington Post* critique of the *Congressional Record*—including the opportunity, when a congressman is absent, for anyone from his office to insert an entry. "I wonder why we do it that way unless it is intended to persuade the voters back home that we are indeed here on the floor, actually making a speech which we can then clip out of the *Record* and send to whoever is interested back home in our district. The fact of the matter is that this document is guilty of virtually all the sins that the network, CBS, has been accused of in the instant citation."

Adams, Eckhardt, Van Deerlin—these men had been heard from before on similar issues. You'd expect them to defend broadcast rights. Now rose a figure most unexpected. The congressman from Kensett, Arkansas rose simply to say, "Mr. Speaker, I have some serious questions in my own mind about the citation, with all due respect to my good friend from West Virginia, the chairman of the Committee."

It was Wilbur Mills.

Mills, chairman of the Ways and Means Committee since 1958, was a key figure in the inner circle of leaders of the House. Indeed, *Congressional Quarterly* has said he "often has been called the most powerful person in the Congress." Virtually every important law on taxes, federal revenue, national debt, import tariffs, foreign trade, Social Security, and health insurance had the Mills touch, in authorship or sponsorship. In his fourteen years as chairman, only three of his bills had failed to pass the House. If the committee chairmen are the Brahmins of the House, the chief Brahmin had now spoken in opposition to one of his fellows. Unprecedented. Not done.

His simple statement about "serious questions" was followed by two more brief sentences, one saying he had tried to inform himself and the other saying he had read the statements from CBS newsmen and wished to insert them in the *Record.* And Mills sat down.

Mills was equally taciturn later with a reporter who asked, "Is this a kind of an earthquake for the members when a committee chairman comes on and in effect opposes the request of another chairman?" Mills replied laconically, "I don't normally oppose a committee because generally a committee is asking for information of a witness that the committee needs in order to legislate. In this case, I don't understand that to be the fact."

The CBS citation was suddenly a live and no longer a foregone issue. Few members of the House would read the statements Mills placed in the *Record* but none would miss that significance of "Wilbur is supporting CBS." The *Record,* however, *is* worth examining for its reflections of how working television journalists viewed the matter.

First—from the remarks of CBS Diplomatic Correspondent Marvin Kalb:

> Discretion is the essence of diplomatic reporting. If a State Department official, dealing in highly sensitive information, part of which he wishes to keep from the Congress, say, U.S. clandestine support of anticommunist guerrillas in Laos, if he were to agree to do a television interview (an unlikely event, but it happens), he would be even more circumspect than usual if he realized that the entire film record, including his "deep background" chitchat preceding the formal interview, or a misspoken thought, or even a simple slip of the tongue, might be

subject to congressional scrutiny. In fact, I suspect he might not even do the interview. It is widely believed that much of the State Department's work—the White House's too—is absorbed with the questionable chore of presenting policy in such a way as to avoid "Capitol Hill" scrutiny or criticism. To legislate congressional access to the "outs" of interviews with "executive branch" officials would not only intrude into the functioning of TV newsmen, converting them, against their will into conduits between two supposedly independent branches of government, it would also drastically reduce the reporters access to the executive branch and his credibility in the long run with the legislative branch. . . .

Congressman Staggers alleges "deliberate distortion" in "The Selling of the Pentagon." He has been encouraging his colleagues to see a conspiracy on the part of the "media" well beyond this one broadcast. He sees the "manipulation of the ballot box," "past proof of fraud and deceit," and the "art of cut and paste." It would appear that he describes too much cunning and machiavellian genius to us—and therefore to a process that is too haphazard, often too rushed, sometimes guileless and thoughtless, combining the immediate needs of the news with a sense of timing and drama, and pushed always by the tyranny of the clock (Broadcasts start on time in this society) that, taken all together, become the rule rather than the exception. Congress should be judging the rule rather than the exception.

Mike Wallace, veteran reporter and co-anchorman on the broadcast "Sixty Minutes":

A story on SIXTY MINUTES this year was a profile of Spiro Agnew, from his childhood on up to the date he became Vice President. While the Vice President, we are told, did not see the broadcast, Mrs. Agnew did and let her displeasure be known. A Republican Congress might have been very interested in what complimentary things were left out of the broadcast; on the other hand, if they clearly had a right to inspect our "outtakes," a Democratic Congress might have been interested in whether uncomplimentary things were excluded. The possibilities, indeed the probabilities, are endless. . . .

Thus far, we in broadcast news have gone about our business in the belief that we are protected by the freedom of the press. It is inconceivable that the men who wrote our Constitution and the Bill of Rights, had someone told them we would some-day communicate ideas and information by electronic means, as well as by the print press, would not have made clear that freedom of the press protected broadcast news.

Mr. Mills led off the CBS statements with remarks from this author, the Washington bureau chief, which perhaps best illus-trate the problems that those of us in charge of news operations saw in all of this:

The actions of the House Interstate and Foreign Commerce Committee have already had a profound effect on our news operation. While our people continue to do their news gather-ing in a professional manner, I sense a growing apprehension over the actions of the Congress. There seems to be a general feeling that continuation of the present trend will result in an unseen Congressional presence in the newsroom, peering over the shoulders of journalists as they make their decisions.

While the nervousness expressed above is difficult to express in specific example, one manifestation is already seen in treat-ment of the very story of the Committee's actions against Dr. Stanton. While most hearings are covered briskly and profes-sionally with editing done similarly, this one series of hearings was not. There was special caution expressed by various par-ticipants in the process, a nervousness that the story might be examined later. This was limited not just to the days of the hearings but to news coverage of the various principals. One day recently an interview with Chairman Staggers was analyzed far beyond its normal due because the producer and correspon-dent feared that the Chairman, who was fumbling as he read, might appear awkward if special care were not taken in the editing. These concerns, while they exist frequently in other cases, took on special meaning and unusual attention because they were in the context of this current controversy.

Haunting news producers, correspondents, and executives in the entire matter of *post mortems* of the editing process is that this will be done, if certain Congressional desires prevail, by

nonjournalists whose motives are not proper presentation of
the news but examination of raw material to see if the news
presented could have favored one side or another as Congressmen would have them favored. Examination of film outtakes, even by fellow professionals, can frequently be a poor
judge of the actual editing without much more information.
Not the least of the elements in this process is the judgment as
to the truth of statements on film. Sometimes there is other
material from equally respected sources which causes one to
avoid using certain quotes, or to use them in juxtaposition
with other material. Ignorance of these and the many other
elements that go into editing decision make examination of
outtakes often a poor way to judge the final product.

There is a feeling which I share with many of my colleagues
that outtakes of film will not be the end. Frustrated as investigators will become with this single source of raw material,
they will seek a mandate to go beyond it to internal memoranda
and individual memory of the editing process. The irony of all
this is that one of our own checks and balances consists of
frequent *post mortems* of story treatment. We are frequently
checking back to see if a story couldn't have been done better
or to make sure that our facts were correct (with resulting
on-air corrections if needed.) Our *post mortems,* done by professionals with day-to-day concern with the story at hand, are
often frustrating because the "evidence" is incomplete, the
outtakes insufficient, the memories a bit hazy, honest men disagreeing.

Investigations *ex post facto* are injurious to a news organization. Each time we conduct our own examination of a single
story or a documentary, we tie up many men for many hours.
Each time government does this, in the acts of federal agencies
or Congressional committees, the hours are multiplied and at-
tentions distracted from the fundamental job of news gathering
and presentation. It saps the energy of CBS News. There has
been a great deal of this in recent years. Many resent the days
spent in gathering material for replies to such government inquiries. Many resent even more the difficulty in catching the
administrative eye for new projects because the news executives are embroiled in lawyers' chores.

When government agents are given the opportunity to come into the newsroom and make these investigations in person and with frequency—the inevitable end, as I see it, of the present push for examination of non-broadcast material—then the greatest damage of all will be done. Courage is the essential ingredient of my craft. It will be replaced with caution. Public service is the heart of what attracts good men to journalism. It will be blunted with concern for the intrusions of investigators and inquisitors. I am convinced that the end result will be the loss of most good men. They will run for newspapers where the First Amendment is yet to be corrupted. Those who remain will no longer operate freely. . . .

A final and personal word. After over two decades of service in broadcast journalism, my zeal for my craft remains high and my respect for my colleagues boundless. It is a tough job they do and they do it well. The days of yellow journalism are long gone. Today's news reporting is of a higher quality than ever before. The sense of honesty and high scruples of all journalists, is unparalleled in our history. It is because of that and because I have witnessed it first hand from the inside, that I bitterly resent the charges by Chairman Staggers of "calculated deception" and "deceit." My colleagues are professionals in their craft and it is a high calling. If there were deception, deceit, fraud or even the merest fudging of the truth, they would speak up strongly and forcefully. They now do when they suspect even honest error. I dread the day when they fear to speak up. This effort on the part of the Congress brings that day closer.

Congressmen were alert to the special nature of the upcoming vote. Many had heard from broadcasters back home (many of them, but not all, solicited by the National Association of Broadcasters to come to the aid of their brothers at CBS). Harley Staggers was to call it the heaviest lobbying campaign he had seen in his twenty-two years in Congress.

But there were other considerations—political ones. One of the top Democrats in the House received a note urging him to support CBS. As his adviser put it, in the confidential memorandum, "The politics of the situation is such that now the Democrats are fighting the networks and the Republican administration is defending them. I realize that castigating CBS is good politics in [your home state] but nationally it's something else."

On the Republican side there was concern of political hazard so soon after the administration had been reversed by the Supreme Court on the Pentagon Papers. According to an intimate of GOP House Leader Gerald Ford, he had moved away from his original thought of supporting Staggers because "If the committee citation had succeeded, it would have put the president and the Justice Department in the embarrassing position of having to prosecute this thing, and we'd be right back as the big, bad administration persecuting the press."

Newsweek reported that friends of Staggers were trying to head him off. A trusted fellow-committeeman, Rep. Torbert Macdonald of Massachusetts, urged him weeks earlier to "Apply the George Aiken principle on Vietnam to this issue: run up the flag, declare a victory—and get out of it." He was also to note, "The networks can be arrogant as is but if this thing went to the Supreme Court and we lost, they would be incorrigible."

Harley Staggers would have none of this. He was determined to have his vote. On Tuesday, July 13, he was to have it.

In the morning, at a leadership conference in Speaker Carl Albert's offices, Staggers learned the extent of defections from his ranks. The leadership wanted to recommit the matter to committee thus killing it. Staggers objected strongly. The Democratic Whip, "Tip" O'Neill, Jr., of Massachusetts told him, "Harley, you haven't got a chance."

Staggers' friend and ranking Republican on the committee, Rep. William Springer, was getting the same message on the Republican side. "Everybody in the leadership was talking about a motion to recommit." Indeed, at noon Carl Albert talked of recommitting to another committee, Judiciary, but this plan was changed since it would be an affront to Staggers. The motion was to recommit to his own committee. Staggers told reporters Albert was "conniving" to defeat him.

The session in Albert's office was a stormy one, a shouting match. "I don't need the leadership," Staggers was quoted as saying, "If you give me my hour, I can convince the House that this is the right thing to do."

And so the House met that afternoon with the members knowing in advance that the session would end with a motion to recommit the contempt citation to committee. But Staggers had his hour—and others had their time—to go over the issue of broadcast rights versus congressional prerogative.

On every seat in the large, lush chamber of the House of Representatives was a 272-page report entitled "Proceeding Against Frank Stanton and the Columbia Broadcasting System, Inc." It was a pretty good summary of the issue, but for many members was their first exposure to any kind of documentation. In it, the Commerce Committee staff outlined its arguments against CBS including those dealing with the First Amendment. There was a minority report, signed by ten members headed by Rep. John Moss of California, father of the 1967 Freedom of Information Act. It noted that the text of Colonel MacNeil's speech and of the interview with Henkin were both in the committee's hands, a look at outtakes was not needed at all. They accused the investigating subcommittee of other motives—"The real purpose of the subcommittee was to review the editorial judgment in the filming of the documentary 'The Selling of the Pentagon,' and other controversial documentaries and news coverage."

Most CBS defenders on the committee and before the full House were quick to damn any possible mistakes made by CBS while defending its right to make them. Rep. Robert O. Tiernan of Rhode Island, however, in a dissent of his own quietly noticed that "our contempt vote and the surrounding publicity has apparently made some of us lose sight of the public service which CBS rendered by disclosing how the Pentagon was using a very substantial sum of the American taxpayer's dollar for propaganda purposes. The documentary was devastating in its portrayal of how the Pentagon has gotten out of hand in its public self-aggrandizement."

More typical were remarks such as those of Rep. Bill Frenzel of Minnesota: "Despite my distaste for the CBS actions and attitudes, I will vote against the contempt citation. I do so because I believe congressional control of the media would be far worse than whatever CBS has done or can do." Similarly Rep. Sherman P. Lloyd of Utah: "I believe there was distortion, possibly malicious distortion. . . . There will undoubtedly be distortion in the future . . . [but] we will be making a mistake if we allow government to push its nose in the tent of a free press."

Most of the speakers—and by House rules, most of the time—went to Chairman Staggers and his supporters. The chairman himself spoke at length—"I think that America is done with this deception. . . . There are those who would like to say that we have all the information that we need. We do not have that information. . . . We do not have the outtakes of any portion of the program. There might be twenty or thirty or forty different places where they misquoted or misplaced these things, we do not know. . . . We want the facts. That is all we want."

The earliest antagonist of "Selling"—Chairman F. Edward Hebert of the Armed Services Committee—rose dramatically and orated. "They cry—'First Amendment.' I believe in the First Amendment and there is nobody in this room who can challenge my standing on that. They have had their First Amendment. They have had their chance to lie under the First Amendment. If it were not for the Frist Amendment, they could not have practiced the deceit that they have practiced. I am one of the victims of that deceit. . . . I agree that the public has a right to know. How is the public going to know if we do not make them show what they have under the table and up their sleeves?"

Rep. Fletcher Thompson of Georgia said if Congress failed here, "the practices will continue. Continue to what? To the era of Hitler's propagandizement of the world that brought so much devastation? I think we must act now to prevent this."

Rep. Henry Gonzalez of Texas, who was from the San Antonio district which was the site of the opening sequence of "Hunger in America" and who had been attacking CBS for it ever since, proclaimed that "CBS assuredly is unwilling to confess it is wrong, or has been wrong, or even that it has an editorial point of view. So who is to protect the truth? . . . We live in a world where the baleful eye of CBS reigns with a mighty hand."

Rep. J. J. Pickle of Texas said, "It is strange" that no one has defended CBS in the mismatching of questions and answers. He noted that CBS, on the very day of the subcommittee vote, issued new guidelines—"In effect, CBS was saying 'We're not guilty—and we promise not to do it again.' "

There were others, many others. The bulk of the remarks on the floor were stinging rebukes of CBS—Edwards of Alabama: "CBS has maligned the South, colored the news, handled coverage of the war in a biased manner"; Hays of Ohio: "There is no degree—and I repeat—no degree in fakery. You either fake or you do not"; Pelly of Washington: "Defrauding the American people through dishonest film editing is reprehensible."

There were some defenders. Rep. Robert Leggett of California called the suggestion that Congress be the arbiter of truth "incompatible with a democratic society . . . with the First Amendment. Furthermore it would be just plain ludicrous, considering the dismal record of untruthfulness the government has accumulated over the past few years."

Rep. Michael Harrington of Massachusetts said, "I disagree with my colleagues who say 'The Selling of the Pentagon' was a deceptive documentary. No one has come forth with legitimate examples of inaccuracies in substance. The documentary raised very serious issues, issues that deserve far more debate before this body than the editing procedures. Why has no one asked if the Pentagon budget can justify so much money for public relations? That is the question this Congress should be considering."

Rep. Abner Mikva of Illinois urged defeat of the contempt citation. "Surely if this resolution is allowed to pass, history will properly judge this House in contempt of the Constitution."

The most important voice in defense of CBS was the oldest voice in Congress. Emanuel Celler of Brooklyn, Chairman of the House Judiciary Committee, eighty-nine years old, and with twenty-five consecutive terms, the most senior member of the House, rose to speak against the contempt citation.

First he recognized the enormity and novelty of one chairman opposing another by saying, "I counter my fellow chairman, the affable gentleman from West Virginia, and that counter leaves an ashen taste in my mouth." He then uttered the one phrase which stood out in the hours of debate and seemed most likely to be recorded in any history of broadcast freedoms. "The First Amendment," he said, "towers over these proceedings like a colossus."

Because of the First Amendment, he said, "no *esprit de corps* and no tenderness of one member for another should force us to topple over this monument to our liberties; that is, the First Amendment."

He proceeded to outline his arguments in legalistic fashion. The First amendment *does* apply to broadcasting. Outtakes and other source materials of broadcasting *are* impervious to government subpoena. There are instances of abuse but the media, even if guilty, *must* have breathing space to survive. Interference with the media *has* a chilling effect on free speech. Finally, Celler concluded with the prediction that if Congress votes contempt, the courts will not sustain it.

There was an amusing moment during Mr. Celler's eloquent and careful presentation which was illustrative of the congressional habit, editing its own *Record*. Citing the president's opposition to the subpoena, Celler mistakenly referred to "President Truman at a San Clemente press conference recently." As he read on, members kept calling out "Nixon not Truman" but in the well of the House, the elderly chairman, not hearing them clearly, waved them off with his hand and continued to read his text.

In the *Congressional Record* the next day, there was no reference to Truman—only to Nixon.

Indeed, the *Congressional Record* is quite a poor record of that actual day's debate. Dozens of members asked for, and received, the right to "revise and extend" their remarks. Defenders of CBS, worried about offending and losing votes by speaking too strongly, became quite passionate *after* the fact—as recorded in the *Record*. On the day after the vote, reporters meeting with Speaker Albert to discuss that day's calendar, noted the *Record's* version of the previous day's debate and asked if they could have the outtakes. Everyone, including Speaker Albert, laughed.

The debate ended with Chairman Staggers having his final say. He bitterly criticized "the greatest lobbying effort that has ever been made on the Congress of the United States" and dramatically pointing to the inscription high above the speaker's chair, said "Mr. Speaker, the slogan up there says, 'In God We Trust.' Are we going to change it to 'In the Networks We Trust?' "

The previous question was moved. Rep. Hastings Keith of Massachusetts rose and offered a motion to recommit. The question was taken. The vote was held. The House of Representatives voted 226 to 181 to recommit. CBS would not be held in contempt then or, likely, ever on this issue.

Harley Staggers was bitter—"Lord, I'm disappointed," he said after the vote. He predicted that sooner or later something will have to be done to prevent "calculated deception" on the television screen. He told *Broadcasting* magazine, "The networks now control this Congress."

He found some sympathy in the nation's news weeklies. *Time* said that the real sentiment of the House may have been expressed by one leader, unnamed, who said in a secret vote, "it would have gone about 5 to 1 against CBS" and *Newsweek* quoted one Democrat saying that in secret ballot, "the vote would be 420 to 15—or worse." *Time* credited "an all-out lobbying campaign" for the CBS victory and concluded—"Asked if he thought CBS executives had 'learned any lesson' in their clash with the House, Staggers replied bitterly, 'Yes, that they have power.'"

Power or not, CBS was badly scarred by the entire affair. The flood of criticism, including the constant accusation of distortion and manipulation, did serious damage to the network's reputation. In the manner of things in Washington, CBS executives knew that the prolonged battle would come up again and again in future hearings. The many critics of television, from the vice-president on down, could be expected to put "The Selling of the Pentagon" into their permanent lexicon.

There were scars internally as well. While CBS news personnel had tremendous admiration for the courage of "the bosses" against the ravages of officialdom, they were conscious also that there would be a closer look at them from the White House, the Pentagon, and the Hill. There was remaining bitterness over the new guidelines, not that they were considered terribly restrictive but simply that they had been issued at this time. There was the problem of dealing with news sources, especially at the Pentagon. The CBS correspondent there, Bob Schieffer, found a frosty reception in many quarters, a marked lack of enthusiasm for dealing with CBS News even on routine matters. An army sergeant tried to stop him from filming a story outside the Pentagon one day. It required intervention by the Public Affairs Office to reassure the soldier that the practice, which went back many years, was proper.

In other places CBS News encountered other problems. A naval public affairs officer on the West Coast permitted a local camera crew to film some destroyer escort ships but told them that they could not share their film with the CBS network without permission from Washington. Secretary Henkin, informed of it, angrily said there was no such order and straightened out an obviously eager navy man.

Morley Safer was in Vietnam on a routine assignment when a memorandum went out warning information officers to "use caution" in dealing with Safer, that he might have "ulterior motives." Safer said he got "the big freeze-out" when he reached Pleiku, that Americans there had apparently been told not to talk to him, and that "the place was like a tomb with us there." When the Associated Press uncovered the memorandum and filed a story, officials apologized and the U.S. Command chief of information, Colonel Robert W. Leonard, personally told Safer, "I wish to apologize for any inconvenience and embarrassment that may have been caused."

"The Selling of the Pentagon" had received more publicity than it deserved and provoked more outrage than it merited. The House vote seemed more important than it was but actually promised no relief from future abuse.

As Julian Goodman, president of NBC, had noted—while it was a strong vote, it still meant that 44 percent of the House voted on legal or emotional grounds against television. "Those 181 members voting against CBS probably had 181 different reasons for being mad at CBS. . . . You can assume charges of bias will continue. Our answer is to keep on doing our news job because we are fair when a politician likes what he sees and biased when he doesn't."

The *Washington Post* used the word "standoff" in reacting to the vote and also saw more trouble ahead. "We are pleased at the outcome. We do not see in it much evidence that the larger confrontation between government and press has been resolved."

More to come was not long in coming. Hastings Keith introduced legislation to provide guidelines for network news, much like the CBS guidelines he said.

Comedian Georgie Jessel was stopped on the "Today" show when he referred to the *New York Times* and the *Washington Post* as "Pravda." Representative Staggers asked for a transcript and Rep. William Harsha of Ohio demanded an investigation saying such "tacit censorship . . . cannot be tolerated on the public air waves."

Within a few weeks of the vote, investigators for the Staggers subcommittee were interviewing CBS employees in Los Angeles, checking on stories to see if the camera crews or film editors could tell them anything about the stories being staged. The subcommittee counsel, Daniel Manelli, denied that this was any "task force project to get CBS." He said that the subcommittee is always interested in getting information on how television networks operate. Among the stories they were reportedly interested in: a Morley Safer report from Vietnam six years earlier.

Fred W. Friendly, a former CBS News president and long-time acquaintance with official efforts to discredit controversial broadcasts, wrote an article in *Harper's* on the subject "The Unselling of the Selling of the Pentagon." He suggested that the "demolition manual" for action goes in several different ways:

1. Enlist friendly Congressmen. See the file on the Farm Bureau's attack on the "Crisis in Abundance" documentary. Avoid the central thrust of the broadcast and pick away at errors of fact, no matter how minor. Finding slight errors helps discredit the whole.

2. Plant news stories, columns, and editorials in friendly trade papers, house organs, columnists. See the follow-up on NBC's documentary on gun control in 1967; also the reaction to Rachel Carson's "Silent Spring" broadcast in 1963. Check the columns of George Sokolsky, Jack O'Brien, and Westbrook Pegler during the Murrow-McCarthy exchange.

3. Organize write-in campaigns to Congress and the FCC. See the attempts against the Bricker Amendment broadcast, "Harvest of Shame", and "The Great American Funeral."

4. Create seeds of doubt over production techniques (see NBC's migrant worker broadcast in 1970) or suggest interviewees were paid (see NBC's "Battle of Newburgh") or attack "scissors and paste" editing (check broadcasts on apartheid in South Africa, the Newburgh broadcast, etc.).

5. Pressure the sponsor. This last, said Friendly, was used effectively during the Joseph McCarthy era but is rarely used now that single sponsors have been supplanted by spot advertisers buying isolated "minutes."

All but the last of these steps, of course, were brought into play against "The Selling of the Pentagon." Friendly adds a "warning" in postscript—"Don't permit spokesmen to enter the arena of central debate of the documentary. Stay on the peripheral issues and ambiguities in narration where the credibility of reporting can be questioned." See, he didn't have to say, "The Selling of the Pentagon."

Friendly concluded his article with the following: "The final verdict on 'The Selling of the Pentagon' will not come from the smokescreen created by all those brush fires of nit-picking doubters. Nor will it derive from the procession of self-serving awards which doubtless will come its way. At the end of the day what will matter most is when another documentary of such impact will be broadcast again. By the answer to that question will be CBS News, its competitors, and its detractors be measured."

Paul Porter, who was FCC Chairman during that agency's years of most stringent regulation in the mid-'40s—including the issuance of the so-called Blue Book asserting FCC powers over programming, had switched to a much different view in the early '70s. He called for a "bill of rights for broadcasters" in his Peabody Award luncheon speech in April, 1971. He said broadcasting "is now under siege from many quarters" but its record was proud and distinguished and could be proclaimed under the caption: "For What The Hell Do We Apologize?"

"I have at long last," said Porter, "become weary of the constant refrain that 'the airwaves belong to the people.' Of course they do. But this should not become a cliché to support any politician or any small group in either the right or left claiming to act in the people's name to throttle free expression of opinion or responsible reporting on the people's air."

The Supreme Court in the late '60s had called the scarcity of licenses the heart of what distinguished broadcasting from newspapers. Anyone can start a newspaper, you need a license to take to the air. A lower court ruling had held differently. The Seventh Circuit Court said that economic factors severely limit the number of newspapers. There are more broadcast stations than daily newspapers and the competition of reporting that they provide was salutary. The court also noted that the "public ownership" concept was the heart of the FCC's sanction of "inhibitory regulation."

There were 1,748 daily newspapers in America as of 1972 while there were 892 television, 4,323 AM radio stations and 2,636 FM stations. There are 27 daily newspapers in cities of over one million population. Those same cities have 55 television, 70 AM and 102 FM stations. There are another 50 daily papers serving cities of half-a-million to a million population. Those same cities have 124 TV, 175 AM and 195 FM stations.

New York has only three dailies (if you omit papers like the *Wall Street Journal* and the *Daily Telegraph*) but it has 9 TV, 17 AM, and 18 FM stations. Chicago is the only city with two morning and two afternoon papers (though they are owned in pairs by two companies) but it has 10 TV, 14 AM, and 18 FM stations. Los Angeles has only two daily papers but has 13 TV channels, 12 AM, and 19 FM stations.

Only 215 cities in the United States have more than one newspaper and in all but 60 of these, the papers have a single owner. On the entire 50 states, three states haven't a single city with more than one newspaper, 16 haven't one city where the two newspapers don't have common ownership and in 18 others there is only a single city with more than one newspaper not commonly owned.

On the other hand, there is not a single city in America beyond the reach of television coverage and in most, several choices of channels are available. With cable TV, many are available and more are coming. There are not only thousands of radio stations but many are heard over a broad area.

In bringing a diversity of voices to America, nothing has served better than broadcasting yet the inhibitions imposed from Washington seem to be increasing not declining. Some have felt it hopeless to defend broadcasting. Bernard Kilgore, president of the *Wall Street Journal,* said some years ago that "[we] are going to get the issue of freedom of the press obscured dangerously if we try to stretch it to fit the radio and television industries that operate and apparently must operate for some time in the future under government licenses. . . . The argument that freedom of the press protects a licensed medium is double talk . . . [and] if we try to argue that freedom of the press can somehow exist in a medium licensed by the government we have no argument against a licensed press."

A similar theme was expressed at about the same time by Walter Lippmann. On March 3, 1960 writing on "Television and Press," Lippmann said, "Networks, which are very few in number, have a virtual monopoly of a whole medium of communication. The newspapers of mass circulation have no monopoly of the medium of print. The situation of freedom is bound to be different, too. Free speech is a cherished principle. But how it can be exercised depends upon where it is exercised."

Lippmann was responding to a speech by Frank Stanton which opposed government intrusion in programming. Stanton had argued that government had no more right to concern itself with broadcast content than it had to concern itself with what was printed. Lippmann disagreed. "This is a thoroughly false argument," he contended. "A television station is not like a newspaper. It is like a printing press. It is a mechanical medium of communication. Now let us suppose that in a whole region around some city there were only, let us say, three printing presses. They would print all the newspapers, all the magazines, all the books, there being no other way to get anything printed. Does Dr. Stanton imagine that under such a condition of virtual monopoly, there would be no public regulation of the printing presses?"

And so goes the argument, reflected in some judicial and much congressional thought that while there are those thousands of individual stations, there are only three networks. Lippmann's analogy, however, is strained. While the networks are comparable to three giant presses, the vast majority of radio and a significant number of TV stations are—in effect—smaller presses. Even network stations have the opportunity, which many exercise, of departing from network programming for broadcasts of their own.

It is true that there are but three commercial networks but this is not the result of government licensing, for technically no network is licensed. It is the result of economic forces comparable to those which have reduced the number of wire services to just two and have kept the number of news magazines similarly small. Government does manage to get to networks through licensing since each owns a number of licensed stations, highly profitable holdings.

This, and the possible direct licensing of networks, usually have inhibited networks from challenging government.

There is nothing to keep someone from starting another network except the economics just as no one is prevented from bringing another newspaper into New York or Chicago except for the staggering cost. Years back when William Randolph Hearst tried and failed to start a successful daily in Atlanta, it was said the loss came to fifty million dollars, a sobering figure to any prospective investor. Today two of the three networks spend that much or more on their news budget alone. Obviously it is no easy task to challenge them and start a fourth network. Yet it can be done. Temporary networks have been set up for special broadcasts. The Hughes Sports Network has had great success with athletic events. Regional networks have worked to cover sports, elections, state inaugurals, etc.

Public Broadcasting, which came alive as a serious network in the late '60s, has shown that a noncommercial network could be created and give competition to existing networks. As the decade of the '70s began, it was still to prove that it could escape from the grasp of the Congress which provided much of its funding. This has been successful in England for a variety of reasons and while there are important differences, theoretically is possible here.

"The situation of freedom" may be different in television but not because networks are few. Their service to stations is not a "condition of virtual monopoly" no more than is the AP or UPI service to newspapers [and stations], services that provide such an extremely high percentage of the actual words printed and broadcast. Choices and editing remain for the users of AP and UPI as well as the affiliates of networks. More important, there are even more choices available to listeners and viewers—more sources of information than at any time in our history.

One rarely hears the Kilgore/Lippmann arguments today, not because newspapermen love television(most despise it) or welcome its competition (most hate it) but because newspapermen have realized—as Eric Sevareid noted some years ago—that to ignore a broadcast journalist's problems with government is to say "Your end of our boat is sinking." The strong defense of CBS by newspapers in the subpoena matter is indicative of a growing concern on their part for the rights of their electronic competitors.

James Reston, writing at the time of the fuss over "The Selling of the Pentagon," said, "The basic assumption of the First Amendment was that the people in a democratic society had a better chance to get a fair presentation of the news from a multitude of free reporters than from reporters regulated by the government. The Founding Fathers had no illusions about the infallibility of the press. Their comments about our stupidity, inaccuracy, and bias make Spiro Agnew's sound almost genial. But they were persuaded that the risks of freedom were less than the risks of legal strictures or government control, and it is hard to argue that this protection should now be guaranteed to the radio and television stations, which now supply a majority of the American people with their first reports of the news."

In the same column, Reston added, "It is ironic that the FCC's 'Fairness Doctrine' was intended to assure precisely that, but everything depends on who is deciding what is 'fair,' and the guess here is that the Founding Fathers would still bet on Walter Cronkite rather than on Agnew."

It is not surprising, as television continues to expand its immense reach into the homes of America, that politicians want to control it. It is disappointing and not just a little bit dangerous in a democratic society, that electronic journalism should be the most susceptible form of journalism. The future of true freedom in broadcast news is not very bright. It is an era when government is unable to resist the urge, unable to keep hands off.

XI

WHOSE BATTLE IS IT—THE PRESS'S OR THE PUBLIC'S?

The role of the press in the United States is the role of an auditor. The press is to give an accounting of what government does and to interpret its meaning.

The role of the political man in the United States is rarely responsive to a full accounting. He recognizes the need for some sort of inventory and the need to provide some information but he feels a full accounting is at the least a nuisance and at the most an injury to running the government. Of course, he believes in a free press. The Constitution tells him he must.

That is not to say that the men in government are not often helpful to the newsman. Many are frequently honest and forthright. There are officials, elected and appointed, who willingly share much of what they know with the press. There are none who share everything. It is a little like the man who says he believes in the Ten Commandments but not all ten at the same time.

It should not be assumed that the men in government are evil men no matter how harshly one measures their view of the press. America is blessed with many able, patriotic men of talent, in-

telligence, and imagination. Men in high places and their subordinates are dedicated to what they consider the public good
but understandably are discomfited by the ever-inquisitive press.

If there is a law in press-government relations, it is that information is provided in reverse proportion to the amount of controversy involved. Cooperation decreases in direct relationship to
the sensitiveness of the subject matter. What the politician does
not share willingly is that material which either reflects unfavorably
on his administration or that which he judges must be kept from
the public for its own good. It is the arrogance of political power
that those who have it always know best when the public should
know least.

Leslie H. Gelb, the former director of Defense Department
Policy Planning and Arms Control, who was head of the study that
became known as the Pentagon Papers, wrote an essay for *Life*
on "Today's Lessons from the Pentagon Papers." In it, he talked
of "governmental credibility." Our leaders, he noted, "made a
major effort to avoid flat lies" but, he added, that is not the point.
"I believe the point is that most of our elected and appointed
leaders in the national security establishment felt they had the
right—and beyond that the obligation—to manipulate the American public in the national interest as they defined it."

The right and obligation to decide what the public should know.
The national interest as they defined it. So it is with political
power.

Gelb had no illusions that the leadership in the 1960s was
unique. "I believe this pattern of concealment and half-truths has
been and still is a way of life in our government."

Traditionally, the people have been more alert to the need for a
free press than have been their leaders. On December 20, 1772
Thomas Erskine defended Thomas Paine before a "special" jury
of upper class Londoners. Paine was in France, being tried *in
absentia* for seditious libel and certain of being found guilty. Said
Erskine, "Government in its own estimation has been at all times
a system of perfection; but a free press has examined and detected
its errors, and the people have from time to time reformed them."
Assured of losing his case (the jury found Paine guilty without
even waiting for the attorney general to respond to Erskine), the

lawyer concluded, "Although my arguments upon the liberty of the press may not today be honored with your or the court's approbation, I shall retire not at all disheartened, consoling myself with the reflection that a season may arrive for their reception." The season was close to arrival. While the authorities quickly condemned his client, a cheering crowd escorted Erskine out of the court room on their shoulders.

It is questionable that a defender of free speech today would find as many ready to cheer. This is an era when the news media, as other institutions, have come under skeptical evaluation. There even seems to be a growing feeling that newsmen are treating politicians unfairly, are "picking on them." The press has grown powerful and is run by a small group of men who would harass the president (so vice presidents say) and must be made responsible to the public—a neat turnabout from the late nineteenth century when Englishmen and their American cousins grew to believe government too powerful and run by a small group of men—and a free press needed to make it responsible to the public.

Where does the power lie today? No matter how you measure it, the greatest power remains with the man in office. As James Reston put it, "We may report the news, but he makes it."

In 1965, the *Wall Street Journal*'s White House correspondent Alan Otten noted that "the image of hard-hitting reporters relentlessly driving a president into the corner with sharp, penetrating questions has always been incredibly overdrawn. Actually the deck is stacked, if at all, the other way. An intelligent, adroit politician almost always has the upper hand at those press sessions—telling little more than he wants to, and little more than he could probably say in a speech, a message to Congress, or a statement released through his press office."

Reston, in his excellent book *The Artillery of the Press,* said the pattern is as true in foreign policy as domestic: "Newspapers, radio, and television stations in the United States influence foreign policy mainly by reporting the actions of government. Acts are more powerful than words in this field and news more influential than opinion. Most of the time, reporters are in the distributing business, transmitting the accounts of what Presidents and Secretaries of State do onto the front pages and into the top headlines, where they undoubtedly influence public opinion. Let me make the news, Franklin Roosevelt said in effect, and you can write all the editorials you like against it."

The cards remain in government's hands, even in a democratic state with a tradition of free press. NBC's David Brinkley once observed that "the press doesn't have the power to subpoena, to investigate tax records or many of the other things that government can do." The press is always on the outside looking in.

Beyond its rather obvious powers, government operates a tremendous publicity machinery. Every agency of government has its press agents variously called "public affairs officer" or "public information officer," and they have giant staffs, giant budgets.

It is difficult to place a dollar figure on how much the government spends in this field. When President Nixon ordered a cut in publicity activities in 1970, the Office of Management and Budget promised to trim 45 million dollars from a total of 164 million but it is not clear how much was included in that 164 million and how much "information" activity was hidden. As one government employee put it, "Did you ever see a speechwriter listed as a speechwriter by any government department?" Four years earlier, the Associated Press estimated that the government may spend as much as 425 million a year to disseminate its news and views.

Of course, federal press agents have been forbidden by law since 1913. In that year, fearful of the executive branch's power of publicity (the government had placed an advertisement for a publicity man to promote new federal highways), Congress attached a rider to an agricultural appropriations bill creating a federal statute (5 USC 54) reading, "No money appropriated by any Act shall be used for the compensation of any publicity expert unless specifically appropriated for that purpose."

Almost sixty years later the Government Information Organization, which is composed of almost three hundred information officers in the federal establishment, promised that it would try to get the law repealed. As Mel White, head of the GIO, put it, "We recognize that no one is out to abolish us. It's just the fact that we are illegitimate. We represent the only function in government for which funds are not directly appropriated. It's not the first law ignored by everybody by mutual understanding."

On November 6, 1970 President Nixon issued his directive to

federal agencies asking that they cut back on public relations expenditures and curtail "self-serving and wasteful public relations activities." The president said, "I want to make it clear that this is not an attempt to single out those who serve the government well by informing the public and preserving the principle of freedom of information. Rather, it is directed at those who are, quite understandably, program advocates, and who, perhaps unknowingly, affront many of our citizens with public relations promotions, fancy publications and exhibits aimed at a limited audience, and similar extravagances."

One year later, the Office of Management and Budget's estimate of cutbacks in the public relations field was a disappointing one. According to OMB, there had been 6,144 "full-time permanent" federal public relations employees. Following the president's directive, almost 1,200 were taken off the public relations rolls but not necessarily placed in different jobs. Since the estimate of 6,144 was low (one OMB source said 10,000 was more like it) and because press agentry in government goes under many names, it was easy to transfer employees by title if not function.

The Pentagon is the largest public relations organization in government and probably in the world. It announced a cutback of 991 employees in keeping with the president's directive. None of the 991 would be dismissed, however. Those in the military would be reassigned to other jobs and civilians would "be protected by civil service."

The Defense Department, as many other agencies, also felt it had not been acting in a "self-serving" way as the president had defined it. Further, it interpreted the presidential directive as exempting such activities as recruiting (The Office of Management and Budget had permitted "help-wanted advertisements for specific vacancies") and legislative-affairs costs—"resources applied to preparation of materials and appearances at congressional hearings, and responses to specific congressional inquiries."

The second largest federal expenditure for public relations was the Department of Health, Education, and Welfare. HEW had over 800 full-time employees in the field and dropped 68 after the Nixon directive but still admitted to spending well over 27 million dollars annually in the field. In 1970, the then-secretary of HEW, Robert Finch, issued an internal memorandum expressing doubts about the amount of printed material coming out of HEW. In the previous year it had published 188 million copies of 6,000 different titles at a cost exceeding seven million dollars. Six months later, 28 million copies remained in bulk storage joining the fifteen to twenty thousand other titles in storage, occupying over 100,000 square feet of space. To handle it all, HEW was employing over one hundred people in these storage areas alone. Said Finch, "We doubt that such a deluge of printed matter is needed to communicate the business of this department."

The president had warned agency heads to make sure "your subordinates carry out the intent of this directive and that they do not attempt to circumvent it through changes in position titles or a reallocation of resources intended for other purposes." Despite this, the fiscal 1971 public relations expenditure was up a million dollars from the previous year. On paper, 1,164 employees had been reduced from the public relations payroll but there was ample evidence, as in the case of the Pentagon, that there had been evasion of the presidents wishes and, further, there was no serious probing into public relations people who go under other names (the FBI's press liaison, for example, is listed as assistant director of the Crime Records Division). At the same time that other areas were asked to cut, the information staff at the White House was increased about 30 percent and became the largest presidential public relations organization in history. The White House information effort was not included in the hundred and sixty-four million dollar figure for full-time federal public relations. Its cost is never made public.

Not all of the thousands of public relations types or the millions of dollars spent annually are arrayed against the press in a massive, coordinated, brainwashing effort. Obviously a part of the manpower and money consists of pure housekeeping functions within government. Much of the effort is truly informational (a word bureaucrats much prefer to public affairs which in turn is preferable to public relations which itself is much better than the taboo phrases of "publicity" and "press agentry") and reporters would complain mightily if there were no one to answer legitimate inquiries.

While the government does service the press and the public with information, much of the mammoth effort is self-serving, whether or not it is so defined by its creators under fear of presidential directive. The real cost, some have estimated, may exceed the total combined budgets of both the AP and UPI, all three television networks, and the nation's ten largest newspapers. When faced with that possibility, one can rejoice in intragovernmental competition and bickering because, if any genius could ever coordinate all the publicity tools of government into a unified effort, it would dwarf anything Goebbels or Lenin ever dreamed of.

When the public begins to wonder if the press is picking on the politician, let it view the vast publicity apparatus and ask "Who holds the cards?."

Government, then, has the opportunity to make the news while the press simply reports it, has elaborate facilities to publicize its efforts, and the special weapon of silence, the opportunity to keep its business from the press. With those cards in the adversary's hands, the press is hard-put to deal with government. Historically, however, it has been more than a match.

The natural allies of the press are the congressmen, who sit on the sidelines overseeing the federal establishment. Since administrations must come to the congressmen for their money and must justify their programs while doing so, a great deal of information is disclosed. Congressmen who consider the press important to their re-election and almost nothing more important than re-election, then tend to share with reporters openly, discreetly, or publicly through congressional hearings.

Congressmen are not altruistic or idealistic in sharing information. They share because it is self-serving to them and they share only that information which serves this end. Their goals, however, are often at variance with those of the administration and that is why they are a reporter's natural allies and most profitable source.

Congress's own use of publicity apparatus may not be as extensive as that of the executive branch but it is considerable. There are many congressional prerogatives to help the politician remain in office. An examination of the 1968 races in the House of Representatives, for example, showed that 96.8 percent of incumbents who sought re-election were re-elected. No small part of this astounding figure is a result of the built-in advantages of incumbency.

To cite one example: very cheap facilities are available to all congressmen to make radio tapes and television films for home-town distribution. The House and Senate recording studios include a payroll of thirty-two employees earning almost $400,000 a year. The cost of a five-minute film to a senator is $36 while comparable films produced in commercial studios in Washington would cost $650 to $1,000. Videotape, which is reusable when the home town station returns it, costs only $13.45 for a special, six-minute color roll and $20 for a five-minute recording session (about 65 percent of the congressmen use videotape and the other third still use film). Additional copies are made by the studio for five dollars per dupli-cate, the congressmen supplying the tape. The same services in a commercial television studio would run hundreds and perhaps thousands of dollars. Radio, of course, is cheaper. They can record a half-hour radio broadcast for less than ten dollars.

This bargain that the Congress makes available to itself is ex-tremely popular. About three-fourths of the House of Represen-sentatives and eighty percent of the Senate use the facilities. About half of Congress uses the studios with regularity.

All of this permits the incumbent congressman to service the home-town radio and television station regularly and at very low prices. Match this with the many other advantages that an incum-bent has and it is little wonder that such a high percentage are re-elected. Congressmen have free mailing privileges, a computerized facility to print, fold, stuff, and address mass mailings including their "non-political" newsletter to constituents—telephone, tele-graph and office equipment all paid for by the government. In addition there are travel allowances for members of the Congress and key staff aides. One member of the House told the New York City Bar Association's Committee on Congressional Ethics that "a challenger needs $25,000 just to get even with me." That esti-mate is low.

While it is easier to get information at the Hill, covering Con-gress can be every bit as challenging as covering the administration. It takes skill for reporters to cut through the barriers erected by the nature of the office and the facilities available to the politician. It is remarkable that so little in government remains hidden despite the best efforts of the worst as well as the best people in public office.

Congress, however, has taken formal steps to diminish secrecy in the executive branch. In 1953, Rep. John Moss of California——then a freshman member of the House Post Office and Civil Service Committee—asked for and was refused information on twenty-eight hundred federal employees discharged for "security" reasons (they were appointed under a Democratic president, were being dismissed by a Republican administration, and Democrat Moss wanted to show that the discharges were not because "their allegiance to the country was in doubt"). Two years later, the Democrats won a majority in Congress and Moss, now on the House Committee on Government Operations, asked its chairman, William L. Dawson to approve a study of secrecy in government.

Chairman Dawson agreed to a staff study. Their research revealed a general trend toward "suppression, nonavailability, or denial of access to information" in areas "untouched by security considerations" which deprived not only the press but congressional committees as well. Moss proposed a special subcommittee continue to look into the matter and was himself appointed chairman of the new group, the House Foreign Operations and Government Information Subcommittee.

In November, 1955 a series of hearings was held and some of Washington's most prominent newsmen testified. So did information specialists in government. Further hearings went into the question of classification of material and heard from scientists. One by one, government departments and regulatory agencies were examined to reveal a pattern of extensive secrecy and widespread censorship of decision making and other agency actions.

In 1960, the Moss subcommittee issued a report on its first five years in the field and noted that its very examination of secrecy had resulted in some improvement. In those five years, the subcommittee uncovered 173 cases of abridgment of freedom of information. In 85 of these, the agency involved removed the secrecy label, usually giving the excuse that a "mistake" had been made. In 10 others there was partial improvement. But in 68 cases, censorship continued despite the subcommittee's admonition that "public business is the people's business." The subcommittee report warned that "the power to withhold the facts of government is the power to destroy that government in a democratic society. . . . A continuing battle must be waged to wipe out the unnecessary pockets of secrecy in administrative regulations, longstanding custom, and bureaucratic attitudes."

In 1960 the Democrats won the White House and the Moss subcommittee was accused of slowing down its efforts. Saul Pett of the Associated Press did a survey of freedom of information some years later and asked Representative Moss to explain the drop in activity during the Kennedy-Johnson years as compared with the Eisenhower years. Moss unabashedly replied, "On the basis of complaints we receive, this administration has a reputation for an almost perfect score in not abusing the handling or withholding of information." However, Staff Director Sam Archibald told Pett, "Yes, there have been improvements. But it is also a fact of life that Democrats are less inclined to clobber a Democratic President." Pett wrote that Archibald authorized the use of his name behind that quote so "Either he has a private income or he must be one of the bravest men in this town, where anonymity is fearless and truth, a sometime mystery of mirrors."

The 1961 Freedom of Information report of *Sigma Delta Chi* said, "It was a gentle Moss who chided the Democratic bureaucrats for their secrecy instead of the old fire-eating Moss of 1955–60 who put scores of Republican bureaucrats on the witness stand and hammered them relentlessly and publicly in behalf of the American people's right to know about their government." It was noted, in time, that the Moss subcommittee had held seventeen hearings during Eisenhower's administration but did not hold a single one after Kennedy's election until 1963.

The 1963 hearings were very important, however. They dealt with the Kennedy administration's handling of the press during the Cuban missile crisis and introduced the phrase "news management." The testimony resulted in great embarrassment for the White House. It is said that a presidential advisor to Lyndon Johnson later wrote a strongly worded memorandum in opposition to any proposed antisecrecy legislation by Moss. The advisor in question was convinced that the Moss inquiry into the Cuban crisis had done serious injury to the Kennedy administration.

The work of the Moss subcommittee culminated in 1966 when it did propose a Freedom of Information Act which passed the House without a single dissenting vote and, despite rumors of presidential veto, met with Lyndon Johnson's approval. The president chose the 4th of July to sign the bill and said on that occasion. "This legislation springs from one of our most essential principles: A democracy works best when the people have all the information that the security of the nation permits. No one should be able to pull curtains of secrecy around decisions which can be revealed without injury to the public interest."

It sounds fine until the proviso "which can be revealed without injury to the public interest" which was an invitation to afford wide discretion in interpretation. The FOI (Freedom of Information) bill itself allows nine exemptions: 1. Executive orders on matters "kept secret in the interest of the national defense or foreign policy," 2. "Matters . . . related solely to the internal personnel rules and practices of any agency," 3. "Matters . . . specifically exempted from disclosure by statute," 4. "Matters that are . . . trade secrets," 5. "Interagency or intra-agency memorandums or letters which would not be available by law to a private party in litigation with the agency," 6. "Personnel and medical files," 7. "Matters . . . compiled for law enforcement purposes," 8. Material relating to "the regulation or supervision of financial institutions," and 9. "geological and geophysical information and data (including maps) concerning wells."

The FOI Act took effect on July 4, 1967. Despite the nine categories of exemptions, it basically demanded that in government, disclosure of information be the rule not the exemption. It placed the burden of proof on the government. President Johnson had said, "I signed this measure with a deep sense of pride that the United States is an open society in which the people's right to know is cherished and guarded." His attorney general, Ramsey Clark, issued a tough forty-seven-page memorandum to government agencies as a guideline on following the new law with the admonition that "Nothing so diminishes democracy as secrecy. . . . Never was it more important than in our times of mass society, when government affects each individual in so many ways, that the right of the people to know the actions of their government be secure."

Two years after the act took effect, however, Ralph Nader, the consumer advocate, issued a twenty-page report saying that it had been "violated systematically and routinely" and was being "undermined by a riptide of bureaucratic ingenuity." Nader cited delay as the common tactic to put off demands for information along with other maneuvers such as complicated appeals processes, high charges for duplicating information, inconsistent interpretation by different agencies, and misclassification to fit under one of the nine exemptions in the law.

Nader gave specifics: the Labor Department denying access to fifteen-year-old violations of the laws dealing with minimum wages and safety standards, the Defense Department refusing to reveal how much oil is pumped from the bilges of navy ships, nineteen instances of the Agriculture Department withholding information which it considers exempt, the Civil Aeronautics Board claiming it had no statistical report on complaints against airlines while another source told Nader's people that the CAB had detailed studies of precisely that, etc. Nader criticized the press harshly for failing to follow through in the courts. In two years, only forty lawsuits had been filed under the FOI Act.

The American Civil Liberties Union, two years after Nader, concluded that "the consensus is that the law hasn't changed things much for the press." It noted that a government agency, the Administrative Conference of the United States, did a study of implementation of the act which itself was classified "not for publication or quotation." The study in question concluded that the press was not using the act very much.

Even John Moss expressed disappointment in its use, saying some people are willing to accept a brush-off and "This includes the news media as well, who sometimes seem disinclined to spend the money and time to win their point by going to court."

Senator Thomas Eagleton of Missouri, after five years of experience with the FOI Act, said that it may have changed the letter of the law but "the spirit of the bureaucrat remains." Speaking to newsmen in St. Louis early in 1972, Eagleton cited ingenuity in circumventing the act including high fees for providing documents, the losing of files, the comingling of non secret with secret documents, and the broadening of interpretations to increase the number of exceptions to the act. The government, he said, fights making material public "right up to the courthouse door" but stops there for fear of court rulings.

Going to court turned out to be less important than the threat of doing so. The greatest value of the FOI Act to date has been the citing of it which has opened doors for newsmen and congressional committees alike. There have been many successes simply as a result of threatening to use the act.

In the first year, *Newsweek* was told that a HEW study of public welfare policies in Mississippi was an "internal working document" and would not be released. The magazine had its lawyer prepare a letter as the first step under the new law and HEW quickly conceded its validity and made the report available. Many reporters found that it wasn't even necessary to write the letter—mere reference to the act was enough. Reporting the matter to the Moss subcommittee also worked wonders.

The Moss subcommittee had become a sort of ombudsman to the press and, now equipped with its FOI law, was even more impressive in responding to reporters' complaints. The subcommittee's probing in 1968, for example, (a) compelled the Defense Department to release the full study rather than just a summary of its survey of defoliation in Vietnam, (b) resulted in the State Department releasing captured Japanese films of the Hiroshima bombing, (c) forced the Office of Economic Opportunity to provide a list of names and salaries of consultants to a newsman earlier refused, (d) managed to get Internal Revenue to release to a magazine writer certain data concerning a university foundation, etc.

In 1969, subcommittee inquiry resulted in (a) the Small Business Administration reversing itself and providing a newspaperman with the names of SBA officials who had approved loans to a company allegedly run by the Mafia, (b) compelled HEW to release information on Medicare reimbursements to hospitals, (c) convinced West Point that a reporter had a right to a copy of the freshman manual of the U.S. Military Academy, (d) arranged for a TV station in the Denver area to film containers of stored nerve gas after it had been denied access, etc.

In 1970, inquiry by the Moss subcommittee resulted (a) in HEW rescinding a policy requiring its officials to report on conversations with newsmen which dealt with "policy," (b) in the Justice Department admitting that an Immigration Service official had no right to prevent TV newsmen from filming in the Los Angeles Federal Building, (c) in the Veterans Administration agreeing to full disclosure of its testing of hearing aids, and (d) in getting the Defense Department to apologize and promise to no longer issue press credentials to government investigators in Vietnam.

The list of successes by the Moss subcommittee is impressive. Even more impressive, if not available, is the list of successes by reporters who simply cite the FOI Act or threaten to go to the Moss subcommittee and get results. It is only when one measures the number of cases going to court that one concludes the law had fallen short of its purpose.

The FOI Act is simply one more means of pressure that newsmen can apply. Bureaucrats who want to avoid newsmen, know that they can engage in a pattern of deception and delay which technically is in accordance with the law but realistically can dampen the reporter's interest. News deadlines are generally incompatible with the time delays that the FOI Act permits and reporters often abandon their inquiries. On the other hand, enough have persisted to make the law a valuable tool.

It is not directed, of course, at its creator—the Congress of the United States. Secret meeting of congressional committees remain commonplace and when the *Congressional Quarterly* issued an eighteen-year survey of this, covering the period from 1953 to 1970, it showed that almost 22,000 of the 59,415 committee meetings in that period were held behind closed doors. Even the Moss subcommittee, in 1971, voted to hold a secret session when it organized. Congress, with that record of 37 percent of its meetings held in executive session, is not likely to bless any actions to extend FOI legislation to its own halls.

Rep. John Moss who led the fight for reform of government information for fifteen years, left the field in 1971 as a result of congressional reform. He was compelled, under new rules to choose between chairmanship of the FOI Committee and an important post as chairman of the Subcommittee on Commerce and Finance. Each congressman was now limited to one chairmanship. He chose the latter and the new FOI chairman was William Moorhead of Pennsylvania, who showed "early foot" in the Moss tradition with his investigations of the Pentagon Papers controversy, most particularly the tendency of the military to overclassify documents.

Members of Congress see no irony in their attempts to open the books of the executive branch while their own are held closed. It doesn't all remain secret, of course, since Congress suffers some of the same problems as the rest of the federal establishment and news leaks are a way of life. Congressmen also share the same frailties as presidents and are as quick to blame the press when the news makes them uncomfortable.

Wes Gallagher, general manager of the Associated Press, has given us Gallagher's Law: "Criticism by the government rises in direct proportion to the amount of news printed or broadcast which reflects unfavorably on government policy." To which Eric Sevareid has added the Sevareid Stipulation: "We will consider alteration of our adversary relationship when two things begin to happen—when political leaders complain they are overpraised and when they admit policy mistakes of a serious nature. That will be the day."

How does the press manage when the public man holds so many cards? There are at least five factors working for the newsman.

First, the nature of advocacy works against the politician. His political foes are eager to share anything they know or suspect with the press. His ideological foes within government compete for their ideas by courting press coverage. Even colleagues who are friendly toward his goals may disagree with his methods and become a source of leaks to the press. Reporters don't need much to get started, an isolated fact here, an opinion there, and soon they are building assumptions with which to confront the politician.

Second, competition within the press is a constant goad to get the story out before someone else does, depriving the politician of time to counter. The tradition of aggressive reporting says be first with the news. Competition comes in differing forms in an era where there is little local competition for the daily newspaper (there is none in 95 percent of our cities) but it exists nevertheless. The tremendous growth in the number of local radio and television news broadcasts makes healthy contributions to competitive reporting. The growth in a national press, networks, and news magazines also serves to keep local reporting alert if it is to satisfy its constituency.

Third, the blessings of bigness are part of the press's strength. We are familiar with the curses of bigness, diminishing the personalized press, encouraging monopolies, centralizing massive power, and eroding intimacy with the reader or listener. Bigness means giant chains of newspapers and mammoth networks. Still, size is not all curse and there are blessings from bigness.

Because of bigness, the reach of the press has grown tremendously and political figures respect the power of that. What the number of daily newspapers in recent years has remained static at about 1,750, the circulation of those papers has not. In the last quarter century, circulation growth has coincided with the growth in adult population, over twenty percent, to a current circulation of 63 million newspapers daily. Radio reaches everywhere and Americans own about 321 million radio sets, over half the world's total and almost two sets per person. As for television, there are 85 million sets in the United States and virtually all television-equipped homes get at least two stations, over half (53 percent) of them get as many as seven stations, and a fourth of the television homes can receive nine or more different stations. Network news audiences are measured in the many millions, not thousands.

Bigness has also brought bigger budgets for news coverage. Advertising revenue has grown tremendously (while newspaper circulation increased 20 percent in the last quarter-century, advertising revenue grew 350 percent in the same period to a present total exceeding five billion dollars annually) and increased news budgets have permitted much more coverage. Hundreds of reporters from small papers and local broadcasters attend national political conventions, for example, to give a "local angle." Large newspapers and networks have continually swelling staffs and send many more people to many more places, increasing competition and widening the scope of reporting. In Washington alone there are over two thousand correspondents. More coverage doesn't mean better coverage but the odds increase.

Fourth, there is the impertinence of the press and its aggressive, inquisitive spirit which constantly demands full disclosure. Politicians may distrust the press, may suspect it, may dislike it, but they also are fearful of rejecting it. When it is strong, they respect it.

Few political figures will avoid press confrontations. In times of crisis, they are compelled to come before the public and explain actions and decisions. When some officials, protected by executive orders or other governmental fiat, avoid congressional or press scrutiny, their superiors generally cannot. When those, in turn, succeed in ducking the press for a time, they rarely succeed in ducking press comment about their tactics. There is a refreshing impertinence to press treatment of officials.

It is different in other countries, even other democracies. Jean-François Revel, in his book *Without Marx or Jesus,* tells of President Pompidou holding a news conference in America and being assailed at every side with disagreeable questions. M. Pompidou reacted with surprise and indignation. "What really outraged him was not the questions themselves so much as the fact that the reporters had a right to ask such questions—and that they were exercising that right."

When Pompidou returned to France, Revel tells us, he was met at the airport by reporters "holding their microphones forward, respectfully, in order not to miss a word of the inanities that were sure to come. 'Gentlemen,' Pompidou said, 'you will understand that I must first make my report to the Council of Ministers, which will meet tomorrow morning.' Obviously, it was good to be home."

The centralization of power in American government has created executives with powers unmatched earlier in our history and the brashness of an uninhibited and unintimidated press is vital to balance this power. It *is* a fourth branch of government when it performs this function, filling a void left as legislative and judicial powers shrink. The press keeps the politician human since it treats him as something less than divinely chosen. The press keeps the politician alert to the scrutiny of his constituents. The press keeps the politician honest.

If these various factors—the nature of advocacy, the competition within the press, the power of bigness, and the tradition of saucy, aggressive reporting—all work to improve the bread, there is a fifth factor, the matter of changing style. As the news manipulators grow more sophisticated, so do the people they would manipulate. The quality of reporting is up just as the quality of manipulating influences has increased. Is it up enough? Some politicians and editors don't think so. A 1969 APME poll of twenty-eight editors and twenty-five public officials showed that two-thirds of them felt newspapers were mistrusted because of "half-told or misleading stories resulting from lax standards for reportorial research and backgrounding of news stories."

There was a time when both groups, the editors and the politicians, would simply say give us the facts, please. Now they insist on research and backgrounding. Walter Lippmann addressed himself to the question in September, 1959 when he spoke to the National Press Club about the job of the Washington correspondent not only as a recorder of facts and a chronicler of events but also "a writer of notes and essays in contemporary history." Said Lippmann:

The old rule is that reporters collect the news, which consists of facts, and that the editorial page then utters opinions approving or disapproving of these facts.

Before I criticize this rule, I must pay tribute to its enduring importance. It contains what we may call the Bill of Rights of the working newspaperman. It encourages not only the energetic reporting of facts. It encourages the honest search for the truth to which these facts belong. It imposes restraints upon owners and editors. It authorizes resistance, indeed in honor it calls for resistance, to the contamination of the news by special prejudices and by special interests. It proclaims the corporate opposition of our whole profession to the prostitution of the press by political parties and by political, economic, and ideological pressure groups, and by social climbers and by adventurers on the make.

But while the rule is an indispensable rallying point for maintaining the integrity of the press, the practical application of the rule cannot be carried out in a wooden and literal way. The distinction between reporting and interpreting has to be redefined if it is to fit the conditions of the modern age.

It is all very well to say that a reporter collects the news and that the news consists of facts. The truth is that in our world the facts are infinitely many, and that no reporter can collect them all, and that no newspaper could print them all—even if they were fit to print—and nobody could read them all. We have to select some facts rather than others, and in so doing that we are using not only our legs but our selective judgment of what is interesting or important or both.

Erwin Canham of the *Christian Science Monitor* has noted that "nothing is more misleading than the unrelated fact, just because it is a fact and hence impressive. Background, surrounding circumstance, prior events, motivation—all are part of the real and basic news. This kind of interpretation . . . is actually the best kind of reporting."

A newspaperman once wrote that he sometimes thought "if the twentieth-century American press had to report the Crucifixion of Christ, the second paragraph would be a straightforward judicial explanation from Pontius Pilate." Many have noted that the problem of dealing with Joe McCarthy was that newsmen were too straight, too objective, and failed to call a lie when they saw one. Elmer Davis said newspapers might precede their stories about McCarthy with the warning, "For the truth about what you read below, see tomorrow's editorial page."

The danger of interpretive reporting, however, is that more and more "selective judgments" are made and selective becomes subjective. The press prides itself on being the adversary of government. There are those who prefer being an advocate to an adversary. They carry selective judgments beyond subjective judgments to support of a cause.

These are the people who feel journalism should do more than report, it should use news columns to push selected goals. They quote the late Ralph McGill who said America is not well informed "for the simple reason that we have been taught to worship a word—objectivity. Truth, I want. But not objectivity. . . . There isn't any such thing as objectivity, and cannot be any such thing."

Another great newspaperman, Herbert Brucker, wrote in defense of objectivity that it was largely a question of defining one's terms. "What they denounce as objectivity," he noted, "is not objectivity as much as an incrustation of habits and rules of newswriting, inherited from the past, that confined the reporter within rigid limits. Within these limits the surface facts of an event may be reported objectively enough. But that part of the iceberg not immediately visible is ruled out, even though to include it might reveal what happened in a more accurate—indeed a more objective—perspective."

Brucker, by the way, had comment on the question of quoting Pontius Pilate. "To report the Crucifixion objectively does in fact require including, along with the Gospel message, whatever further information aggressive questioning might have pried out of Pilate."

Kingman Brewster of Yale once spoke of the academic approach to objectivity in terms which apply fully to newsmen as well. "Cynical disparagement of objectivity as a myth," he said, "seems to me both naive and irresponsible. Any claim of novelty to the observation that men are fallible at best, corruptible at worst, is naive. Its irresponsibility lies in the conclusion that, since the ideal is unattainable, it should not be held up as a standard to both practitioners and critics."

News people spend a lot of time debating the values and shortcomings of objectivity, interpretive reporting and advocacy journalism while public men see no debatable question; they are convinced that news is not objective but increasingly one-sided. In the third year of his presidency, Richard Nixon said, "I respect the individual members of the press—some of them, particularly the older ones, who have some standards of objectivity and fairness. And the individual competence of many of the younger ones, I respect that too, though nowadays they don't care about fairness, it's the 'in' thing to forget objectivity and let your prejudices show. You can see it in my press conferences all the time. You read the Kennedy press conferences and see how soft and gentle they were with him, and then you read mine. I never get any easy questions—and I don't want any. I am quite aware that ideologically the Washington press corps doesn't agree with me. I expect it."

George Reedy, once press secretary to Lyndon Johnson, wrote "If censorship ever comes to the United States, it will explode out of the frustrations of a political leader convinced that the public good is being thwarted by self-serving reporters distorting the news."

The growing resentment of political figures towards advocacy journalism is understandable. There are some who also claim that the growing skepticism of the reader and listener is a rebellion against subjective reporting. The fact is, however, that advocacy journalism is minimal in today's press, is common only in small circulation, opinion journals. While there has been a tremendous growth in interpretive journalism, this broader use of the reporter's function has reflected a basic desire to be fair rather than a passion to press pet ideas. There have been exceptions but they are not general.

Covering the public man demands more than simple reporting of facts easily gathered and generally furnished by the news source himself. It calls for determined and aggressive questioning of the source, careful and intense research for background material, and serious and thorough examination of contrasting views.

One proponent of advocacy journalism said that objectivity is "the classic cop-out from choice making." The job of the journalist is to present the choices, not to make them. Readers and listeners should make the choice. Perhaps the fairness syndrome which pervades broadcasting is, if we dismiss government regulation of it, the best description of the spirit that should be embraced by interpretive reporting. Is it fair to all sides? Are all views being expressed? Fairness must mean, first of all, fair to the public. It means inclusion of as many pertinent elements as the reporter can gather, with assurance that one side or the other is not being ignored. These elements include "background, surrounding circumstances, prior events, motivation" not simple, formal, official facts.

The history of government-press relations weighs against reporting in such a manner, for those with political purpose much prefer to limit coverage to simple, formal, official fact. Reuven Frank, president of NBC News, has noted that politicians in America always tell us that "a free press means a responsible press, a constructive press, a patriotic press, an evenhanded press, a restrained press—all the noble words used to describe the press in the official utterances and even the constitutions of every dictatorship in the world, of right or left. A free press, they will tell us, is a press which deserves to be free. That is what President Nyerere said when he fired the editor of the *Dar es Salaam Standard;* that is what prime minister Lee Kuan Yew said when he shut down the *Singapore Herald.*"

At the time of the Pentagon Papers, James Reston of the *New*

York Times said in a television interview, "Well, you know, I have been very troubled through these last few weeks about this whole business because it seemed to me that the government assumed in some way that we were indifferent to the security of the Republic or that somehow we loved our country less than the people in government. That is not true. . . . I bitterly resent the idea that we are any less concerned about the security of the Republic than the attorney general or anybody else in Washington."

There are newsmen who bitterly resent the implication that they are less concerned about fairness in reporting than the vice-president or anybody else in Washington. There are journalists who bitterly resent the implication that they care less for good government than a president or anybody else in Washington.

From the perspective of the newsman, the more the public knows, the greater the ventilation of ideas and proposed actions, the better the government. If this makes the operation of the people's business a bit more difficult, it also assures that it is a great deal more open.

The late Hugo Black said in his James Madison lecture on the Bill of Rights:

> Since the earliest days, philosophers have dreamed of a country where the mind and spirit of man would be free; where there would be no limits to inquiry; where men would be free to explore the unknown and to challenge the most deeply rooted beliefs and principles. Our First Amendment was a bold effort to adopt this principle—to establish a country with no legal restrictions of any kind upon the subjects people could investigate, discuss and deny. The Framers knew better perhaps than we do today, the risks they were taking. They knew that free speech might be the friend of change and revolution. But they also knew that it is always the deadliest enemy of tyranny. With this knowledge they still believed that the ultimate happiness and security of a nation lies in its ability to explore, to change, to grow and ceaselessly to adapt itself to new knowledge born of inquiry free from any kind of governmental control over the mind and spirit of man. Loyalty comes from love of good government, not fear of a bad one.

In a society as immense and diverse as the American society of the twentieth century, there is no device other than the press to reach the far corners of the land and report on the people's servants and their stewardship of the people's business. Libraries and universities can help individuals explore the unknown and challenge basic principles but the vitality of such exploration and challenge also depends ultimately on widespread dissemination. In a system where advantages are weighted on the side of the governors, the press as their censors must stand tough. As some have said, this will remain the land of the free only so long as it is the home of the brave.

All of this was the intent of the men who gave us the tradition of a free press and those who wrote it into the First Amendment. It is a freedom, it should be repeated, not for the newspaperman or the broadcaster but rather for the reader and listener. It is not to protect newspapers from government supervision but to protect the American people from having their news supervised by government.

Editors and publishers, broadcasters and reporters can wave the banner of free speech until they fit Churchill's definition of a fanatic—one who can't change his mind and won't change the subject—but the ultimate victory of emancipated speech rests with the public. When the public wavers in its support, the politician is quick to smell it. When the public, frustrated or frightened in times of stress, permits free speech to become atrophied, the politician moves in. Without carping criticism, they'll make the trains run on time, efficiency will return to government.

Every generation has these moments of stress. Every generation faces its crisis in free speech. The difficult part is that when the public support is least, free speech is needed most. Tolerance for dissent is always high in calm days. The true test of a man's respect for his neighbor's views comes in stormy times.

In contemporary America, much of the public is disillusioned with the press. In various ways, opinion polls show shrinking support and growing skepticism about the press, its fairness, its choice of subject matter, its role. Many observers are convinced that the public is inclined to blame the messenger, not the message; is less concerned about the role of the news media than the nature of the

news. It is a society which cannot stand its own news. There is
some question whether a society which cannot stand its own news
can long stand as a democratic community.

It is difficult for a frustrated American to welcome news of matters which disturb him, which he finds disagreeable. It is hard to
accept the premise that suppressing the disagreeable matter in the
press only invites suppression of other matters tomorrow. He is
perplexed, he is puzzled, he is uncomfortable. He does not see a
ready connection between his own freedoms and a press that is
inhibited or restrained. It is not obvious to him that when a single
reporter hesitates because his next sentence might offend a powerful source or a single broadcaster pauses to listen for the footsteps
of government behind him, then free speech has already been
seriously compromised.

The battle is for reporters who do not hesitate and broadcasters
who do not pause. The wisest men in American history, many of
them suffering the sting of an impertinent press themselves, recognized that the safety of a democratic state rests in the rights of
that impertinent press—even its right to be wrong. They knew
that the imperfect device of a public press was a vital balance to
the imperfect device of popularly elected government.

The descendants of those wise men of two centuries ago are
bothered, baffled, frustrated, uncomfortable, and being asked to
be gentle with the very itch they want to scratch. But it is really
not too much to ask. It simply calls for an understanding that the
right to speak and the right to be heard are but two parts of free
speech—the third part is the right to hear others.

In the unique form of government devised in this land, there is
a haunting truism to buttress this tolerance for what others have
to say. It is that no other freedom is safe once the first freedom,
that of free speech, is lost.

INDEX

DATE DUE